D0336329

A CONCISE ENCYCLOPEDIA OF THE SECOND WORLD WAR

The Yalta Conference, February 1945. Seated, left to right: Winston Churchill, Franklin D. Roosevelt and Joseph Stalin; prominent behind them are Anthony Eden, V. M. Molotov and Averill Harriman (Photo: Imperial War Museum).

A CONCISE ENCYCLOPEDIA OF THE SECOND WORLD WAR

Alan Reid

BOOK CLUB ASSOCIATES
LONDON

This book was designed and produced by
Alban Book Services Limited,
147 London Road, St. Albans, Herts, England

Unless otherwise specifically indicated,
all photographs are reproduced by courtesy of
the Imperial War Museum, Lambeth Road, London

This edition published 1975 by
BOOK CLUB ASSOCIATES
By arrangement with Osprey Publishing Ltd.

Filmset in 8/9 pt. Times New Roman 327
Printed in Great Britain on 118 gsm paper by
W. S. COWELL LIMITED
at the Butter Market, Ipswich, England

ISBN 0 540 07004 1

CONTENTS

FOREWORD

But war's a game, which were their subjects wise,
Kings would not play at.

William Cowper: The Task

Ambitious kings and unwise subjects have constantly plunged their countries into war, and even the war that was to end all wars only set the scene for the Second World War. The 1914–18 war was history's most tragic and senseless waste of youth. The war of 1939–45 was the most horrible, barbaric holocaust inflicted on man by man. Some would forget them, but forgotten history reminds by recurrence.

Whatever ineptitudes caused the war or, through isolated decisions, led to needless casualties, military or civilian, it was the twisted mind of one inexplicably powerful man that brought a new, extraordinary inhumanity to the Second World War. Other leaders in history have been callous in their sacrifice of others to achieve selfish or dubious aims. But Hitler surpassed them all in his deliberate, highly organised efforts to murder, work to death, or simply let die millions of people who were innocent of any crime whatsoever.

. . . Hitler has shown us that Hell is still here on Earth. He has, in fact, taken the lid off Hell, and we have all looked into it. That is his service to the human race.

Field Marshal J. C. Smuts: 1944

The war became truly global when the Japanese conflict spread beyond China into the Pacific and against America. That sudden war brought horror, pain and loss as any war does, and the deaths of millions. It is no consolation to those who found in Japanese prison camps anguish, misery and suffering, to know that they were victims of a culture whose values and life-style were so different from their own that death was considered a true beginning rather than an end, and surrender an ultimate humiliation. And yet the Japanese also wept in grief when their innocent died in Tokyo, Hiroshima, Osaka and Nagasaki.

Unfortunately war also brings with it glory, excitement, comradeship, achievement and the personal self-satisfaction of facing ultimate dangers and surviving. Somehow war's attraction seems to balance war's repulsion, and it remains captive in Mankind's sphere. The pity is that the horror is unpalatable and therefore either poorly remembered, or ignored by tacit consent. Those who look for heroism and glory in war can find an awesome number of accounts of it (and it would be a heartless person who did not stand in awe of heroism and sacrifice, especially if he were the beneficiary of it). It is unfortunate, however, if each account of glory is not balanced with an account of shame and suffering. The lessons of a selective history are more damaging than ignoring history altogether.

As far as possible, this book is a factual account of how the war began, what main events took place during its course, the mechanism of war, its leaders, and some of the war's consequences. Perhaps the sheer accumulation of 72 months' activities during which millions of people tried their hardest to kill millions of others will convey war's senseless barbarity. If it does, I hope it will also convey a wonder at the individuals who fought the war in innocence, and a pity for those who suffered it in innocence.

On a practical note, I hope that the layout of the Chronology will make it far easier than previously has been possible for people to follow the progress of the war – whether month by month in its entirety, or by following particular campaigns while also being able to see quickly what else was happening. This should avoid the confusion of backtracking or jumping too far ahead. Thus the Chronology is written as if by some detached global diarist who recorded the happenings of each month on the month's last day. Thus events in progress at that time are recorded in the present tense.

The subdivision into four main areas is self-explanatory and made clearer by the map below. Geographical accuracy has been sacrificed for simplicity, and the "Russia" area throughout infers the Russian front – thus Berlin and Poland begin under "Europe", but move into "Russia" as the Russian front sweeps over them.

A. R.

GLOSSARY

AA	Anti Aircraft (gun)
Abwehr	German Military Intelligence
A.D.C.	aide-de-camp
A.O.C.	Air Officer Commanding
B.B.C.	British Broadcasting Corporation
B.E.F.	British Expeditionary Force
Big Six	Japanese Supreme Council for the Conduct of the War
C.G.S.	Chief of General Staff
C.I.G.S.	Chief of the Imperial General Staff
C-in-C	Commander in Chief
CINCPAC	Commander in Chief, Pacific
COSSAC	Chief of Staff, Supreme Allied Command
D-Day	Commencement of Allied invasion of Europe (6.6.44)
G.C.	George Cross – British medal for civilian bravery
G.O.C. (-in-C)	General Officer Commanding (-in-Chief)
H.M.S.	His Majesty's Ship
H.Q.	Headquarters
Kriegsmarine	German Navy
Luftwaffe	German Air Force
MTB	motor torpedo boat (Germany, E-boat; U.S.N., PT-boat)
Nazi	National Socialist German Workers' Party
OKH	*Oberkommando des Heers* (German Army High Command)
OKW	*Oberkommando der Wehrmacht* (German Armed Forces High Command)
Operation Anvil	Allied invasion of southern France (re-named Dragoon) 15.8.44
Operation Attila	German occupation of Vichy France 11.11.42
Operation Avalanche	Allied capture of Naples 1.10.43
Operation Barbarossa	German invasion of Russia 22.6.41
Operation Citadel	German armoured offensive at Kursk 5.7.43
Operation Dragoon	See Anvil
Operation Dynamo	Evacuation of B.E.F. from Dunkirk 27.5.40
Operation Jupiter	Projected British invasion of northern Norway in 1942
Operation Manna	British aid to liberation of Greece 4.10.44
Operation Marita	German invasion of Greece 6.4.41
Operation Overlord	Allied invasion of Normandy 6.6.44
Operation Sealion	Projected German invasion of England in September 1940
Operation Shingle	Allied landings at Anzio 22.1.44
Operation Sledgehammer	Projected Allied capture of Cherbourg in 1942 (replaced by Torch)
Operation Torch	Allied invasion of N.W. Africa 8.11.42
Operation Typhoon	German attack on Moscow 2.10.41
Operation Winter Gale	Projected relief by Manstein of German 6th Army in December 1942
p.o.w.	prisoner of war
R.A.F.	Royal Air Force
R.N.	Royal Navy
rpm	rounds per minute (machine guns, etc.)
SA	*Sturmabteilungen* (Storm Troops)
SAS	Special Air Service
SD	*Sicherheitsdienst* (security service of SS)
S.E.A.C.	South East Asia Command
S.H.A.E.F.	Supreme Headquarters Allied Expeditionary Force
S.O.E.	Special Operations Executive
SS	*Schutzstaffel* (German elite para-military force)
U.N.	United Nations (the Allies)
U.S.A.A.F.	United States Army Air Force (also U.S.(A).A.F.)
U.S.N.	United States Navy
U.S.S.	United States Ship
V.C.	Victoria Cross – British medal for bravery in service
W.A.A.F.	Women's Auxiliary Air Force
W.R.N.S.	Women's Royal Naval Service

1. A CHRONOLOGY OF THE SECOND WORLD WAR

PRELUDE

For what can war but endless war still breed?
John Milton: Sonnet on the Lord General Fairfax

20.4.1889 Adolf Hitler born in Austria near Bavarian border.

1909–1913 Hitler footloose in Vienna. Early political thoughts and anti-Semitism became established.

1914 The Great War. Ended by Armistice with demoralised and mutinous Germany 11.11.18.

28.6.19 Treaty of Versailles signed. Germans humiliated and embittered by loss of European territory, overseas territories, enforced disarmament and severe restrictions on rearmament, occupation of demilitarised Rhineland, and decision to extract reparations.

1920 Hitler became committee member of National Socialist German Workers' Party (NSDAP), designed Nazi flag and chose swastika as party symbol.

April 1921 Allies presented reparations bill of 33,000 million dollars. German mark began to drop in value.

5.10.21 SA stormtroopers – brownshirts – formed. By end of 1921 NSDAP included Roehm, Goering, Hess, Rosenberg.

1921–1922 Mark continued to fall in value. January 1923 France occupied Ruhr in effort to enforce payment of lapsed reparations. Mark, at 75 to 1 dollar in 1921, fell in value to 4,000 million to 1 dollar in November 1923. Little effect felt by Government and industrialists, but embittered and suffering German people turned resentment towards the Weimar government, and above all kept smarting from the slap given at Versailles.

1921–1922 In Washington Conference on Far East, U.S.A., Great Britain, France and Japan agreed on each others' rights in islands of Western Pacific, and agreed not to fortify any island. U.S.A., Britain and Japan also agreed to limit their navies, but ratio of 5:5:3 on capital ships angered Japanese. Agreement never honoured by Japanese, who commenced massive naval shipbuilding programme and fortified their islands.

8 & 9.11.23 Munich Beer Hall Putsch. Hitler and SA under Goering attempted coarse, ill-timed putsch in Munich. Ended in chaos – most leaders, including Hitler, arrested. Hess and Goering fled.

26.2.24 Hitler used his trial as political platform, and received only 9 month sentence. In prison, began composition of *Mein Kampf*, outlining his aims for German supremacy.

The Nazis used the years before the war to build armaments and to whip-up nationalistic pride. Military parades, speeches, brilliant propaganda and the omnipresent symbols of the regime contrasted startlingly with the pre-Hitler years of poverty, disorder and humiliation.

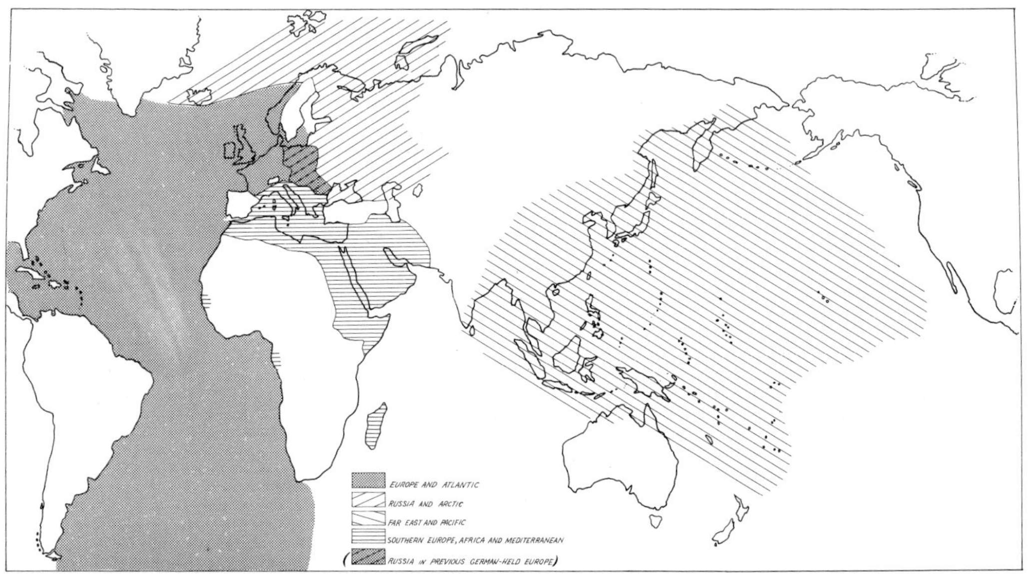

Map showing the geographical divisions adopted for the area-by-area treatment of the Chronology.

24.10.24 Wall Street crash marked beginning of world-wide Depression.

1925 Hitler rebuilt NSDAP and set up elite personal corps of SS (*Schutzstaffel*).

1.12.25 Treaty of Locarno signed – formed Anglo-French alliance, reaffirmed French alliances with Czechoslovakia and Poland, and also established concord between France and Germany. Peace and hope brought temporarily to Europe. 1929 Reparations revised downwards. 1929 Himmler took over SS, then 200 strong.

1930 Allied occupation forces left demilitarised zone of Rhineland – 5 years ahead of planned date. Germans demanded further recognition and equality.

14.9.30 In Reichstag elections NSDAP became second largest party.

13.7.31 All German banks closed. Over 6 million in Germany unemployed. Hoover moratorium of 1931 suspended reparations for 1 year – after which Lausanne Conference decided to end them altogether.

18.9.31 Japanese occupied Manchuria, theoretically part of China, though China had not played any rôle in that country's affairs for some time. China appealed, fruitlessly, to League of Nations; but by 1933 she had resigned herself to loss of Manchuria, and peaceful relations between China and Japan were re-established.

22.2.32 Hitler began his bid to win election as President against Hindenburg.

14.4.32 SA outlawed.

1.6.32 Conservative Franz von Papen named Weimar Chancellor.

15.6.32 Ban on SA lifted, followed by brutal political thuggery and intimidation throughout Germany.

31.7.32 Renamed National Socialist Party became largest party in new Reichstag elections, but lacked overall majority. Hitler snubbed by Hindenburg in his demand to be made Chancellor. There followed months of trickery, cajolery, resignations, elections, rigging, plots, cabals, and counterplots leaving the country bewildered and to all purposes leaderless. On 31.1.33 Hindenburg relented and made **Hitler Chancellor of a Coalition Government.**

27.2.33 Reichstag burnt down, possibly by Nazis, but immediately used by Hitler as excuse to wipe out Communists and other threatening groups.

21.3.33 Ceremonial opening of **first Reichstag of the Third Reich** (the "Thousand Year Reich"). "Enabling Act" forced through Parliament gave its powers to Hitler, making him virtually a dictator.

1.4.33 National boycott of Jewish businesses proclaimed by Hitler. Dr. Schacht began to use his revolutionary economic genius to bring full employment back, mainly by massive Government expenditure on secret rearmament.

14.10.33 Hitler used lack of disarmament by Allies as excuse to withdraw from Disarmament Conference and League of Nations. France alone opposed any measure of German rearmament; to most other countries a strong Germany was an essential part of the balance of power in Europe – and none believed that rearmament could take less than a decade, by which time Germany would no longer be a "problem". In 1934 Germany and Poland signed a Non-Aggression Pact, which removed threat of Polish support for France. Hitler saw Italy as his main potential ally, to the extent that he let Italian–Austrian alliances take precedence over his Austrian ambitions.

14.6.34 Hitler met Mussolini, already a ruling Fascist full of military pomp, and he persuaded Hitler to moderate the Austrian Nazis. Hitler's poor showing against Mussolini aggravated him into vicious response to the increasing Nazi in-fighting, and to widespread criticism of the brutal methods of Roehm and his SA.

30.6.34 Night of the Long Knives. Roehm and possibly up to 1,000 real, potential or imaginary opponents of Hitler were butchered, along with most powerful SA leaders, by Himmler's SS. Remaining SA incorporated into SS which was made responsible only to Himmler and Hitler. Majority of 50 or so concentration camps then existing were centralised into fewer, larger units (Dachau, Ravensbruck, etc.), run by SS under Theodor Eicke.

2.8.34 President Hindenburg died. Army consented to Hitler's immediate assumption of powers of head of state and Commander-in-Chief of Armed Forces. **Hitler proclaimed Fuehrer** and Reich Chancellor. All armed forces compelled to take oath to Fuehrer and Germany. Increasing number of anti-Semitic decrees passed, and Nazification or Subjugation of Churches began.

25.7.34 Austrian Chancellor Dollfuss shot by Nazis in attempted Vienna putsch. German war industry had become well established with enormous armament and civil engineering programmes.

October 1934 Pierre Laval succeeded the murdered Barthon as French Foreign Minister, and put emphasis on friendship with Italy.

16.3.35 Hitler brought in conscription, causing last gathering of Britain, France and Italy over this final break with Treaty of Versailles. Saar (separated after 1918) voted unanimously to be reunited with Germany, and confident Hitler repudiated Versailles and the last shackles on Germany. This confident trust that no country would ever call his bluff, and that he could get his way by repeated moves and patient waiting, became the basis of Hitler's foreign policy – accompanied by

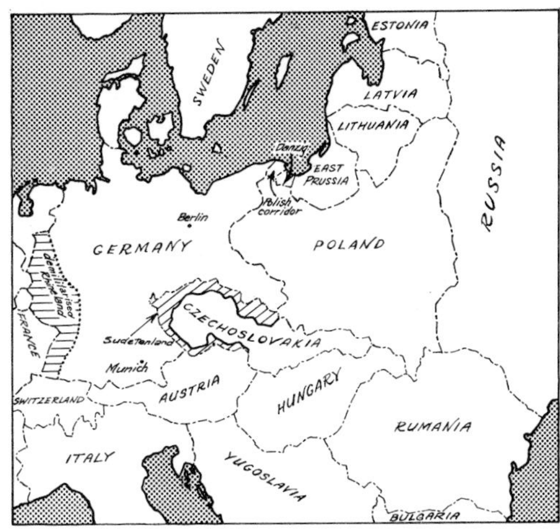

Central and Eastern Europe from 1921 to March 1936.

varying amounts of sabre rattling.

October 1935 Despite threat of League of Nations Sanctions, and pleas and offers from Britain, Italy attacked Abysinnia.

7.3.36 German troops reoccupied the demilitarised Rhineland – once again no country raised more than brief vocal protest, though Hitler's move meant that the last of the props for security against German aggression had been swept away.

1.5.36 Abyssinian slaughter ended as Emperor Haile Selassie fled his country. Mussolini proclaimed the birth of a "new Roman Empire". It was also the death of the League of Nations' effectiveness, for 52 nations had been unable to save Abyssinia.

16.6.36 German police forces unified and placed under Himmler's SS, and therefore beyond the reach of the judiciary.

11.7.36 Papen, made ambassador in Vienna after Dollfuss' murder had strained relations, engineered German and Austrian "Gentleman's Agreement" of mutual trust and respect.

July 1936 Spanish Civil War. Rebels led by Franco received arms and planes from Italy and Germany, while Russia supplied Republic forces.

July 1937 Japanese "influence" in China turned into open warfare. China appealed to League of Nations, but received little concrete help, and by the end of 1938 Japanese held most of the China coast. America took the opportunity to confirm her policy of isolationism.

5.11.37 Hitler expounded his views on *lebensraum* and natural German supremacy to his Minister of War (Blomberg), Foreign Minister (Neurath), and C-in-Cs of Air Force, Army and Navy (Goering, Fritsch, Raeder); based his long term plans mainly on opportunism and by winning constant concessions.

8.12.37 Hitler humiliated by resignation of Schacht as Minister of Economics and covered it up by simultaneous sacking, through concocted damaging evidence, of Blomberg, Fritsch, Neurath, Papen and Hassell (Ambassador to Italy).

1938

12.2 Schuschnigg (Austrian Chancellor) met Hitler to discuss co-operation but Hitler took aggressive role and achieved increased German dominance over Austria.

9.3 Schuschnigg abruptly announced immediate plebiscite on Austrian independence in an attempt to put it through before Hitler could act. Hitler was aware that plebiscite would favour independence and on 11.3 closed German–Austrian border. Schuschnigg received little support from Italy or Britain over German threats and demands to abandon plebiscite. Agreed to postpone it. Goering instructed Nazi Seys-Inquart to take over as Chancellor. Schuschnigg resigned in despair and Goering threatened armed intervention when President Miklas refused to appoint Seys-Inquart. 8.45 p.m. order was given to invade Austria.

12.3 Seys-Inquart appointed himself Chancellor and vainly tried to stop invasion. Hitler drove into Austria and in Linz announced the *Anschluss* – the inclusion of Austria in the Third Reich.

13.3 Austria ordered out of existence by its own self-appointed Chancellor. *Anschluss* aroused nationalistic sentiments of 3 million Sudeten Germans in Czechoslovakia and Hitler encouraged them to make more and more demands with every concession given.

10.4 Daladier became new Prime Minister of France, and, with British Prime Minister Chamberlain, ignored Czech position and Russian suggestion of talks on crises in Europe.

20.5 Czech reservists called up and frontier manned.

4.9 President Beneš offered Sudeten leaders everything they wanted, knowing they had no valid arguments, and hoping rest of Europe would see Hitler in his true light as a "Conqueror".

15.9 Chamberlain flew to Munich to attempt to appease Hitler.

18.9 Chamberlain and Daladier met to discuss partition of Czechoslovakia.

21.9 Czechs accepted Anglo–French proposals for appeasement of Hitler – who immediately stepped up his demands. By 28.9 practically every diplomat had made fruitless appeals, when finally Mussolini persuaded Hitler to postpone military action for 24 hours, pending a conference on Czechoslovakia in Munich between Britain, France, Germany and Italy (the Czechs were not invited). The four nations agreed to the occupation of Sudetenland by 10th October – instead of Hitler's first demand of 1st October. Czechs could only accept.

30.9 Chamberlain signed statement of agreement with Hitler, pledging desire for peace – "Peace in our time". But "Munich" soon became synonymous with betrayal and weak appeasement.

In Russia, Stalin's ruthless purges came to an end with over 1 million dead, and the army cleared of virtually all its experienced generals.

1939

Hitler's attention turned east again – this time towards Poland, and especially the self-governing city of Danzig across the "Polish Corridor". Much of Germany's pre-1914 territory was then held by Poland, and Hitler gradually began to build up an obsessed desire to crush Poland and her inhabitants.

9.3 Czecho-Slovakia (so called since Munich) finally broke up and Slovaks got independence.

15.3 Bohemia became a German protectorate. Hitler occupied Prague – a move which resulted in increased anti-German feeling in Britain.

30.3 Chamberlain assured Beck that Britain and France would support Poland against any military threat to her independence, but no formal agreement signed. Danzig became a symbol of independence to the Poles, and from then on its future was never rationally discussed. To Hitler, it also meant far more than the city itself, and there was little doubt that he would have asked for more even if he had been given Danzig.

3.4 Hitler told German armed forces to prepare for attack on Poland, for any date after 1st September, provided Poland stood alone.

28.4 Hitler repudiated the 1934 Non-Aggression Pact with Poland, and the 1935 Anglo–German Naval Agreement.

22.5 Italy and Germany signed a formal alliance ("Pact of Steel"). Long but futile talks on Anglo–Soviet pact began again.

In the East, the Japanese threat increased as more and more of China was occupied by Japanese troops. All Chinese ports were in Japanese hands, and the Chinese were only supplied by land over the Burma road, and by air.

July Sporadic clashes between Russian and Japanese forces on Mongolian border developed into extended conflict, which ended in August with Japanese defeat and loss of 18,000 troops.

7.7 Mussolini warned Britain that Italy would side with Germany if Britain fought on the Polish side over "the Danzig problem".

12.8 Ciano tried to get Hitler to achieve Polish aims through an international conference, such as Munich over Czechoslovakia. Hitler became determined to smash Poland.

17.8 Talks between Britain and France, and Russia broke down.

19.8 Fourteen U-boats sailed from Germany for North Atlantic.

20.8 Hitler sent personal message to Stalin asking for pact to be considered. 21–24.8 Pocket battleships *Graf Spee* and *Deutschland*, with more U-boats, sailed for South and North Atlantic.

23.8 Germany and Russia signed non-aggression pact, and agreed on the future division of Poland.

24.8 Swede Dahlerus sent by Goering to London as last-minute negotiator. British Parliament recalled.

25.8 Hitler ordered immediate attack on Poland, but cancelled order when he heard of formal signature of Anglo–Polish alliance.

26.8 British Admiralty assumed control of merchant shipping.

27.8 German merchant fleet ordered home or to neutral ports. Diplomatic activity between London, Paris, Rome and Berlin increased to frantic pace. Dahlerus was constantly to and fro, but much taken in by Hitler's surface sincerity.

29.8 Hitler offered to deal directly with Poland, but only if a Polish Plenipotentiary arrived within 24 hours – which Poles would not do.

31.8 At 12.30 p.m. Hitler issued Directive No. 1 for Conduct of War, ordering attack to begin the following day. 4.00 p.m., confirmed orders. 6.30 p.m. Polish diplomat in Berlin, Lipski, saw Ribbentrop in first German–Polish contact since March. Meeting fruitless as Lipski did not go as Plenipotentiary. In Britain, evacuation of children from London ordered. $1\frac{1}{2}$ million German troops moved up to Polish border. 8.00 p.m. SS soldiers in Polish uniforms carried out mock raid on German radio station at Gleiwitz, leaving concentration camp "victims", in German uniforms, on the scene. This satisfied Hitler that Poland was the aggressor.

1.9 Friday 4.45 a.m. First air attack began on Poland. 5.45 a.m. German invasion of Poland began with rapid

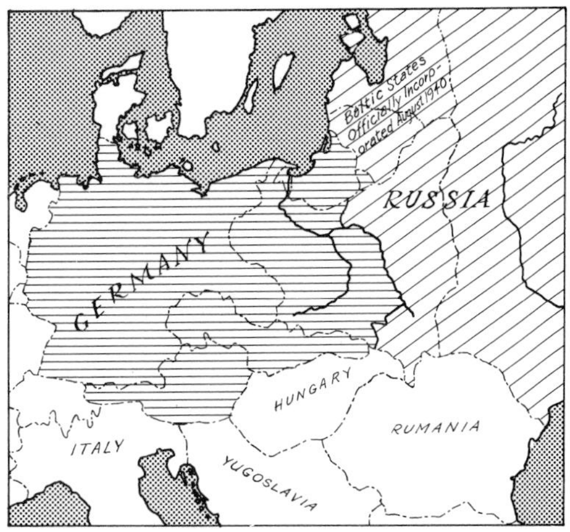

Central and Eastern Europe, October 1939.

blitzkrieg attack against out-numbered, under-equipped, and poorly deployed Polish armies. German and Polish navies clashed. **Britain mobilised her army.**

2.9 Frantic efforts made by Italy to prevent escalation of war, by diplomatic activity in Berlin. German advance continued rapidly, and Polish air force was already largely destroyed.

WAR

Even if we could not conquer, we should drag half the world into destruction with us, and leave no one to triumph over Germany . . . we may be destroyed but if we are we shall drag a world with us – a world in flames.

Adolf Hitler, 1934

SEPTEMBER 1939

EUROPE and ATLANTIC

(3rd) The British ultimatum to Germany for withdrawal from Poland expired at 11.00 a.m., when Britain declared war on Germany. France followed suit at 5.00 p.m. At 9.00 p.m. the extent of the coming war was foreshadowed when *U30* sank the liner *Athenia* en route for Montreal from Liverpool – 112 passengers died, including a number of Americans.

Poland was rapidly overrun by the force of *blitzkrieg* against their inferior forces, and their hopeless reliance on counter-attack instead of defence. Russia mobilised

(8th) and Poland's end became inevitable when Russia invaded Eastern Poland (17th). The Polish Government and High Command took refuge in Rumania the following day, exhorting their subjects to "fight on". Warsaw fell (27th), though prolonged guerilla resistance still continues. The large concentration of Polish troops at the Modlin fortress were defeated the next day. In Moscow Ribbentrop and Molotov agreed on the partitioning of Poland: Russia took its oil supplies, 77,000 square miles, and 13 million people. Germany kept the industrial sector and took over 22 million people in 73,000 square miles. Some 180,000 Poles managed to escape across neutral borders.

Britain and France began talks on how Germany could be attacked, and relied on the Maginot line for their defences. The British Expeditionary Force (B.E.F.) advance units crossed to France (4th and 9th), but the French mobilisation was laboriously slow. An offensive intended to withdraw pressure from Poland only began when Poland was almost defeated (17th), and then it was confined to useless efforts against the well-defended Siegfried Line, in order not to violate Belgian territory.

By contrast, the war at sea began rapidly and in earnest. R.N. carriers sailed to hunt U-boats (3rd); but after *Ark Royal* was narrowly missed by *U39* – which was then sunk by escorts (14th) – and after *Courageous* was sunk by *U29* with the loss of 514 men and 48 aircraft (17th), the carriers were sensibly withdrawn from this role. The blockade of Germany began the day war was declared, and Bomber Command carried out its first raid (4th), causing little damage to German warships in harbour. The first Trans-Atlantic convoy sailed (15th) and on the following day *U31* sank the *Aviemore* in the first submarine attack on a convoy. By the end of the first week of war, nearly 40 ships had been sunk by submarines and mines. In the Baltic, all U-boats were withdrawn (7th) and the Russian tanker *Metallist* was sunk (26th) – possibly by Soviet torpedo boats to "excuse" Russian threats against Estonia. *Admiral Graf Spee* claimed its first victim (30th), and the battleship is a major threat to shipping in the South Atlantic.

OCTOBER 1939

EUROPE and ATLANTIC

The war is being called the "Phoney War", and "Sitzkrieg", but there has been nothing phoney about the war at sea. Hitler declared all-out war on camouflaged or armed Allied merchant ships (4th); this was later extended to all except passenger ships (17th), and then authority was given to attack without warning any Allied ships in convoy (29th). Hitler's War Directive no. 7 (18th) emphasised need to smash British merchant and naval shipping. Eight groups of R.N. and French Navy ships, 22 in all, hunted in vain for *Graf Spee*, which had sunk four more ships. In an extraordinary act of daring and skill, *U47* penetrated the defences of Scapa Flow in the Orkney Islands and sank the battleship *Royal Oak*. 833 seamen died including the Captain and Rear Admiral Blagrove. Both the R.N. in the North Atlantic, and the German Navy in the Baltic, halted, inspected, and frequently appropriated hundreds of merchant ships. Magnetic mines laid by Germans had sunk 50,000 tons of shipping. The sinking of 3 U-boats by mines in the Straits of Dover marked the closure of the English Channel to U-boats. The pocket battleship *Deutschland* sank its first merchantman.

In Poland the last large force surrendered (5th) and Hitler, already eyeing Russia, marked Poland as the assembly area for "future German operations". He also looked to the west and issued Directive no. 6, preparing the attack on France and Britain, via the neutral countries of Luxembourg, Holland and Belgium. Britain and France continued thinking in terms of an attack on Germany, believing that the Germans could never penetrate the Maginot Line, and that they would not dare abuse Belgium's neutrality. The Allies also ignored the tentative peace feelers put out by some Germans, and did not realise there were some non-Nazis in high Army posts. Brauchitsch and Halder regarded Hitler's desire to attack France with dismay, and predicted such a move would lead to a full-scale world war and German defeat. Their intentions to lead a march on Berlin to oust Hitler and the Nazi echelon failed through lack of essential support from Fromm.

RUSSIA and ARCTIC

Russia became anxious about her vulnerability and concluded Pacts with Estonia, Latvia, and Lithuania (10th) to secure her Baltic flank. Russia also made territorial demands from Finland (14th) which would have strengthened her northern approaches while not weakening Finland, who would also have been given twice as much land in exchange. Finland was antagonistic to such plans.

NOVEMBER 1939

EUROPE and ATLANTIC

The war at sea continued with a ferocious contrast to the lull on land. *Graf Spee* caused destruction and fear among shipping in the South Atlantic, and the British, Australian, and French navies made extensive patrols to search for her. Many ships continued to be sunk by mines – on one typical day (18th) mines laid by German destroyers off the Thames estuary sank a destroyer, a trawler and seven merchant ships. *Sturgeon* became the first R.N. submarine to sink a German ship (20th), but the next day the cruiser *Belfast* was badly damaged by a mine laid in the Firth of Forth. A massive North Atlantic hunt began (23rd) after *Scharnhorst* sank the auxiliary cruiser *Rawalpindi*, but a violent storm (26th–

27th) allowed *Scharnhorst* and *Gneisenau* to slip through to the North Sea. By the end of the month 27 Allied ships had been sunk by mines, but the finding of an undamaged magnetic mine led to degaussing, an effective countermeasure which neutralises a ship's magnetic field.

In Germany Gen. Brauchitsch again appealed to Hitler not to invade France (5th) but Hitler demanded invasion should begin on 12th. Worsening weather, however, caused a postponement (7th). Hitler seemed frustrated by lack of action and (23rd) accused the Generals of lack of will, repeating his demands for the subjugation of West Europe, and expressing his fears of Russia.

The U.S.A. repealed the Neutrality Act, allowing "Cash and Carry" whereby Britain could buy war material from America, but only for transport in British ships.

RUSSIA and ARCTIC
Territorial discussions between Russia and Finland grew steadily more strained, when Finland also refused to lease or sell to the Russians the port of Hanko, at the junction of the Baltic and Gulf of Finland. The Russians cancelled their non-aggression pact (28th) and two days later invaded Finland. Finnish harbours in the Arctic and Baltic are being attacked by Russian naval fleets, and on the ground the Finns face forces over 30 times larger than their own.

DECEMBER 1939

EUROPE and ATLANTIC
Another month of "The Phoney War" – except at sea. Between the 2nd and 7th *Graf Spee* sank three big ships in the South Atlantic. But she was intercepted (13th) off the estuary of the River Plate by R.N. cruisers *Ajax*, *Achilles*, and *Exeter*. Outgunned and vulnerable, the cruisers harassed the pocket battleship, with *Exeter* drawing most of the fire until she was put out of action, losing 61 lives. *Ajax* was also badly damaged, *Achilles* less so, but together they had 11 seamen killed. *Graf Spee* was severely damaged by the darting cruisers and, with 36 dead and 60 wounded, she sailed into the neutral port of Montevideo for repairs (14th). On 16th three more R.N. cruisers and the naval Force "K" were ordered to the River Plate. The three-day anchorage given by Montevideo expired (17th) and *Graf Spee* sailed with a skeleton crew. Before reaching open water, Captain Langsdorff ordered the ship scuttled, and later (20th) committed suicide. Her defeat brought an enormous boost of morale to Britain and France, for the Allied losses at sea were steadily mounting. Morale was further boosted when the 32,581 ton German passenger ship *Columbus* was scuttled to avoid capture by the R.N., which had been guided to her by U.S. destroyers escorting her from U.S. waters.

Elsewhere at sea Allied losses continue. The "hero of Scapa Flow", *U47*, sank three more ships, for instance, and *U48* sank 4 – all within less than two weeks. Britain is still refraining from sinking German merchant ships, and this deprived them of the liner *Bremen* after the R.N. submarine *Salmon*, its captor, was forced away by German aircraft (12th). An escort of battlecruiser, battleship, carrier and 12 destroyers guided the first Canadian troop convoy, with 7,400 men of the 1st Canadian Division, across the Atlantic (10th–23rd).

Constant bad weather again postponed Hitler's plans to invade France, and he decided to wait until early in the New Year. Quisling arrived in Berlin, initially seeing Admiral Raeder to whom he confided his fears of an Allied occupation of Norway. Quisling also met Hitler (16th and 18th). The R.A.F. flew a disastrous reconnaissance operation over Wilhelmshaven, and lost 12 of 24 Wellingtons.

By the end of the year, since the morning of 1st September, about 18,000 Poles, including several hundred women, have been executed for various "offences".

RUSSIA and ARCTIC
Russia's invasion of Finland continues to fare badly. Her troops are ill-prepared and the fierce resistance by the Finns has caused concern and disruption. The Finnish ski-patrols (the "White Death") continue to inflict heavy losses on Russian troops. Only at sea have the Finns come off worst.

On 14th the Soviet Union was expelled from the League of Nations.

1940

JANUARY 1940

EUROPE and ATLANTIC
On 10th Hitler decided to begin the attack on France on 17th, but also on 10th a German major bearing the complete Nazi Western-attack plan, was caught in a heavy storm on a flight from Munster to Bonn and made a forced landing in Belgium. He was unable to destroy all his papers and when the German air attache in the Hague reported a long phone call between the King of Belgium and the Queen of Holland, Hitler decided (16th) to change his plan completely. There was speculation that the "accident" was arranged by Admiral Canaris, who was bitterly opposed to attack on France. General von Manstein, despite opposition from the Army High Command (OKH), had his plan of attacking through Belgium and the Ardennes approved by Hitler. This plan was designed to follow much of the 1914 route, bypass the Maginot Line, and meet mainly French instead of English troops. On 27th Hitler ordered preparation of plans for the possible invasion of Norway.

U-boats and mines continue to take heavy toll of Allied shipping – some 70 were sunk this month. R.N.

submarine operations in the Heligoland Bight (off Hamburg) were stopped (9th) after three were sunk in three days.

RUSSIA and ARCTIC
Russo–Finnish war goes on. Red Army thrusts in northern areas diverted a large proportion of Finnish troops away from the Mannerheim Line across the Karelian Isthmus, while the Soviets continue a massive build-up for an assault on the Line.

FAR EAST and PACIFIC
Japan has by now occupied almost all north-east China, and still holds all China's sea ports.

The first contingent of Australian and New Zealand troops left Wellington (6th) for Suez.

FEBRUARY 1940

EUROPE and ATLANTIC
Despite finding the German's original Western plans in the January air crash, Allied Commands did not expect Germany to attack in any way other than against the Maginot Line, as that would have meant violation of neutral countries; therefore they made no alterations to their defensive plans. On the same day however (5th), both a Special German staff group, and the Allied Supreme War Council held meetings – the former to discuss possible invasion of Norway (to prevent the Allies from doing so and getting access to Sweden's steel), and the latter to plan a landing at Narvik in March with the same objectives. Then, in Norway itself, *H.M.S. Cossack* under Churchill's direct orders made a dash up the Jössing-Fjord (16th), and released over 300 prisoners from the German supply ship *Altmark* – all of whom were from ships sunk by *Graf Spee* in the South Atlantic. This unchallenged violation of Norway's waters convinced Hitler that Norway was Britain's accomplice, and resolved him to occupy the country. (He was not concerned that his ship's "cargo" and arms also violated Norway's waters.)

The first Australian and New Zealand troop convoy of 13,500 reached Suez safely, but merchant seamen continued to be involved in a more brutal war than their compatriots in the services. *U53* alone accounted for 6 ships by mines and torpedoes, but was then sunk by the R.N. destroyer *Gurkha.* Bizarre tragedy struck a German destroyer flotilla when it was accidentally attacked by Luftwaffe He III's. During the attack and attempts at evasion (22nd–23rd) two destroyers were sunk by the planes and by British mines with heavy loss of life.

RUSSIA and ARCTIC
Russia attacked Finland (1st), beginning with a massive artillery barrage on a ten mile sector of Finland's Mannerheim Line in the south near Summa. Marshal Timoshenko gathered 27 divisions along the Line, and for two weeks the slamming tactics gradually broke through the Finnish defences. An assault was also mounted across the frozen Gulf of Finland to the rear of Viipuri. The Franco–British expeditionary force, almost ready to sail to Finland's help, was too late.

MARCH 1940

EUROPE and ATLANTIC
But for the continuing terror and sufferings of Jews and opponents of the Nazis, especially in Poland, there was little land evidence of a war between great European powers. Again, it was for the men at sea alone that the war was anything but "phoney". In the first attack by German aircraft on shipping in the southern part of the English Channel (2nd) a passenger ship was set on fire, while around the Shetland and Orkney islands at least 9 U-boats pursued R.N. ships, and sunk 6 merchantmen. U-boats also hunted, unsuccessfully, large numbers of R.N. and French submarines in the North Sea and off Norway – at times 13 U-boats hunting an even greater number of Allied submarines (14–29th). The Luftwaffe sent 34 planes to bomb ships in Scapa Flow (16th) but caused only slight damage. German merchant ships are still scuttling themselves when threatened with capture in the British blockade of Germany. By the end of March, 222 Allied ships – 764,766 tons – have been sunk, for the loss of 18 U-boats.

Paul Reynaud replaced Daladier as Prime Minister of France and at London meeting of Allied Supreme War Council (28th) he urged action in Norway. Chamberlain and Churchill concurred and it was decided to mine Norwegian waters and land forces at Narvik, Trondheim, Bergen and Stavanger. 8th April was set as departure date for troops. (The British War Cabinet had hoped for earlier landings, using the excuse of going to Finland's aid for violation of Norway's neutrality. But this plan was upset by developments in Finland.)

Hitler issued (1st) a directive for the preparation of invasion of Norway and Denmark, though he would still have preferred Neutrality there, with consequent saving of troops. By the middle of the month, however, he was convinced the Allies were planning the same step as he was.

RUSSIA and ARCTIC
Once Russia had smashed through the Mannerheim Line, it was obvious Finland could be completely wiped out, and on 6th the Finnish Government requested peace negotiations with Russia. While the terms were stricter than her original territorial demands, Russia was anxious not to have a really hostile neighbour, and let the Finns off very lightly. **On 13th, the Peace Treaty** was signed. The 3½ month war had cost Finland about 25,000 lives and 61 planes from its meagre air force. Some

200,000 Soviet Russians had died, however, and over 700 planes and 1,500 tanks were destroyed.

APRIL 1940

EUROPE and ATLANTIC

Germany invaded Denmark and Norway (9th) and Denmark had no option but to capitulate (Hitler himself had previously ensured a non-aggression pact). Kristiansand, Narvik, Trondheim, Bergen, and Stavanger were rapidly taken. In Oslo resistance was fiercer – the new cruiser *Blücher* was sunk with over 1,000 men, and the pocket battleship *Lutzow* badly damaged. Eventually the city fell to a large force of airborne troops.

The invasion was preceded, and accompanied, by fumbling Allied attempts to thwart the Germans. After French doubts and haggling, the mining of Norwegian waters only got under way on the 5th, postponing the whole Allied plan, which would have resulted in them landing in Norway before the Germans. The mining operation was extensive, and during it (7th) a large German battle force sailed into the North Sea. The British Home Fleet immediately set out from Scapa Flow and by concentrating on the whereabouts of the battle fleet (among it the battleships *Scharnhorst* and *Gneisenau*) it missed the invasion fleet. On 9th the battlecruiser *Renown* briefly engaged *Scharnhorst* and *Gneisenau*, causing some damage to the latter. More ships arrived to join the Home Fleet, and there were some fierce air-to-sea and sea engagements off the Norwegian coasts. The Luftwaffe sank the destroyer *Gurkha* and damaged two cruisers, while 15 British Skua divebombers sank the cruiser *Konigsberg* in Bergen harbour. Early in the morning of 10th five R.N. destroyers made a daring surprise attack up Ofotfjord, sank two German destroyers and damaged a number of other ships. Two of the British destroyers were sunk; the others escaped, only one being undamaged.

Off the coast the search for the German naval force continued. *Gneisenau, Scharnhorst* and *Admiral Hipper* were spotted by air reconnaissance, but in bad weather escaped both R.N. ships and 92 bombers of Coastal Command. Part of the R.N. force eventually ran into the remaining destroyers of the German Narvik group and sank all 8 ships and a U-boat (13th). No British ships were sunk, but many were badly damaged.

British landings on Norway began on 13th, at Namsos and Harstad, and the following day north of Narvik. More landings followed on 16th and 18th, with the objective of cutting off northern Norway from the strong German concentrations in the south, and using Narvik as the centre of non-German Norway. But the British troops are inadequately trained, and almost at a loss in the thick snow in the north. All crack British troops are in France with the B.E.F., and, despite being outnumbered on land and having the seas commanded by the British, German troops have rapidly dominated ground positions; at Narvik the Germans are facing a force over three times as big.

Quisling immediately tried to set himself up as the new leader of Norway, and while given certain prominence by the Germans, he has not got the role he sought, and is finding very few supporters among his countrymen – who, despite Britain's poor showing in this campaign, are rapidly becoming her strong allies.

MAY 1940

EUROPE and ATLANTIC

Blitzkrieg. At 4.00 a.m. on the 10th paratroopers and Stuka dive-bombers began the **invasion of Holland, Belgium and Luxembourg**, and at 5.30 a.m. the first land forces crossed the borders. (As with the invasion of Norway, the Allies were given warning of the attacks, perhaps originating from Admiral Canaris. But once again, they were not taken seriously). The German Army Group B under Bock led the attack in the north, while Army Group A under von Rundstedt attacked towards France. Anglo–French forces were inadequately prepared – the B.E.F. comprised only 10 divisions and had few tanks, while the French, numerically superior to the Germans, were badly led by generals who could not comprehend the differences between 1914 and 1940. The Belgians were forced back to the Antwerp–Louvaine Line and were joined by a division of the B.E.F. On 13th von Kleist's Panzer Divisions advanced through the Ardennes and by the following day there was **a breach of 50 miles in the French line**. The Germans simply bypassed the Maginot Line.

In Holland the populace tried to flood the low areas and demolish dykes and bridges, but most key positions were quickly occupied by German troops. Belgium fought on, with hopeless appeals to Britain for help. With defeat inevitable, Queen Wilhelmina and the Dutch Government escaped on British destroyers to England (13th). The next day German bombers shattered the centre of Rotterdam while peace negotiations were going on. The massive raid killed over 800 civilians, injured several thousand, and made 78,000 homeless. The Dutch Army surrendered almost immediately thereafter, with 100,000 killed or wounded – about a quarter of its total strength.

Belgium fared no better, and on 16th Antwerp and Brussels were abandoned to the Nazis. The surprise attack through the Ardennes gave the German *blitzkrieg* tactics huge advantage and by 18th Guderian, disobeying von Kleist's orders, but backed by von Rundstedt, had pushed forward with his Panzer corps to the old Somme battlefields. By 20th he had reached the Atlantic.

In Britain, Chamberlain resigned (10th) and a coalition Government with Churchill as Prime Minister was formed. Reynaud, French Premier, took over the

Ministry of National Defence and reorganised his top generals (18th) – but far too late.

Amiens fell (20th) and the Germans advanced on Channel ports. Then von Rundstedt halted 4th Army, a decision approved by Hitler who visited the front on 24th. The next day OKH authorised continued advance, but von Rundstedt kept his forces away from Dunkirk. When Calais fell, 20,000 British, French, Belgian and Dutch soldiers surrendered (26th). On 25th King Leopold warned Churchill Belgium could no longer hold out. The next day he asked for armistice, and ceasefire between Belgium and Germany was declared.

Lord Gort, C-in-C of the B.E.F., decided to evacuate all possible forces from certain destruction or capture, and at 6.57 p.m., 26th, the Admiralty ordered the beginning of Operation Dynamo – the evacuation of the B.E.F. from Dunkirk, though they expected to rescue no more than 35,000 before the area was taken. Countless ships and boats set out, and are now taking thousands off the beaches at Dunkirk. The Luftwaffe is bombing with Stukas, but the weather and R.A.F. fighters are effectively against them. On the 31st alone, 68,014 got off the beaches, and the evacuation continues.

The ill-fated British campaign in Norway was marked by the evacuation from Aandalsnes and Namsos (1st and 2nd). After a long struggle, British, French and Polish troops finally took Narvik (28th) and they are holding it tenuously. Having already occupied Faroe Islands with Denmark's consent in April, Britain has now also occupied Iceland.

The R.A.F. bombed Freiburg (11th) and the Ruhr (15th).

The *Blitzkrieg* that struck the Low Countries was as devastatingly effective as the destruction of Poland. Paratroopers played a decisive rôle in conquering Holland by capturing vital bridges, canals and dykes for the oncoming Panzers and infantry. (The Allies never copied the frequent German infantry use of large numbers of bicycles, though they proved highly effective in Western Europe – and even in Malaya.)

JUNE 1940

EUROPE and ATLANTIC

Evacuation from Dunkirk ended on the 4th after 338,226 troops were rescued. Loss of life, of naval ships and of dozens of small boats was heavy, but the evacuation of ten times more than were expected was considered miraculous. The German advance through France again speeded up, and on the day the Germans crossed the Seine (10th), Mussolini announced **Italy's declaration of war with France and Britain**.

On the 12th the French Government declared Paris an open city, moved to Tours and then to Bordeaux. But on 16th Premier Reynaud resigned and Marshal Pétain took over. The next day he asked the Germans for an Armistice. Much of the remainder of the B.E.F. as well as over 20,000 Polish troops managed to escape from France – a total of 156,000 soldiers and 310 guns were taken off from Cherbourg, but over 3,000 died when the liner *Lancastria* was bombed at St Nazaire. On the 17th Gen. de Gaulle also escaped to Britain.

In the railway carriage where Marshal Foch dictated the Allied terms to Germany in 1918, in the forest of Compiègne, on 22nd **France accepted Hitler's harsh Armistice terms**, and Pétain became the head of Vichy France. The capture of France had cost the Germans only 156,556 killed and wounded. (Vichy-France was the area south of Occupied France, the "border" running roughly from Bordeaux to Geneva, with Lyon north of it. Pétain's Govt. sat at Vichy.)

With Britain now alone against Germany and Fascist Italy, Churchill made his famous "their finest hour" speech to Parliament (18th), preparing his country for the Battle of Britain. In spite of general pessimism over Britain's chances, the U.S.A. increased its supply of weapons. Desperate attempts to get the French fleet to sail from France were in vain.

Allied forces in Narvik proved unable to resist massing German land forces, and the **evacuation of 25,000 Allied soldiers from Norway** began (4th). The German navy tried to intercept evacuation fleet, but only found a subsidiary convoy – on it, however, they inflicted very heavy damage and great loss of life. On 9th **Norway capitulated**, though its ships, especially its large merchant navy, escaped to Britain. But the capture of Norway gave Germany excellent North Sea bases, and the whole western coast of Europe, from the Bay of Biscay to the North Cape, was in Hitler's hands. The capture of Norway had cost the Germans 5,300 lives, the Allies (mostly Britain and France) 2,740.

Near Cracow, in Poland, the Germans opened the Auschwitz concentration camp; its initial purpose being to supply the new I.G. Farben Industrie factory with a regular workforce of 100,000 (this being a "turnover figure" as the inmates were expected to work to death).

The first British commando raid, for morale-boosting purposes as much as for a military objective, took place against the small French port of Le Touquet (23rd–24th).

RUSSIA and ARCTIC

On 26th Russia issued an ultimatum to Rumania demanding the restoration of Bessarabia and northern Bukovina. Within 24 hours, and under reluctant German advice, Rumania withdrew her troops and Russia moved in.

AFRICA and MEDITERRANEAN

"Force H" of the British fleet assembled at Gibraltar to try to prevent the French Mediterranean fleet in Oran, Algeria, being taken over by Germany or Italy. With Italy in the war, the Africa front opened and in an air raid on Tobruk, Marshal Balbo, commander of the ¼ million Italian troops in Libya, was killed (28th). His place was taken by Marshal Graziani.

JULY 1940

EUROPE and ATLANTIC

Hitler's thoughts were increasingly on a landing on Britain, and he decided on the 2nd that invasion would be feasible once the R.A.F. was defeated. On the 16th Hitler issued Directive No. 16 – the initial plans for Operation Sealion – the landing on and occupation of England. (Hitler always referred to "England", and never to "Britain"). The directive called for preparation to be completed by mid-August; and the Battle of Britain had already begun when German bombers attacked Allied convoys in the English Channel (10th).

Although occupied with the problem of defeating Britain, Hitler also expressed his anxiety (21st) over Russia right at his rear while he was dealing with Britain. Then, on 31st, he revealed to his Army chiefs that he would attack Russia in Spring 1941.

SOUTHERN EUROPE, AFRICA and MEDITERRANEAN

Admiral Somerville, in charge of Force H from Gibraltar, was unable to persuade the French Fleet in Oran to come over to Britain, to hand over their ships, to sail them to neutral countries, or to scuttle them. Eventually the British Force H opened fire on the French navy. 1,300 Frenchmen were killed, and the battleship *Bretagne* blew up. Six warships escaped to Vichy-held Toulon, but the French fleet was largely immobilised in other ports.

AUGUST 1940

EUROPE and ATLANTIC

Hitler ordered intensification of air and sea warfare

against Britain ("England") in Directive No. 17 (1st). Prime importance was put on the destruction in air and on ground of the entire R.A.F., but a major strategy was total war on the British economy – therefore ports and shipping were also to be hit. Air warfare was planned to reach maximum power soon after 5th, and Goering foresaw little difficulty. On 8th there were intensive attacks on convoys in the English Channel, and then raids began on fighter airfields in South and South East England. The desperate determination of the fighter pilots, aided by the considerable advantage of radar's early warning which avoided wasteful flying and also let them get above the incoming planes, reduced the R.A.F.'s disadvantage against the far greater numbers in the Luftwaffe. German bomber and fighter losses were consistently higher than British losses, although it was clear that the R.A.F. could not long sustain its own rate of destruction. On **the Battle of Britain's busiest day** there were five major actions, and almost 1,000 planes attacked southern England and Tyneside. German losses that day were 76, against 34 British planes. Goering is embarrassed by the failure of his Luftwaffe to achieve rapid success, and the raids continue.

At sea U-boats and mines continue to take a mounting toll of shipping. On the 17th Germany announced a total blockade of a large area around Britain, in which all ships are liable to be sunk without warning. With the failure to knock out the R.A.F., and after internal differences among war leaders, Hitler decided (27th) on a landing on the "smaller front" – some 100 miles of England's South East coast nearest to France. Operation Sealion (the invasion) was still scheduled for 15th September, but on 30th the harassed German Navy reported that it could not be ready before 20th Sept. at the earliest. The first preparatory studies were also compiled for the German assault on Russia.

RUSSIA and ARCTIC

Estonia, Latvia and Lithuania became states of Soviet Russia, giving Russia a wide frontage on the Baltic (3rd–6th). On the 5th a Soviet submarine escorted by ice-breakers and a tanker set out from Murmansk for Vladivostok via the Northern seaway – the first submarine to sail this route.

FAR EAST and PACIFIC

Japan compelled France to allow her to undertake "protective" occupation of strategic positions and services in French Indo-China.

SOUTHERN EUROPE, AFRICA and MEDITERRANEAN

Italian forces invaded British and French Somaliland (5th). The main British position near Tug Argan was attacked on the 11th, and three days later British evacuation of Somaliland began. By the 19th some 7,000 civilians and troops had sailed from Berbera to Aden, and Somaliland was in Italian hands.

Mussolini demanded (unsuccessfully) that Greece should denounce Britain's guarantee of Greek independence. He branded Greece for having an "unneutral" attitude, and Italian troops stationed in Albania ("annexed" by Mussolini in April 1939) massed on the Greek border. A Greek cruiser was torpedoed and sunk (15th) by an unknown submarine. Italy denied responsibility over the attack.

SEPTEMBER 1940

EUROPE and ATLANTIC

Between 1st and 5th, the Luftwaffe made 11 major air raids on R.A.F. fighter airfields and on factories. Heavy loss of British planes and destruction of vital sector-stations left the R.A.F. very nearly beaten. Germany did not realise the full significance of the radar stations and failed to destroy them. This, plus a change of tactics on 6th, probably saved the R.A.F. – though it was still inflicting crippling losses on the Luftwaffe. The **6th of September was a decisive day**: Britain learnt for certain that Germany was massing an invasion fleet; the U.S.A. handed over the first eight of its old destroyers to the Royal Navy; and the Luftwaffe switched its attentions away from airfields and aircraft factories and onto London. That night 68 bombers attacked the city, but on 7th came the first mass air raid. At 5 p.m. over 300 bombers and twice as many fighters began to pound London, and two hours later 250 more bombers dropped their explosives. Attacks continued until the early morning and left 430 civilians killed and 1,600 severely injured. **The Blitz had begun.** The bombers returned the next night, and a further 412 died . . . the raids continued nightly, and are still going on.

One of the worst days – though also for the Luftwaffe – was the 15th when a massive daylight raid ruined thousands of London homes. But the Germans lost 56 planes, and Goering realised his force could not long take such losses. That night R.A.F. bombers carried out their heaviest raid – on invasion ports from Boulogne to Antwerp, sinking many barges and small craft. Two days later (17th) Hitler ordered Operation Sealion postponed indefinitely "but inconspicuously" – having on the 3rd accepted 21st as the probable date.

Allied convoys are still suffering heavy losses from U-boats, and from mines "sown" by U-boats or aircraft. Italian and Vichy French submarines have joined forces under the Commander of U-boats, Vice-Admiral Doenitz. Britain signed the Destroyer/Naval Base Deal with America, and received 50 destroyers in exchange for the American use of British naval bases in the western Atlantic.

A Vichy French naval force sailed for Gabon (9th) to attempt to win back the colony from de Gaulle and the Free French. A British and Free French naval force, which had sailed from the Clyde on 31st August to try to win for the Free French the Vichy colony of Dakar (Operation Menace), received orders to intercept the Vichy fleet, but that fleet put into Dakar before it was located. On the 18th British ships intercepted two of the Vichy fleet sailing from Dakar to Libreville, and took them under escort. Three Vichy cruisers were shadowed and when one slowed down with engine trouble, it was also taken under escort. The last two Vichy cruisers abandoned the Gabon attempt and returned to join the considerable French naval force in Dakar. On 22nd Operation Menace began with R.N. shelling off Dakar. Attempts by de Gaulle (by wireless) were unable to get the Vichy force to change sides, and a fierce two-way naval bombardment went on for two days, before Churchill ordered the attempt to be given up.

FAR EAST and PACIFIC

Japan signed the Tripartite Pact with Germany and Italy (27th), in Berlin. Hitler saw in Japan a buffer against the U.S.A. and a distraction for Russia, while Japan, beginning the occupation of French Indo-China, saw an opportunity to take over "defeated" Europe's colonial possessions in the East.

SOUTHERN EUROPE, AFRICA and MEDITERRANEAN

Italian troops continued to mass on the Albania/Greece border, and 40,310 troops, plus horses, vehicles and 33,500 tons of supplies arrived safely in Albania from Brindisi (12th). In North Africa, Italian troops advanced just into Egypt (13th), and Graziani built 7 forts which were, however, sited ineffectually.

The beginning of the Blitz of London marked the R.A.F.'s victory in the Battle of Britain, for Fighter Command was able to build-up its depleted forces and repair its airfields. The sprawling miles of London never became an overfamiliar sight to many Luftwaffe bomber pilots.

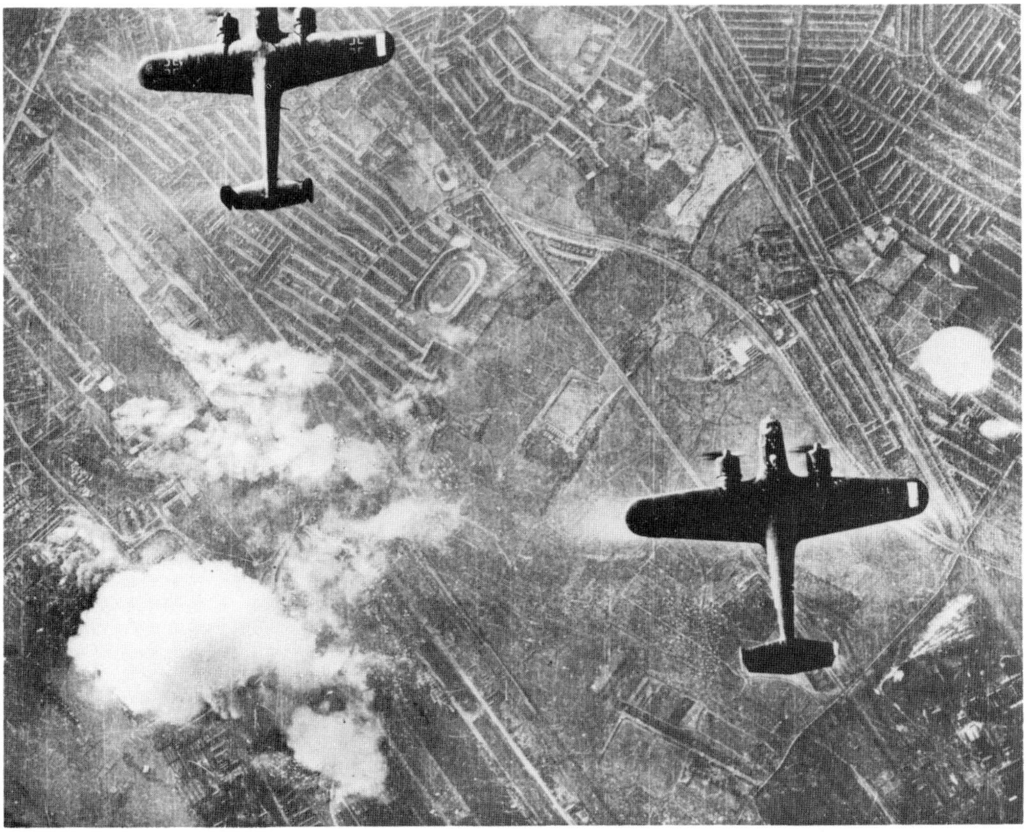

Vichy French aircraft from Morocco bombed Gibraltar (24th and 25th) as reprisal for the Dakar bombardment and dropped over 100 tons of bombs, but caused little damage.

OCTOBER 1940

EUROPE and ATLANTIC

Reichsmarshal Goering lost considerable prestige when it became clear any invasion fleet would still have to face massive R.A.F. attacks, and with winter approaching Hitler called off Sealion (12th), arbitrarily choosing Spring 1941 as the new date, though there was little conviction that it would ever take place.

Hitler met Franco (23rd) in a bid to get Spanish help against Britain, seeking especially the capture of Gibraltar, but Franco remained firm on Spanish neutrality. The next day Hitler met Marshal Pétain who signed an agreement under which Vichy France would collaborate with Germany in the defeat of Britain. Hitler then went on to meet Mussolini (28th) and learnt of the Italian invasion of Greece (see below). This surprise infuriated Hitler. He knew Mussolini would need German help, and that would delay his own attack on Russia. To Hitler, Mussolini's was a senseless act, offering scant reward for the effort, unlike Germany's "very useful" (and peaceful) occupation of Rumania (7th).

The Battle of the Atlantic continued with unrelenting viciousness. The ordeal of eastbound Atlantic convoy HX 79 was a typical example. In one night (19th–20th) – and despite a strong escort – a pack of five U-boats sank 11 merchant ships, while almost equal havoc was simultaneously being wreaked on the westbound convoy OB 229.

SOUTHERN EUROPE, AFRICA and MEDITERRANEAN

On the 28th Mussolini presented Greece with an ultimatum alleging a list of "wrongs" perpetrated by Greece against Italy, and demanded that Italian troops should be permitted to occupy certain strategic positions in Greece. Without waiting for a reply, **the Italians invaded Greece from Albania**. Britain promised support for Greece, and landed Army and R.A.F. units on Crete (31st).

The Italian navy again had little good fortune. Having missed a Malta convoy, an attack was mounted (11th–12th) on the R.N. escorts returning to Gibraltar. An initial surprise attack was made by three torpedo boats on the cruiser *Ajax*, but two were sunk almost immediately. A destroyer which had come up in support was severely damaged and easily sunk the next day, after its crew had been warned to abandon it.

NOVEMBER 1940

EUROPE and ATLANTIC

The war at sea continued its ferocity, and with the continuation of bombing of cities, merchant seamen and civilian losses have been higher than in the fighting forces. The centre of Coventry was practically wiped out in a massive night air-raid (14th–15th), which marked the beginning of a new German bombing strategy. Almost 500 bombers took part, and some 400 people were killed. London had twelve quiet nights – its first since the Blitz began, but was very heavily bombed again on 15th. Luftwaffe strategy of hitting industrial centres then selected Birmingham (19th–22nd) and killed nearly 800, injuring three times as many. Southampton was another centre that suffered badly (23rd, 24th and 30th). Worst attack of all was the incendiary raid on London (29th) in which a great part of the City of London was destroyed, and St. Paul's Cathedral only just saved. The R.A.F. made a 127 bomber raid on Hamburg (16–17th).

In the Atlantic U-boats and mines again took a heavy toll, while *U99* under Lt. Cdr. Kretschmer has begun to establish a chilling reputation for destruction. The German heavy cruiser *Admiral Scheer* attacked a convoy of 37 ships bound for Britain, east of Newfoundland. The R.N. auxiliary cruiser *Jervis Bay* sacrificed herself by holding the *Scheer* while the convoy tried to scatter under a smoke screen. The German ship then sank five merchant ships, damaged three, and escaped into the South Atlantic.

SOUTHERN EUROPE, AFRICA and MEDITERRANEAN

Mussolini hoped for a rapid victory in Greece, and while the R.A.F. was establishing bases in Crete, the dictator poured 200,000 troops into Greece from Albania It should have been the end, for the Greek defences faced Bulgaria. But Mussolini underestimated his victims, who rapidly mobilised and switched to the offensive. The Italian setbacks began when their crack Alpine Division lost 5,000 in a Greek trap sprung in the Pindus Gorges of N.W. Greece. Allied reinforcements of 3,400 troops from Alexandria arrived in Piraeus (16th) and by the 22nd the Greeks had pushed into Albania, taken Koritza and captured huge quantities of equipment.

The Italian Navy were no better off – on Italy's worst day in Greece (11th), part of the British Mediterranean Fleet led by the carrier *Illustrious* made a raid on the Italian Fleet in the harbour of Taranto. Swordfish aircraft inflicted heavy damage, sinking three battleships. Two planes were shot down. Another part of the Mediterranean Fleet sank four merchant ships in the Strait of Otranto.

Free French forces comprising mainly Foreign Legion units under Col. Leclerc, made a seaborne attack on Libreville (7–9th) while the R.N. blockaded Gabon. The

Vichy Navy suffered heavy loss and by 14th all French Equatorial Africa was controlled by de Gaulle.

DECEMBER 1940

EUROPE and ATLANTIC

Wat at sea claimed many more lives and thousands of tons of shipping. German auxiliary cruisers, generally disguised to look like merchantmen, continue to take a heavy toll of unescorted ships, especially in the South Atlantic and Indian Oceans. The German heavy cruiser *Admiral Hipper* slipped unnoticed through the Denmark Strait to hunt merchant ships in the North Atlantic. On 25th *Hipper* engaged the cruiser *Berwick*, an escort of a troop convoy south-bound far west of Finisterre, and inflicted some damage on her and two merchantmen. *Hipper*, outnumbered and with faulty engines, then withdrew, sinking an independent ship on the way. She arrived in Brest on 27th, and is a constant threat to Channel shipping and Mediterranean-bound convoys.

Mines have again sunk many ships. Three operations by the Luftwaffe (12–19th) dropped 300 mines in the Thames estuary and they claimed 12 ships before the end of the month. The battleships *Gneisenau* and *Scharnhorst* tried for the first time to break out into the North Atlantic, but heavy storm damage to *Gneisenau* off Norway postponed the attempt.

December saw the first concentrated R.A.F. bombing attacks on Mannheim, Bremen and Kiel, among other industrial centres. The Luftwaffe carried out heavy raids on Liverpool harbour (20th–22nd), sinking one ship and damaging 19. Hitler ordered Directive no. 20, which planned the reinforcement of Rumania to counter British strength in the Balkans.

FAR EAST and PACIFIC

The German auxiliary cruiser *Schiff 45 Komet* shelled the small British island of Nauru (700 miles north-east of Solomon Islands) and destroyed oil tanks, the phosphate loading mechanism, and other installations.

SOUTHERN EUROPE, AFRICA and MEDITERRANEAN

Allied troops were in a major offensive against the Italians in North Africa (7–11th). Its success was greatly due to the daring tactics of Gen. O'Connor who began an advance over the 70 miles separating the forces in Egypt on the 7th and engaged far larger Italian forces on the 9th. After breaking through a gap in the defences, O'Connor's tanks defeated the Italian tank forces. Advances and captures continued rapidly, and by 11th Gen. Wavell estimated 5 Italian divisions were out of action. The advance was assisted by R.A.F. attacks on Italian airfields, and by R.N. ships bombarding Sidi Barrani and the coastal road.

The British Mediterranean Fleet still had as its major concern the escorting of convoys to Malta, but it also carried out operations on Axis airfields in the Aegean, and shelled the Albanian port of Valona. Germany transferred some Luftwaffe units to Southern Italy and Sicily. By the end of the month, about one quarter of Albania is in Greek control.

1941

JANUARY 1941

EUROPE and ATLANTIC

Germany continued its build-up in Rumania in readiness to aid Italians in the Mediterranean areas, but Mussolini, already humiliated, persuaded Hitler to leave the struggling Albanian offensive to Italian forces.

The German Army High Command drew up its first preparatory directive for Barbarossa – the invasion of Russia (31st).

At sea German raiders are as big a hazard to unescorted ships in southern waters as U-boats and mines are to convoys in the north. The heavy cruiser *Admiral Scheer* captured three British merchant ships (18–20th) and the auxiliary cruiser *Schiff 33 Pinguin* captured three Norwegian whaling factory ships with 22,200 tons of whale oil, and 11 whalers. A British auxiliary cruiser captured a Vichy French merchantman – one of the frequent, tragic brushes between British and French at sea. Allied maritime hazards increased when *Scharnhorst* and *Gneisenau*, under Admiral Lütjens, slipped out from Kiel.

Hitler finally gave up hopes of being able to capture Gibraltar – a conclusion also reached by the Italians. On 29th secret Anglo–American talks began in Washington on the joint conduct of the war in the event of the U.S.A. being drawn in.

There was a very heavy air raid on Plymouth (10–11th).

SOUTHERN EUROPE, AFRICA and MEDITERRANEAN

After heavy shelling from three battleships, eleven destroyers and several gunboats, Bardia was evacuated by the Italians who began a headlong retreat along the Cyrenaica (Libya) coast. Generals O'Connor and Wavell decided that O'Connor's troops should take the opportunity – and risk – of short-cutting south west across the diameter of the Cyrenaica bulge, to cut off the Italians, and at the end of the month they have almost reached the head of the Italian retreat. British and Australian troops occupied Tobruk after heavy bombardment from R.N. and R. Australian Navy ships, (22nd) and captured 25,000 Italian soldiers and 50 tanks.

Wavell's offensives against the Italians in Abyssinia

and Somaliland have begun. Thinking the British had huge forces in Sudan, the Italians quit Kassala and crossed the Abyssinian border into the Eritrea area. Allied forces in Sudan went on to defeat Gen. Frusci at the battle of Agordat, east of Kassala, but many Italians took refuge from it all in the mountainous area of Keren (31st). Lt. Gen. Sir Alan Cunningham and the Allied forces in Kenya began their advance from the south (24th) and crossed the border into Italian Somaliland (29th).

FEBRUARY 1941

EUROPE and ATLANTIC

Again it was merchant seamen who suffered the brutality of warfare in this sector; and Jews and Communists who underwent the barbarities of the Nazis in German-occupied Europe. The heavy cruiser *Admiral Hipper* left Brest (1st) on her second Atlantic hunt, and returned on 15th, having sunk 7 out of 9 ships in an unescorted North Atlantic convoy (12th). The fearsome duo of *Gneisenau* and *Scharnhorst* slipped unnoticed through the Denmark Strait (4th) and cruised the North Atlantic, where they sank 5 merchantmen (22nd).

SOUTHERN EUROPE, AFRICA and MEDITERRANEAN

Gen. O'Connor's daring attack which routed the Italians finished its headlong advance when the Italian forces capitulated at Beda Fomm, 50 miles south of Benghazi. Advance Allied units had cut the coast road on 5th, and 5,000 Italian soldiers had been taken prisoner. The next day Australian troops stormed Benghazi as the main Italian force began to march into the Beda Fomm trap. On the 7th the 62-day drive was over, and 2 Allied divisions had routed 10 Italian divisions. 130,000 were taken prisoner, and nearly 400 tanks and some 850 guns were captured. The price paid by the Allies was the loss of 555 soldiers, and nearly 1,400 wounded.

In the battle of Juba River (16th) Cunningham's forces defeated the bulk of the defenders of Italian Somaliland. The relatively small force then covered the 275 miles to Mogadishu in 2½ days, and found enormous fuel stocks on their arrival (25th). Further north in the Eritrea province of Abyssinia, 30,000 of the best Italian troops established themselves firmly in the mountain fortress of Keren.

Greece was persuaded to accept British troops as reinforcements against the Italians (24th) who were receiving increasing German support. Gen. Wavell, burdened with the almost impossible task of conducting fronts in Somaliland, Abyssinia, Libya and Greece, also had to face the **arrival of the first German troops in North Africa**, who garrisoned Tripoli (12th) under the direction of Gen. Rommel, who had arrived on 2nd.

Part of the R.N. Mediterranean Fleet shelled Genoa (9th), sank four merchant ships in the harbour and caused considerable damage in the city. Bad weather prevented the Italian Fleet from finding any of the British ships.

Malta suffered one of its early attacks by the Luftwaffe (7–8th).

MARCH 1941

EUROPE and ATLANTIC

The U.S. Senate passed **the Lend-Lease Bill** under which America would supply Britain with equipment, notably ships, on a "freely lent" basis. This gave Britain access to enormous resources, without getting even deeper into debt. On 30th, all German, Italian, and Danish ships in U.S.A. harbours were seized.

Gneisenau and *Scharnhorst* put in to Brest (22nd), having sunk or captured 22 ships in two months. As soon as their presence in harbour was confirmed (29th), Brest was blockaded by the R.N. Air raids began as well, R.A.F. bomber offensives being diverted almost entirely to the battleships, though with little real success.

RUSSIA and ARCTIC

Hitler clarified his eastward "lebensraum" aims to his Service chiefs and senior generals, and emphasised as well that the war against Russia was to be one of "ideologies and racial differences" which would have to be conducted with "unprecedented, unmerciful and unrelenting harshness". He excused in advance any breaking of international laws, since Russia had not participated in the Hague convention.

British Commandos raided four ports in the northern Norway island group of Lofoten. They blew up fish oil factories, sank two ships, captured 225 prisoners and took back 315 Norwegian volunteers, without suffering any casualties.

FAR EAST and PACIFIC

Japan was strongly urged by Hitler to attack the British at Singapore.

SOUTHERN EUROPE, AFRICA and MEDITERRANEAN

Gen. Cunningham continued his rapid move through Somaliland and into Abyssinia, encountering Italian forces again only at Dagabur, 590 miles from Mogadishu (10th). A small Allied force from Aden reoccupied Berbera on the Gulf of Aden (16th), and the next day Cunningham's forces took Giggia, almost due west. With the benefit of a new, short line of communication, they soon took Harar. In 30 days, Cunningham's forces had covered over 1,000 miles.

The Allied push southwards into Eritrea met repeated Italian counter attacks, but on the 27th the seige of the Keren fortress ended with its capitulation. The hard defence had cost the Italians over 3,000 dead, and after that resistance in Eritrea collapsed steadily.

Hitler consolidated his eastward expansion by compelling Bulgaria to join the Tripartite pact (1st). The Italians tried to regain the initiative against Greece (9th), and eventually Hitler forced Yugoslavia to join the Axis powers as well (24th). But two days later Gen. Simovic overthrew the Government and set up a new one in the name of King Peter – giving Britain a much-needed ally in this sector. Hitler then issued Directive No. 25, ordering the destruction of Yugoslavia as well as Greece.

The Axis build-up in North Africa continued, while large numbers of Allied troops were taken out of the line to fight in Greece. Rommel, with one German and two Italian divisions, attacked a depleted British line near El Agheila, 150 miles south of Benghazi, and is driving them back.

Further British troops arrived in Greece (5th). The Italian navy tried to intercept another convoy, but met Admiral Cunningham's Mediterranean battle fleet off **Cape Matapan**. Air attacks slowed the Italian Fleet. Late the next night (28th), three Italian cruisers were spotted unsuspectingly crossing the front of the R.N. battle fleet, which suddenly lit up the cruisers and two escorts with searchlights and at virtually point blank range opened fire on the surprised Italians. All three cruisers and the two large destroyers were sunk within minutes. The British ships were almost unscathed, but 2,400 Italian sailors were lost with the five ships, only 900 being rescued.

APRIL 1941

EUROPE and ATLANTIC

Bombing raids by both the R.A.F. and the Luftwaffe continued regularly. Plymouth suffered heavy bombing (21st–28th) in which 1,000 were killed and injured, and some 40,000 left homeless. London had a number of raids. The R.A.F. bombed Kiel and Wilhelmshaven (24–25th), hoping this time to also hit the pocket battleship *Admiral Scheer* which returned to Kiel (1st) from a cruise during which she sunk 17 ships. Bombing attacks, and mine laying operations, continued against the two battleships in Brest, and four bombs hit *Gneisenau* (10–11th).

RUSSIA and ARCTIC

Hitler set the date for Operation Barbarossa (the invasion of Russia) as 22nd June, and expected it to take not more than 10 weeks, although he already resented the delay caused by the Balkan campaign.

FAR EAST and PACIFIC

Japan signed a treaty of neutrality with Russia (13th), and tried to persuade America to recognise special rights for the Japanese throughout the Far East. The U.S.A. insisted that all military activity in China should first stop.

SOUTHERN EUROPE, AFRICA and MEDITERRANEAN

The Germans invaded Yugoslavia (6th), hurling 33 divisions against the Yugoslav's 28, of which three were cavalry divisions. The country's defences were thinly dispersed and rapidly fell to the *blitzkrieg* tactics. In "Operation Punishment" the completely defenceless city of Belgrade was murderously bombed into a shattered ruin, a rubble grave for some 17,000 Yugoslavs. On 13th Belgrade was taken and soon after Yugoslavia surrendered (17th).

Simultaneously with the invasion, German troops had gone into Greece to aid the Italians. The German attack from Bulgaria soon resulted in the fall of Salonika (8th), while other attacks came across the Yugoslavia border, and with the Italians through Albania. The rapid fall of Yugoslavia put extra pressure on the widely spread-out Greek and British troops. The British, Australian and New Zealand forces withdrew to Mount Olympus (13th). The Greeks also came under strong attack and the defence line retreated rapidly south. Heavy bombing by the Luftwaffe was a constant part of the assault; a great deal of damage was caused in Piraeus, and many valuable supplies destroyed. The R.A.F. was compelled to quit all Greek airfields, and on 21st the Greek army surrendered. The British forces began a difficult evacuation without air cover (24th). German paratroops cut off the Peloponnese by siezing the bridge over the Corinth Canal (26th). The next day the Germans entered Athens, the **Greek Government surrendered**, and the Swastika flew above the Acropolis. The King of Greece went to Crete, but Hitler had already issued a directive for the capture of the island (25th), an intention confirmed by agents in occupied Athens. The majority of the Greek navy escaped, including all its submarines.

Africa. Rommel's assault on the meagre British force under Gen. Neame in Libya forced them back to Agedabia (2nd), and a separate German attack towards the main Allied fuel dump at Msus forced the garrison to destroy it (3rd). This also deprived the British of most of their mobility. Benghazi was abandoned and the Germans and Italians began to overhaul the retreating British. On the night of 6th, a German patrol captured Gen. Neame and Gen. O'Connor. It was decided (6th) to hold Tobruk and it was reinforced, mainly with Australian troops. The garrison, of about 23,000, was besieged on 11th. Two days later, Bardia, well to the east, was evacuated by the Allies.

Three battleships and a cruiser of the R.N. Mediterranean Fleet from Alexandria bombarded Tripoli in the night of 20th, and caused extensive damage in the port. Four R.N. destroyers intercepted an Axis convoy off the

Tunisian coast and destroyed it completely, losing one destroyer (16th). Approximately 1,800 of the 3,000 troops on the five merchant ships died.

Asmara in northern Abyssinia (Eritrea) fell and 10,000 Italians were taken prisoner (1st). The important Red Sea port of Massawa was captured three days later, and this released large numbers of South African troops to reinforce the hard-pressed Allies in Egypt. On the same day (4th) the Italians abandoned Addis Ababa, capital of Abyssinia. Cunningham, from the south, captured Dessie (20th) and closed on the remaining Italians led by the Duke of Aosta (who are fortifying themselves in Amba Alagi), while Gen. Platt closes in from his success in Eritrea.

After a revolt, the new Prime Minister of Iraq announces his intention to confirm the treaty allowing the British on Iraq.

MAY 1941

EUROPE and ATLANTIC

Under the command of Admiral Lütjens the battleship *Bismarck* and the heavy cruiser *Prinz Eugen*, with preliminary escorts, sailed from Gdynia (18th). The fleet was sighted by air reconnaissance and the Battle Cruiser Squadron under Vice-Admiral Holland, and comprising the battle-cruiser *Hood* and the battleship *Prince of Wales* with escorts sailed from Scapa Flow (21st). The following day the Home Fleet, with the battleship *King George V*, the carrier *Victorious* and numerous cruisers and destroyers under Admiral Tovey also put to sea. The German ships were sighted passing through the Denmark Strait (23rd) and the next day was engaged by the Battle Cruiser Squadron. Almost immediately a shell from *Bismarck* struck *Hood* and penetrated her after-magazine. *Hood* exploded, and disappeared in three minutes, leaving only 3 survivors. Vice-Adm. Holland was among the 1,416 who died with the ship. The *Prince of Wales* was damaged but her shells had hit *Bismarck*, which slowed and began to lose oil. She was later hit by a torpedo from a plane off *Victorious*, but was not sighted again till the 26th when a torpedo attack by Swordfish aircraft off *Ark Royal* damaged her steering gear. Hemmed in by dozens of ships of the R.N. (27th), shelled by the battleships *King George V* and *Renown*, Hitler's largest battleship was finally sent to the bottom by torpedoes from the cruiser *Dorsetshire*, and 2,100 perished with her.

Rudolf Hess "appropriated" a fighter and flew to Scotland, in what he explained was his bid to make a settlement. Imprisoned, he was then virtually ignored by the British, while Hitler overcame the embarrassment by references to Hess's mental instability.

Air warfare over Britain and Europe continues in intensity each month. Liverpool was very heavily bombed (1st–7th), Clyde port installations were hit (6–7th), and a massive raid on London (10–11th) caused some 2,000 fires. The R.A.F. carried out its biggest ever night raid (8–9th) on Bremen and Hamburg, and two nights later 110 bombers returned to attack Hamburg.

A break in the war at sea came with the capture of *U110* (9th) together with numerous code books, etc. Lt. Cdr. Lemp, who had sunk the *Athenia* on the evening of the first day of war, was killed during the engagement.

"Gustav Siegfried Eins," Britain's "black propaganda" radio station began its broadcasts and received rapid "success" with German troops.

RUSSIA and ARCTIC

German leaders carried out the final preparations on their plans for the occupation and exploitation of Russia. Keitel issued a directive in Hitler's name (13th) by which suspected Russian civilians could be summarily "tried" by German officers and shot if necessary, while prosecution of German soldiers for offences against Russian civilians was not obligatory. Another directive accorded to Himmler the carrying out of "special tasks" prior to the administration of occupied areas – i.e. the extermination of Jews and other "undesirable elements". Goering was to be responsible for exploitation of the country and its assets. The planners acknowledged that millions of Russian civilians would have to go without adequate food, which would be needed for Germans. Despite rumours, troop build-ups, and even direct reports from his agents and from Britain, which even gave him the actual date, Stalin refuses to believe that Germany is planning an attack on Russia.

FAR EAST and PACIFIC

The Chief of the Imperial General Staff urged reinforcement of Singapore's defences, but Churchill would not cut back on allocations to Egypt.

SOUTHERN EUROPE, AFRICA and MEDITERRANEAN

The evacuation of Greece ended (2nd) with 11,000 men and great quantities of equipment being left behind; but 43,000 did manage to get away since the evacuation began on 24th April. The decision was taken to attempt to hold Crete, and Maj. Gen. Freyberg was put in command of the rather meagre defences (4th), which were strengthened by troops from Greece and by Royal Marines who were to hold Suda Bay. After heavy bombing of the airfields by the Luftwaffe, the last few R.A.F. fighters left Crete (19th).

Elite German paratroops were dropped on Crete in the war's first massive airborne invasion, and fighting was ruthless and ferocious (20th). Almost the complete first wave of 3,500 paratroops was killed, but the unopposed Luftwaffe soon smashed the anti-aircraft guns and turned on the defenders. A second wave of 3,000 Germans managed to establish a foothold. After the fiercest

Above: Left to right: Hitler, Ribbentrop, Himmler and Göring (Photo: Properfoto Limited). Below: Field-Marshal Bernard Montgomery and Marshal Georgi Zhukov in Berlin, 1945 (Photo: Imperial War Museum).

fighting, Maleme airfield was captured (21st), and German planes with reinforcements and supplies began to land at the rate of 20 per hour. The Germans attempted a seaborne invasion the next day, but R.N. cruisers and destroyers intercepted the fleet of small boats, and sank 15 of them and an Italian destroyer. Approximately 4,000 soldiers were drowned, the weight of their equipment dragging them under. Another invasion was attempted, and although massive air cover sank two R.N. cruisers and three destroyers, the invasion was repulsed and no more attempts by sea were made. By 28th the Germans were rapidly establishing superiority and the Heraklion garrison was evacuated to Alexandria, with heavy losses at sea inflicted by the Luftwaffe. By the following morning 5,000 had left, and that night (29th) another 6,000 were safely evacuated – the escape to Alexandria continues.

Emperor Haile Selassie became the first Facist-deposed sovereign to return to his capital when he arrived at Addis Ababa (5th). The duke of Aosta surrendered the last Italian stronghold of Amba Alagi (18th). He was granted the supreme recognition of "the honours of war", but insisted on clearing their minefields, and then handed over all arms. Guerilla warfare and sporadic resistance continues inland in the Gondar province. The Allied campaign against the Italians in Somaliland and Abyssinia was conducted with rare chivalry, and there was very little destruction in towns and villages.

Iraq went back on her word and besieged the British military base at Habbaniya (2nd). Germany established air bases in Syria with French connivance, and bombed Habbaniya. A British and Arab Legion force from Transjordan relieved the besieged base, and went on to take Baghdad (31st).

JUNE 1941

EUROPE and ATLANTIC

Hitler, Goering, Himmler and Heydrich finalised plans and briefed subordinates for the "final solution" of Jews. Auschwitz was chosen to be the chief extermination camp.

RUSSIA and ARCTIC

Stalin continued to disbelieve rumours and reports of an imminent German invasion and even broadcast denials (14th), accusing Britain of trying to split Germany and Russia. In Berlin on the same day Hitler held an all day conference going over the Barbarossa plans with his Chiefs and leading generals. On the evening of 21st Molotov received German Ambassador in the Kremlin and mentioned his concern about Germany's seemingly strained relations with Russia. Early the next morning the Ambassador delivered the declaration of war which he had just received from Berlin. Simultaneously the Soviet Ambassador in Berlin was informed by Ribbentrop that German "countermeasures against Soviet threats" had begun. At 3.00 a.m. Ciano was given an explanatory letter from Hitler for Mussolini, who then also declared war on Russia.

Operation Barbarossa began at 3.30 a.m., 22nd with a massive artillery barrage along hundreds of miles of the front. Russia was so taken by surprise that her artillery did not return fire for several hours. Many Red Army troops were overrun before they could deploy for action, and many hundreds of Russian planes were destroyed on the ground. Russian losses were enormous, and tens of thousands of prisoners of war filed back into Germany. The formerly superior Soviet air power was completely shattered, and its leader committed suicide. The German *blitzkrieg* tactics once more seem invincible, and the Russians are falling back rapidly. Already Brest-Litovsk has been taken (24th).

SOUTHERN EUROPE, AFRICA and MEDITERRANEAN

The R.N.'s **evacuation of Crete** saved some 16,000 British, Australian and New Zealand troops, but after 1st no more ships could approach, and about 10,000 Allied soldiers (about half of them Greek) fell into Axis hands. The capture of Crete cost Germany dear – up to 17,000 soldiers may have been killed and wounded, and the Army generals were particularly distressed by the slaughter of the crack paratroops. The Allies also suffered badly. The R.N. lost three cruisers, six destroyers, many smaller craft, and 2,000 were killed and wounded.

In "Operation Battleaxe" the Allies tried to relieve Tobruk (15th) but after initial success Wavell had to fall back before Rommel's counter-attack (17th). Gen. Auchinleck relieved Gen. Wavell as C-in-C Middle East (21st) and Lt. Gen. Cunningham took over the newly-created 8th Army.

The **British invaded Syria and Lebanon** (8th) with the support of de Gaulle, and met strong Vichy French resistance. Damascus was captured by Australian troops after a daring commando attack behind enemy lines (21st).

Germany and Turkey signed a treaty of friendship (18th).

JULY 1941

EUROPE and ATLANTIC

The U.S. Navy began reconnaissance of north west Atlantic (1st), while an American fleet sailed with troops to relieve the British garrison on Iceland.

RUSSIA and ARCTIC

German advances in Russia were rapid, and Stalin soon reversed his long anti-British tendencies to begin clamouring for every assistance, as well as a diversionary second front. The Russians carried out a scorched-earth policy during their retreat. The **German armies advanced 400 miles in 18 days**, but when they advanced towards Smolensk on 10th, resistance began to stiffen. Hitler, however, was confident Russia would soon collapse, and issued a directive about an imminent reduction in Army strength (14th) and a greater concentration of production on ships and planes for the destruction of Britain. But then the Red Army brought into use its formidable Katyusha rockets and when the Germans reached Smolensk (16th) there was bitter fighting. The Luftwaffe also began to meet stronger opposition.

Stalin reacted furiously over the retreat and there was a purge of officers whom he felt had failed and a number of them were shot. The Germans had captured nearly 150,000 Russian soldiers, as well as over 1,000 tanks and 600 guns by the end of the month.

The newly formed SS Action Groups (*Einsatzgruppen*) operating behind the advancing Germans, were given their first listings of thousands of Jews, agitators, and Communist Party officials, with orders from Heydrich that they were to be shot. The barbaric treatment of the Russian civilians within German territory is sickening – and it is also foolish. Some Russians are at first pleased to be out of Stalin's iron grip, but rapidly discover anything is better than the Nazis.

FAR EAST and PACIFIC

Roosevelt's adviser, Hopkins, asked Churchill to strengthen Singapore defences, but Churchill still insisted on giving Egypt priority. Roosevelt froze all Japanese assets in the U.S.A. (26th) and put an embargo on oil supplies to Japan. When Britain and the Dutch Government in London followed suit, Japan was deprived of practically all her supplies of oil.

From the very first day of the war, death was a close companion to merchant seamen crossing the Atlantic, and U-boat commanders and crews became Germany's heroes as ship after defenceless ship was sent to the bottom. The U.S. Lend-Lease Act, however, gave the Royal Navy many desperately needed escorts.

SOUTHERN EUROPE, AFRICA and MEDITERRANEAN
Allies achieved superiority in Syria and after an approach by the Vichy French, an Armistice was signed (14th) giving Allies occupation of Syria and blocking the German path to the Persian Gulf and India. Allied casualties were over 4,600 killed and wounded, while Vichy French and Syrians had 6,500 casualties.

AUGUST 1941

EUROPE and ATLANTIC
Roosevelt and Churchill met on *Prince of Wales* in Argentia Bay, Newfoundland, and drew up the **Atlantic Charter** (12th) agreeing principles of self government and freedom of choice for all countries. U.S. aid was also promised in the patrolling of W. Atlantic waters.

Atlantic convoys still suffer regular losses from U-boats' attacks and mines. The auxiliary cruiser *Schiff 36 Orion* sailed into the Gironde estuary after an operation of 510 days in which she sank 12 ships in the three major oceans.

RUSSIA and ARCTIC
German advances continued. Hitler named the Leningrad industrial complex as the primary objective (4th), but already some German generals have become concerned by the growing ferocity of Russian resistance roused by German treatment of civilians, and by the enormous numbers of reinforcements that keep replacing Russian army losses. Hopes of a political upheaval in Russia faded. Against often powerful argument by his generals, Hitler issued orders for the attack on Kiev (21st), and decided not to head immediately for Moscow. The push to Leningrad to link with the Finns, and the southward drive to cut off the food sources of the Ukraine and the Caucasus oil fields, thinned the German lines.

Sea warfare moved to the Baltic and the Black Sea. An air attack on a Soviet Baltic convoy sank a ship carrying 2,500 wounded troops (14th). The Russian naval base of Nikolaev in the Black Sea was evacuated and uncompleted ships blown up or towed away (14–17th). The Russian navy dominates the Black Sea, and is frequently used to support land troops. The defence of the Estonian port of Tallinn was supported by the Soviet Baltic fleet (23rd–28th), but the port eventually had to be evacuated. In attempting to reach Kronstadt, there were very heavy losses in the extensive minefields laid by German and Finnish forces. Luftwaffe attacks caused further catastrophe, and few ships reached Kronstadt intact. Some beached on islands in the Gulf of Finland and saved their troops. On 30th the Baltic fleet was concentrated to form an artillery barrage in the defence of Leningrad.

The first Russian-bound convoy from Iceland successfully reached Archangel.

A R.N. force from Scapa Flow evacuated Norwegian and Soviet colonies from Spitzbergen. Canadian and Norwegian commandos destroyed installations and 450,000 tons of coal.

FAR EAST and PACIFIC
Japan tried to begin negotiations for the lifting of the oil embargo, but America insisted on Japan's withdrawal from China and Indo China. The oil embargo was extended by the U.S. and Britain to cover all raw materials, and subsequently all trade.

SOUTHERN EUROPE, AFRICA and MEDITERRANEAN
Soviet, and British and Indian troops entered Iran and rapidly broke down the weak resistance. The Allies captured a considerable tonnage of Axis shipping in the Iranian ports.

The R.N. took 6,000 fresh troops to besieged Tobruk, taking off 5,000 wearied soldiers. A constant activity in this sector is the struggle for Allies to supply Malta and Egypt, and for Axis to supply Rommel. R.N. superiority results in Rommel losing some 35% of his supplies and reinforcements.

SEPTEMBER 1941

EUROPE and ATLANTIC
While land battles flare up and die down, the war at sea and the war in the air continue with horrible consistency. Over a ten-day period (18–28th), for instance, two Atlantic convoys lost 15 ships to U-boat attacks. U-boat strength is now about 150. The German capital ships in Brest continued to be a concern to Britain, and were once again the targets of a concentrated R.A.F. raid (13th). Bremen, Hamburg and Wilhelmshaven suffered in heavy raids (15th).

The U.S. destroyer *Greer* was attacked near Iceland by *U652* (4th) after a British aircraft had dropped depth charges. Roosevelt authorised attacks on sight of any Axis ships in "U.S.-interested" waters (11th). The first 14 Liberty ships were launched in U.S. ports, and a further 312 have been ordered. The U.S. Navy took over the escort duties of some convoys between Newfoundland and Iceland.

The poison-gas Cyclon-B was used for the first time to kill detainees in Auschwitz.

RUSSIA and ARCTIC
The heavily-reinforced German Army South made steady progress against very fierce Russian opposition in the Ukraine, pushing beyond Kiev to the north and south. When Kiev fell (19th) parts of the German army were 150 miles east of the city. Marshal Timoshenko took over command of the threatened troops, but the Germans completed a brilliant pincer movement and captured 665,000 Russians.

Hitler eventually gave in to the urging of his Chiefs, and suddenly became impatient to get to Moscow, ordering immediate preparations for an advance (5th). He did not deflect from his intentions against Leningrad, though, and emphasised that no surrender of the city was to be accepted (18th). Hitler subsequently ordered (29th) that Leningrad and its population were to be "wiped off the face of the earth". But German advances north of the Ukraine have begun to slow down, though the Russians have abandoned the Karelian Isthmus and Leningrad is cut off by land from the rest of Russia. The Gulf of Finland was heavily mined to prevent the Soviet Baltic Fleet breaking out should Leningrad fall.

An Anglo–American delegation, including Lord Beaverbrook and Averell Harriman arrived in Archangel on the cruiser *London* (27th) on their way to discuss military aid with the Soviet Government, who were pleading for a second front, as well as thousands of tons of raw materials, and aircraft and tanks.

SOUTHERN EUROPE, AFRICA and MEDITERRANEAN

Tobruk is still besieged, but a convoy changed over another 6,000 Australian troops in the garrison, and delivered 2,000 tons of supplies. The first U-boats to operate in the Mediterranean passed Gibraltar (24th). An Italian submarine penetrated the defences of the Bay of Gibraltar and launched three "human torpedo" teams, which sank two merchant ships and severely damaged another (20th).

OCTOBER 1941

EUROPE and ATLANTIC

Amid the constant Battle of the Atlantic, the U.S. destroyer *Kearney* was mistakenly torpedoed and badly damaged by *U568* (17th). Aircraft are playing a bigger role in sea warfare – by reconnaissance for ships and convoys, by bombing submarines and surface vessels, and by sowing mines.

Admiral Lord Mountbatten was appointed to the new position of Chief of Combined Operations (27th) to instigate and co-ordinate raids on German-held territory by the large forces gradually gathering in Britain.

Hamburg and Bremen were repeatedly bombed by R.A.F. Bomber Command.

RUSSIA and ARCTIC

"Operation Typhoon", Hitler's planned cyclonic advance and capture of Moscow, began (2nd), and initially made quite rapid progress. But again the Army chiefs had argued with Hitler, for he ordered simultaneously that: Leningrad be captured; that German and Finnish troops were to go north to cut the Murmansk railway; that in the south the Crimea should be taken; that Rostov and the Maikop oilfields captured; and that the Caucasus finally cut off by capturing Stalingrad. The initial rapid advance and the bombing raid on Moscow (6th) led to some panic in the Russian capital, and the Soviet government moved out to Kuibyshev, 500 miles to the east, though Stalin stayed in the Kremlin. In the first two weeks the Germans reported the capture of about 650,000 Russians, 5,000 guns and 1,200 tanks. Spearheads of the advance were soon within 40 miles of Moscow (20th).

Leningrad became completely besieged, and German troops penetrated the outskirts. In the south, as German and Rumanian troops began to overrun the Crimea, Odessa was successfully evacuated (3rd–14th). Thousands of Russian troops, guns, etc., and the Black Sea fleet, moved to Sevastopol, which held out against the Germans.

The first snow of the winter fell early, and half-way through the month heavy rains began. The German advances slowed in the mud and eventually almost came to a halt. Troops were inadequately clothed and supplied, and guns and even tanks became bogged down. Morale is sinking rapidly, and Russian resistance becomes fiercer and fiercer. The heavily-armoured T-34 tanks are almost invulnerable before the German tanks. Partisan attacks and sabotage in occupied areas are increasing and cause considerable disruption and losses. Reprisals are immediate and barbaric, but only intensify the hatred for the invaders.

FAR EAST and PACIFIC

Gen. Hideki Tojo became Prime Minister of Japan (16th), and began to refine his plans for the Japanese empire. This involved an early war against America in which her Pacific Fleet would have to be destroyed to allow unhindered occupation and reinforcement of a large defensive ring, after which a peace treaty would be negotiated.

SOUTHERN EUROPE, AFRICA and MEDITERRANEAN

Operations by R.N. surface ships and submarines, and by aircraft flown from Malta and carriers took a heavy toll of Axis shipping and about 63% of Rommel's supplies and reinforcements were lost or had to return to their bases. A large Luftwaffe force arrived in Sicily, and there are now 25 U-boats operating in the Mediterranean.

British commandos carried out a daring but costly raid from submarines on Rommel's H.Q. A number of German officers were killed, but Rommel was not at his H.Q. that night (14th).

NOVEMBER 1941

EUROPE and ATLANTIC

America changed its Neutrality Laws to allow its merchant ships to enter previously self-prohibited war zones, and to be armed (18th). In the South Atlantic one of Germany's most successful auxiliary cruisers, *Schiff 16 Atlantis* which had sunk 22 ships, was surprised by the

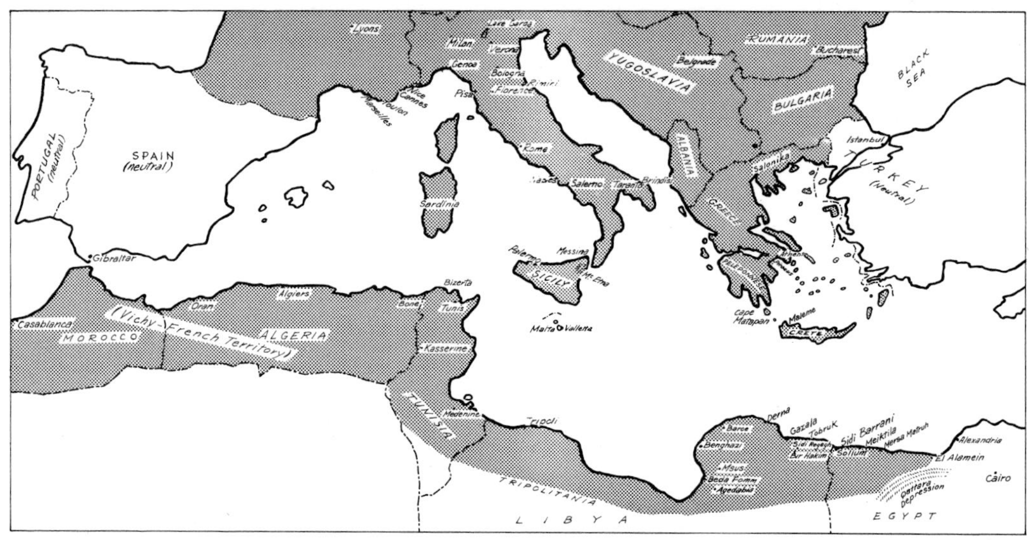

Southern Europe, the Mediterranean and North Africa: the shaded area indicates the furthest extent of Axis conquest (and influence, in the case of unoccupied satellite states).

R.N. cruiser *Devonshire* while replenishing a U-boat. *Atlantis* scuttled herself, and the U-boat – which submerged when *Devonshire* was sighted – towed the crew to safety in their lifeboats.

RUSSIA and ARCTIC

The parallel with Napoleon's offensive of 1812 escaped no-one, especially when the severity of winter came early. Stalin made his "Holy Russia Speech" which recalled to many Churchill's appeal for courage in 1940. The lack of winter clothing, and even such necessities as anti-freeze for engines almost halted the Germans in the north. Horses and men became practically the only tractive power, and morale, even at senior officer level, fell rapidly. But Hitler was resolute. He absolutely forbade any retreat and eventually ordered a new attack on Moscow (15th). Despite atrocious conditions and extreme exhaustion, the Germans gradually got closer to the city, and are now within sight of the outskirts. Hitler is convinced one last push will achieve his aims.

Stalin's Tokyo spy advised him that Russia need fear no immediate threat from Japan, and Zhukov, commanding Moscow's defence, brought the crack mountain troops from the Manchurian border to help defend Moscow.

In the south it was slightly warmer but equally wet, and Russian resistance grew more intense. German tanks eventually reached the objective of Rostov (21st), but Field Marshal von Rundstedt knew it could not be held for long, and within five days it was retaken. Rundstedt was ordered by Hitler not to retreat, but he offered his resignation rather than sacrifice his army. Hitler relieved him of his command (30th).

By the end of November German casualties have risen to over 745,000, which is 23% of the average total strength. Dead total some 200,000.

FAR EAST and PACIFIC

The Japanese Pearl Harbor Striking Force under Vice Adm. Nagumo sailed for Hawaii, taking a distant northerly route to escape detection. The fleet consists of 6 aircraft carriers, 2 battleships, 9 destroyers, 1 cruiser, 3 submarines, and 8 tankers.

Negotiations between U.S. and Japan continue in strained atmosphere. U.S. experts broke the Japanese code and now intercept all messages from Tokyo to the Japanese Ambassador. It is obvious to some that hostilities are likely, but no-one knows where they will begin, and many are sceptical and complacent. A war-warning was sent to commanders in Hawaii and the Phillipines (27th), and the U.S. Army and Navy was put on the lowest level of combat readiness (28th). Convoys for merchant ships in the Pacific were made compulsory.

SOUTHERN EUROPE, AFRICA and MEDITERRANEAN

The Allies began an offensive in Libya (18th) and established a strong position at Sidi Rezegh, south of Tobruk (19th). German armour reinforced the Italians, but Sidi Rezegh was held by the Allies (21st). Another Allied force worked behind Axis-held Sidi Omar on the Egyptian frontier, and the Tobruk garrison broke out to threaten Rommel's rear. Sidi Rezegh fell to the Axis after fierce tank battles (23rd), and when Rommel sent forces through Allied lines to rescue his garrison at Bardia, he caused tremendous confusion among the Allied forces, which began a muddled retreat into Egypt. Then Auchinleck flew in from Cairo and forbade further retreat. Maj. Gen. Ritchie took over command of the 8th Army, and the R.A.F. consistently attacked Rommel's transports. The Axis forces withdrew to their supply bases between Bardia and Tobruk; the Allies launched another attack (26th), and are preparing for a further assault.

The aircraft carrier *Ark Royal* was torpedoed by *U81* (13th) after delivering Hurricanes to Malta. She was taken in tow, but sank 25 miles out from Gibraltar (14th). Only one of the crew was not saved. *U331* penetrated the escort screen around three R.N. battleships off Sollum and sank *Barham*, with the loss of 861 lives.

Provisioning Malta is still a struggle for the Allies, and Malta itself is constantly bombed by German and Italian planes. But the Axis are also struggling to supply their own forces in North Africa, and are now making increasing use of large Italian submarines as "merchantmen" and "tankers".

DECEMBER 1941

EUROPE and ATLANTIC

Following the Japanese attack on the U.S. Pacific Fleet (see below), **Hitler declared war on the U.S.A.** (11th). Germany, Italy and Japan signed a new Tripartite Pact, pledging the defeat of the U.S.A. and Great Britain.

RUSSIA and ARCTIC

Germany massed a huge concentration of tanks and troops and launched a desperate, three-pronged assault on Moscow (1st). A reconnaissance battalion penetrated the suburbs the next day, and were able to sight the spires of the Kremlin. In the morning (3rd), they were driven back and the German commanders realised their objective was hopeless. On 5th the German army was at a complete standstill – halted by fierce resistance and a temperature of −36°C. Then Gen. Zhukov flung his fresh, fully-trained and well-equipped mountain forces from the Manchurian border at the Germans along the whole 200 mile front (6th). The surprised, exhausted and shattered German forces staggered back further and further. Hitler forbade a general withdrawal to a new line of defence, and carried out a purge of generals who disobeyed or disagreed with his orders. Bock, Guderian, Hoepner, Sponeck followed Rundstedt's earlier departure, and even von Brauchitsch resigned – Hitler taking over his role as Chief of the Army High Command (OKH). Hitler is now Fuehrer and Head of State, Minister of War, Supreme Commander of the Armed Forces, and Commander in Chief of the Army.

The Russian counter offensive was fierce and they retook Kalugo, Kalinin and Volokolansk – where eight partisans were found hanging from makeshift gallows. In the south, Reichenau – who had replaced Rundstedt – was given permission to retreat 50 miles from Rostov to the Mins river.

Some estimates put Russian killed or wounded by the end of the year at about 4½ million.

FAR EAST and PACIFIC

At 7.50 a.m. on **Sunday the 7th the first Japanese bomb fell on Pearl Harbor**, while in Washington the Japanese Ambassador was still decoding his country's declaration of war against the U.S.A. The attack by fighters and dive-bombers in two waves off the Japanese carriers lasted 2 hours and put out of action the entire U.S. Pacific Fleet's battleship force. Four battleships were sunk and four more severely damaged while several smaller ships were also lost. The U.S. Navy and Marine Corps lost 2,117 men (about half in the battleship *Arizona*), the Army 218, and there were 68 civilians killed. Over 1,200 people were wounded. The Japanese lost 29 planes out of the attacking force of 354, as well as five midget submarines which carried out simultaneous but unsuccessful attacks. Nearly 200 American aircraft were destroyed, virtually all while still on the ground.

Due to blunders, complacency, incredulity and a general lack of communication and preparedness, the attack took the American forces completely by surprise, and it was only about five hours after the attack ended that an attack warning was received by the Commander at Pearl Harbor. While many Japanese were elated with the easy destruction, some realised that a second attack would have been able to destroy vital fuel dumps and ship-repair facilities, and that the chance absence on manoeuvres of the Pacific Fleet's aircraft carriers meant that the U.S. retained a significant force. Adm. Yamamoto also forecast, when he heard the attack had preceded the declaration of war, that the full fury of the U.S.A. would destroy Japan, since this act completely united all factions in America.

The Japanese offensive began even earlier, by error, on the **Malay Peninsula** when a bombardment began two hours before the Pearl Harbor attack. But London was not immediately alerted and could not warn America – Churchill actually learned of Japan's attack on Pearl Harbor via the B.B.C.

Numerous other offensives rapidly got under way. Air attacks on the main **Philippine island of Luzon** (7th) caused massive damage to U.S. airfields and planes. The next day there were extensive landings on Malaya which met little opposition. Attacks on the British base at **Hong Kong** also began on 8th. The second line of America's defence after the Pacific Fleet was MacArthur's Far East Air Force in the Philippines, and this was largely destroyed in the Luzon attack. Japanese landings on Luzon soon followed (10th).

On the same day, the last Allied mobile force in the Pacific and Indian oceans was severely crippled. The R.N. Force Z under Vice Adm. Phillips, off the east coast of Malaya, was attacked by Japanese aircraft. The Allied fleet had no air cover, and the battlecruiser *Repulse* and the new battleship *Prince of Wales* were both rapidly sunk. It cost the Japanese only four aircraft. Phillips, and 800 others, went down with the ships, but 2,000 were saved.

The Japanese overran the U.S. garrison on **Guam in the Marianas** (10th), but an attack on Wake Island, further east, was repulsed by 500 marines (11th). Wake was eventually captured on 23rd. The Japanese also made landings in **Burma and Borneo**. Hong Kong surrendered (26th) and the rapid advances on Luzon are forcing MacArthur to retreat towards the Bataan Peninsula, having declared Manila an "open city". Even so, it was heavily bombed by the Japanese (27th).

Attacks on Burma were carried out by repeated heavy bombing raids on Rangoon, which caused tremendous damage.

SOUTHERN EUROPE, AFRICA and MEDITERRANEAN

The British and Commonwealth forces launched another attack against Rommel and his German and Italian divisions (2nd), and forced the Axis to withdraw, leaving behind 36,500 prisoners and nearly 400 tanks, and suffering 24,500 dead and wounded. Tobruk was relieved (9th) and Cyrenaica is once more in Allied hands – at the cost of 18,000 killed and wounded.

1942

JANUARY 1942

EUROPE and ATLANTIC

Roosevelt, Churchill, Litvinov, and Soong (for China) signed the **United Nations Pact** affirming the principles of the Atlantic Charter and pledging co-operative defeat of the members of the Tripartite Pact (1st). A further 22 countries signed the Pact, by which it was also agreed that no signatory would make a separate peace treaty with any of the Axis.

The Battle of the Atlantic continues with many Allied shipping losses, and new types of U-boats achieve many sinkings.

RUSSIA and ARCTIC

The Germans retreated step by step from Moscow, in temperatures of 30 degrees below zero and battered by ferocious Russian attacks. Every fall-back had to be pleaded for time after time, Hitler constantly insisting that there must be no retreat regardless of lives lost. Some generals grew so desperate in their futile attempts to hold the Russians, that the use of poison gas was once raised (7th).

The first U-boat group, a pack of three, operated against Arctic convoys and sank a Soviet minesweeper, a merchantman and a R.N. destroyer. The British persuaded greater Russian participation in the convoys.

Besieged Sevastopol received numerous supplies and reinforcements from the Soviet Black Sea Fleet, which also shelled German land positions. Attempts to relieve Sevastopol via landings in German territory north of the city (5–8th) resulted in the landed forces being wiped out or captured by the Germans. Other landings on the eastern end of Crimea, near Feodosia, were carried out simultaneously. Further Russian landings in the middle of the month were initially more successful, but the Germans soon recaptured lost territory.

FAR EAST and PACIFIC

The Japanese captured the town and naval base of Cavite on Manila Bay (2nd) and MacArthur withdrew further to make a last stand on Bataan Peninsula. Japanese naval superiority makes it impossible for supplies to be brought in, or an evacuation to be attempted.

Japanese tanks broke through defences north of Kuala Lumpur on the Malayan Peninsula, forged ahead and cut off 4,000 British troops (7–8th). After a brief stand – the first serious resistance to the Japanese offensive in Malaya – **Kuala Lumpur was abandoned** (11th).

Wavell passed through Singapore (8th) on his way to Java as Supreme Commander of the newly formed ABDA Command (American, British, Dutch, Australian) and decided to form a defence line on Johore. All the Singapore defences had been built facing the sea, and the rear was practically unprotected. The Japanese can not be held, and troops are crossing the narrow strip of water to Singapore. Few civilians have been evacuated. The British have already lost 25,000 troops – mainly taken prisoner.

Japanese troops attacked Burma from Thailand (Siam), advanced on Moulmein, in the south, and announced an alliance with Thailand (21st). Moulmein was occupied on 31st, and the defenders only narrowly escaped.

Japan landed forces in **New Guinea and the Solomon Islands** (23rd).

FEBRUARY 1942

EUROPE and ATLANTIC

The battleships *Gneisenau* and *Scharnhorst*, and the heavy cruiser *Prince Eugen* slipped out of Brest at night with a large escort (11–12th). During the day there was also constant air support, but, largely through constant luck, the convoy was not spotted by the British till it was off Le Touquet. Coastal batteries failed to score any hits, and an attack by five MTBs from Dover was also unsuccessful. Bad liaison and communications, plus an element of sheer illfortune, caused delay and confusion among the British, and a desperate, heroic attempt by a squadron of six Swordfish torpedo aircraft only resulted in them all being shot down. Eventually larger groups of bombers and torpedo aircraft were sent out, but none of them found the German ships. Five destroyers sent out from Harwich made an attack, but scored no hits. *Scharnhorst* and *Gneisenau* were however damaged by mines, but all the ships arrived on 12th at Wilhelmshaven and the Elbe estuary. *Prinz Eugen* was later damaged by a torpedo during an attack by R.N. submarines as she was being transferred to Norway. R.A.F. bombers severely damaged *Gneisenau* in a raid on Kiel (27th).

In New York harbour one of the world's biggest troop ships, the former liner *Normandie*, caught fire and capsized (9th).

RUSSIA and ARCTIC
The Russian counter-offensive lost momentum towards the middle of the month, and the Germans were able to sort themselves out after their retreat. German losses (excluding other Axis armies on the Russian front) from Barbarossa are 1,005,636. Of these at least 202,250 were killed, and almost 50,000 are missing. Frostbite has taken a huge toll.

FAR EAST and PACIFIC
After bombarding Singapore, Japanese troops began to cross the straits (8th). British defences were poor and by nightfall thousands of Japanese were ashore in Singapore. The British forces were without air cover and every counter-attack failed. On the 15th **Singapore, with 85,000 Allies, surrendered** to the Japanese. Apart from the British, Australian, and Indian troops, 15,000 foreign non-combatants were taken prisoner.

A huge Japanese fleet sailed to invade Java (25th) which was defended by 120,000 troops who had no air defences. The Allies formed a Combined Striking Force (CSF) of 5 cruisers and 14 destroyers under Rear Adm. Doorman and met the Japanese in the **Battle of Java Sea** (27th). The Japanese force was far superior, and the flagship and three other CSF ships were sunk. Doorman died with his ship. The next day 2 Allied cruisers intercepted Japanese transports and sank 2 before a large Japanese naval group arrived and sank both cruisers. The cruiser *Exeter*, although damaged, put to sea with two destroyers and engaged four Japanese heavy cruisers and three destroyers in a battle lasting 1½ hours before the three Allied ships were sunk (29th). Only 4 ships of the CSF survived, and the invasion was delayed no longer than 24 hours. The first Japanese landings, on the north coast of Java, began on 28th and more troops are now pouring ashore.

The U.S.N. made its first offensive strike in the Pacific when carrier-borne planes attacked Kwajalein in the Marshall Islands (1st). The Japanese commander of the island was among those killed; a transport ship was sunk and nine others damaged.

In Burma, the Japanese initially met fierce resistance from British and Indian troops at the Sittang River (17–19th), but on 23rd they blew up the vital Sittang Bridge, stranding many Allied troops, and advanced rapidly towards Rangoon.

MARCH 1942

EUROPE and ATLANTIC
British commandos raided the port of St. Nazaire on the Bay of Biscay (28th). U-boat pens were damaged and the only dry dock big enough to take the battleship *Tirpitz* (then in Norway) was successfully blocked by ramming the gates with an explosive-laden ship. The Commandos suffered heavy losses.

The Japanese onslaught in the Far East took the British as much by surprise as it did the Americans at Pearl Harbor. The Japanese advance down the Malayan Peninsula was rapid. Many prisoners were taken on the way to Singapore – where the massive defences pointed impotently seawards.

Himmler received his first reports of medical experiments being carried out on Dachau concentration camp inmates and encouraged further work.

The R.A.F. carried out an area attack on Lübeck with enormous destruction. Germany has now suffered as much from bombing raids as Britain has.

RUSSIA and ARCTIC
Arctic convoys face increasing dangers, apart from vicious conditions at sea. *Tirpitz* tried to intercept a Murmansk-bound convoy but missed it in bad weather. The British Home Fleet sailed to hunt *Tirpitz*. Poor visibility prevented an engagement, and a torpedo attack by aircraft off *Victorious* was unsuccessful. *Tirpitz* eventually put back into Trondheim (12th).

On the Russian front, both armies are bogged down by the mud of the Spring thaw.

FAR EAST and PACIFIC
Gen. Alexander arrived in Rangoon to conduct the **retreat out of Burma** (5th). Rangoon had been judged indefensible, and defences have been concentrated in the Mandalay area. Alexander ordered Rangoon to be evacuated (6th) and the city was taken over by the Japanese two days later. Lt. Gen. Slim took direct command of the newly arranged troops and made two counter-attacks against the Japanese (21st and 27th). Heavy bombing of all airfields forced the R.A.F. to quit Burma. Mandalay was subjected to concentrated bombing and Chinese troops under Gen. Stilwell were forced to abandon Toungoo, on the Sittang north of Rangoon.

The Japanese, with unchallenged air superiority, quickly overpowered the Dutch defences of Java and the **surrender of Java**, together with 98,000 Dutch, U.S. and British troops, took place at Bandoeng (9th).

Gen. MacArthur was ordered to escape from the Philippines to set up a new H.Q. in Australia, and he left Corregidor island in Manila Bay by MTB (11th), arriving in Australia on 17th. The Japanese on Luzon are relentlessly forcing back the Bataan defences, and the underground passages of Corregidor are filled with wounded.

Allied commanders decided Ceylon could be a vital point, and put together a scratch naval force under Adm. Somerville. The Japanese did not include Ceylon in their plans, but decided to destroy this new threat to their Burma operations. Colombo harbour was attacked by over 100 planes (5th). Two cruisers were sunk and the harbour greatly damaged. Somerville's aircraft carriers arrived too late to intervene, and the naval force was deployed in East Africa and Bombay.

SOUTHERN EUROPE, AFRICA and MEDITERRANEAN
The siege of Malta constantly escalates, and the island is bombed almost daily.

APRIL 1942

EUROPE and ATLANTIC
The arrival of America in the theatre of war has increased the hunting grounds for U-boats, and there are still heavy losses in many parts of the Atlantic. The first convoy under a new system using regular ocean escort groups sailed from Halifax (20th).

Hitler's summer plans mainly involve Russia, but he also ordered the increased garrisoning of the west coasts of Europe.

RUSSIA and ARCTIC
Hitler issued Directive No. 41 (5th), reaffirming his original Russian aims – capture of Leningrad and break through to the Caucasus, with the Caucasus operation to start first. Hitler ordered that Stalingrad, too, should be taken, or at least destroyed by shelling and bombing. Hitler relied extensively on the capture of the Caucasus oilfields, but in Moscow Stalin knew that he needed them just as much, and began his own plans for a Russian summer offensive.

Hitler reinforced the tremendously depleted German armies with thousands of troops from Hungary, Italy and Rumania. Ribbentrop confided to Ciano (30th) that 270,000 Germans had been killed in Barbarossa, but Ciano believed the figure could be as high as 700,000. Some 5 million Russians, troops and civilians, have been taken prisoner since the invasion of Russia. Most have been sent to Germany as slave labour, and they are dying in their thousands from starvation and maltreatment.

FAR EAST and PACIFIC
The **U.S. army on the Bataan Peninsula in the Philippines surrendered** (9th) in the face of certain annihilation. Gen. Wainwright is holding out in the old fortress on Corregidor, and prevents the Japanese use of Manila Bay.

The total force surrendered to the Japanese numbered nearly 76,000, of which 35,000 were Americans. Under brutal conditions, with little food or water and frequent vicious assaults by the guards, the prisoners began the infamous Bataan Death March to prison camps at Cabanatuan. Some managed to escape on the journey, but sickness, starvation and summary execution took up to 10,000 lives, 2,330 of them Americans.

In Burma the Japanese advanced rapidly. Alexander decided not to defend Mandalay and began a 200 mile withdrawal towards India (26th), with the objective of reaching Assam before the monsoons. The Japanese took Lashio, the Burma Road terminus (29th), and the next day the retreating Allies crossed to the west of the Irrawaddy River.

Lt. Col. Doolittle led 16 B25s on a bombing raid on Tokyo off the carrier *Hornet* 668 miles away, and flew on to land in China. The Japanese relocated four fighter groups for the defence of Japan. (Not much damage had been done, but the presence of enemy aircraft over their capital was a tremendous shock for many Japanese military leaders as well as civilians.

SOUTHERN EUROPE, AFRICA and MEDITERRANEAN
Malta endured another bitter month, and King George VI of Britain awarded the people of the island the George Cross. The month began with only 6 aircraft left. A Mediterranean U.S.N./R.N. convoy flew off 47 Spitfires (20th), but 30 of the 46 that landed in Malta were destroyed on the ground before they could be refuelled.

MAY 1942

EUROPE and ATLANTIC
The R.A.F. made the first "1,000 Bomber Raid", sending 1,074 bombers at night over Cologne (30th). Six hundred acres were devastated, and 39 bombers shot down. Civilian casualties were very high.

Himmler's SS deputy, Heydrich, newly made "Reichsprotektor" of Bohemia and Moravia, was critically injured in Prague by a hand grenade thrown by a Czech agent (27th). In the next few days the Germans killed 1,357 Czechs in reprisals, and 657 "died" during interrogation.

Prinz Eugen managed to get to Kiel despite many attempted air attacks (18th).

RUSSIA and ARCTIC
Marshal Timoshenko launched a Russian attack on the south-west front near Kharkov (12th), but this played into the hands of the main German force. Stalin forbade a retreat (17th), until the Germans launched a massive counter-attack (19th). But by then Russians were caught in a pincer trap, and 241,000 were taken prisoner.

In the Crimea, the Germans launched an attack on the Kerch peninsula, which was still held by the Russians (8th). By 16th it was captured and except for the besieged city of Sevastopol, all the Crimea is in German hands.

Germany's Eastern Sector intelligence expert, Gehlen, estimated (1st) that Russia had lost, since their attack on Finland, some 7½ million killed, wounded, or taken prisoner – but this still leaves approximately 9½ million available to the Russian armed services.

FAR EAST and PACIFIC
A new era in sea warfare began in **the Battle of Coral Sea**. It started with the Japanese capture of the Australian island of Tulagi in the Solomons (3rd). The next day U.S. planes off *Yorktown* bombed Tulagi. Japanese planes sank an American destroyer and an oil supply ship, but believed they were an aircraft carrier and a cruiser (7th). All the Pacific Fleet carriers were in fact still unharmed, and on the same day planes off *Yorktown* sank a Japanese light carrier and a light cruiser, for the loss of five planes. U.S. and Australian ships patrolled the Coral Sea searching for the Japanese invasion fleet known to be heading for Papua and New Guinea. On the 7th the Japanese lost 26 planes in aerial combat, landing accidents, and 6 which mistakenly tried to land on *Yorktown* in the gathering darkness. The evenly-matched carrier forces met on the 8th. Cloud conditions favoured the Japanese and the U.S. carrier *Lexington* was badly damaged, abandoned, and then sunk by a U.S. destroyer. The Japanese carrier *Shokaku* was bombed, and retired unable to launch aircraft. With far more Japanese than U.S. planes lost, Vice-Adm. Inouye recalled the invasion fleet, being unable to give adequate air cover. In the whole Coral Sea battle, all combat took place by plane – the first time no surface ships took part in a naval engagement. The Japanese regretted more than ever that the U.S. carriers had not been in Pearl Harbor in December.

In Burma, Mandalay was successfully evacuated (1st) and the British and Indian troops fought a fierce rearguard action to cover the crossing of the Chindwin River at Kalewa (10th). Two days later the monsoon broke, enabling the dismal evacuation to be completed without Japanese intervention. On the 20th, all **Burma was under Japanese control**. The 900 mile retreat had cost the Allies 13,000 killed, wounded or missing; the Japanese casualties were about 4,600.

In an attempt to entice the U.S. Pacific Fleet into close battle before it could make up its Pearl Harbor losses, the Japanese H.Q. ordered (5th) the occupation of the Western Aleutian and the Midway islands. With its knowledge of the Japanese codes, the Americans were able to prepare for the offensive.

SOUTHERN EUROPE, AFRICA and MEDITERRANEAN
In North Africa, Auchinleck was coming under strong pressure from Churchill to attack Rommel's Afrika Korps from the 8th Army's Gazala Strip, west of Tobruk. The decision was taken out of his hands when Rommel launched a surprise attack (26th). His armoured divisions, unable to penetrate against numerous new Grant tanks in the centre, swung south and set up an advance base behind the Gazala Line, south of Tobruk near Bir Hakim (27th). Heavy bombing of this base left Rommel with few more tanks than half the British force of 420. But Ritchie, commanding the 8th Army, used his armour in small abortive attacks instead of massing them. With Italian forces now attacking the main Gazala lines from the west and German armoured divisions behind the line, the Allies are in a precarious position.

The month began with **Malta seemingly on the point of collapse**, its food, ammunition, fuel, and aircraft practically finished. The German Command issued a directive for the capture of Malta (4th). Later in the month 17 Spitfires arrived safely, and towards the end of the month more convoys were approaching. The Axis powers have equal difficulty in getting supplies across the Mediterranean to Benghazi.

JUNE 1942

EUROPE and ATLANTIC

One of the worst-ever months for Allied shipping losses in the Atlantic, with 627,000 tons sunk. But escorts are becoming increasingly efficient, and a number of U-boats were sunk or driven away.

Gen. Eisenhower arrived in England to take command of all U.S. Forces in Britain.

Heydrich died in Prague (4th) of his injuries received in May and as a reprisal the nearby village of Lidice was reduced to rubble and ploughed into the earth, 192 boys and men shot and its 296 women and children sent to concentration camps. Eighty-two of the children were soon gassed at Chemnitz in Austria. At least four other villages in Europe have had the same "treatment".

RUSSIA and ARCTIC

The German 11th Army under von Manstein began a major attack on Sevastopol (8th) and land, sea and air forces of both Russia and Germany and Italy were soon engaged. Soviet ships reinforced Sevastopol and evacuated wounded amid constant attacks by Axis MTBs, submarines and aircraft. On the 27th *Tashkent* with 2,300 evacuees and wounded aboard was bombed, but reached Novorossiysk in tow before sinking. The Soviet command eventually gave the order for a general evacuation (30th), but only a few managed to get away in small ships and submarines before **Sevastopol fell to the Germans**, who now hold all the Crimea.

A large German offensive was launched towards Voronezh and the Don (28th) and is rapidly making progress.

FAR EAST and PACIFIC

The Japanese plan for its new offensive set the 6th as Midway invasion day, and it was to be carried out by an armada of 160 warships under Adm. Yamamoto. Against this were 76 U.S. ships led by Adm. Nimitz. Japanese aircraft bombed Midway (4th) but most U.S. planes took off in time and attacked the Japanese ships, though with heavy losses. U.S. torpedo planes off carriers unsuccessfully attacked the Japanese carrier force, with the loss of 35 out of 41 planes. Then almost immediately 37 dive bombers off *Enterprise* and *Yorktown* attacked and severely damaged the carriers *Kaga*, *Akagi* and *Soryu* – all of which sank later on that day (4th). In the afternoon Japanese aircraft off *Hiryu* crippled *Yorktown*, but aircraft from *Enterprise* and *Hornet* bombed and set fire to *Hiryu*. During the night (4–5th) Yamamoto called off the Midway invasion but ordered bombardment of the islands. Two Japanese cruisers collided in this operation while avoiding an American submarine. One was sunk the following morning, and *Yorktown* was also finally sunk (7th). The Battle of Midway again emphasised the power of aircraft at sea – and the outcome ended Japan's naval dominance of the Pacific.

During Midway, the Japanese occupied the Aleutian islands of Attu and Kiska (7th), but lost 3,500 dead and 253 aircraft. The U.S. Navy lost 307 men and 150 aircraft.

SOUTHERN EUROPE, AFRICA and MEDITERRANEAN

Rommel launched a strong attack against the Free French forces at Bir Hakim, supported by constant Luftwaffe sorties (1st and 2nd). The British counter attacked in fierce tank battles against Rommel's centre – "The Cauldron" – which caused heavy casualties on both sides, but ended unsuccessfully for the British. The Free French resistance at Bir Hakim ended (10–11th), and the Allies were heavily outnumbered in tanks for the first time. On 14th Ritchie withdrew from the Gazala line, and in his retreat left Tobruk surrounded by Axis forces. The Luftwaffe, commanded by Kesselring, carried out devastating Stuka raids on Tobruk, accompanied by an artillery barrage (20th–21st). On 21st Germans penetrated the Tobruk defences and captured an Indian brigade. That evening the senior officer **Maj. Gen. Klopper, surrendered Tobruk** with 35,000 Allied soldiers, and enormous quantities of supplies. Only a group of Coldstream Guards managed to break out. The fall of Tobruk had tremendous, and opposite, effects on the morale of the Allied and Axis forces, and an exultant Hitler promoted Rommel to Field Marshal.

Pressing his attack, **Rommel crossed into Egypt** (23rd), and two days later Auchinleck flew to the front from Cairo and relieved Ritchie of command of the dispirited troops. The Allies formed a defensive position at Mersa Matruh, and once more had numerically superior forces of infantry as well as tanks. Auchinleck planned a more mobile campaign, but Rommel struck again (26th) and captured more troops than he had in his own attacking force. Rommel's Afrika Korps is now only 60 miles from Alexandria.

More ships managed to get through to Malta, and 59 Spitfires arrived from carriers (3rd and 9th). Mussolini convinced Hitler and his own staff to postpone the invasion of Malta till September.

JULY 1942

EUROPE and ATLANTIC

The Battle of the Atlantic moved very far westwards when *U132* slipped into the Gulf of St. Lawrence and sank four ships (6–20th), and when *U166* laid a barrage of mines off the estuary of the Mississippi River (25th). The submarine then went on to torpedo and sink four ships in the Gulf of Mexico.

RUSSIA and ARCTIC

The German summer offensive continued its momentum and soon reached the Don on either side of Voronezh (5th), while in the Crimea Manstein moved into Sevastopol (1st). The 6th Army under Paulus moved towards Stalingrad, supported on its left flank by the 4th Panzer Army. Army Group A led by List moved rapidly south-east through the Don-Donetz corridor. Then Hitler, desperate to make certain of the Caucasus oilfields, ordered the 4th Panzer Army to go south and assist in the crossing of the Don and the taking of the oilfields (13th). The Panzer Army therefore had to move right across the front of Paulus's 6th Army which was advancing to Stalingrad. This caused tremendous confusion, seriously delayed Paulus, and also removed his main left-flank defence. Hitler's generals tried vainly to point out the need to keep up the Stalingrad attack.

The Germans moving south under List crossed the Don (22nd) and took Rostov the next day.

Meanwhile the Russians were rapidly reinforcing Stalingrad and preparing a strong defence line – having, as so often before, received advance information of the German moves through their agent "Lucy" in Switzerland, who has inside information at a very high level.

Paulus resumed the 6th Army drive on Stalingrad, initially making good progress. Hitler then issued Directive No. 45 (23rd), which once again changed orders for the 4th Panzer Army, again sending it to attack Stalingrad, but this time from the south. Hitler, however, did not change his oilfield objectives, even though he had now deprived List's Army Group A of much of its strength, having also sent some divisions far North to help the Leningrad front. Paulus and the 6th Army were soon within 40 miles of the Volga (28th), but resistance has now begun to increase. Hitler's vacillations have meant that the 6th Army faces a much-strengthened Stalingrad defence, while a weakened Army Group A is committed to the conquest of the enormous Caucasus territory.

Having twice swept Axis forces from Egypt to Tripolitania, the Allies (now formed into the new 8th Army) were once again driven back towards Egypt by Rommel. After the defensive Gazala Line fell, and then Tobruk, six months passed before the Allies were to drive the Axis back for the third and last time.

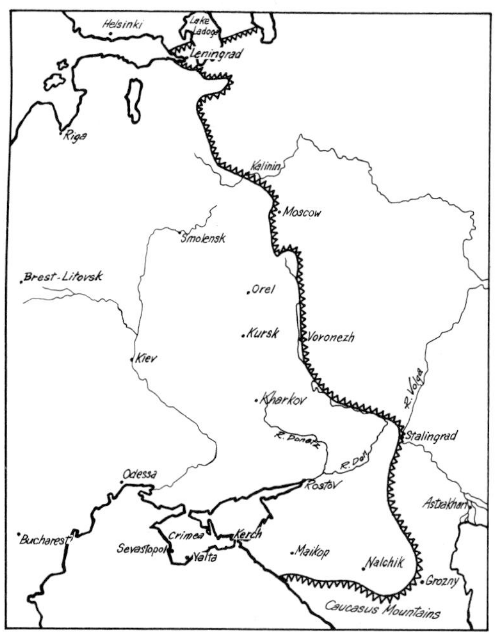

The extent of German conquests in Russia.

In the Arctic, convoy PQ17 of 36 merchant ships with an escort of destroyers, corvettes and smaller craft, on its way from Reykjavik to Archangel, was located by a U-boat, and a group of nine U-boats were deployed to intercept it (1st). The distant-covering escort of the battleships *Duke of York* and *Washington*, the aircraft carrier *Victorious*, two cruisers and 14 destroyers headed north from Scapa Flow. The next day a German force comprising the battleship *Tirpitz*, a cruiser and four destroyers set out, and was joined by the pocket battleships *Lützow* and *Admiral Scheer* with 6 destroyers (3rd). *Lützow* and three destroyers ran aground on the Norwegian coast, while further R.N. surface ships and submarines arrived in the area. German air attacks on the convoy sank five ships (4–5th). The Admiralty then expected a major surface attack and Admiral Pound, the First Sea Lord, ordered the destroyers of PQ17's escort to join the cruiser force. The convoy was ordered to scatter and very soon lost 12 ships to attacks by aircraft and submarines. Under Hitler's orders not to take risks, the German naval C-in-C recalled the German surface force, and ordered the convoy to be attacked by aircraft and U-boats. It was the 15th when the last U-boat returned to base, and by then U-boats and aircraft had sunk 24 ships from convoy PQ17 – a loss of nearly 144,000 tons of shipping and many lives. Among the cargoes lost were 430 tanks, 210 aircraft, 3,350 vehicles and some 100,000 tons of war equipment.

FAR EAST and PACIFIC

Japan suddenly found itself going over to the defensive, and orders were given to hold all positions in the Solomons and in New Guinea. Burma was the only front where Japanese strikes continued, to prevent counter-attacks being mounted from India. Amid some acrimony over the respective roles of the Army and of the Navy and Marines, MacArthur and Marshall, with Admirals Nimitz and King, planned a U.S. offensive to seize two of the Solomon Islands (2nd).

SOUTHERN EUROPE, AFRICA and MEDITERRANEAN

Rommel's headlong advance was finally brought to a halt by Auchinleck at El Alamein, on a front between the coast and the Qattara Depression (1st). In Cairo the apprehensive British Embassy and Army H.Q. began to burn their secret documents. Fighting continued sporadically throughout the month, but now a stalemate has been reached.

Allied leaders decided (24th) to invade North Africa (Operation Torch), giving the Americans their first combat against Germany. Gen. Eisenhower was appointed Commander.

AUGUST 1942

EUROPE and ATLANTIC

In a **disastrous raid on Dieppe**, 6,000 commandos – mainly Canadian – attacked the very heavily-defended port (19th). The beaches were covered with obstacles, and enfilading fire was possible from German positions overlooking the beach. Only one small group achieved comparative success, and the final batches of reinforcements were mercifully not sent in. The force withdrew in the afternoon and managed to rescue only a few from the attack. The assault cost the Allied commandos 3,670 killed, wounded and missing, while the R.N. had 550 casualties and the R.A.F. 153. A destroyer, 29 tanks, many landing craft and 106 aircraft were lost. The German defenders had only 590 casualties and lost 48 planes. Many Allied commentators claimed afterwards that the failure of the raid was inevitable and should have been foreseen. It did, however, emphasise the dangers in attacking similar strong points without a heavy advance bombardment and without complete air superiority. The Dieppe raid will doubtless influence the planning of any further amphibious attacks.

The Battle of the Atlantic, and the sufferings of merchant seamen, continue relentlessly. Convoy SC94 from Canada lost 13 of its 36 merchant ships through U-boat attacks (5–10th): 2 U-boats were sunk and two damaged. The gradually mounting U-boat losses provide some solace for the Allies, though neither side can replenish at the rate of loss.

The arrival of the U.S. 8th Air Force in England – mainly in East Anglia bases – has greatly increased the Allied air power over Europe.

RUSSIA and ARCTIC

The German Army Group A continued its advance towards the Caucasus oilfields, but reached the Maikop oil field, 200 miles south of Rostov, only to find it in flames (9th). The speed of the advance began to slow noticeably (17th), though the foothills of the Caucasus 150 miles south-east of Maikop were reached. The long supply line is further complicated by the German and Russian railways operating on different track widths. The command of the Crimea can cut many miles off the route for some supplies.

The Russian Black Sea Fleet is still very active and frequently shells German supply lines. Resistance increases in ferocity as the Germans now face Caucasus Russian troops, who are fighting for their home ground. Hitler's insistance on the advance being pushed over the Caucasus to Batumi, and the capture of the whole neck of the Caucasus between the Black Sea and the Caspian Sea, gives Army Group A a vast and difficult area to conquer.

Bitter fighting has marked every **advance by Paulus's 6th Army on Stalingrad**. The 4th Panzer Army got into position and the first major assault on Stalingrad began (19th). As in other rapid German attacks, there were some full scale Russian desertions, though most Russian prisoners of war face starvation and death in labour camps. Deserters going from the front to the rear chance instant execution at NKVD checkpoints. In Moscow, Stalin resolved that Stalingrad should be held to the last. A German spearhead eventually penetrated the northern suburbs (22nd) and reached the west bank of the Volga the next day. That night (23rd–24th) the Luftwaffe carried out an enormous terror-bombing raid on Stalingrad, using high explosives and just as many tons of incendiaries on the town's many wooden residential areas, dry as tinder after the hot, dry summer. The holocaust was a terrifyingly brutal foretaste of the hell Stalingrad has become. The whole city seemed to blaze amid the vast devastation. In the few hours of the raid, almost 40,000 men, women and children were blown to pieces, crushed or burnt to death. To the Germans, it seemed as if the city would be theirs within days, but the leaders of the defence of Stalingrad – Generals Chuikov and Yeremenko and Commissar Nikita Kruschev – proclaimed a state of siege (25th), and prepared to defend the city to the last pile of rubble.

Partisan activity has increased in far greater proportion than has the number of deserters, and strikes behind the lines cause severe damage and disruption. Hitler subsequently issued Directive No. 46 (18th), ordering the severest treatment, and giving sweeping powers to the SS and Police.

FAR EAST and PACIFIC

U.S. Marines landed on Guadalcanal and Tulagi in the Solomons (7th). The landing met little resistance on Guadalcanal and the new airstrip was soon captured; but this was only the start of a bitter, frustrating struggle against soldiers who would usually choose death before surrender. In an air battle between U.S. and Japanese planes off aircraft carriers, 16 Japanese and 12 American aircraft were shot down. Both sides tried to reinforce their positions on Guadalcanal, and a Japanese cruiser force fleet was seen setting out from Rabaul in the afternoon. Japanese torpedo aircraft attacked U.S. ships taking part in the landing (8th). A U.S. destroyer was sunk, but U.S. planes and AA fire brought down 17 of the 26 Japanese planes. Through bad communications, and inexplicable lapses on the part of the Allies, the Japanese cruiser force slipped into the narrows between Savo Island and Guadalcanal without being detected and took by surprise both the southern and northern Allied covering forces (8th). In the chaos, the Allies lost 1,270 killed and 709 wounded. Four cruisers and one destroyer were sunk, and a number of others badly damaged. Japanese ships suffered little damage, but on its way back to Rabaul the cruiser *Kako* was sunk by the U.S. submarine *S44*.

The Japanese were under the impression that there were only about 3,000 U.S. troops on Guadalcanal (there were in fact some 17,000), and sent in an assault reinforcement of 900 men (18–19th). In the resulting battle, they were all killed, for the loss of only 34 Marines. A much larger landing force planned for the 21st was postponed for two days by the arrival of U.S. carriers and escorts for U.S. transport ships.

The Japanese intended landing 1,500 soldiers on Guadalcanal under cover of the Combined Fleet, and a diversionary force to lure the U.S. carrier force, and two large groups to intercept it, formed east of the Solomons (23rd). Inconclusive skirmishes between sea, air and under-sea groups on each side carried on for days, mainly with Japanese losses, and it was only on the nights of 28–30th that Japanese troops were able to land.

The Japanese tried simultaneously to establish themselves on Papua and 1,300 soldiers were landed on Goodenough Island preparatory to the battle for Milne Bay (24–25th). A further 1,100 landed on the Papuan peninsula the next night. The Australians and Americans put up a very fierce defence, even when Japanese cruisers made a sortie on 29th. After some success at first, the Japanese were driven back, and on the 31st the Japanese command decided to concentrate on Guadalcanal. Evacuation of the Japanese Papua landing force is now under way.

In the North Pacific, America has begun attacks to win back occupied Aleutian Islands.

SOUTHERN EUROPE, AFRICA and MEDITERRANEAN

Unhappy with the conduct of the war in North Africa, Churchill and Chief of the Imperial General Staff, Field Marshal Sir Alan Brooke, visited Cairo with Gen. Smuts. Gen. Alexander was given the Middle East Command, with Gen. Gott as the new Commander of the 8th Army (6th). But the very next day Gott was killed when his plane was shot down on the way to Cairo. Churchill, C.I.G.S. and Smuts unanimously decided on **Gen. Montgomery to lead the 8th Army**, and he took command on 13th. Alexander relieved Auchinleck two days later, and the build-up of the 8th Army's forces began in earnest. On 29th air reconnaissance reported Rommel's Afrika Korps moving into battle positions and the next day the Axis forces attacked, attempting to swing round the southern flank of the Allies. Extensive minefields and heavy bombardment from the R.A.F. and artillery units caused considerable losses to the Afrika Korps and Italian divisions. Montgomery, expecting the attack, had made preparations and the battle for the commanding site, the Alam Halfa ridge, is now raging, with the Axis forces meeting fierce resistance.

Conditions on Malta have begun to improve, though out of a heavily escorted convoy of 13 merchant ships that passed Gibraltar on 11th, only 5 reached Malta, after four days and nights of almost constant attacks by submarines, MTBs and aircraft. The carrier *Eagle* was sunk and *Indomitable* too badly damaged to fly off planes. *Furious*, however, managed to send 37 Spitfires to Malta, and for some reason "armour piercing" bombs dropped on *Victorious* bounced off the flight deck. The last ship that arrived in Malta was the heavily-laden tanker *Ohio*, severely damaged and almost sinking, but with its desperately-needed cargo intact.

Axis convoys and forces at sea fared even worse. Many German and Italian submarines were sunk, and few of Rommel's requirements have managed to get through. His fuel position is especially critical.

SEPTEMBER 1942

EUROPE and ATLANTIC

The westbound convoy ON127 with 32 merchantships was attacked constantly by a group of 13 U-boats (10–14th). Every U-boat in the group made an attack – the first time in the Battle of the Atlantic this has happened. Twelve freighters and a destroyer were sunk, but only one U-boat was damaged. The attacks were eventually stopped as the convoy came under increasing air cover from Newfoundland.

In the South Atlantic, north-east of Ascension Island *U156* sank the troopship *Laconia*, which was carrying 1,800 Italian prisoners of war. Under a "no-attack" agreement, the U-boat radioed for assistance and other U-boats, French warships from West Africa and a British merchant ship came to the rescue. But a U.S.A.A.F. bomber escorting the British ship received confusing signals and orders, and attacked *U156*, in spite of Red Cross flags and the lifeboats it was towing. Eventually, 1,083 survivors of *Laconia* and the U-boat were rescued. Admiral Doenitz ordered that in future U-boats should not attempt rescues (17th). Thus the war at sea has lost a little more of its comparative chivalry.

After constant differences of opinion, especially over the Russian campaign, and incensed by his professional detachment and realism in the place of the requisite Nazi ardour, Hitler finally sacked the Chief of the Army General Staff, Gen. Halder (24th).

RUSSIA and ARCTIC

The German 6th Army came up against the full strength and determination of **the Russian defence of Stalingrad**, and a desperate street-by-street battle in the outer suburbs has turned into a house-by-house, building-by-building struggle in the more central and the industrial areas. Hitler has become obsessed by his wish to capture the city, and forbids any talk of withdrawal, or limited objectives, despite the risk of the 6th Army's encirclement, and the fact that the 4th Panzer Army is unable to get through Russian defences to join Paulus. The loss of men and materials in the 6th Army is enormous, and replenishment is not coming through in any quantity, but Paulus has been urged to make every effort to take the city.

In the Caucasus, Kleist's 1st Panzer Army (part of List's Army Group A) tried to make a breakthrough from Mozdok towards the rich oilfields of Grozny, not 50 miles away. But the resistance has become stronger and replacement equipment has deteriorated. Hitler was dissatisfied with Army Group A's progress towards its three different objectives, and he sacked List, taking over the Army Group himself (9th). Kleist's east flank comes under constant attack – even by cavalry, and bombers from Grozny cause much damage. The Russians are rapidly laying a railway line south from Astrakhan to reinforce the Caucasus. Every attempt made by Kleist to break through is repulsed, though the German flag has been planted on the highest peak in the Caucasus mountains.

In the Arctic Ocean the disaster that befell convoy PQ17 was fresh in the minds of the Admiralty when convoy PQ18 sailed. Its 43 freighters and tankers had an escort and a close support force totalling 20 destroyers, a light cruiser, four corvettes, two submarines, three minesweepers, two anti-aircraft ships and four trawlers. Not far away was a covering force of three heavy cruisers, while two battleships, a light cruiser, and five more destroyers formed the distant cover. German reconnaissance spotted the convoy on 12th and attacks by U-boats and planes began the next day. Only two out of the next six days and nights were without attacks on the convoy.

A good deal of the battle took place in the air, and on one occasion a Hurricane launched by catapult off *Empire Morn* shot down two He115s. Thirteen ships in the convoy were sunk – 10 of these by planes, and three by U-boats. Four Hurricanes were shot down, but the attack cost Germany three U-boats and 27 aircraft.

FAR EAST and PACIFIC
The battle for Guadalcanal raged all month. The Japanese 2nd and 3rd Fleets, of considerable might, sailed from Truk (9th) to cover Japanese landings and the planned attack against the U.S. forces on the island. Two U.S. task forces joined up (14th) on their expeditions to reinforce U.S. Marine positions and land more aircraft. Reports of the formidable Japanese fleets caused the U.S. convoys to hold back, but they ran into a Japanese submarine group, and the carrier *Wasp* was sunk (15th). The Japanese fleets were eventually recalled to Truk, having missed the U.S. task forces, which made their landings on 18th.

The Japanese land attack was launched as planned (12th), with "Edson's Ridge" as its main objective. The ensuing battle was typically furious, and almost proved successful. As it was, the U.S. Marines repulsed the Japanese who lost almost 2,000 men – some 10 times as high a casualty rate as suffered by the Americans. Both sides continue their efforts to build up their island forces, and to thwart each other's efforts.

SOUTHERN EUROPE, AFRICA and MEDITERRANEAN
The Battle of Alam Halfa built up to a climax when Rommel made an attack on the ridge itself which was Montgomery's stronghold, having been misled by a "planted" map showing any other route to be unsuitable for tanks. Plagued by softer sands and deeper minefields than he had been led to believe, troubled by fuel shortages, and faced with very powerful resistance, Rommel called off his attack and withdrew (7th). The 8th Army's morale was enormously boosted by this reversal of its recent headlong withdrawal, and Montgomery began a massive build-up of forces, determined to achieve superiority in every aspect before attacking. On 23rd, Rommel fell ill, and went home to Germany on leave.

The Allies attempted a raid on Tobruk, with disastrous results (13–14th). After a night of R.A.F. bombardment, Allied soldiers tried to land, but only a few got ashore. A simultaneous Commando attack also failed. The Allies lost 576 taken prisoner, and two destroyers, a cruiser, three MTBs and two launches were sunk by Axis bombers and the Tobruk shore batteries.

Off Southern Africa, in the Indian Ocean, an Allied naval force carried out the occupation of Madagascar, then controlled by the Vichy French. Troops were landed at Majunga (10th) and Morondava on the island's west coast. Some began an overland march to the capital, Tananarive, while the naval group picked up the soldiers from Majunga, and made a landing at Tamatave, on the east coast (18th). Tananarive was occupied on 23rd, and the French Vichy Governor withdrew. A South African regiment landed in Tuliar (29th) and the French forces are being pursued from the north and the south. An Allied destroyer sank two French transports south of Madagascar (24th and 30th).

OCTOBER 1942

EUROPE and ATLANTIC
Forces continue to build up and train in Britain for Operation Torch – the invasion of North Africa. In occupied Europe it is civilians who suffer so heavily from the Allied air offensive over Germany, and from the insidious evil of Nazi dogma and practice.

In the Atlantic, U-boat groups patrol widely and continue to take a heavy toll of shipping and merchant seamen's lives. Increasingly, however, long range air support and long experience are giving convoy escorts successes in sinking attacking U-boats. Stragglers are always easy prey, and if the North Atlantic route proves too costly to the U-boats, the South Atlantic frequently offers rich pickings. Off the South African coast, a group of four U-boats accounted for 27 ships.

RUSSIA and ARCTIC
The hideous and terrifyingly **ferocious battle of Stalingrad** continues with little let up. Despite a steady reduction in its numbers of tanks and aircraft, the Germans pressed the Russian defenders closer and closer to the west bank of the Volga, and on 14th it seemed as if the last Russian defenders must be trapped. But the timely arrival of a Russian Guards division blocked any further advance. The Russians are still pressed close to the west bank, but as winter approaches, morale in Paulus' exhausted 6th Army drops lower and lower. Supplies of all kinds are dwindling, and Paulus senses the vulnerability of his weak flanks. This has been noted by the Russians as well, who are now planning a counter-offensive. In the shattered city, house-to-house fighting has given way to desperate room-to-room struggles.

In the Caucasus, Army Group A continues to try for its three still-distant objectives, but the mountains' defenders constantly repulse the attacks. Eventually Kleist's 1st Panzer Army switched tactics and attacked on its right flank, instead of constantly going for Grozny on its left, and advanced far enough to capture Nalchik.

FAR EAST and PACIFIC
Attempts to build up their forces on Guadalcanal dominated the activities of both the Japanese and the Americans. The naval Battle of Cape Esperance went marginally in the Americans' favour, but it was by no means decisive (11–12th). Both sides managed to land more

troops, but far more U.S. troops were brought in. The Japanese lost a cruiser and two destroyers; the U.S.N. a destroyer, with three cruisers damaged. At the same time the Japanese Combined Fleet left Truk for Guadalcanal to support a planned major offensive. The Fleet was a formidable force, and part of it split off to bombard Henderson Airfield on the island (13–14th), causing a great deal of damage to the airfield itself, and destroying over half of the 90 aircraft at the base. Henderson was again shelled the following night, while another part of the fleet landed well over 4,000 men. On 15th both sides lost transport ships, and the Americans were unable to get much-needed fuel to the island. Henderson Airfield again came under attack, and though U.S. forces were able to inflict damage and losses on Japanese ships, the Japanese Combined Fleet dominated the area.

Roosevelt put priority on the reinforcement of Guadalcanal, and additional planes and ships were sent to the South Pacific. Japanese land attacks on Henderson Airfield on 22nd were repulsed by fierce resistance from the U.S. Marines. Another naval engagement, the Battle of Santa Cruz (25–27th) resulted in a tactical victory for the Japanese Combined Fleet, but it also suffered considerable damage. In particular, it lost a large number of its aircraft, and had to return to Truk to refuel. The Japanese land attacks were unsuccessful, and with the departure of the Japanese Combined Fleet, U.S. forces once again dominate the area.

SOUTHERN EUROPE, AFRICA and MEDITERRANEAN

The 8th Army continued to build up armour and equipment, and Montgomery began rigorous training routine for the offensive against the Axis at Alamein. In the midst of his preparations (6th) he reversed his original plan, and decided to attack on the Axis flanks and hold the German armoured units, rather than attempt a central breakthrough. The **battle of Alamein** opened on the night of 23rd with a massive artillery bombardment, immediately followed by an infantry attack.

In Rommel's absence, the Axis were commanded by Gen. Stumme who was thoroughly confused by the sudden, violent bombardment. Travelling north up the front, he came under fire from Australian troops and later died of a heart attack, leaving his army virtually leaderless. In the night of 24–25th the British armoured divisions began their crucial attempt to break through, but were halted by strong resistance. Montgomery insisted, early in the morning, that the attack should be kept up, and by dawn the armoured forces and a New Zealand division had got through to the west of the minefields. Very strong resistance slowed up the Allied advance (26th), and casualties were severe. On his return, Rommel began to plan a counter-attack, and this was launched against the northern line (27th). R.A.F. bombing raids, and a bristling defence of heavy armour and anti-tank guns stopped the counter-attack, and Rommel lost nearly 40 tanks. Two days later Australian forces launched a diversionary attack in the north and Rommel brought up reserves from the centre and from the south. Montgomery's numerical superiority over Rommel in every aspect is now enormous – his tanks, for instance, outnumbered Rommel's by about nine to one.

NOVEMBER 1942

RUSSIA and ARCTIC

The Russians' desperate hold on a thin line of shattered factories and buildings on the west bank of the Volga persisted despite the tens of thousands of casualties suffered in October. Although his 6th Army had captured most of Stalingrad, Paulus grew increasingly concerned by the possibility of encirclement. His troops were exhausted and supplies of food, ammunition, fuel and clothing were running out fast.

In Moscow, Zhukov, Vasilevsky and Stalin planned a pincer movement to isolate the Germans, and began to build up their forces north of the Don, and in the south opposite the German 4th Panzer Army. On 11th, Paulus launched a last, desperate attack on Russian positions in the northern industrial area, using his best troops. The losses on both sides were enormous, thousands being killed in bitter, hand-to-hand combat. Intelligence reports made it clear to Paulus that the Russians were about to launch a pincer attack, and eventually it came from the north-west with a massive armoured assault on the thin, Rumanian-held flank (19th). Despite German counter-attacks and fierce resistance, the Russian attack faltered only momentarily, and it rapidly flung the Axis forces panic-stricken towards Stalingrad. The next day the Russians broke through the south-eastern flank of the 6th Army, which was also held by Rumanian troops. With his army almost totally encircled, Paulus begged Hitler (22nd) to authorise a retreat through the narrow gap still left in the south-west, but Hitler was adamant that Stalingrad should not be given up. The gap was closed the next day, trapping the German 6th Army in a rather pear-shaped area of steppe and city, about 30 miles from its tapered western tip to the Volga, and about 20 miles across at its thickest point.

Goering confidently boasted that the Luftwaffe would be able to supply the surrounded army with 500 tons of food, fuel and ammunition a day. Hitler ordered Manstein – in charge of the newly formed "Army Group Don" – to break through to the 6th Army, but still forbade any evacuation. In Stalingrad the exhausted German and Rumanian troops are feeling the effects of constant effort on reduced rations. Sniping, skirmishes, and fierce fighting for every yard of rubble becomes a daily routine. The Russians on the west bank are cut off from the east bank by huge drifting ice flows on the Volga, and are also faced with shortages.

In the Caucasus the onslaught of winter halted Kleist's

last attempt at a breakthrough. Then the Russians launched a strong counter-offensive, and Kleist has now fallen back to his September positions.

FAR EAST and PACIFIC
This was the decisive month for both sides in the struggle for Guadalcanal, and there was fierce fighting on the island, as well as at sea and in the air. Both sides amassed powerful naval forces to escort fresh troops to the island. Some U.S. forces were put ashore on 11th, but another disembarkation the next day was cut short by the approach of part of the Japanese fleet. The **sea battle of Guadalcanal** began, carrying on intermittently for three days and nights. Both naval forces suffered considerable losses in ships and men, but the U.S. emerged numerical victors, having sunk two Japanese battleships, two destroyers, and six transport ships, for the loss of two cruisers and four destroyers. Both sides managed to land considerable numbers of troops, but the repeated Japanese shelling of Henderson Airfield was relatively ineffective.

SOUTHERN EUROPE, AFRICA and MEDITERRANEAN
The **Battle of Alamein** continued with an armoured assault on the centre of the German line at night, while Rommel was diverted by the Australian attack in the north (1st–2nd). The Allied advance came up against a strong anti-tank screen, but Rommel saw the need to withdraw and form a new defensive line. As usual however, Hitler forbade any retreat. Eventually the 8th Army broke through (4th), but rainfall two days later enabled Rommel to escape the threatened encirclement. With such a vast superiority in troops and especially, by then, in tanks, Montgomery could easily have trapped the Axis army and captured the entire Afrika Korps. But, afraid of extending his supply line too quickly, Montgomery began a cautious westward pursuit of the German and Italian forces. The Allies took some 30,000 prisoners (of which about one third were Afrika Korp troops), and there were about 15,000 Axis, and 13,500 Allied casualties. Vast quantities of guns, vehicles and tanks were abandoned by the Axis for lack of fuel. Rommel's retreat, despite Montgomery's cautious pursuit, was steady and soon Benghazi was abandoned (20th). Not long after that, Rommel went to Germany to recommend to Hitler that the Afrika Korps should withdraw from Tripolitania altogether, and attempt defence – or evacuation – in Tunisia.

At the same time that Rommel was carrying out his evacuation of Egypt, **"Operation Torch" began** at the other end of North Africa, with the landing of American forces on either side of Casablanca, and of American and British forces at Oran and on either side of Algiers (8th). Attempts to guarantee a rapid French surrender were foiled when the anti-British Admiral Darlan unexpectedly returned to North Africa two days before the invasion. The Allies therefore met fierce French resistance. At Casablanca the unfinished and immobile battleship *Jean Bart* engaged the U.S. battleship *Massachusetts* while all available French ships and aircraft went out to engage the American Fleet. Seven French warships and three submarines were sunk, the *Jean Bart* was gutted, and over 1,000 French lives were lost before the city surrendered (11th). There was fierce fighting in the port of Algiers, but Darlan surrendered the city in the evening (8th). Oran put up much more determined resistance and caused many American casualties before surrendering on the 10th. In other places, the Allies had co-operation from anti-Vichy leaders – Blida Airfield, for instance, was held by the Fleet Air Arm with the aid and co-operation of the French Commander.

Darlan was persuaded to order all French commanders to surrender to the Allies (9th), but a number decided he no longer had authority. The landing of fresh German and Italian troops on El Aouina airfield at Tunis on the same day complicated matters. Eisenhower wanted to take Tunis as soon as possible, and additional Allied forces landed at Bougie (11th) and Bone (12th). The first clashes with German patrols from Tunis came on 15th, but the Allied advance was eventually halted about 30 miles south-west of the city (25th).

The **captitulation of the French forces in North Africa** speeded up Germany's long-planned total occupation of France, and **German troops advanced into southern France** aiming to take over the powerful French Mediterranean Fleet in Toulon. This included a battleship, two battle cruisers, seven cruisers, 29 destroyers and torpedo boats and 16 submarines. Rival French factions argued the fate of the ships – which had almost sailed to attack Eisenhower's invasion forces. Pro-British influences were not strong enough to persuade the Fleet to join the Allied navies, but with only hours to spare before the arrival of the Germans, they were able to scuttle the Fleet, and 73 ships sank in Toulon harbour (27th).

In Madagascar, the last Vichy-French troops surrendered to Allied forces at Ihosy (5th).

DECEMBER 1942

EUROPE and ATLANTIC
Forty-three ships were sunk in the Atlantic by U-boats this month and eight by E-boats (German MTBs) operating in the English Channel and the North Sea. Only seven U-boats were destroyed – including one which was accidentally rammed by another U-boat. The use of air cover, however, has prevented submarines taking an even higher toll of shipping. 1942 has been the worst year for the Allies in the Battle of the Atlantic – nearly 8 million tons of merchant shipping has been sunk.

RUSSIA and ARCTIC

The Luftwaffe has been unable adequately to supply the besieged 6th Army at Stalingrad, where conditions in the *Kessel*, as it has come to be called (Cauldron), deteriorate daily. Only a small proportion of the necessary supplies needed every day have got through. Many aircraft could not take off in bad weather, and dozens never reached the *Kessel*. Cold, hunger and exhaustion take almost as high a toll as the daily sniping, fighting and shelling. Manstein's efforts to achieve a breakthrough were brought to a halt 35 miles from Stalingrad – and by then Paulus had only enough fuel for his army to travel 20 miles. Hitler constantly refused to allow Paulus to attempt an evacuation, and would only talk of a link-up with Manstein.

Then the **Russians launched a massive onslaught against the Italian** 8th Army which held the territory between the east and west sweep of the Don. The Italians broke in panic against impossible odds (16th). Manstein abandoned his already futile attempt to get through to Paulus, and concentrated on preventing all the Axis forces in the Caucasus from being encircled by the Russians. The Russian advance rapidly took the important German airfield at Tatsinskaya, and amid desperate attempts to get airborne, 56 transport aircraft collided with each other or were hit by artillery and tank fire. Tens of thousands of Italians were killed and even more taken prisoner, and these are being marched into captivity in Russia. Hundreds, exhausted and starving, drop out to rest and are immediately shot, while many freeze to death each night.

On Christmas Eve German troops hanged two teenage boys and a girl for spying – incredibly, nearly 2,000 civilians are still living in the murderous city. On Christmas Day, the Russians launched a ferocious artillery and *Katyusha* rocket barrage on the north-east of the *Kessel* and penetrated a few miles, killing some 1,300 Germans. It is obvious to most of Paulus' officers that there is no longer hope of rescue for the 200,000 men of the 6th Army who are still alive.

In the Arctic, the Murmansk-bound convoy JW51B, of 14 merchant ships and an escort of destroyers and corvettes, was intercepted by the German heavy cruisers *Lutzow* and *Admiral Hipper* and four destroyers (31st). The German force only managed to sink a destroyer and a minesweeper in a skilful evasion carried out by the R.N. destroyers. The convoy's close escort of two light cruisers and a destroyer then arrived, sank one of the German destroyers, and badly damaged the *Admiral Hipper*. The Germans broke off the engagement and are returning to Norway.

FAR EAST and PACIFIC

Both commands continued to attempt to reinforce Guadalcanal, but the U.S. forces' hold on Henderson Airfield helped them to achieve superiority. Gen. Patch took over the command of Guadalcanal (9th). Japanese troops now have very little food left – some have none at all. In Tokyo, the Imperial Head Quarters decided to abandon the island (31st).

Australian troops, aided by the Dutch Navy, made landings in Papua, but the Japanese also built up their forces.

Calcutta suffered its first air raid from Japanese planes.

In the year since Pearl Harbor, U.S. submarines have sunk 139 Japanese merchant ships.

SOUTHERN EUROPE, AFRICA and MEDITERRANEAN

A combination of heavy rains and the rapid reinforcement of German strengths in Tunisia has resulted in the opposing forces there reaching a stalemate, and Eisenhower gave up his objective of the immediate capture of Tunis. An R.A.F. raid on a Tunisian airfield by nine aircraft was intercepted by 50 German fighters, and all R.A.F. planes were shot down (4th). Rommel's retreating army has been constantly harried by aircraft, and a sweep by a New Zealand division caused considerable disruption and almost cut off his line of retreat (13th). To Hitler and Mussolini, Rommel is no longer the infallible Field Marshal. Montgomery, having advanced 1,200 miles since Alamein, is still wary about letting a light advance force get too far ahead of his concentrations and supply columns.

Admiral Darlan was assassinated, and his place at the head of the navy was taken by Giraud.

U.S. aircraft carried out their first raid on Naples (4th).

1943

JANUARY 1943

EUROPE and ATLANTIC

Hitler reacted hysterically to the defeat of the German navy's attempt to destroy the Arctic convoys (1st) – being especially furious over the JW51B debacle of the day before. His screaming demands for the High Seas Fleet to be broken up for scrap led to a showdown with Raeder, who always struggled with Hitler's lack of appreciation of (and interest in) naval matters. Raeder resigned (6th) and Doenitz was appointed the new C-in-C (30th).

The U.S.A.A.F. carried out its first bombing raid over Germany, when it attacked Wilhelmshaven and neighbouring targets (27th). R.A.F. Mosquitos carried out a daylight raid on Berlin (30th).

RUSSIA and ARCTIC

The Russians began the New Year with a tremendous artillery barrage on the Stalingrad *Kessel*. The new commander of the overall Russian campaign, Marshal Rokossovsky, offered Paulus 24 hours to surrender (8th) (on the 46th day of the 6th Army's encirclement), promising food, and repatriation at the end of the war. Paulus would still not act without Hitler's consent, and was told that the longer he held out, the better it would be for the rest of the German army. Very few planes were getting through – over 400 wrecked aircraft litter the flight path into the *Kessel*.

Manstein desperately held Rostov in his bid to rescue the Axis forces in the Caucasus, while the **fate of the abandoned Stalingrad soldiers was sealed** on the morning of 10th. A shattering barrage from about 7,000 heavy-artillery pieces was accompanied by wave after wave of Russian bombers. Thousands died instantly, and the German perimeter rapidly gave way as panic stricken and hysterical soldiers reeled from the assault and rushed towards the buildings of Stalingrad. By the evening, the whole army was on the run across the steppe, pursued by lines of tanks and infantry. The vital Pitomnik airfield soon fell to the Russians (16th), and while hundreds tried to break out on their own, or else surrendered individually, Hitler still refused Paulus permission to capitulate (22nd), and even refused to acknowledge the true position of the 6th Army.

By then the rubble of Stalingrad was the last refuge of over 100,000 Germans. They were lice-ridden, starved and exhausted, but their fear of Russian ill-treatment, the conviction of many that they would be shot on surrendering, and the overriding memories and rumours of how the Russian people had been treated by their fellow Germans, kept the 6th Army more or less united, though the number of suicides increased. The chance of even the worst wounded being evacuated steadily decreased, but over 40,000 had been flown out. By 28th the last morphine had been used and a Russian mortar attack on the central positions brought a new toll of deaths, suicides and flights into capture or immediate execution. On the 10th

"Private Armies" were usually discouraged, but under extraordinary leaders and in special circumstances they could achieve more than conventional units. Lt. Col. Stirling's SAS desert raiders in North Africa, and Maj. Gen. Wingate's "Chindits" in Burma (pictured here) are the two most famous. The Chindits harassed the Japanese under appalling conditions, but Wingate's early death curtailed their controversial activities.

anniversary of the 3rd Reich (30th), Paulus dutifully sent Hitler a message of congratulations, and the next morning Hitler made him a Field Marshal, mainly in the hope that Paulus would remember that no German Field Marshal had ever capitulated. However, Paulus voluntarily surrendered to the commander of a Russian tank parked near his basement H.Q. and was taken to Gen. Shumilov to formally surrender the remnants of the 6th Army – fewer than 110,000 men. As they were rounded up for the march into captivity, most were treated comparatively sympathetically, but many met their deaths.

So **the Battle of Stalingrad has come to an end**, and with it the German offensive in Russia. It has cost the Russians nearly $\frac{3}{4}$ million dead, wounded and missing, while some 850,000 Axis soldiers are dead or marching into captivity. No-one knows how many civilians have died – at least 40,000 were killed in the first bombing raid, and the following months doubtless took an equal, if not greater toll. The bustling industrial city which was home to over 500,000 before the evacuation and battle, is now 99% rubble, with a civilian population of 1,500.

The Italian and Rumanian prisoners taken in the earlier breakthrough began their long march into the frozen wastes of Russia. With no food, often stripped of their clothing by Russian civilians, and shot if they drop out of line to rest, their numbers diminish by some 300 every day.

FAR EAST and PACIFIC

The rapidly worsening Japanese position on Guadalcanal and on Buna, due mainly to American air domination, had persuaded the Emperor to agree to the evacuation of both places, and the Guadalcanal evacuation got going (14th) in the face of steady advances by the U.S. Marines. Resistance all the way was intensely fierce, and the Japanese made a futile and suicidal counter-attack (22nd). The next night (23rd), the front line defence withdrew through the next line of defence, as the evacuation from Cape Esperance speeded up. Not realising that the Japanese were evacuating, the Americans did not pursue the withdrawal, and on the following night the Japanese "leap-frogging" back towards Cape Esperance continued, with a few rear-line scouts giving the impression of a strong line. The approach of a large number of naval ships was presumed by the Americans to herald the landing of troop reinforcements, and not, as was the case, a mass evacuation.

SOUTHERN EUROPE, AFRICA and MEDITERRANEAN

The Casablanca Conference was held between Churchill and Roosevelt (14–24th), together with Chiefs of Staff, etc. It was agreed that there could be no invasion of Europe for a considerable time, but the invasion of Sicily was decided on. Inevitably there was argument over which theatre of war should receive most attention. It was emphasised again that Germany must be conquered as soon as possible (as part of this, decisions were taken to do everything possible to end the damaging effects of the U-boats), while the Pacific effort should be directed towards containment rather than conquest. The policy of clearing minor Pacific islands, and of weakening larger concentrations by disrupting communications, was laid down. Roosevelt afterwards caused considerable stir by stating to the Press that the Allies would insist on the "unconditional surrender" of Germany, though this was not part of the joint policy declaration. The phrase is open to so many interpretations and is resulting in much controversy.

Continuing his pursuit of the rapidly-escaping Rommel and his Afrika Korps, Montgomery and the 8th Army made a triumphant entry into Tripoli (23rd).

FEBRUARY 1943

EUROPE and ATLANTIC

The defeat of the 6th Army at Stalingrad was announced to the German people, and Hitler proclaimed four days of national mourning, closing theatres, cinemas, etc. (3rd). The **three great defeats suffered by Germany** – Stalingrad, Alamein, and the North African landings, have been the first major setbacks to the seemingly invincible German armies.

RUSSIA and ARCTIC

The last pockets of German resistance in Stalingrad were mopped up (2nd) and two days later the city's citizens and workers began to return to rebuild the ruins. No longer tied down by the extraordinary German tenacity at Stalingrad, the Russians were able to widen their offensive against their invaders, and recaptured Kursk (7th). Kharkov was recovered within two weeks. Further south, Rostov was finally retaken (14th), and there are no longer any German combatants in the Caucasus.

To the north-east, march the long lines of the 107,000 soldiers of the 6th Army taken into captivity. Many are dying of cold, exhaustion and starvation. Sometimes, especially in villages, the guards fire a round or two each into the miserable columns of men. The paths taken by the Germans, the Italians, the Rumanians, the Hungarians, are clearly marked by hundreds and hundreds of frozen corpses.

FAR EAST and PACIFIC

Convinced a new, reinforced Japanese offensive was about to be launched, the U.S. Marines on Guadalcanal kept away from the thin Japanese rearguard, while empty landing craft crept ashore to take off nearly 5,500 weary, half-starved Japanese soldiers (1st). Three days later another 5,000 left virtually unmolested. Only when the last forces had left (9th) did the Americans realise the bitter struggle for Guadalcanal was over. Although the

Japanese managed to evacuate over 13,000 soldiers, 25,000 had died holding the island. The U.S. forces had lost 1,600 Marines and GIs. For the Japanese, it was a considerable disaster. It proved they were not invulnerable, and although each side had lost approximately 25 warships each, the Americans' losses could be far more easily replaced. For the Allies, Guadalcanal has boosted morale and, most important, the routes to Australia and New Zealand have been kept open. But the extremely fierce resistance put up by the Japanese for every foot of land, even against great odds, allows no-one to think the clearance of the occupied islands is going to be an easy task.

In Burma Brig. Orde **Wingate led his "Chindits"** on their first expedition of guerilla warfare against the Japanese (8th). On the 14th they crossed the Chindwin, and were well into enemy territory.

SOUTHERN EUROPE, AFRICA and MEDITERRANEAN

To establish a unified force with the German garrison at Tunis, Rommel attacked U.S. positions south of Tunis (14th) and after fierce fighting **the Germans broke through the Kasserine Pass** (20th) and began to threaten the British lines. The Axis advance was halted however, and then forced back (23rd). American morale suffered badly from defeat in their first conflict with German troops. The U.S. forces were new and ill-trained, and their support mainly consisted of poorly armed Free French soldiers.

In the last week, Gen. Alexander took command of the whole Allied front, against Rommel who had been put in charge of all Axis forces in Africa. Air Marshal Tedder took command of the Allied Air Forces, and the battle for Tunisia is now at its height, for despite his setback after the Kasserine breakthrough, Rommel still fights fiercely against the "Torch" Allies to the west, and against the 8th Army to the east.

MARCH 1943

EUROPE and ATLANTIC

On the night 5–6th R.A.F. Bomber Command opened Air Marshal Harris' night bombing offensive against Germany with an accurate attack by nearly 450 aircraft on Essen. Thus **the Battle of the Ruhr began**.

The Battle of the Atlantic reached its worst period for Allied shipping losses. In the first 20 days alone, 43 ships were sunk. Around the world, over 100 merchant ships – a total of some 625,000 tons – were destroyed.

RUSSIA

Manstein forced a desperate counter-attack against the Russians, and Kharkov again fell into German hands (11th). All the German withdrawals have considerably shortened their lines, and given them a powerful defence – while it is now the Russians who are overstretched along a massive front, with a conspicuous bulge westwards around Kursk. The Spring thaw has immobilised the two forces, who are strengthening their positions and building up reserves. Stalin and Zhukov expect a German counter-attack on the Kursk bulge, and are planning accordingly.

FAR EAST and PACIFIC

A large Japanese convoy with 7,000 troops left Rabaul on New Britain for an invasion of New Guinea. U.S. and Australian planes, mainly from Papua, attacked the convoy in **the Battle of the Bismarck Sea** (3rd) and launched an even bigger attack the next day, in which they were joined by U.S. PT boats. All the transport ships, and four Japanese destroyers were sunk. Over 3,500 Japanese soldiers and sailors died in the attack, which cost the Allies only five aircraft.

In Burma, Wingate's Chindits cut the Mandalay-Myitkyina railway line in 75 places during the month.

In an attempt to reduce the number of cargo ships sunk by U.S. submarines, the Japanese formed a second convoy escort.

SOUTHERN EUROPE, AFRICA and MEDITERRANEAN

The 8th Army clashed with Rommel's Axis forces at Medienne (6–8th) in four major Axis attacks, all of which were beaten back in severe fighting. Rommel, by then severely ill, was recalled to Germany, and the Allies moved up to the Axis' main defences, the Mareth Line (originally constructed by the French). The Battle of the Mareth Line began in the third week, and involved artillery barrages and air bombardment, followed by frontal and left flank attacks by the 8th Army and Free French forces. The flank has been turned but heavy and complicated fighting against the concentrated Axis forces continues.

APRIL 1943

EUROPE and ATLANTIC

This month saw the ending of U-boat dominance in the Battle of the Atlantic. Apart from being able to escort every convoy for the full duration of their voyages, the U.S.N. and R.N. are now able to operate independent flotilla groups which can go to the aid of any convoy which is being attacked by a U-boat group. Air cover has also substantially increased, and although over 230 U-boats are in action, fewer and fewer have carried through full-scale attacks. A major factor in limiting U-boat activity is the increasing use of centimetric radar in aeroplanes, by which U-boats travelling on the surface at night can be located and sunk or forced to dive.

In the Jewish ghetto in the devastated Polish capital of Warsaw, the 60,000 remaining Jews (of the 400,000 who had been confined in it in 1940) rebelled against the Nazis

(19th) who were daily dragging more and more away to be murdered or worked to death in concentration camps – mainly Treblinka. Furious at the thought of Polish Jews killing German soldiers and destroying tanks, **Himmler ordered the utter destruction of the Warsaw ghetto** – a walled-in part of the city of less than one square mile. Stroop, the SS officer in charge, began to burn down the ghetto (24th). The next day the Germans captured 27,500 Jews and despatched them to Treblinka. Over the following days, many were killed as they were captured, yet now resistance continues in the sewers and the rubble. There are few unburnt buildings left.

Gen. Guderian (recalled from the front to be Inspector General of Armoured Troops) and Speer have speeded up production of *Panzer IV* tanks to nearly 2,000 a month, and have ordered the manufacture of *Panthers* and *Tigers*. The tanks are mainly meant for Russia.

RUSSIA and ARCTIC

The increasing daylight hours have caused heavier losses on Arctic convoys, and the presence of most of the German Fleet in Norway – including the huge battleship *Tirpitz* – adds to convoy dangers. The decision has been taken to stop Arctic convoys until winter, but supplies to Russia will be sent via the Persian Gulf.

The quiet stalemate continues on the long Russian front, as both armies build up their forces and prepare for the fighting days of summer.

Since the 1st of February, over 400,000 Germans, Italian, Rumanian and Hungarian prisoners of war have died. In the prison camps, some have become cannibals.

FAR EAST and PACIFIC

The Allies intercepted, and as usual decoded, a message about an intended tour of the Solomon Islands to be made by the highly respected Adm. Yamamoto, architect of Japan's Pearl Harbor attack. A force of 16 U.S. planes intercepted the Japanese group over Bougainville Island. Despite the 62 Japanese fighter escorts, Yamamoto's plane was shot down and he was killed (18th). Coming so soon after Guadalcanal, Yamamoto's death has a very damaging effect on Japanese morale.

SOUTHERN EUROPE, AFRICA and MEDITERRANEAN

The two Allied forces – from Operation Torch, and those with Montgomery from Egypt – joined together when two patrols met (4th), after clearing the Axis forces from almost 2,000 miles of North Africa. In a desperate attempt to supply the trapped troops in Tunisia, a huge German air convoy of 100 transport planes set out from Sicily (18th). Attacking British and U.S. fighters scattered the convoy and destroyed over 50 planes. The next day South African fighter aircraft shot down 15 out of a flight of 18 planes. Another German attempt was made (22nd), but 30 of these – many heavily loaded with petrol – were destroyed.

The U.S., Free French, and 8th Army forces are continuing their pressure on the German and Italian positions, making gradual headway.

MAY 1943

EUROPE and ATLANTIC

The Battle of the Atlantic has ended – for the present – with Doenitz's recall of all Atlantic U-boats to base (22nd). The new era of Atlantic crossings came with the eastward convoy SC130 from Halifax which did not lose a single ship, although its escort sank 5 U-boats. In the whole month 50 merchantmen were sunk – for the loss of 41 U-boats. The night-time use of radar-equipped aircraft has played a major part in the U-boat defeat. The frequent need to dive during vital battery-charging surface runs on their diesel engines severely limited ranges, and the ability to form groups and the favoured surface attacks also became increasingly hazardous. Doenitz is now working out new strategies, and designers are planning new submarines. In the meantime the Southern Atlantic and the Indian Ocean offer occasional prey in the form of unescorted merchantmen, but the simultaneous defeat of the Axis in North Africa means more shipping can forsake the "round Africa" route for the direct Mediterranean–Suez route to the east. The R.A.F. attacks on the U-boat pens and construction yards which began in January have had little effect on the enormous concrete roofs covering the complexes, although nearly 20,000 tons of high explosives and incendiaries have been dropped on them.

In a highly skilled night raid using special bombs released under precise but very dangerous conditions, R.A.F. bombers of the specially-formed **617 Squadron attacked the Mohne, Sorpe and Eder dams** in north-west Germany (16–17th). The bombs and their delivery technique were conceived by Barnes Wallis, and they successfully damaged all three dams. The Mohne and Sorpe walls were breached, flooding the Ruhr valley, drowning 1,200 people and putting much industry out of action. Of the 19 Lancaster bombers which took part, eight were destroyed.

The **Warsaw ghetto uprising** ended when the destruction of the last building and sewer was followed by blowing up the Warsaw synagogue (16th). One hundred and eighty Jews were "destroyed" on that day, and the SS commander of the annihilation, Stroop, boasted that 56,065 Jews from the ghetto had been killed in the month of the uprising – about 13,000 in the ghetto itself, and the remainder on the way to, and at Treblinka.

At the Trident Conference in Washington, Churchill, Roosevelt and their military advisers met to discuss war priorities (12th). Churchill was most anxious to relieve German pressure on the Russians, and pressed for the invasion of Italy after Sicily. The invasion of Europe had been preliminarily fixed for 1.5.44, and Churchill was only too aware of Stalin's reactions if the Western Allies accomplished little until then. Roosevelt was not keen on Italy, and a number of Staff Chiefs also preferred Sardinia. Churchill argued that the defeat of the Italians would draw away large numbers of German divisions to replace Italian forces in Italy and the Balkans. No agreement could be reached in Washington, and Churchill left with Gens. Marshall, Bedell-Smith and others to consult Eisenhower in Algiers (27th) (see below, AFRICA).

RUSSIA
As Stalin and Zhukov had anticipated, Hitler and his Chiefs decided on a large scale attack on the Russian bulge at Kursk, and began to assemble tanks and troops – while the Russians were doing likewise.

FAR EAST and PACIFIC
In the North Pacific U.S. forces landed on Attu in the Aleutian Islands. Despite being outnumbered by about four to one, the Japanese defended with their typical desperation, and eventually even launched a suicidal counter-attack. Only 26 Japanese were captured alive – over 2,500 had died fighting.

Wingate's Chindits returned from their three-month penetration into Japanese-held Burma. The expedition scored a psychological rather than a military success – it had taken on the Japanese in jungle warfare, and caused a good deal of damage and disruptuion, though nothing of a permanent nature. But the Chindits boosted Allied morale and caused the Japanese the inconvenience of not being able to regard the Burmese jungle as a safe place. The losses to the Chindits, mainly through tropical illnesses, accidents, etc., were very heavy.

SOUTHERN EUROPE, AFRICA and MEDITERRANEAN
Gen. Alexander launched a final assault on Tunis with a pre-dawn bombardment by aircraft and 1,000 guns. In the dark Sappers cleared minefields and cut defensive wires, and before first light the Allies had overrun the Axis outposts (6th). The main positions were cleared before noon, and by the evening of 7th Tunis was captured. U.S. forces took Bizerta on the same day, while the Axis rushed towards the natural defensive position of the Cape Bon Peninsula. They were closely pursued and attacked by Alexander's forces, and one of his armoured divisions made a rapid, moonlight drive splitting through the centre of the Axis forces, causing tremendous confusion. Allied naval and air movements ensured the Axis could not arrange a "Dunkirk" evacuation. On the 13th, all German and Italian troops were surrendered – over 250,000. The final battle in Africa had cost the Allies 70,000 killed and wounded. **The African continent is now free of Axis forces.**

Churchill met Eisenhower in Algiers, and with their advisers continued the discussions on post-Sicily tactics (29th). Air bombardment of Pantelleria Island, south-west of Sicily had already begun (26th), and it was decided that if the conquest of Sicily was rapid, and the "foot" of Italy did not appear to be heavily guarded, the invasion of the "toe" would follow immediately.

JUNE 1943

EUROPE and ATLANTIC
For the first time, not a single North Atlantic convoy was attacked this month, but 17 U-boats were sunk. In the U-boat pens, newly-designed U-boats take shape, while others are being fitted with *Schnorkel* devices to enable their diesel engines to operate while the submarines are below the surface.

FAR EAST and PACIFIC
Gen. MacArthur and Adm. Halsey began their two-pronged drive towards Rabaul and the Phillipines by attacks on the central Solomon Islands. The New Georgia Group with the Munda airfield was the first objective, and concentrated landings (30th) achieved rapid success.

In the North Atlantic, the Aleutian Island of Kiska was heavily bombarded.

SOUTHERN EUROPE and MEDITERRANEAN
Gen. Eisenhower, as overall commander, prepared for the invasion of Sicily. Gen. Alexander commanded the Army Group (comprised of Patton's U.S. 7th Army and Montgomery's 8th Army); Air Chief Marshal Tedder the Allied Air Force; and Admiral Cunningham the Allied naval forces. In the first stage the island of Pantelleria, south-west of Sicily, was captured with its garrison of 11,000 Italians (11th). The 6,570 tons of bombs dropped on the island had done remarkably little damage.

JULY 1943

EUROPE and ATLANTIC
Heavy night raids on Hamburg by R.A.F. bombers began (24th) and were repeated on three further nights. With the raids continuing, it is impossible to estimate casualties, but nearly one million civilians have fled the city. Huge areas have been destroyed by the Allies' alternate use of high explosive bombs and incendiaries. A new R.A.F. trick, the dropping of clouds of thin metalised strips (called "Window") so far completely confuse German radar screens, and the R.A.F. are losing comparatively few aircraft. The Ruhr has also been heavily attacked – the fifth major raid since the bombing offensive on Germany's industrial centre began in March. Duisberg, Krefeld, Düsseldorf, Essen, and others have suffered severe damage, as have a number of Krupp armament factories.

RUSSIA
With nearly 1,000 planes and the latest tanks at his disposal, Manstein launched an attack on the Russian bulge at Kursk (4th). Zhukov and the Russians were fully prepared with far more, if inferior tanks. They also had some 20,000 artillery pieces, from heavy guns to anti-tank guns, and enormous troop concentrations. Crack SS Panzer divisions in the new *Panther* and *Tiger* tanks spearheaded the typical German *blitzkrieg* wedge assault, meeting extremely fierce resistance. After a week the Germans seemed to be about to break through, and they had been achieving a two to one success rate over the Russian tanks in the biggest, most ferocious tank battles ever fought – at one time, almost 3,000 tanks were engaged on the flat grasslands. But then the Russians threw a completely fresh tank army into a furious eight-hour battle, and there seemed to be no end to the Russian replacement ability (12th).

The next day, even Hitler agreed that Manstein should withdraw, since the whole German armoured strength was liable to be wiped out. Manstein wanted to make a general retreat and set up a strong defensive line on the Dnieper River, but Hitler would not tolerate such a long retreat, and Manstein was forced to fight and retreat without being able to consolidate his forces. The Russians also widened the Kursk bulge by launching a northwards attack towards Orel.

FAR EAST and PACIFIC
MacArthur, with his largely untried GIs, continued the Central Solomons Campaign with the landing of 34,000 troops against a garrison of 8,000 Japanese near Munda. Japanese reinforcements were landed, and slowed up the American advance.

In the Aleutians, the Japanese evacuated their garrison of 5,000 from Kiska – to the ignorance of the U.S. forces, who continued to bombard the island on and off for 2½ weeks.

SOUTHERN EUROPE and MEDITERRANEAN
By considerable ingenious and meticulous subterfuges, the Axis had been led to expect an Allied invasion of Sardinia, or an Aegean assault. Nevertheless Sicily was defended by some 350,000 Axis troops – about ¾ Italian – when the Allies launched heavy air attacks on the island's airfields (3rd). **The invasion of Sicily** began in bad weather with the night landings of paratroopers and glider-borne assault troops on the south-east apex to secure a landing for the 8th Army drive on Syracuse (9–10th). Bad weather conditions and inexperience resulted in 69 of the 137 gliders landing in the sea, and many soldiers in them were drowned. Only twelve gliders arrived at one of the most important bridge objectives. It was seized by eight officers and 65 soldiers – when they were relieved 12 hours later, only 19 were still alive.

The American landings on the south-west apex were also widely scattered, but this added to the enemy's confusion as well as to the paratroopers'. All the sea-borne landings (10th) were entirely successful, though sometimes opposed. The U.S. 7th Army soon took Licata, and the British 8th Army captured Syracuse (11th), and Augusta (13th). German reinforcements, including some elite troops such as the *Herman Goering Division* arrived in Sicily. The rapid 8th Army advance came to a halt on the verge of the Catania plain which was guarded by very strong German defences on the slopes of Mount Etna. Patton's U.S. 7th Army continued its rapid advance and took Palermo (22nd) but also began to slow down as it neared the Etna and north-east stronghold.

Churchill and Roosevelt made a surrender appeal to the Italian people (16th), emphasising that there would have to be no unconditional surrender. After dropping warning leaflets, Rome was bombed by 270 planes of the U.S.A.A.F., the marshalling yards being the primary target (19th).

After Fascist rebels in the Grand Council voted for the restoration of a Constitutional Monarchy, King Victor Emmanuel III dismissed Mussolini (25th), dissolved the Fascist Party, and entrusted the Italian Government to Marshal Badoglio (28th). He began negotiations with Allies, having imprisoned Mussolini. It is clear that Italy is on the verge of surrender.

AUGUST 1943

EUROPE and ATLANTIC
At the Quebec Conference, Roosevelt and Churchill met with their advisers and decided on the invasion of Italy early in September and confirmed "Operation Overlord", the invasion of Europe, with a target date of 1.5.44.

R.A.F. Bomber Command carried out one more night raid on Hamburg. Since the attacks began on 24th July, 3,095 bombers have dropped some 8,000 tons of bombs on Hamburg, losing 87 aircraft. Upwards of 50,000 Germans, mostly civilians, have been killed and 40,000 injured – the evacuation of 1 million saved many lives. Sixty-two thousand acres have been obliterated.

Six hundred R.A.F. bombers attacked the German rocket establishment at Peenemünde (17–18th). Considerable damage was done and many scientists and technicians killed in the night attack. The raid cost 57 bombers shot down near the target and crashed on returning to base. The ball-bearing factories at Schweinfurt-am-Main, and the Messerschmitt aircraft factory at Regensburg were bombed by large U.S.A.A.F. bomber formations, which lost 59 aircraft.

Since the beginning of June, 74 U-boats have been sunk in the refuelling area north-west of the Azores, mostly by planes off U.S.N. escort carrier groups. The Indian Ocean is now practically the only fairly safe hunting ground for U-boats.

Above: Royal Navy 20-mm "Pompom" multiple anti-aircraft guns and crew (Photo: Imperial War Museum).
Below: British 5·5-inch gun in action at night (Photo: Imperial War Museum).

RUSSIA

With the Battle of Kursk over, the Russians turned entirely to the offensive. Orel was abandoned by the Germans (4th) and they retreated steadily. For the second – and final – time Russian troops liberated Kharkov (23rd). The Germans are unable to halt the Russians, yet are not allowed to fall back to a strong defensive line.

FAR EAST and PACIFIC

Munda in the New Georgia group of the Solomons was finally taken by U.S. forces (5th). Landings were then made (15th) on Vella Lavella to use it as a fighter base. Very fierce resistance was again met, and the slow advances due to Japanese tenacity were responsible for MacArthur's decision to bypass Kolonbangara with its much larger garrison. Also, Vella Lavella was only 100 miles from the Japanese stronghold of Bougainville – the island to which the Japanese from the Central Solomons were retreating.

U.S. planes raided the Japanese base at Wewak on the north coast of New Guinea, and destroyed over 100 planes (17–18th). Continuing the "leap-frogging" policy of isolating some islands, it was decided that no land attack will be made on Rabaul in the Bismarck Archipelago, which has a Japanese garrison of at least 10,000.

In the North Pacific Aleutians, the U.S. eventually stopped bombarding Kiska, and landed 34,000 troops – who discovered the island was empty.

South-East Asia Command (S.E.A.C.) was formed (2nd) with Admiral Lord Mountbatten Supreme Commander. Gen. Slim was put in command of the newly-formed 14th Army, Wavell became Viceroy of India, Auchinleck succeeding him as C-in-C India (responsible for troop training). S.E.A.C. had its air strength reinforced, and its primary objective was to re-open land communications with China.

SOUTHERN EUROPE and MEDITERRANEAN

British reinforcements from Tunisia arrived in Sicily and captured Adrano, a key position in the approach to Mt. Etna (6th). The U.S. Army began to move forward again and captured Randazzo (13th). The Germans and Italians began an evacuation across the Messina Strait to the Italian mainland, and soon Patton was on the outskirts of Messina, which fell to the U.S. on the 17th. Seven thousand German troops were taken prisoner – but 60,000 escaped to Italy. The 39 days campaign cost the Germans 30,000 dead and wounded, and the Italian forces had 130,000 killed, wounded, or taken prisoner. There were 31,158 Allied troops killed and wounded.

While German troops were sent into Italy and the Balkans in anticipation of Italy's surrender, representatives of America, Britain and Italy met in Lisbon. The U.S.A.A.F. once again bombed Rome (13th), which the next day was declared an open city.

SEPTEMBER 1943

EUROPE and ATLANTIC

The giant German battleship *Tirpitz* fired its guns for the first time in a bombardment, with *Scharnhorst*, of Spitzbergen (8th). *Tirpitz* subsequently anchored in Altenfjord, and six British midget submarines were sent in to attack her (22nd). Two managed to penetrate the defences and put charges on the hull. Their detonation severely damaged the *Tirpitz*'s main turbines, and put the ship out of action. (The only dry dock capable of accommodating the ship is at far-away St. Nazaire – and that is still useless after the British Commando raid in March 1942. It seems as if *Tirpitz* is out of the war for good.)

Doenitz sent 28 U-boats back into the Atlantic to renew the blockade of Britain. They met fierce opposition, but one group managed to sink six merchantmen and three escorts for the loss of three of its submarines.

RUSSIA and ARCTIC

The Russians are continuing their massive and relentless pressure on the steadily retreating Germans. Poltava, 70 miles west of Kharkov, was retaken (22nd), and after furious fighting, far to the north, Smolensk was once again in Russian hands (25th). The Germans are now back on the Dnieper line, which is where Manstein wanted to set up a strong defence. But with the Russians close on their heels, there is no opportunity to prepare for a stand.

The sole Russian supply route during the cessation of Arctic convoys was the laborious and limited approach via Persia, and the massive battles against the Germans used up enormous supplies. Molotov therefore urgently pressed, and virtually demanded, that the Arctic convoys should be resumed without delay (21st). The Russian attitude angered Churchill, especially since many convoys received little Russian assistance, and British sailors and essential permanent forces in Archangel and Murmansk were subjected to extremely severe restrictions of movement and frequent unpleasant treatment. Excessive bureaucratic red tape caused endless delays, and it was difficult to replace or rotate Russian-based men. Churchill therefore asked Stalin to review this aspect, but also notified him that convoys would resume in November, and that four were planned over four months. The disabling of *Tirpitz* has considerably diminished Arctic convoy dangers.

FAR EAST and PACIFIC

MacArthur's battle for New Guinea, after the air attacks in August, began with a landing of Australian troops east of Lae as a preliminary to the attack on Huon Peninsula (5th). The next day U.S. paratroopers made the Pacific war's first airborne assault when they captured Nadzab airfield. The overland advance on Salamaua continued and it fell on 11th. Lae was evacuated by the Japanese

(15th), and the Allies pushed towards Madang. The clearance of this part of New Guinea will give the Allies some control of the Dampier Strait and provide a launching base for operations against the island of New Britain.

In mid-September the Japanese Imperial G.H.Q. revised their ambitions and laid down new borders which they considered would be the minimum area needed to fulfil the Japanese war aims. New Guinea, the Bismarck Islands (the main one is New Britain), the Solomons, Gilberts and Marshalls are eventually to be given up, but the G.H.Q. ordered their retention for at least six months while an "impenetrable" inner ring is established.

Allied superiority in sea, land and air power steadily increases. The Allies now have 20 Divisions in the South-West Pacific against six Japanese Divisions. In China, Japan has 26 Divisions, and 15 in Manchuria. U.S. submarines continue to take a heavy toll of Japanese merchant ships – over 172,000 tons were sunk this month.

SOUTHERN EUROPE and MEDITERRANEAN

An Armistice with Italy was signed, but not announced (3rd), and on the same day the invasion of Italy began with practically unopposed landings across the Strait of Messina. Reggio rapidly fell and the 8th Army advanced quickly up the Calabria. After Allied pressure the surrender of Italy was announced by Badoglio (8th). Further British landings in the Gulf of Taranto were unopposed (9th), but on that day Gen. Mark Clark and the U.S. 5th Army met very fierce German opposition against their landings in the Gulf of Salerno. The battle was almost decided in the German's favour (11th), and the Luftwaffe carried out many bombing raids on the invasion ships. But Allied air superiority was eventually established, and the beachhead was firmly consolidated (15th).

Allied plans to land airborne troops near Rome were abandoned, as the Germans, with 15 divisions in Italy, and obviously prepared for Italy's capitulation, moved rapidly and took Rome (10th). King Emmanuel and Badoglio managed to escape to Brindisi in R.N. corvettes. Mussolini, who had been interned variously on islands in the Mediterranean, was taken to a mountain resort in Central Italy in August. In his haste to get out of Rome, Badoglio must have forgotten about Mussolini,

The extent of Japan's conquests in the Pacific and South-East Asia.

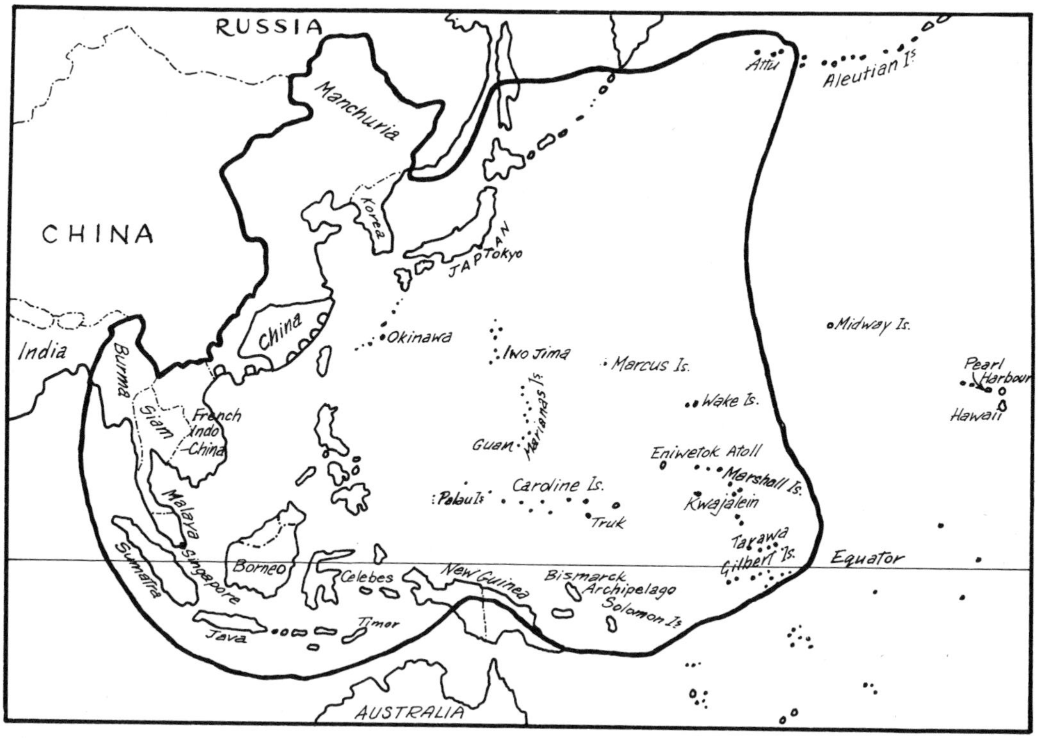

and on the 12th 90 German paratroopers landed by glider and freed the former dictator, taking him to meet Hitler. Mussolini proclaimed himself leader of a new Republican–Fascist Party (15th), and set up his new H.Q. near Lake Garda, deep in German-occupied Italy. Many resistance movements have broken out, and there is considerable internal conflict going on in Italy.

The 8th Army encountered very little resistance, and after covering 200 miles in 13 days, an advance guard joined up with the U.S. 5th Army south-east of Salerno (16th). The Allied advance up the east coast from Taranto to Brindisi was equally rapid, and soon the army reached Bari (22nd). By the time Foggia had been reached (27th), there were many important airfields under Allied control. It was only when the River Biferno was reached that strong German resistance was encountered.

Unlike France, Italy once rid of Mussolini was pleased to see its Navy pass into Allied control, and on the night of the announcement of surrender (8th) the Italian Fleet left Genoa and Spezia bound for Malta. The next morning it was attacked by German bombers, and the flagship *Roma* blew up and sank, taking with her many lives. A British naval force met the Italian Fleet (10th), and the next day escorted it into Malta. One of the British ships which had met the Italians, the battleship *Warspite*, was subsequently disabled (16th) by the new type of radio-controlled glider-bomb which had been so effectively used against *Roma*.

The fall of Italy significantly altered the balance of power in the Balkans and Aegean. Both Hitler and Churchill pressed for grabbing the initiative in the Aegean – Hitler, being a dictator, has begun to establish German superiority, while Churchill argues with little success against Roosevelt and Eisenhower, who are reluctant to release anything which might be needed for Overlord (the invasion of Europe).

In the Balkans the Italian forces were taken by surprise on the sudden surrender, and many were trapped between partisan forces and German troops who immediately regarded them as potential enemies. The 7,000 strong Italian garrison on Corfu was practically wiped out by the Germans. The Cephalonia garrison fought on, but were eventually overwhelmed (22nd) and the survivors shot or deported. In the days following the Armistice, some 40,000 Italian soldiers were killed in the Balkans and the Aegean, while thousands more were deported to work camps in Germany.

OCTOBER 1943

EUROPE and ATLANTIC

The renewed U-boat offensive met little success. A large, "double" convoy with a considerable number of escorts and extensive air cover crossed the Atlantic with the loss of only one merchant ship, while six U-boats were sunk. In the past two months, nearly 2,500 merchant ships crossed the North Atlantic, and only nine were sunk. A further help for the Allies in controlling the Atlantic came with the granting by Portugal of naval and air base facilities in the Azores.

Nearly 290 heavy U.S. bombers carried out a daylight raid on the ball-bearing factory at Schweinfurt (14th). The group flew without fighter escorts, the "Flying Fortress" planes being supposed to carry out their own defence. Although great damage was done to the factories, 60 bombers were shot down – an unacceptably high loss.

Sir Andrew Cunningham succeeded the very ill Sir Dudley Pound as Britain's First Sea Lord.

RUSSIA and ARCTIC

The Russian armies continue to push back the Germans. The front-line generals' hope of a stand on the Dnieper vanished when the Russians crossed the river with scarcely a pause. Early in the month, it was crossed north of Kiev. Zaporozhe in the far south was recovered (14th) and when Melitopol was liberated (23rd) the only German troops east of the Dnieper were those near the river mouth. Then the Russians recaptured Dnepropetrovsk, their first major town west of the river (25th), and the large Crimean garrison, together with the east-bank forces, was cut off from safe retreat. The Russian advance has a snowballing effect – Manstein's army has lost 133,000 men since Kursk, and has only received 33,000 replacements. Russia, on the other hand, has innumerable manpower reserves, and masses of Allied equipment.

Churchill adopted a hard line against Stalin over the Arctic convoys and the treatment of British forces in Russia. In Moscow, Molotov pleaded with Eden for the resumption of the convoys (19th) and when Churchill prevented escort destroyers from sailing to begin escort operations, Molotov persuaded Stalin to relax his conditions. Agreement was reached, and the first convoy sails next month.

FAR EAST and PACIFIC

The Japanese evacuated Vella Lavella in the Central Solomons (6–7th), and **the Central Solomons campaign came to an end** with a fierce sea battle fought off the island. The U.S.N. have lost six warships in the struggle for the Solomons so far, against the Japanese loss of 17.

On New Guinea, U.S. and Australian troops have got to within 50 miles of Madang. Heavy air raids on Rabaul began (12th) and are still continuing regularly.

The Americans began a heavy bombardment of the Japanese airfields on Bougainville, the largest of the Solomon Islands. The Japanese forces on the island now number about 60,000.

SOUTHERN EUROPE and MEDITERRANEAN

The civil strife in divided Italy took a new turn when Badoglio's Italy declared war on Germany (13th). More than half of Italy is therefore now occupied by "enemy" troops – this time the Germans commanded by F. M. Kesselring.

The U.S. 5th Army continued its advance from Salerno, and took Naples (1st). On the east coast British commandos took Termoli, behind enemy lines, and the 8th Army pushed the Germans back from the Biferno. On the advice of Kesselring, Hitler altered his previous plan which allowed only for the defence of northern Italy, beyond Rome. The Germans are now preparing a defensive line along the north bank of the Sangro in the east to the mouth of the Garigliano in the west.

NOVEMBER 1943

EUROPE and ATLANTIC

Berlin came under heavy night air raids (18–29th). A total of over 1,200 bombers took part, and 43 were shot down.

Hitler issued Directive No. 51 which drew attention to the threat of an invasion on Western Europe – and so diverted attention from the worsening situation on the Russian front. The Directive picks out the Calais area as being the most likely invasion point. (Allied deception strategy plans to pinpoint Calais as the target.)

RUSSIA and ARCTIC

The Russian advance liberated Kiev and took many Germans prisoner, but Hitler still forbids a strategic withdrawal to set up a strong defensive line. The Russians outnumber the Germans by 5·7 million to 3 million, and have a huge superiority of numbers in guns and tanks.

The first Arctic convoy since March reached Russia

The Germans' third winter in Russia was as marked by hardship and defeat as had been the first two. They had been beaten back from Moscow in the first winter, suffered a disastrous defeat at Stalingrad in the second, and in the third their northern line was broken and Leningrad relieved. In later tank battles the Germans were sometimes more effective than the Russians, fielding such formidable equipment as the PzKw VI Tiger, but they did not have the Russians' endless reserves of manpower and industrial capacity.

without mishap, and an "empty" convoy was safely returned.

FAR EAST and PACIFIC
Under Gen. MacArthur and Adm. Halsey, the two-pronged drive to the Philippines continued its slow advance with Halsey's landing of 14,000 Marines on the heavily guarded island of Bougainville (1st). A Japanese fleet sent to disrupt the invasion was attacked by the U.S.N. and lost a cruiser and a destroyer (2nd). At the same time heavy air attacks were made on Rabaul, and on a Japanese fleet of seven cruisers seen heading for Bougainville. All the cruisers were badly damaged (5th). Japanese planes from Rabaul attacked a U.S.N. task force, but suffered the loss of many aircraft. After that, the Japanese withdrew their aircraft and warships from Rabaul to Truk Island, 875 miles north in the Caroline Islands. The 60,000 Japanese forces on Bougainville did not attack the Americans, believing the landings were a deception prior to an imminent main assault. The Bougainville build-up continued, and soon there were 34,000 U.S. troops ashore (14th). Off New Ireland, in the Bismarck Archipelago, the U.S.N. sank three Japanese destroyers, without receiving a single hit (25th).

The disagreement between Gen. MacArthur and Adm. Nimitz on how Japan should be defeated leads to two separate lines of attack – MacArthur largely by land, via the Philippines, while Nimitz favours capturing a number of small but well-placed islands, and to rely on superiority of naval and air forces to cut Japan off from her "empire", and cut the islands off from supplies. Nimitz began his "Central Route" drive in the Gilbert Islands with tremendous gun barrages on Tarawa and Makin islands from ships of the 5th Fleet (12–20th). Makin was only defended by about 800 troops, but the U.S. soldiers, poorly-trained and led, took four days to clear the island, losing 66 lives (20–24th).

On Tarawa, the U.S. Marines faced a very tough defending force of almost 5,000, most of whom were trained, experienced soldiers. The first wave of Marines met extremely heavy fire, despite a dawn barrage of 3,000 tons of shells (20th). By noon 5,000 Marines had landed and both sides suffered many casualties. More troops were brought in the next day, and gradually the ferocious Japanese resistance was overcome. When fighting ended (26th) only 17 Japanese and 129 Korean labourers out of the islands original garrison of 5,000, were taken prisoner.

The next islands in Nimitz's path are the 32 island groups of the Marshalls, and Nimitz has decided to leapfrog the first two major atolls and make an attack on Kwajalein, the largest island in the group (and the world's largest coral atoll).

Japanese merchant shipping losses due to American submarines reached a record 265,000 tons this month.

SOUTHERN EUROPE and MEDITERRANEAN
The Big Three, **Churchill, Roosevelt and Stalin, met at Teheran** (28th). Stalin above all wanted to push for the opening of a second front to divert German attention from the costly Russian battle, and was well pleased to be told about the Overlord plans for May 1944. For the first time there was some conflict between Churchill and Roosevelt, who was overly anxious to appease Stalin, in so doing putting undue emphasis on Churchill's aims in Italy and their possible effect on Overlord.

Churchill and Stalin began informal discussions on the future of Europe, and, despite their protestations in the Atlantic Charter, it is clear that the Big Three are going to draw up mutually satisfactory boundaries for others. An overriding concern is that German unity and military strength should be curbed forever. The conference is still going on, the month ending with Churchill giving an enjoyable and informal dinner to celebrate his 69th birthday.

In Italy, the Germans fell back on their Garigliano defensive line, and the Allied advance has practically halted.

DECEMBER 1943

EUROPE and ATLANTIC
Following positive identification of "flying bomb" launching sites in Peenemünde and on the French coast, the first of many bombing attacks by the Allies was launched (20th). U.S. Air Forces sent almost 1,500 aircraft on raids into Germany and to Schipol, Amsterdam (13th). For the first time bombers were given prolonged fighter protection, the new Mustang fighters having a greatly increased range.

Eisenhower, Montgomery, Bradley and Tedder arrived in England from the Mediterranean (24th) to begin planning Overlord. Eisenhower is to be Supreme Commander, Tedder his Deputy, and Montgomery will be in charge of the landings. Lt.-Gen. Spaatz has been put in command of the U.S. Strategic Bombing of Germany.

RUSSIA and ARCTIC
The Russian winter has temporarily stopped the Russian advance, and only in the Crimea and south of Kiev do the Germans hold territory east of 32°E.

The December Arctic convoy to Russia was intercepted by *Scharnhorst*, Germany's only mobile heavy ship in Norway, south of Bear Island (26th). *Scharnhorst* was escorted by five destroyers, but faced the convoy escort of 14 destroyers and a covering escort of three cruisers. Nearby was the C-in-C, Admiral Fraser, in the battleship *Duke of York*. *Scharnhorst* attacked the convoy twice but withdrew after being engaged by the R.N. cruisers and destroyers. Both *Scharnhorst* and the R.N. cruiser *Norfolk* were hit. After dark *Duke of York*, approaching at high speed, detected the battlecruiser by radar. *Scharnhorst* was unaware she was being tracked until, at 12,000 yards, *Duke of York* fired a star shell and opened fire on the German ship. Adm. Fraser sent in four destroyers and a running battle ensued in which *Scharnhorst* received several hits and began to slow down. Eventually four torpedoes struck the ship and *Duke of York* approached and knocked out the German guns. Destroyers then moved in and sank the battlecruiser with torpedoes. Of her 1,970 officers and men, the R.N. was only able to save 36 men. The destruction of *Scharnhorst* freed the Home Fleet from its need to wait and watch over the German capital ships in northern waters.

FAR EAST and PACIFIC

Allied landings on the south-west coast of New Britain cut off 8,000 Japanese from reaching Rabaul (15th) and further landings by U.S. Marines on Cape Gloucester gave the Allies complete control of the Dampier Strait between New Guinea and New Britain (25th). Landings on Bougainville continued, and by mid-December the Allies had 44,000 troops on the island.

SOUTHERN EUROPE and MEDITERRANEAN

The Teheran Conference ended (1st) and Eisenhower and Churchill went to Cairo for further discussions. A major decision was the confirmation of the dual drive on Japan, with emphasis on getting island bases near Japan to permit bombing raids.

The departures caused by Overlord resulted in changes of command in Italy – Gen. Maitland-Wilson succeeded Eisenhower and several divisions were withdrawn. Nevertheless 7 divisions of the 8th Army and 13 divisions of the U.S. 5th Army now face Kesselring with his 18 German divisions (of which 5 are tied up in North Italy by outbreaks of partisan activity).

1944

JANUARY 1944

EUROPE and ATLANTIC

Some 800 U.S. bombers escorted by fighters made a raid on German aircraft factories at Halberstad and Brunswick. Although 38 German fighters were shot down, the Americans had heavy losses – 56 bombers and 6 fighters.

The Luftwaffe returned to night raids on London and other cities in Britain (21st) – the "Little Blitz", with usually fewer than 100 bombers used on each raid.

RUSSIA and ARCTIC

The 890 day siege of Leningrad was relieved by the Russian winter onslaught, which re-established land communications with the city (19th). Since the siege began in September 1941, nearly 200,000 were killed by the German bombardments, and over 630,000 died from starvation, cold and exhaustion. The toll would undoubtedly have been higher had the Finns not stopped at their original border with Russia – a response to Russia's halt after breaching the Mannerheim Line in February 1940. This permitted tenuous and hazardous access to Leningrad across Lake Ladoga.

The relief of Leningrad was part of a massive Russian offensive along the whole front. Novgorod, south of Leningrad, also fell, and in the south the area between Kiev and the mouth of the Dnieper is being steadily cleared of the invaders.

FAR EAST and PACIFIC

The landing of 7,000 U.S. troops at Saidor, near Madang on New Guinea, enabled a beachhead to be secured for further landings (2nd). This move has cut off the large Japanese forces on the Huon Peninsula, who cannot hope for evacuation with Allied control of the nearby seas.

In preparation for the attack on the Marshall Islands, four U.S. aircraft carrier task forces approached the islands and occupied Majuro for an anchorage (31st). Of the 100 islands in the Marshalls group, 19 are occupied by Japanese troops. The attack on Kwajalein, the biggest, is due to begin at any moment.

SOUTHERN EUROPE and MEDITERRANEAN

In what was meant to be the decisive stroke in cutting communications to the Garigliano line, and hasten the German defeat in Italy, the U.S. Maj. Gen. Lucas with 50,000 **U.S. and British troops landed at Anzio**, between the German line and Rome (22nd). The landing met little opposition, and one scout patrol even got as far as Rome itself. Despite urging, and the ideal opportunity to make a major and decisive move inland, Lucas stalled and methodically built up his beachhead. Far faster-moving was Kesselring, who sent eight German divisions to Anzio. When Lucas at last decided to push inland, the Germans had formed a powerful perimeter, and easily held back the Allies (30th).

Concentrated Allied attacks on the Garigliano line began (17th), and there were some successful crossings made, though U.S. forces suffered many casualties crossing the Rapido (20th). The major approach to the north, the Liri valley, is defended by powerful German positions at Cassino, especially on the slopes of the dominating Monte Cassino, which is topped by an ancient Abbey. A second attack on the Cassino stronghold was also rebuffed (24th).

FEBRUARY 1944

EUROPE and ATLANTIC

Air warfare continues to dominate Western Europe. German raids on London and other cities continue, but with nowhere near the intensity of the day and night raids on Germany. After reports indicated that there were 74,000 dead and injured, and 3 million homeless in Berlin alone, there was some condemnation in Britain of these tactics. A typical attack was the night raid by almost 900 R.A.F. bombers on Berlin factories (15th). Much damage was caused, but 42 bombers were shot down, and 17 crashed on return to base. The effect of bombing raids becomes difficult to measure, as the Germans disperse manufacturing plants away from concentrated areas.

RUSSIA and ARCTIC
The Russian offensive rolled back the Germans inexorably. In the south, Nikopol on the west bank of the Dnieper was taken (7th), and a large German force was almost captured when Zhukov's armies recaptured Krivoy Rog. Between there and Kiev, 30,000 Germans were taken prisoner in the fall of Cherkassy, and a desperate tank drive narrowly prevented another 30,000 falling into Russian hands. Acting out of frustration and anger, Hitler has decided to replace Manstein with Gen. Model. At the end of February, Army Group South has its back against the River Bug.

In the north, Hitler ordered the Army Group to fall back to defensive positions on the Estonian borders.

The Arctic convoys still face U-boat dangers, and the harshness of winter seas. In the February convoy Capt. Walker R.N. sank his fourteenth U-boat.

FAR EAST and PACIFIC
Adm. Spruance, in charge of the Marshalls invasion planned by Nimitz, launched a gigantic bombardment of Kwajalein with bomber sorties and heavy shelling from U.S. warships. Apart from the bombs dropped by waves of aircraft, 36,000 shells struck the island (1st). The island was defended by 8,500 Japanese, but few were front-line combat troops as the Japanese Command had not expected the attack on the Marshalls to begin with Kwajalein. Nevertheless, it took the 41,000 Americans who landed on Kwajalein over a week before the last Japanese died or surrendered. Of the 8,500, only 35 were taken prisoner.

U.S. bombers attacked the Truk Island bases with devastating results – about 200,000 tons of merchant shipping, two destroyers and 275 aircraft were destroyed (17–18th). This move enabled the invasion of Eniwetok Atoll to go ahead without Japanese air interference (17th–21st). The atoll (about 300 miles west–north–west of Kwajalein) was as strongly defended as others had been, and 2,677 Japanese died trying to hold it. U.S. forces lost 339 men.

When U.S. forces took Los Negros in the Admiralty Islands, on the western edge of the Bismarck Archipelago (29th), the Japanese withdrew all their aircraft from Rabaul. Meanwhile, on Bougainville, the Japanese garrison began moving into position to attack the large U.S. force.

In marked contrast to their fortunes in the Pacific islands, the Japanese launched an offensive in the Arakan province of **north eastern Burma** (3rd). This put extra emphasis on the Central Pacific drive to get within bombing range of Japan, since the re-occupation of Burma, and the re-opening of ground communication with China is now bound to take longer.

SOUTHERN EUROPE and MEDITERRANEAN
The third concentrated Allied attack on the Cassino defences also ended in failure (11th), and although there was no evidence to suggest that the Abbey itself was providing cover for the Germans, Allied leaders decided to bomb it, and warned the occupants to evacuate the buildings (14th). Over 200 bombers dropped 576 tons of high explosives on the monastery (15th) and more bombing and an artillery barrage followed when defensive fire proved to be unabated (18th). In yet another very determined attack, the Allies suffered heavy losses – especially among New Zealand and Indian troops. All that the complete destruction of the Abbey achieved was to let the Germans into the ruins, where the rubble afforded perfect barricades and shelter. The German line remains intact.

Gen. Clark visited the Anzio beachhead where the U.S. and British troops were surrounded by German forces. A breakout attempt (7th) proved fruitless, and then Kesselring made a determined assault against the Allies (16th). The fighting was fierce, and both sides suffered heavy casualties. Further German attacks (18th and 20th) were equally ferocious, and at first they almost drove the Allies back to the beaches. The final attack was determinedly met by U.S. troops, and the Germans withdrew having suffered some 2,500 casualties.

MARCH 1944

EUROPE and ATLANTIC
Over 600 fighter-escorted bombers of the U.S.A.A.F. began a new series of air raids on Berlin (6th). Losses on both sides were heavy – 68 bombers and 13 fighters, for 53 Luftwaffe fighters. Further raids followed and extensive destruction has been done to Berlin. But Allied plane losses were heavy. The night bombers of the R.A.F. have also encountered formidable defences.

The Atlantic war has continued in favour of the Allies – 29 U-boats have been sunk, but very few merchant ships have been attacked.

RUSSIA
The German Army Group North halted the Russian advance on the defensive line drawn up on the border of Estonia (1st). In the South, however, only a desperate breakthrough by Manstein prevented the Russians capturing a large part of Group South against the Black Sea. By the time Model arrived to take over from Manstein, much of the army had fallen back across the Rumanian border. Some 50,000 died or were taken prisoner in the frantic escape from encirclement.

FAR EAST and PACIFIC
The long awaited battle on Bougainville, in the Solo-

mons, began when the Japanese attacked the U.S. forces in the Empress Augusta Bay area. The attack was fierce, but with 27,000 U.S. forces by then on the island it soon died down (17th). Another attack was equally ineffective (23rd), and the Japanese withdrew from the Bay area, having lost about 8,000 soldiers, against 300 American casualties. The Americans decided not to make a counter-attack, but to make Bougainville another island where Japanese forces would be left to "wither away".

The superb anchorage of Manus Island in the Admiralty Islands, much closer to Japan than Rabaul, was captured (25th) after large U.S. forces had made landings in the Admiralty Islands (9th) in support of the division that landed on Los Negros in January. In New Guinea, Australian troops are approaching Madang. The Rabaul Japanese garrison has no ships or planes, and is also being left to wither.

The struggle in Burma intensified with Japanese movements towards Assam in the north west. The Chindits had re-formed as Long Range Penetration groups (LRPs), and a force parachuted behind enemy lines north-east of Indaw (5th). With overland reinforcements, they constructed a landing strip ("Broadway") in the jungle, and eventually there were 9,000 Allied troops deep in Japanese territory (13th). However the Japanese launched an attack towards the Brahmaputra Valley to capture the airfields from which the Allies were flying supplies over "the Hump" to China. "Broadway" was a strong threat to the Japanese plans, and the field, together with most of the Spitfires flying from it, was destroyed (17th).

The overland Japanese force of some 155,000 crossed the Chindwin (8th) and headed for Imphal, some taking the route via Kohima, which was on the British supply route. Gen. Slim hurriedly despatched reinforcements to Kohima, which was soon besieged, and then the major part of the Japanese force surrounded the Imphal forces (29th). The LRP concept eventually proved ineffective, when they were repulsed in an attack on Indaw (26th). Wingate's death in an air crash (24th), added to the speed of their demise.

SOUTHERN EUROPE and MEDITERRANEAN

The German hold on Cassino resisted 1,400 tons of bombs, heavy shelling and a third major attack (15th), before constant rain made tank and infantry assaults almost impossible, and the attacks were called off (23rd).

The Germans finally abandoned their attempts to break up the Allies' position at Anzio (4th), and rain brought the battle to a standstill there as well.

APRIL 1944

EUROPE and ATLANTIC

The Allied air forces in Britain have built up their strength to well over 1,000 heavy bombers, but bombing raids are now directed at objectives concerned with Overlord, and the Germans are hurriedly repairing their damaged factories, etc., in the main cities.

RUSSIA and ARCTIC

While the Germans held firm against the Russians in the north and centre of the front, Army Group South was not able to establish a defensive line. Advance Russian troops followed retreating German elements into Rumania (2nd), while further east they began their offensive to clear the Crimea (8th), driving the Germans back into Sevastopol. The westward sweep in the south liberated Odessa (10th) – two and a half years after German and Rumanian troops captured it.

Aircraft from the R.N. carriers *Victorious* and *Furious* carried out a bombing raid on *Tirpitz* anchored in Altenfjord, northern Norway, following indications that she was being prepared to move to the Baltic. The raid was successful and *Tirpitz* is once again disabled. Three planes were shot down, while there were about 400 German casualties.

FAR EAST and PACIFIC

The garrison at **Kohima in Assam was besieged** by part of the large Japanese force which had crossed the Chindwin in March. Although only 2,500 strong, the British and Indian troops kept the Japanese at bay until reinforcements arrived (20th). By that time the defenders had been squeezed back onto the small Garrison Hill, even the sick and wounded bearing arms against the attackers. The Japanese lost 4,000 men. At Imphal, the Allies continue their stand against the powerful Japanese force which almost encircles them. Disagreement between Japan and Chandra Bose's "Indian National Army" prevented simultaneous attacks springing up behind Allied lines.

On New Guinea, the Australian cross-country troops captured Madang, while MacArthur with 52,000 men landed in Dutch New Guinea and took Hollandia, an excellent naval and air base. The attack took the 11,000 Japanese defenders – few of them combat troops – completely by surprise, and there was virtually no resistance.

In China, the Japanese renewed their offensive (17th), attacking in the east in an attempt to divide China, capture airfields and railheads, and separate U.S. and Chinese forces.

SOUTHERN EUROPE and MEDITERRANEAN

The stalemate at Anzio and Cassino continued all month, and both sides have been regrouping and reinforcing. The main Allied forces – all the U.S. and French Divisions in Gen. Clark's 5th Army, and most of Gen. Leese's 8th Army – are between Cassino and the west coast, but Kesselring has his defences covering the width of the front from coast to coast, uncertain of where the attack will come. The Allies have carried out many air raids on railway lines both north of Rome and between Rome and the front, but the Germans managed to get many supplies through by road and by coastal shipping.

MAY 1944

EUROPE and ATLANTIC
D-Day has been set for 4–6th of next month, and an enormous invasion force is rapidly building up in southern England. Elaborate deception plans have been evolved to keep the invasion point secret. Hitler's constant anxiety about an attack on Germany through Norway caused him to reinforce his garrison – there are now some 372,000 German troops practically idle in Norway. Hitler has also emphasised his belief that the invasion will strike around Calais. Rundstedt and Rommel have considerably strengthened the Atlantic Wall, as Rommel feels that the Allies must be stopped on the beaches, and not further inland.

The Allied air forces decided to make concentrated attacks on German oil production, and initial strikes were very successful.

RUSSIA
Russian forces recaptured Sevastopol (9th), and the whole Crimea is again in Russian hands.

FAR EAST and PACIFIC
The siege of the 60,000 British and Indian soldiers on the **Imphal plateau** continued throughout the month, and attempts to fly in supplies were sometimes thwarted by the monsoon. Other Allied troops are struggling to reach Imphal and attack the encircling Japanese from the rear.

SOUTHERN EUROPE and MEDITERRANEAN
The Allied offensive on the Garigliano Line in Italy began with an artillery barrage by 2,000 guns on the German positions between Cassino and the west coast (11th). The barrage, launched at night, caught the Germans unaware. The attack, after dawn bombing (12th), was launched with considerable desperation, as the Allies want a breakthrough well before the planned attack on southern France (Anvil) which is to assist Overlord. After very fierce fighting Cassino was outflanked, and a force of **Polish soldiers stormed and captured Monte Cassino** and the Abbey ruins (18th). Kesselring hurriedly sent for reinforcements, but these were put into the battle piecemeal as they arrived and made little difference to the Allied aggression, which eventually forced the Germans into rapid retreat (25th).

At the same time as the Cassino assault began, the six divisions on the Anzio beachhead broke out, with the intention of cutting reinforcement lines to the main front and trapping the German divisions. The race for Rome, however, took preference, and many Germans are managing to escape the trap. Mountainous country does not allow the 8th Army to use its armour to the fullest advantage, and German rearguard resistance prevents their retreat being turned into a rout.

King Victor Emmanuel III of Italy abdicated in favour of his son, Prince Umberto.

JUNE 1944

EUROPE and ATLANTIC
D-Day (6th). Operation Overlord, the invasion of occupied Europe, got under way after a last minute postponement of 24 hours caused by bad weather. Under the overall command of Gen. Eisenhower, the invasion began with airborne troops being dropped soon after midnight to be in positions to prevent counter-attacks on the Normandy beachheads. Montgomery was in charge of the landing of the U.S. 1st Army under Bradley and the British 2nd Army under Dempsey. The American landings on "Utah" beach and the British and Canadian landings on "Gold, Juno and Sword" beaches went well, but the "Omaha" landings met stiff opposition. This was made even more devastating as a result of the landings being started far too far offshore. Many landing craft were swamped and sunk, while others were swept off course. A large number of soldiers reached the beaches violently seasick and then had to face vicious crossfire. The Americans did not use flail-tanks, etc. to clear beach obstacles and mines, as the British did, and the engineers sent in to clear Omaha suffered terrible casualties. The distant landings also resulted in 27 out of the 29 tanks sent off being swamped and submerged before they reached shore. Eventually the landings were virtually restarted, much closer inshore, and by night-fall Omaha was sufficiently held to allow more landings during the night. But casualties at Omaha were over 3,000, and 50 tanks and 26 guns were lost, as well as 60 landing craft and small escorts.

The British and Canadian landings on Gold, Juno and Sword were backed by very heavy and accurate R.N. bombardment. Landing craft were brought close inshore and made accurate landings. By nightfall Dempsey had penetrated up to six miles inshore, but then the Allies came up against the main German reserves which were being rushed into the area.

By the end of D-Day, over 145,000 soldiers were ashore and consolidation of the beachheads began. German defences were slow to respond due to the lengthy chains of command that orders and requests had to pass through, and to Hitler's conviction, even after D-Day, that the main landings were still to come. Some German counter-attacks were made, but the potentially effective Panzer Group West suffered a severe setback when an R.A.F. attack destroyed their H.Q. (10th). Total Allied air superiority was a decisive factor in establishing the landings.

After the beachheads were linked (11th) more men and equipment came ashore, and six days after D-Day some 326,500 men had been landed, along with 54,200 vehicles and over 104,000 tons of supplies. When the landings had put a total of over 587,500 Allied soldiers on Normandy, the worst gales for 40 years lashed the coast (19th–22nd). The "mobile" harbours – the concept was given the name "Mulberry" – held firm off Arromanches, but the U.S. Mulberry was destroyed, and many vessels with it.

Rundstedt and Rommel were thwarted in their plans to pull massive reinforcements down to Normandy by Hitler's precaution against another landing, by heavy bombing of rail and road links, and by extensive sabotage carried out by the French Resistance from the moment D-Day began. U.S. troops wheeled west towards Cherbourg and defeated the four German divisions that were being sent to reinforce the port (13–15th). A tremendous, wearying assault on Cherbourg ended with the garrison's surrender (26th), followed the next day by the Naval surrender. However, the Germans blew up as much as they could before surrendering, and it will be some time before Cherbourg can be used.

After their quick and strong landing, the British and Canadians made very little progress against massive armoured resistance around Caen. As the British are held on the eastern point of the landings, the U.S. forces pivot round to begin pushing west.

The German Navy made an attempt to interfere in the landings (9th), but enormous air and sea superiority cleared the Channel for the Allies. Hitler conferred with Rundstedt and Rommel not far from Rheims (17th) but went back to Berchtesgaden after a V1 "flying bomb" veered off-course and landed near the H.Q.

The first ten V1 flying bombs (V for *Vergeltung*, meaning Retribution) launched against Britain (12th) failed to reach the country, but early the next morning the first of the 1,435 that hit Britain this month exploded in south-east England. The following day the R.A.F. found they could be intercepted and exploded in mid-air, and many have been shot down by planes, as well as by AA batteries.

RUSSIA

On the 3rd anniversary of Barbarossa, Russia hit back at its German invaders with massive force along a 450 mile front (22nd–23rd). Enormous numbers of well-trained Russian troops sent the Axis forces reeling back and Finland's Mannerheim Line was overwhelmed, though the Russians pushed no further than Viborg – the line of the 1940 surrender. It was in Belorussia that the offensive was fiercest – greatly assisted by paralysing sabotage and ambushes by nearly 150,000 partisans active behind German lines. Even though the Russians broke through the German line in several places, Hitler ordered the Army Group Centre to stand fast till the last man. It was another example of his insane and disastrous refusal to admit defeat, for the Russians made a huge break in the German lines and encircled the whole of Army Group Centre. It was an impossible trap to get out of, and 350,000 Germans were captured (28th). With the loss of a whole Army Group, the German line is crumbling rapidly.

FAR EAST and PACIFIC

The island-hopping advance by Nimitz through the Central Pacific went ahead with an attack on the Marianas, where the principal objectives are Guam and Saipan. Bombing from U.S. aircraft carriers and shelling from the Pacific Fleet was followed by the landing of **20,000 U.S. Marines on Saipan** (15th). Resistance at first was strong and the Americans had 2,000 casualties – but the total forces available in the invasion numbered over 125,000, against under 32,000 Japanese, many of whom were wounded when two troopships in their convoy to

The extent of Axis occupation of Western Europe.

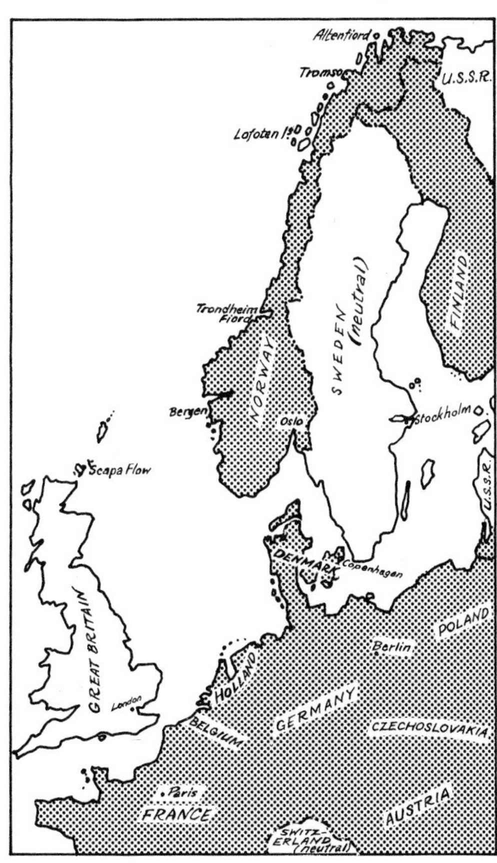

Saipan were sunk by U.S. submarines. The Japanese again relied mainly on defence of the beaches, which became a suicidal battle in retreat as the superior U.S. numbers, planes, tanks and shelling drove relentlessly forward. Eventually the Japanese on the island were split into two groups (18th), but casualties from the battle and from the natural hazards of the tropical island claimed many American lives.

Having learnt of the invasion of Saipan, the Japanese commanders ordered the U.S. Pacific Fleet to be "destroyed" and, although vastly outnumbered, the Japanese Mobile Fleet engaged the Pacific Fleet between the Philippines and the Marianas (19th). It became the biggest carrier battle of the war to date – U.S. submarines sank 2 Japanese carriers, and this, combined with U.S. air superiority, caused terrible destruction to the Japanese, who lost 346 planes against 30 U.S. planes on the first day. The next day the U.S. carriers pursued the Japanese Fleet, and torpedo aircraft sank another carrier and destroyed many more planes. The pursuit was broken off by the Task Force's commander – whose orders were to protect Saipan – after the Force had destroyed three carriers and a total of some 475 planes. U.S. losses were two small vessels and 130 planes – 80 of these were lost on or near their carriers as they struggled to find the fleet in the dark after the final engagement (20th). The horribly easy full-scale destruction gave the **Battle of the Philipinnes Sea** the gruesome nickname of "the Great Marianas Turkey Shoot".

In New Guinea, MacArthur's offensive continued with the capture, after two weeks of bombardment, of the small island of Biak, which gives a command of the entrance to the largest and best bay in New Guinea. Biak also has excellent airfields and was defended by 10,000 soldiers. MacArthur's landing there unwittingly helped Nimitz take Saipan, as the Japanese tried to reinforce Biak instead of anticipating the attack on the Marianas.

In Assam the siege of Imphal entered its third month with the Allied position growing weaker until it seemed as if reserves would finally run out. But the relief columns finally linked up with the beleaguered forces, and convoys of supplies and men rolled in (22nd). The Japanese circle cracked and they are fleeing back across the Chindwin, with Gen. Slim's forces in close pursuit. The breaking of the Japanese stranglehold marked the end of the Japanese attempt to reach India, and although Slim's 14th Army had 16,700 killed, wounded and ill, the Japanese losses have been disastrous. On the Imphal battlefield alone 13,000 Japanese lay dead, and it is likely that as many as 65,000 may die before this campaign is over. The tracks back to the Chindwin are becoming littered with abandoned guns and equipment, and with the dead and dying.

American B-29 "Superfortress" bombers carried out their first raid on Japan, bombing steelworks on Kyushu (16th).

SOUTHERN EUROPE and MEDITERRANEAN

In Italy the Cassino and Anzio breakouts flung back the Germans, and Kesselring declared **Rome an open city** (4th) in order to save it bombardment. On the same day U.S. troops reached Rome, followed closely by the British 8th Army. Kesselring, with 25 divisions still in Italy, fell back 150 miles to the Gothic Line, which runs along the Arno River at Pisa, to Rimini on the east coast. (It was built by the Todt organisation with Italian forced labour.) Alexander decided to attempt a breach of the Northern Apennines before German defences could be made too secure, and the Allies advanced 110 miles. The U.S. forces had a hard battle against a Panzer Korp; and the British 8th Army, after taking Perugia (20th), fought a fierce battle before breaking through the German defensive Line at Lake Trasimene (28th).

JULY 1944

EUROPE and ATLANTIC

Hitler narrowly escaped an attempt on his life, when a bomb planted by Col. Count von Stauffenberg in Hitler's conference room in the "Wolf's Lair" H.Q. exploded, killing four of the 20 officers present (20th). Hitler suffered only minor injuries, but Stauffenberg and some other conspirators, convinced he had been killed, tried to set in motion the long-planned army take-over. A number of SS units were disarmed, but some Army men in key posts would not act until Hitler's death had been confirmed. When his survival was announced that night, the plot collapsed, and the arrest of hundreds of officers and officials began. Eight of the plotters were shot almost immediately; others were hanged on loops of piano wire, and Hitler later enjoyed the film made of their slow strangulation.

The Allied invasion forces continued their build-up on the Normandy beachhead. Rundstedt, who was forced by Hitler to rely entirely on the Atlantic Wall for defence, realised that with the wall so widely breached, nothing would now hold back the Allies. When a counter-attack by four SS Panzer divisions was held on the British and Canadian front, Rundstedt told Keitel that the only course open was to surrender (1st). Von Kluge almost immediately replaced Rundstedt. Kluge could not stop the Allied advance either, and **Montgomery eventually took Caen** after a long and hard struggle (9th). U.S. forces captured St. Lô (18th) and after that Patton and the U.S. 3rd Army broke out from the beachhead area (26th) and moved into Brittany, crashing south through the Avranches front at the end of the month.

Rommel's car was attacked along a country road by a lone fighter plane apparently with R.A.F. markings, and he was severely injured (15th). His criticisms of Hitler had become increasingly outspoken, and it was probably only his great public popularity (and his injuries) that saved him from the wave of arrests after the 20th July plot failed.

The month marked new eras in air warfare – V1s landed on England (mainly on London) with terrible regularity, and the first 2,754 flying bombs launched since mid-June killed a total of 2,752 people. In the whole of July, 2,453 V1s landed on England. Great hopes in the defeat of the V1s were put in the formation of the first Allied all-jet aircraft squadron, using Gloster Meteors (12th).

In a low-level strafing attack on a fuel depot in Occupied France, U.S.A.A.F. fighters were the first to use Napalm bombs, consisting of "jellied-petrol" which engulfs large areas in a fierce blaze.

RUSSIA

The Russian advance continued as rapidly as it had begun in June. Minsk fell with the loss of 100,000 German casualties, and the Russian advance – often up to 15 miles a day – soon crossed into Poland (18th). Lublin was retaken (23rd) and then Brest-Litovsk (28th) with a further 35,000 German casualties. Army Group North are isolated in Estonia, and the Russians are poised to capture Riga on the Baltic. Further south, Lvov fell (27th), and with crossings over the Bug and the Vistula secured, the Russians are within reach of Warsaw.

Hitler's interference with the movements of German reserves meant that once a breakthrough had been achieved the Allied advance was rapid. Here British crews of Sherman tanks pause during their offensive. For the retreating Germans, there was not always time to bury their dead.

FAR EAST and PACIFIC

The bitter fight for Saipan came to an end (9th) after at least 30,000 Japanese troops had died in trying to resist the U.S. might flung against them. Total American casualties (dead and wounded) were about 14,000. The Japanese resistance had been typically, and eventually needlessly fierce. The hundreds of caves into which the garrison and the civilian population retreated, presented the Americans with endless dangerous skirmishes against defenders who, if they were not killed fighting, usually preferred suicide to surrender. The most tragic aspect of the battle for Saipan was the death of well over 20,000 Japanese civilians – many killed in defending their island with bamboo sticks against American guns, grenades and flamethrowers; and many jumping to death from the cliffs.

The next island in the Marianas to be attacked by U.S. Marines was Guam, the southernmost island in the group, which had been frequently bombarded before landings began (21st). Three days later, Marines landed on Tinian, the tiny island on the southern tip of Saipan.

On top of steadily worsening conditions in Japan for civilians, the loss of Saipan was a bitter blow, and under strong pressure Gen. Tojo resigned, together with most of his Cabinet (18th). Gen. Koiso has replaced him.

While the remnants of the Japanese besiegers of Imphal struggle back to safety, Gen. Stilwell and his Chinese-American army is slowly advancing towards Myitkyina, in northern Burma, in a bid to capture forward supply bases for the renewal of deliveries to China.

SOUTHERN EUROPE and MEDITERRANEAN

After disagreement over priorities, Roosevelt and the U.S. Chiefs of Staff were able to get Operation Anvil – the Allied invasion of southern France – ordered for August 15th (2nd). (Its code name was then changed to "Dragoon" in case "Anvil" had become known to the Germans.) This resulted in Gen. Alexander, commanding the Italian campaign, having troops taken away at the time that his opposite number, Kesselring, was being assured by the German High Command that reinforcements were on their way. The Allied advance began to slow down as they approached the German Gothic Line on the Arno and across to Rimini. But Polish troops captured Ancona on the Adriatic Coast (18th) and the following day U.S. troops took Leghorn (Livorno) on the west coast. After the harbour facilities had been repaired, this port greatly shortened the Allies' supply line, and helped in the occupation by the U.S. of Pisa (23rd).

AUGUST 1944

EUROPE and ATLANTIC

In two entrapments by rapid wheeling movements of U.S. forces, the German Armies lost tens of thousands of

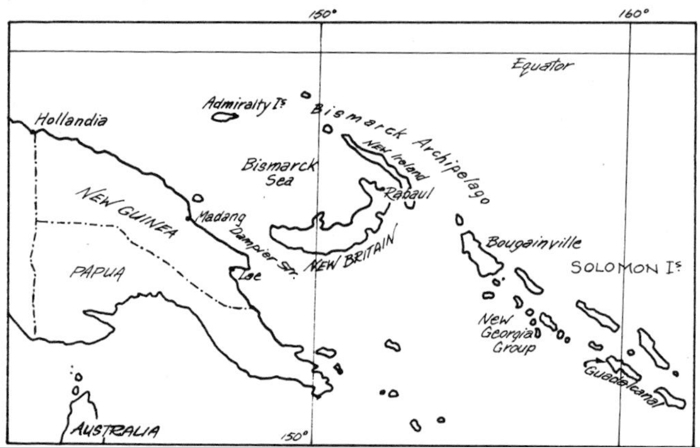

Left, New Guinea and the Solomons.

Opposite, the mainland of South-East Asia.

men. A futile counter-attack on Avranches (the town itself was taken by U.S. forces on the 1st) led to a trap as U.S. troops split either side of the Germans and caught them in a pincer movement. Near Falaise, a large pocket of German troops were caught as the U.S. forces pivoted swiftly round the fierce Anglo–Canadian battle against the main German forces between Caen and Falaise. After Avranches, U.S. forces followed the coast westwards and captured St. Malo (17th), while the rest of the invasion forces fanned out into France.

The rapid Allied advances, and the success of the Mediterranean landings (see below), set off a revolt in Paris (19th), when the Gendarmerie, French Forces of the Interior, and assorted bands of civilians fought the German garrison. Hitler ordered the city destroyed, but the German commander did not carry out the order. With the main Allied forces on the outskirts, **the 10,000 Germans in Paris were surrendered** by Gen. von Choltitz to Gen. Leclerq (25th). The next day de Gaulle and Leclerq, together with Resistance leaders, headed the Free French and other Allied liberators in a triumphal march down the Champs Elysées.

With the Russians within sight of Warsaw, leaders of the Polish Resistance began an uprising against the Germans, hopeful that the Russian advance would speed the Germans out of the city. But the Russians made no effort to assist the Poles, halted their advance, and even refused overflight and landing requests for R.A.F. and U.S.A.A.F. planes to help the Poles. Initially the Poles had considerable success and much of Warsaw was in their hands by the 6th. But then Hitler put an SS officer in command, and sent in a force of the roughest SS troops (8th). The Germans then began to destroy the Poles, and the city of Warsaw, with determination and cruelty. Despite every appeal by the Allies, Stalin refused to go to the help of the Poles, though the Russians could probably have easily taken the city The pitiful struggle by the long suffering people of Warsaw still goes on, against the most vicious counter-measures. Guderian, the new Chief of the Army General Staff, has appealed in vain to Hitler to stop the brutality.

The Allied liberation of Normandy and the Mediterranean landings caused Hitler to replace the faltering Kluge with F. M. Model as C-in-C West (17th). Two days later Kluge sent a letter to Hitler begging him to end the war, and then he committed suicide.

By the end of the month, the Allies have established many crossings of the Seine, and the momentum after the breakout from the beachhead seems to gather speed. German losses have been devastating: over 200,000 dead or wounded and another 200,000 taken prisoner; 20,000 vehicles, 1,300 tanks, and 1,500 artillery pieces.

New types of fuses are giving AA batteries in Britain excellent chances against V1s – in one 24 hour period (27–28th) ground defences shot down 69 flying bombs (out of 96 launched; aircraft shot down a further 18).

RUSSIA

In the south, Russia attacked through Moldavia and into Rumania (20th). The Rumanians rapidly responded to a *coup d'etat* in Bucharest led by King Michael (23rd), and turned on their former comrades – with the Russians, cutting off and destroying 16 German divisions. By the end of the month, the Russians were in Bucharest. Apart from enormous quantities of tanks and weapons, the Russians took over 60,000 German lives, and 106,000 prisoners.

In the north, German resistance in Estonia is rapidly being overcome; and Finland has asked for an armistice with Russia (25th).

FAR EAST and PACIFIC

In the Marianas, Tinian fell rapidly (1st) and after the usual Japanese self-destructive defence, **Guam passed**

into U.S. hands (8th). The Americans suffered over 7,000 casualties in the campaign. By mid-August, the whole Marianas group was under the Allies, and Japan was within reach of land-based bombers.

In **Burma**, Stilwell's Chinese–American army captured Myitkyina, and the last Japanese troops were cleared out of Assam.

SOUTHERN EUROPE and MEDITERRANEAN
Operation Dragoon (ex-Anvil) began early in the morning on the 15th with the landing of 10 divisions of French and U.S. troops and a mixed U.S. and British airborne division on the coast of the French Riviera between Cannes and Hyères, and mainly at St. Tropez. A massive naval force stood offshore to bombard the German-held territory, but there was little opposition. The French Resistance operated inland, while Allied aircraft were active over the retreating Germans. A Panzer division at Montélimar provided the only strong resistance as the Allies swept up the Rhone valley, passing Grenoble within two weeks of the landing. A pocket of German troops defending Marseilles had been left relatively unmolested, but with escape by land, sea or air clearly impossible, the troops eventually surrendered (28th).

In Italy the British 8th Army took Florence (4th), but the departure of French mountain troops for the Riviera landings prevented the Allies from following through the breaks in the Gothic Line. The lack of opposition met by the Allies in southern France, plus the fact that the landings were made far later than planned, and that they therefore had little if any effect on the Normandy landings, made Churchill and the Italian campaigners (Clark and Alexander) disappointed and angry. If they had not been deprived of so many troops, they would easily have broken the Gothic Line, and have been able to push up towards Austria. Nevertheless Alexander launched an offensive with the British 8th Army and the remnants of the U.S. 5th Army (26th), and gradual headway against Kesselring's Gothic Line is being made.

SEPTEMBER 1944

EUROPE and ATLANTIC
The direction of the Allied war in West Europe was taken over by Eisenhower (1st), on the same day that Canadians – this time by land – took Dieppe and avenged the bloody raid of August 1942. Two days later **Brussels was liberated** by British forces, and then they went on to take Antwerp (4th), where the rest of the month was spent clearing mines in the Scheldt estuary, and attacking the strong German resistance along the South Beveland isthmus. This was taken by the end of the month, with 12,500 prisoners.

Von Rundstedt came back as C-in-C West (5th) but that did not stop the Allies taking Moselle (7th), or Liege, and Ostend (8th).

Operation Market Garden, the Allied attempt to surprise and outflank the Germans on the Siegfried Line by quick movement, depended on capturing intact the strategic bridges of Holland. U.S. airborne landings at Eindhoven and Nijmegen (17th) secured the bridges across the Maas and Waal, but the British paratroopers dropped over **Arnhem** landed a considerable distance from the bridge, and also came up against a SS Panzer

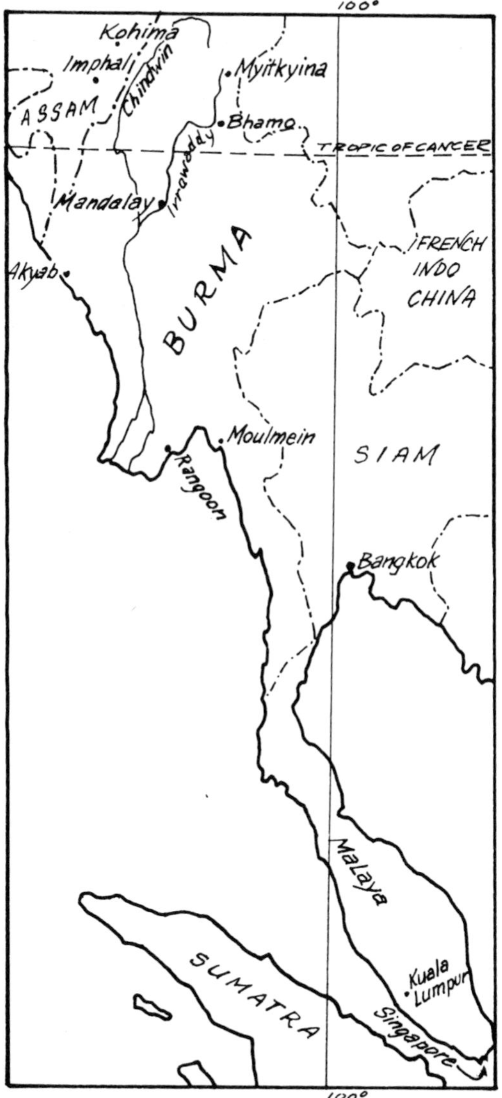

Division. The airborne troops fought fiercely against the Panzers, while a British armoured division tried to battle through deep enemy lines to relieve their comrades. The uneven, desperate battle lasted just over a week, until about 2,000 managed to break out to Allied lines (night of 25–26th). Approximately 10,000 landed; 1,130 were killed, and 6,450 taken prisoner. The German division had over 3,000 casualties. The ferocious battle of Arnhem marked the end of the Allies' rapid advance in Western Europe, though Boulogne and Brest were both retaken (18th) and the cut-off pocket at Calais surrendered on the last day of the month.

The first V2 rocket launched against the Allies landed near Paris (8th) and was followed later by two landing on widely separated points in London. Unlike the V1 flying bombs, the V2 rockets cannot be heard or seen approaching, and they have a bigger explosive warhead. All the V1 sites in France have been captured in the Allied advance.

At the second Quebec Conference (12–16th), Churchill and Roosevelt and the Joint Chiefs of Staff made decisions primarily affecting the war in the Pacific (see below).

The terrible tragedy of the Warsaw uprising has gone on all month – thousands have died, and now the fighting, so reminiscent of the horrors of the Warsaw ghetto, has moved into the city's sewers.

RUSSIA and ARCTIC

The Russian sweep in the South barely faltered as it covered Rumania. Bulgaria, aware of its possible fate, sued for an armistice and even declared war on Germany (7th), but that country, too, was overrun by the Russians.

R.A.F. bombers flying from Archangel attacked *Tirpitz* in Altenfjord, Norway, with 12,000 lb. "blockbuster" bombs (15th). *Tirpitz* was badly damaged, and has been towed to Tromsöfjord for its guns to be used against the still expected invasion of Norway.

In the North, Estonia and Latvia were freed from German control, and Stalin once more had the Baltic States he had grabbed in his early dealing with Hitler. In Finland there was a ceasefire, and the Finns then signed an Armistice with Russia and Britain (19th).

FAR EAST and PACIFIC

The numerous raids launched from carriers of Adm. Halsey's U.S. Third Fleet against Japanese air bases were extremely effective, and Halsey persuaded Nimitz to recommend that the invasion of the Philippines should be brought forward. This was approved by MacArthur, who could hardly wait to return, and at the Quebec Conference the Joint Chiefs of Staff set October 20th as the date for the invasion of Leyte, the key central island of the group between Mindanao and Luzon.

MacArthur continued his advance from New Guinea to the Philippines with the unopposed occupation of Morotai (15th). On the same day, however, Halsey's Marines met tremendous resistance when they landed on **Pelelieu**, one of the Palau Islands at the western edge of the Caroline Islands. Pelelieu has a warren of caves, and in them groups of Japanese (in one cave, over 1,000) are resisting and fighting with suicidal ferocity. Marine losses are mounting as the caves are cleared one by one. Flame throwers are proving the most effective mechanisms of destruction at the Marines' disposal.

SOUTHERN EUROPE and MEDITERRANEAN

Alexander's Italian offensive surprised the Germans, and a 20 mile gap was punched through the Gothic Line (1st). The eastern end of the Line was turned back by the 8th Army, and the U.S. 5th Army penetrated the centre of the Line (18th). But reinforcements are arriving for Kesselring, and the Allied troops are suffering many casualties.

The Greek Government-in-exile moved from Cairo to Caserta in Italy, after rumours of an impending evacuation of Greece by the Germans caused rival factions to prepare to take control once the Germans went. The Greek Government appealed to Churchill for aid, and an agreement (the Caserta Agreement) was reached in which Greek guerilla leaders declared they would obey the Greek Government, which in turn placed the direction of military matters under the British commander, Gen. Scobie.

OCTOBER 1944

EUROPE and ATLANTIC

Increasingly-stiff resistance by the Germans maintained the halt of the Allied advance, which also began to feel the effects of a tightly-stretched supply line from the distant coast, where there are still no good port facilities. The Allies concentrated on building up supplies for an offensive in November, but U.S. forces attacked and captured Aachen, 50 miles west of Cologne and the Rhine (21st).

The battle to clear the approaches to Antwerp moved to the attack on Walcheren Island at the mouth of the estuary. The saucer-shaped island, much of it below sea level, was defended by a German garrison of 10,000, and after four years of occupation it bristled with mines, anti-tank traps, wire obstacles and at least 30 artillery batteries. R.A.F. attacks early in the month blasted a huge gap in the dyke on the western edge, and the centre of the island was immediately flooded. The remaining massive defences were attacked at the end of the month by three groups of Royal Marine Commandos, supported by an intensive naval bombardment, by artillery barrages across the estuary, and by rocket attacks from aircraft. There have been many casualties, and fierce fighting is still going on.

The Germans finally forced the abandoned Warsaw resistance fighters to surrender (2nd). Almost 300,000 townspeople have been killed, and Hitler completed his last act of hatred by ordering Warsaw to be razed to the ground (9th). So much was already in ruins before the uprising but artillery, bombs, and demolition teams have now demolished nine tenths of the ancient Polish capital. To the east, the Russians watch the columns of smoke, and get ready to advance again.

Rommel's support for the July 20th plotters was discovered. Rather than arrest Germany's most popular commander, Hitler promised Rommel his family would be unharmed, and he would be given a hero's funeral, if he took his own life. Under supervision of two of Hitler's staff, Rommel took poison and died immediately (14th).

RUSSIA

Churchill went to Moscow (9–17th) for discussions with Stalin. The main objects of the talks were to come to some agreement about the different spheres of influence after the war, the two countries' obligations to other countries, and the special problem of Poland. Churchill was most concerned about Poland – Britain had gone to war with Germany because Poland's borders were violated, and yet Russia had also crossed into Poland and shared the country with the Nazis. Churchill and Stalin came to ready agreement on the Balkan countries. Russian dominance was acknowledged for Rumania and Bulgaria, British dominance for Greece, and Yugoslavia and Hungary were to be "shared" equally. But over Poland, disagreement, dissatisfaction and mistrust prevailed.

Tito's Yugoslav partisans aided by Allied arms drove out the Germans and won back Belgrade (20th).

FAR EAST and PACIFIC

The Philippines campaign began with air raids on Japanese aircraft bases between the islands and Japan (10th) which resulted in numerous very fierce air battles involving land-based and sea-borne aircraft (12–16th). Most of the fighting took place over and near Formosa, and the U.S. planes devastated the Japanese. Many Japanese planes, originally intended for the aircraft carriers, were sent to reinforce the Formosa groups, and were also destroyed. The Americans lost less than 80 planes, but destroyed up to 500 Japanese aircraft in the air and on the ground.

The Japanese were expecting Leyte to be attacked, and planned to lure away the main U.S. fleet with a decoy approach near Luzon, and then attack the invasion fleet from two directions. The Japanese Fleet set sail to prepare the trap (17th), and when MacArthur began the landing on Leyte under the protection of ships and planes of Adm. Kincaid's invasion fleet (20th), the main U.S. Fleet under Halsey lay east of Luzon. On the 23rd the Japanese Centre Force approaching from the south-west was intercepted by U.S. submarines, which sank two heavy cruisers (one was Adm. Kurita's flagship) and damaged a third. The next day (24th) planes from Halsey's carriers also attacked this force amid the islands north-west of Leyte, sank the huge battleship *Musashi*, and damaged other ships. The Centre Force then turned back.

On the same day the Japanese Southern Force was approaching Leyte from the south through the Mindanao

The Philippines.

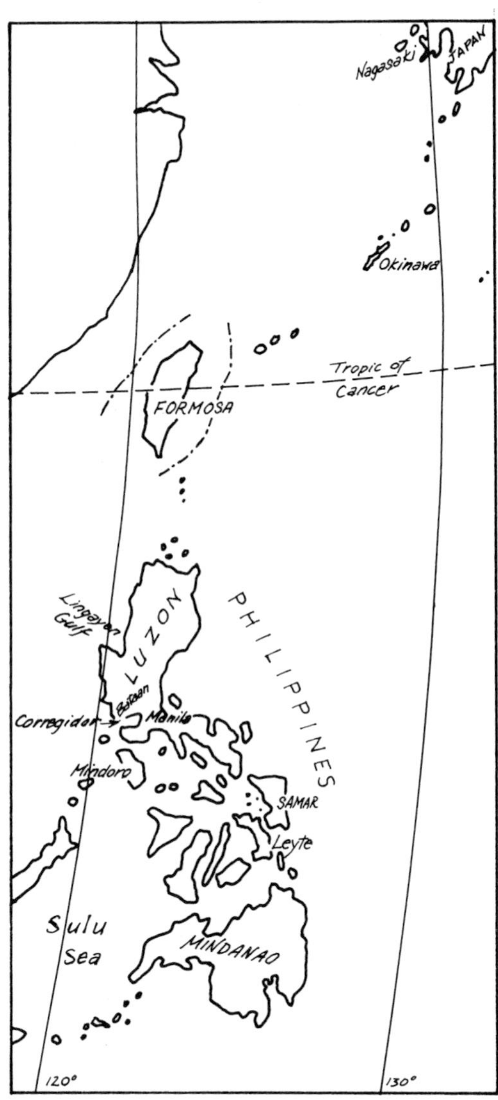

Sea, while Halsey's fleet, off Luzon, was coming under air attack by Japanese naval planes. Since there were no carriers in the two Japanese fleets already sighted, Halsey decided to look for a third fleet. The U.S. carrier *Princeton* was severely damaged and had to be abandoned, and Halsey ordered an air search to the north. The Japanese decoys (the Northern Force), sailing south, were spotted in the afternoon (24th), but although it had carriers, there were few aircraft, as the ones attacking Halsey were actually flying from Luzon, having come on the 23rd from Formosa. Halsey sailed north towards the Japanese trap at midnight (24th) – at the same time that the Japanese Centre Force under Kurita once again turned east to sail around Samar and approach Leyte from the north-east.

The Japanese Southern Force split into two groups and approached Leyte that night (24th), and a tremendous sea battle began between it and Kincaid's U.S. invasion fleet (which included two Australian warships). The Japanese force, having lost two battleships, a cruiser and three destroyers turned away. Early the next morning (25th), U.S. escort carriers covering the invasion were surprised by Kurita's Centre Force, and fought a desperate retreat which cost them two carriers, three destroyers and over 100 planes. (One of the carriers was the first ship to be sunk by a *kamikaze* suicide bomber attack.) The Japanese Centre Force lost three cruisers. At that moment Kurita's Centre Force could have carried on to Leyte virtually unopposed, and wrecked MacArthur's invasion force. But Kurita, perhaps thinking he was about to be caught between the fleets of Halsey and Kincaid, and knowing the Southern Force had been beaten off, turned about and retraced his passage between Luzon and Samar. Halsey had turned back in response to calls from the invasion fleet, leaving two carrier groups to attack the decoy force. On the 26th and 27th U.S. planes pursued the Japanese and heavy losses were again inflicted.

The Battle of Leyte marked the end of any real threat to the Allies from the Japanese by sea or air. Apart from the tremendous losses of aircraft, the Japanese had lost the last important elements of its Fleet – three battleships, four carriers, ten cruisers, nine destroyers, and a submarine. The U.S. losses amounted to three carriers, three destroyers and a submarine. And now they are well ashore on Leyte.

Fierce **fighting continues on Pelelieu**. The combination of fanatical defence and the natural features of the island are making this one of the Pacific's bitterest struggles, though the numbers involved are not great. After the first four weeks of battle, 1,121 U.S. Marines had been killed.

The Joint Chiefs of Staff issued a Directive for the capture of Iwo Jima, between the Marianas Islands and Japan, to be used as a fighter base for bomber escorts on raids over Japan, and as an emergency landing base.

In Burma, differences of opinion between Chiang Kai-Shek and the blunt, controversial Lt. Gen. Stilwell resulted in Stilwell ("Vinegar Joe") being recalled to Washington – a placatory gesture to Chiang, who felt the Big Three were not treating him as befitted his involvement in the war.

SOUTHERN EUROPE and MEDITERRANEAN

British Commandos were sent into Southern Greece, and Allied troops occupied Patras on the Pelepponese (4th). On the day after it was learnt that the Germans were evacuating Athens, paratroopers landed on Megara airfield, west of Athens (13th). Further paratroopers arrived the next day, and occupied Athens (14th) while naval forces with the main body of troops entered Piraeus. Two days later **the Greek Government went to Athens**, but although Churchill had "bought" Russian non-intervention, emergence from the occupation proved difficult. The Germans wrecked bridges, roads and railways as they retreated, there were desperate shortages of food, and despite their agreement on the Caserta decision, Communist guerilla leaders paid little attention to the Greek Govt. Unrest grows steadily, and the Greek people are in difficult mood. British troops have gone on half rations to help feed the Greeks.

In Italy Kesselring launched a number of counter-attacks on the Allied positions, and combined with very heavy rainfalls, these have made Allied advances practically impossible. Clark and the U.S. 5th Army almost managed to cut in behind the German line facing the British 8th Army at Bologna (20–24th). But the weather worsened, the Germans held firm, and the Italian campaign has reached a stalemate.

NOVEMBER 1944

EUROPE and ATLANTIC

In the battle for Walcheren to open the port of Antwerp, two Commando forces linked up after house-to-house fighting through the town of Flushing (3rd) and when the island finally passed into Allied hands, 8,000 prisoners were taken (8th). Minesweeping began immediately, but although up to 100 craft were used, it was three weeks before the approaches were clear and **the first convoy entered Antwerp** (28th). Like London, Antwerp has also become the target for flying bombs and rocket attacks.

There has been considerable disappointment in the Allies' slow advance towards Germany this month – heavy rains and the problem of long supply routes have added to the difficulties of meeting very stiff German resistance. In the air war, however, constant bombing raids on communications and on oil depots and refineries by the U.S.A.A.F. by day and the R.A.F. by night, are having considerable effect. On the ground, gradual advances with strong forces in the north and south have only succeeded in moving the whole Allied line up to within a few miles of the Rhine, or against the defences of the Siegfried Line.

Despite constant and devastating Allied air raids, Germany made more U-boats this month than in any previous month. Speer's brilliant organising ability overcame shortages of materials and ruined factories to arrange the manufacture of different parts of submarines all over Germany. These are then assembled into completed U-boats in huge bombproof pens in Baltic ports.

RUSSIA and ARCTIC
An attack by 32 Lancasters with 12,000 lb. "Tall-boy" bombs on *Tirpitz* in Tromsöfjord in Norway scored hits and very near misses (12th). The misses gouged out the fjord alongside *Tirpitz*, deep enough to enable her to capsize; when she did, nearly 1,000 of her crew were trapped and died.

FAR EAST and PACIFIC
The battle for Leyte has raged all month, but the rapid build-up of U.S. Forces makes the Japanese defeat inevitable and imminent. By the 1st there were already over 101,500 U.S. troops ashore, and now there are almost 200,000. The conqueror of Singapore, Gen. Yamashita arrived to conduct Leyte's defence, which is as fierce as Americans have come to expect in all engagements against the Japanese. By the end of this month, about 24,000 Japanese have been killed – U.S. deaths are over 2,250, and tropical sicknesses are also claiming many lives.

The last **resistance on Pelelieu ended** when the commander of the defence committed suicide, followed by his few remaining companions who had not already died in suicide attacks (25th). The battle lasted over two months – the whole Japanese garrison of 5,300, and 1,950 Americans have died on the tiny island. Someone worked out that for every Japanese killed, the U.S. forces fired nearly 1,600 rounds of heavy and light ammunition.

Kamikaze attacks – practically the only air/sea striking power left to the Japanese – increased this month, and four carriers were badly damaged. At the end of the month, B-29s from the Marianas made bombing raids over Tokyo, and there have been a number of carrier-borne attacks on Japanese shipping.

SOUTHERN EUROPE and MEDITERRANEAN
The German evacuation of Greece continued with the withdrawal from Florina (1st), and before the middle of the month the last of the invaders had crossed the northern borders. Internal disorder then threatened, with conflict between the one "Democratic" party and the two Communist-controlled groups, and Gen. Scobie declared Athens a military area (15th). By the end of the month, there was a deadlock over the disarmament of guerillas and of the Cabinet troops, and the situation has become very tense.

In Italy, where von Vietinghoff has replaced the injured Kesselring, the situation remained virtually unchanged, though the Allies gained some ground after an offensive on the 21st. The troops are exhausted, and the wet conditions make advances almost impossible.

DECEMBER 1944

EUROPE and ATLANTIC
The "Battle of the Bulge" – the German counter-offensive in the west – took the Allies completely by surprise, and recalled the first *blitzkrieg* over the Ardennes. Hitler held his final briefing for the battle (11th–12th), and since he had effectively put an end to most of his opponents – whatever their objectives – after the 20th of July plot, he was able to shout down the few voices raised in protest over his grand plan to smash through the Allied lines, split them in two, and recapture Antwerp. In spite of his lack of enthusiasm for the scheme, Rundstedt was recalled to be put in charge, and he launched the battle with 250,000 soldiers and all the tanks he could muster (16th). The main Allied offensives had been in the north and south, and the centre of the Allied line, along the Ardennes, was thin, protected by new, inexperienced troops and by older, battle-weary ones, using their spell on the quiet stretch for a rest period.

Within 48 hours of the attack being launched 50 miles of the Allied front was pushed back up to a depth of 15 miles. Pockets of resistance were by-passed, and the whole town of Bastogne was eventually isolated by Rundstedt's Panzer Armies, becoming a beleaguered Allied outpost deep in enemy territory as the Germans swung north-west towards Liege and the Meuse. The German offensive was assisted by heavily overcast weather, and the enormous Allied air superiority could not be used until the German advance had drawn to a halt (24th). By then they had made a cut into Allied territory to a depth of about 65 miles, ranging in width from about 10 miles to about 50 miles, with the furthermost tip only 3 miles from Dinant on the River Meuse.

Eisenhower rapidly strengthened the bulge with extra divisions – the thrust had cut Bradley's 12th Army Group in two. Montgomery led all the troops on the north of the Bulge, while Bradley commanded the southern troops which included Patton and his 3rd Army. The clearing of the weather allowed in the planes which carried out many damaging attacks on the German troops. With the outward push held, Bastogne, reinforced by a U.S. airborne division, became the target of the German assault. The brunt of the German attacks are being met by U.S. forces, and Patton is now slowly pushing north with the 3rd Army to relieve Bastogne.

The Allied air offensive over Europe has reduced German monthly oil production from 662,000 tons in May, to 260,000 tons this month.

RUSSIA and ARCTIC
The techniques that defeated the U-boats in the Atlantic were used to defeat them in Arctic waters, and with the German surface navy destroyed the greatest hazards faced by the Arctic convoys are the winter storms and seas. In the second half of this year, all Russian-bound convoys got through intact, and only a few homeward-bound ships have been torpedoed. Nine U-boats were sunk along the Arctic route.

The Russian army in the north continued building up its strength and perfecting its supply lines in readiness for the final assault on Germany. Remembering their own defence of their homeland, and aware that for the first time in the war German soldiers will be fighting on their own land, the Russian command is prepared to meet very fierce resistance. In the south-east their Balkan gains are being consolidated.

FAR EAST and PACIFIC
The Americans are now only a step away from Luzon, the scene of their tragic defeat in April 1942, having landed on Mindoro, south of Manila Bay (15th). With U.S. forces so close, the Japanese decided to move the American prisoners taken on Bataan deeper into Japanese territory. They crammed over 1,600 weak, emaciated men into the closed holds of a small cargo ship. In this floating black hell, at least 300 died in two days from thirst, starvation, suffocation, or simply being crushed or bashed to death. (In the first year at the Cabantuan prison camp on Luzon, 2,644 Bataan prisoners died.)

The Allied pursuit of the Japanese in **Burma** relieved Kalewa (3rd), crossed the Chindwin, and while the Japanese retired to the Irrawaddy, Slim confused the Japanese defence by moving south and crossing the Irrawaddy south of Mandalay.

Mountbatten, S.E.A.C.'s C-in-C, is rapidly building up a decisive superiority of land and air forces, and has also supplied arms to numerous groups of anti-Japanese factions in S.E. Asia.

SOUTHERN EUROPE and MEDITERRANEAN
Communist supporters in Athens staged an illegal demonstration (3rd) and after skirmishes with the police, a Greek civil war became a certainty. Gen. Scobie ordered the Communist groups to leave Athens and Piraeus, but their troops and many civilians attempted to capture the cities. On the 5th, Churchill ordered Scobie to intervene and suppress the Communist rebels by force, though Scobie's forces were heavily outnumbered. Alexander arrived to assume overall control (12th) and British reinforcements were sent (15th). Alexander urged talks for a settlement to avoid an escalation of the war; Churchill arrived (24th) and a conference began under the control of the Archbishop of the Greek Church. The Archbishop was approved as Regent by the King of Greece, in London, and as a new Government was being formed at the end of the month, the British drove the Communist rebels out of the city. Fighting continues in the country.

In Italy the battle still proceeds with little real progress. Canadian troops took Ravenna (4th) but the U.S. 5th Army has not yet been able to take Bologna. The Allies wait for Spring to launch an offensive.

1945

JANUARY 1945

EUROPE and ATLANTIC
The German offensive in the Ardennes became a defence and then a retreat. Patton's 3rd Army broke through to Bastogne and turned the corridor into a salient (3rd), while the U.S. 1st Army made strong attacks on the northern line. Considerable German withdrawals were made on the 9th, and these were speeded up when the Russian offensive in the east began (12th). At the same time U.S. forces north and south of the "Bulge" met, and for the rest of the month "mopping up" operations were carried out until the original line was restored (28th). Allied casualties, killed and wounded were almost 77,000. Hitler's offensive cost him over 70,000 German soldiers, killed and wounded, about 50,000 taken prisoner, almost 600 tanks, thousands of vehicles and guns, and about 160 planes.

Even at this stage, however, the Luftwaffe was able to inflict damage. In a large scale offensive against Allied airfields in northern Europe involving 800 planes of every type, the Luftwaffe destroyed close on 300 Allied planes (1st). German losses were about 100 fewer, but whereas the Allies were able to replace their losses almost immediately, the German force was permanently weakened.

With the Allies pressing against the whole German border in the west, and Russia gaining ground steadily in the east, Hitler made his first public broadcast for some time (30th) – and it may be his last. Characteristically, it was in no way defeatist or even conciliatory. But his enthusiasm and confidence were not wholly infectious, and thousands of civilians have begun to flee from Berlin and other towns in eastern Germany, towards the west.

Hitler's talk of secret "super weapons" had considerable effect in Britain – especially in London – which received some 220 V2 rockets.

RUSSIA
In the middle of Germany's renewed Western offensive, Churchill asked Stalin to begin an Eastern offensive to relieve pressure on the U.S., British and Canadian troops (6th). Stalin stepped up preparations, and at 10 a.m. on the 12th the guns of **the Russian Armies roared the**

resumption of battle. The Ardennes offensive, and an abortive attempt by Hitler to recover some lost ground in the south-east, left Guderian with a weakened defence in the north. Nothing could stop the Russians. The ruins and the unburied dead of Warsaw were covered by the Russian wave (17th); Modlin fell (18th); then Cracow (19th). From the south, the drive for Budapest began. In the north, Marshal Rokossovsky swept over East Prussia and Danzig; Zhukov ploughed through central Poland. Before the Russians, fled the refugees fearful of rumour, fact, and the remembrance of guilt. The Russians have almost reached the Oder, and have already entered Silesia.

One of the hundreds of towns and villages, camps, strongholds and other sites cleared of Germans by the Russians, was **Auschwitz** concentration camp – most brutal of the Nazi camps designed for the "Final Solution" to their hatred of Jewry and Bolschevism, where more than 1,000,000 and perhaps as many as 2,000,000 men, women and children were deliberately and systematically murdered.

FAR EAST and PACIFIC

MacArthur's return to Luzon began with the traditional pre-invasion bombardment (6th), and the landing of four divisions began three days later in Lingayen Gulf – where the Japanese had come ashore three years ago. Initially, resistance was slight since deception tactics had made it impossible for the Japanese to know where the U.S. forces would land. But on the way to Manila, resistance is becoming stiffer. Japanese suicide-plane attacks reached their peak in these operations, the Australian cruiser *Australia* being the most unlucky ship in being hit five times in a few days. But even these desperate measures decreased as Japanese forces on the Philippines began to run short of planes and pilots willing to man them

American forces rapidly recovered from the shock of Germany's Ardennes offensive, launched in December 1944. Fighting in the "Battle of the Bulge" was fierce and tanks played an important part. By the end of January U.S. forces had forced the Germans back to the November line, and the push towards Germany resumed.

The Japanese again suffered defeat in Burma, being completely disrupted in the Arakan by the Allied capture of Akyab (3rd), and the Commando landings at Kangaw (22nd). A vital Allied accomplishment was the completion of the Ledo Road (7th) which was started in December 1942. It links the railhead at Ledo, Assam, with Myitkyina and at Bhamo joins a branch of the Mandalay road to China.

SOUTHERN EUROPE and MEDITERRANEAN
The British troops in Greece quickly overwhelmed the Communist guerilla fighters once they had been driven out of Athens (5th), and a truce was signed on the 11th.

In Italy the Allied troops, resting and building up for a Spring offensive, are also overcoming the depressing effects on morale caused by depletion of their forces for other theatres.

FEBRUARY 1945

EUROPE and ATLANTIC
Dresden, in eastern Germany, was bombed in perfect weather by successive waves of R.A.F. bombers at night and U.S.A.A.F. bombers by day – a total of 1,800 sorties (13–15th). The city had escaped bombing throughout the war and was being used as the main communications centre for the German armies fighting on the Russian front, though few air defences had been arranged. Its industry had benefitted from the unusual respite, and some 200,000 refugees from the advancing Russians had joined the 630,000 inhabitants. The bombing – a destructive mixture of high explosives and incendiaries – caused a terrible firestorm. The explosions, the hurricane-force winds and the searing heat destroyed over 1,600 acres of the city. No-one will ever know for certain how many died in the holocaust – almost certainly more than Hamburg's 50,000, perhaps as many as 140,000.

On the Western front, in mainly terrible weather conditions, the Allies have gradually pressed forward. The Luftwaffe, now practically non-existent, was unable to prevent the devastating raids on German lines of communication. Nor could it do much to prevent the 1,000 U.S. bomber raid on Berlin (3rd). On the south-west front, Patton's U.S. 3rd Army cleared the Saar-Moselle area, and the Rhine's west bank.

For Britain, it was the worst month of the deadly, silent V2 rockets – 232 landed in south-east England.

RUSSIA
After a preliminary meeting in Malta, Churchill and Roosevelt (with advisers, Chiefs of Staff, etc., totalling some 700 people) joined Stalin for the "Big Three" Yalta Conference (5–11th). The question of Poland's boundaries and her system of government occupied the major part of the Conference. A measure of agreement was reached by which Russia would take over some Polish territory (to the "Curzon Line" – running roughly north-south through Brest-Litovsk), but that Poland in turn should be given some German territory. Churchill, mindful of Britain's obligations to Poland, remained ill at ease, for Stalin would not consent to any direct participation by the west in aiding Poland, or in seeing the operation of a fair election. The question of the partitioning of Germany was also discussed, and the general divisions and spheres of interest, raised at Teheran, were elaborated on. The third major topic was the Dumbarton Oaks scheme for future world security – the basis of the United Nations. The Big Three agreed on the principle of the Veto for the major powers in Security Council voting procedures. Stalin also agreed to join the war against Japan after the defeat of Germany.

The Russian armies in the north reached the banks of the Oder (3rd) and are establishing bridgeheads west of the river. In the south, Hitler flung every available reserve against the Russians in trying to hold Budapest, but this too fell (13th). In Silesia, even boys' brigades are involved in trying to hold back the Russian advance towards the Niesse.

FAR EAST and PACIFIC
The preliminaries to the **assault on Iwo Jima** began at last. However the attack was anticipated by the Japanese almost as long ago as the Americans decided to capture it, and extensive defences had been prepared. The pre-invasion bombardment of the island was extremely heavy – nearly 7,000 tons of bombs and well over 20,000 shells had exploded on the little island by the 15th. The arrival of the massed sea power of the U.S. (17th) made it even clearer that the invasion was imminent, and the commander of the defence, Kuribayashi, replied with a barrage of his own. For the first time the Americans were able to pinpoint actual targets, and achieved far more successful shelling (18th).

The landing operations on the 19th were preceded by one of the war's heaviest bombardments. For two hours, starting at 6.30 a.m., 25 ships and gunboats fired shells, rockets and mortars at the island while planes dropped bombs and napalm. Nevertheless, the Marines met heavy fire when they went ashore, and by nightfall they were confined to a beachhead about 2½ miles long and well under a mile inland at its deepest point. An expected counter-attack did not materialise, but the day's losses were heavy – a "suicide" sniper hiding in the wreck of a boat caused many deaths. The night was one of terror and death for the troops on the beach, for they were exposed to constant and very accurate mortar and artillery fire from the defenders. Desperate fighting gradually took the Marines to Mount Suribachi (22nd), and the next morning, after hours of combat and hand to hand fighting up the old volcano, the U.S. flag was planted on the summit – resulting in one of the war's most famous photographs. The remainder of the island was still in

Japanese hands, and with attackers fighting as hard as the defenders, losses on both sides are heavy.

A *kamikaze* attack caused serious damage and destroyed 42 planes on the giant U.S. carrier *Saratoga*.

MacArthur's battle to regain Luzon continued with steady success. Yamashita had ordered Manila to be evacuated, but a Japanese Rear Admiral has organised resistance with 20,000 men from the naval base. This is resulting in a lot of damage to the city. Mirroring the Japanese victory of nearly two years ago, U.S. troops recaptured Bataan (16th), and finally won back Corregidor in Manila Bay (28th).

The Allied campaign to push the Japanese from **Burma** centred around the vital communications centre of Meiktila, south of Mandalay, where fierce fighting is going on.

SOUTHERN EUROPE and MEDITERRANEAN
In preparation for a Spring offensive, the Allied air forces in northern Italy carried out many effective raids on German communications and supply dumps.

MARCH 1945

EUROPE and ATLANTIC
The first Allies crossed the Rhine into Germany when an advance section of a U.S. armoured division captured the Luderdorff Bridge at Remagen (between Bonn and Cologne) before German engineers could blow it up (7th). The rest of the division and several other divisions rushed across before frantic German shelling and bombing, and the enormous loads, collapsed the bridge (17th). Hitler dismissed Rundstedt and brought Kesselring in from Italy, largely as a result of this costly German blunder. By the time the Remagen bridge broke, the Allies occupied the whole of the west bank of the Rhine. The fighting in the north was fierce, and the British and Canadian troops fought hard against determined resistance. But by the time Montgomery was ready to cross the Rhine, the German losses since their Ardennes offensive were about 60,000 killed and wounded and over 290,000 taken prisoner.

At the point where Montgomery was to cross the Rhine, the river is over 400 yards wide, and his offensive started in typical waterborne invasion style, with a massive artillery bombardment of the opposite shore (from north to south of Wesel) (23rd). After an hour's shelling, commandos crossed the river and captured Wesel, while U.S. and British landings were made in the region. The next day over 1,500 planes with paratroopers, and 1,300 gliders took **thousands of U.S. and British troops across the Rhine**, and Montgomery is now heading for the great industrial heart of Germany, the Ruhr.

In the south, Patton and the U.S. 3rd Army, advancing at great speed each day, began to cross the Rhine south of Mainz, where the swift advance found little resistance (22nd). Fanning out across the old demilitarised zone, the **U.S. forces reached Frankfurt and captured Mannheim** on the 29th.

Persuaded by Speer that defeat is imminent, Hitler ordered the "scorched earth" destruction of Germany. Only Speer's strenuous disobedience prevented this catastrophe.

A landing party from the German garrisons on the Channel Islands made a surprise attack on the port of Granville on the Cherbourg Peninsula, until recently Eisenhower's H.Q. (8–9th).

The war at sea has hardly slackened, though there are far fewer sinkings. The number of U-boats in operational condition reached its highest figure – 463 – but they have not been able to regain even a semblance of their early successes. Mines took a far higher toll than U-boats did – in particular a new group sown by German E boats in the English Channel. German surface ships from west Holland attempted an attack on Allied shipping in the Zeeland approaches to Antwerp, but were driven away from the estuary.

German oil production dropped to only 80,000 tons this month, as a result of constant Allied air raids. A 1,000 bomber raid by the R.A.F. on Dortmund dropped 4,800 tons of bombs (12th).

The V2 campaign also came to an end (27th) after 212 dropped during the month. The total that fell on Britain was 1,115 – almost half of which hit London. They killed 2,855 people, and seriously injured over 6,000. Two days later the last V1 was shot down. Of the 6,000 flying bombs that crossed the Channel, 3,957 were shot down. The remainder killed 6,139 and seriously injured 17,239. All launching sites are now destroyed.

In Oregon, U.S.A., a woman and five children were killed by a balloon-borne bomb launched from a Japanese submarine off the west coast – the only American civilians to be killed on the mainland by enemy action (5th).

RUSSIA
The Baltic port of Gdynia fell before the Russian advance (28th) and nearby Danzig was captured two days later. In the south, the Russians swept into Austria. The noose around Germany is rapidly tightening.

FAR EAST and PACIFIC
Japanese counter-attacks on Iwo Jima were repulsed and fierce fighting continued until a proclamation to cease hostilities was read (14th). Of the original Japanese garrison of 21,000, only 216 were taken prisoner. Some 3,000 remained in caves, where they died in "mopping up" operations, or met their death in desperate *banzai*

charges, until Kuribayashi committed *harakiri* by stabbing himself in his stomach, and bowing his head for decapitation by one of his staff officers (27th). American casualties on Iwo Jima were proportionately the highest of the war – 4,554 Marines and 363 Navy men were killed.

The **next objective of the U.S. forces is Okinawa**, and bombardment of the island and its 100,000 Japanese defenders began on the 24th. By the time it ended (31st), over 27,000 shells of five inches or larger had been fired. The U.S. 10th Army with 172,000 combatants is poised for the invasion.

In Burma the Allies captured Meiktila, and moved north to win back Mandalay (20th).

A night raid by over 270 heavy U.S. bombers on Tokyo (9–10th) dropped thousands of incendiaries and created a vicious firestorm. This devastated a quarter of Tokyo and killed almost 72,500 civilians. Night raids on Nagoya, Osaka, Kobe and Yokohama followed, causing widespread destruction and thousands of deaths.

The U.S. Army's 173 day **battle for Luzon ended** with the last clearance of Manila, now a horribly ruined city (4th). The Allies lost nearly 40,000 killed and wounded, including many Navy casualties.

The British Pacific Fleet joined the U.S. Pacific Fleet (26th) for the final onslaught on Japan. Carrier-borne raids on Japan (18th–21st) suffered retaliation from suicide attacks, but 160 attacking planes were shot down.

SOUTHERN EUROPE

The Allied air offensive on German supplies and communications in northern Italy continued. Gen. Mark Clark issued orders for the Allies' Spring offensive, which initially aims at clearing the Germans to beyond the Po, and taking Verona.

APRIL 1945

EUROPE and ATLANTIC

Germany began to disintegrate rapidly. Allied armies met in a pincer movement round the Ruhr at Paderborn (1st), which trapped Model and his forces in a noose 80 miles across. As the Allies tightened the knot, resistance collapsed, and by the 18th 400,000 Germans had surrendered. Model was not among them – he shot himself in a wood near Duisberg (21st).

After the Ruhr encirclement, U.S. forces raced westwards, and when they reached the Elbe (12th) they were only 60 miles from Berlin. Further south, Nuremberg, sacred to the Nazi's memories, was overrun (20th). Patton reached the Czechoslovakia frontier (23rd) and within two days advance parties of the U.S. and Russian forces had met at Torgau, north-east of Leipzig.

President Roosevelt died from cerebral haemorrhage (12th) and was succeeded by Harry Truman.

In Hitler's bunker beneath the Chancellery, the last days of the Third Reich played out their bizarre and hysterical ceremony. Hitler's last Order of the Day (16th) claimed that fresh units were replacing losses. Mentally and physically the Fuehrer had been rapidly disintegrating, and he continually sent out orders to no longer existent units of the Army and the Luftwaffe. Goebbels and Bormann remained with Hitler, and when Goering, safe out of Berlin, telegraphed Hitler to suggest that he should take over command of the Reich, Bormann prompted Hitler to depose the Reich Marshal, and then also ordered the SS to arrest him. Goering was not the only one to ignore and upset Hitler – Speer still refused to carry out a scorched-earth policy throughout Germany (23rd); and the final, greatest insult that infuriated Hitler was the discovery that Himmler had been attempting to arrange a surrender, through Count Bernadotte of Sweden.

On the morning of the 29th, Hitler married Eva Braun, and the guns of the approaching Russians could already be heard. Later in the day, he heard of Mussolini's death. He wrote his will, had his dog killed, and appointed Doenitz as the new President of the Reich. At 3.30 p.m. **Hitler shot himself** in his mouth, and Eva Braun took poison. Their petrol-soaked bodies were burnt outside the bunker, and their ashes scattered by Russian shells.

The war at sea, so quick to begin, is going on to the bitter end. Forty-four U-boats sailed from Norway during the month, and sank 10 merchantmen and two small escort ships. Twenty-three U-boats were sunk, though none of the new very dangerous Type 23 submarines were caught. In the Bay of Biscay a new airborne anti-submarine device – a retro-rocket on a bomb allowing a straight fall, sank a U-boat (30th).

R.A.F. bombers began to drop thousands of tons of food and clothing to the struggling people in Rotterdam and other centres in Holland (29th), where thousands have already starved to death.

Among thousands of other starving, maltreated, dying Jews, Communists and "enemies of the state", U.S. forces liberated Halder, Hitler's former Chief of the Army General Staff, who had been sent to Dachau concentration camp after the 20th of July Plot in 1944.

RUSSIA

The Russian Battle for Berlin, directed by Zhukov, was launched from the Oder with a massive artillery barrage (16th), and made steady progress. At the end of the month the Russians are almost in the centre of Berlin, only a few hundred yards from Hitler's bunker. Civilians are trying to flee to the west, away from the guns and the revengeful Russian soldiers. Often, they are joined by German soldiers who have flung away their weapons, and by officers who have stripped insignia of rank from their uniforms.

Russian troops met the Allies' west front for the first time when they joined U.S. soldiers at Torgau, north-east of Leipzig (25th). Further south in Czechoslovakia the Russian line overran Brno (26th).

FAR EAST and PACIFIC

On Easter Sunday (1st) **the invasion of Okinawa** began with 1,300 ships taking part. The Japanese had been driven back by the naval barrage and scarcely opposed the landing. By nightfall, with a loss of only 28, nearly 60,000 U.S. troops were ashore. The Japanese had drawn up a horrifying plan to crush the U.S. forces which called for mass suicide by many thousands of their men. Together with suicide attacks by Japanese soldiers, there were to be massed *kamikaze* flights, given the name *Kikusui* (floating chrysanthemum), while the massive battleship *Yamato* and the remnants of the Japanese fleet would bombard enemy positions, if necessary beaching the ships rather than letting them sink (*Yamato*'s guns had a range of 25 miles).

The Japanese attack on the Okinawa invasion fleet was launched (6th) with 340 bombers and over 350 *kamikaze* planes, but did not cause the expected large-scale destruction. On the following day U.S. ships located the Japanese Fleet and launched a carrier attack. *Yamato* was blasted by bombs and 12 torpedos. After 2 hours the enormous battleship sank, taking with her nearly 3,000 men. A cruiser and four destroyers were also sunk. The cost to the Americans was 15 aircraft. The U.S. forces were able to establish land bases for additional aircraft and by the 19th, 160,000 U.S. troops were ashore, and most of Okinawa had been captured. But the remaining defence – especially from fortified positions in the neck of the island – is typically tough, and the island is far from won.

Russia informed Japan it would not renew their Neutrality Pact (5th), although technically it should still be in operation until 13th April 1946.

SOUTHERN EUROPE

The war in Italy has ended. The Allied offensive began on the 9th when the 8th Army followed a tremendous artillery and air bombardment with a rapid armoured advance. Tanks and troops with flamethrowers caused chaos, and five German battalions on the Senio were practically wiped out. The U.S. 5th Army opened its offensive on the 14th and also made great advances, soon taking Bologna, together with Polish troops (21st). A British force had moved north to cut off the retreat from Bologna, and as the German army began to disintegrate, large numbers surrendered (25th).

Partisan activity began in earnest, and quickly Verona and Genoa fell, then Milan, and Venice. At the same time (26th) the Brenner Pass was sealed. Mussolini, his mistress Carla Petacci, and a number of companions tried to escape to Switzerland, but were discovered by a partisan group near Lake Como. The next day (29th), the partisan leader shot Mussolini and Carla Petacci, and their bodies were taken to Milan where they were hung by their heels outside a garage on Piazzale Loreto – scene of the recent hanging of partisans.

On the 29th, as the 5th Army entered Milan, the German unconditional surrender was signed by plenipotentiaries at Alexander's headquarters in the presence of senior British, American and Russian officers.

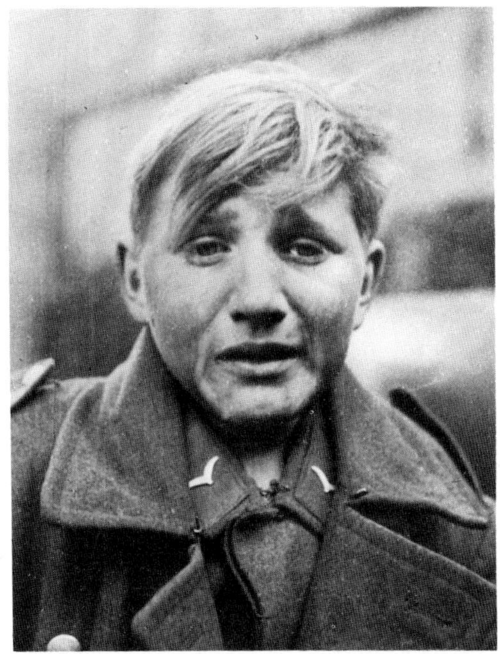

In the last months of the Third Reich, younger and younger boys were thrown into the front line. Years of indoctrination motivated many – for the others, there was the fear of the roving courts-martial and their instant executions of "deserters and traitors".

MAY 1945

EUROPE, ATLANTIC, RUSSIA and SOUTHERN EUROPE

The war in Europe is over. Early in the morning of the 1st, Gen. Krebs set out from Hitler's bunker for the nearby Russians to attempt a negotiated surrender, but was told that surrender would have to be unconditional. Later in the day Doenitz heard from Goebbels for the first time that Hitler was dead. At 8.30 p.m. Goebbels poisoned his six children and had himself and his wife shot by an SS guard. Their bodies were not properly burnt, as the last of the entourage fled the bunker in panic. Bormann was seen rushing towards Russian lines, and a shell exploding near-by may have killed him. Hitler's death was announced on the radio (a "fighting death"), and Doenitz made a pathetic attempt to pick up the reigns of leadership.

The following day (2nd) Berlin fell to the swarming Russians; the remains of the bunker and the blackened corpses of the Goebbels family were found, and the Soviet flag flew above the Chancellery ruins. Also on the 2nd, British, U.S. and Russian troops met at Lübeck near the Baltic, and on the 3rd British troops occupied the devastated wastes of Hamburg.

On the 4th Admiral Friedeburg, Doenitz's emissary, arrived at Montgomery's H.Q. on Luneberg Heath, and surrendered the German forces in north-west Germany, Holland, Schelswig-Holstein, Norway and Denmark. At 2.40 a.m. on the 7th, the total unconditional surrender of Germany was signed at Eisenhower's Rheims H.Q. by Lt. Gen. Bedell Smith and Gen. Jodl, for all hostilities to cease at midnight, 8th May. In the early hours of the 9th, the formal ratification by the German High Command was signed in Berlin by Air Chief Marshal Tedder (as Eisenhower's Deputy), Marshal Zhukov, and Field Marshal Keitel.

In Italy, remnants of the German armies surrendered to the Allies (2nd), having lost 556,000 killed and wounded in the 600 days of the Italian campaign. At sea, 156 U-boats obeyed Doenitz's call to surrender, while 221 were scuttled by their crews.

Most of the senior Nazis and officers of the armed forces were in captivity or otherwise accounted for when Himmler confessed his identity to the British, in whose custody he then was (22nd). In spite of being searched, Himmler avoided more than cursory questioning by biting into a concealed cyanide capsule. He died instantly (23rd). On the same day Doenitz, Jodl and other members of the Doenitz Government were arrested.

In the strange silence of peace, devastated Germany – its cities so much rubble, its people homeless, hungry and bewildered – is gradually becoming aware of what has happened. The presence of foreign uniforms, the confirmation of rumours, the millions of corpses in the concentration camps, the dead and missing members of families – all rise to obscure memories of military bands, of red, white and black flags, of the beloved Fuehrer.

In the bunker, two days before Hitler's suicide, one German, Gen. Burgdorf, spoke a judgement on the Nazi leaders that would have found many assenters in Germany, though it did not go far enough – perhaps through lack of knowledge. In a tirade against Bormann, Burgdorf was heard to say:

Our young officers went to battle filled with faith and idealism. They went to their deaths by the hundreds of thousands – but for what? For their Fatherland, for the greatness and future of Germany? For a decent life? In their hearts, perhaps they did, but nowhere else. They died for you, for your benefit, for your extravagant ambitions . . . our youth bled to death on the battlefields of Europe, sacrificed millions of innocent lives, while you, the Party leaders, grew richer and richer, lived like lords, accumulated vast riches . . . deceived and milked the nation. Our ideals, our morals, our faith, our souls – these you have ground into the dirt. Mankind was but a stepping stone for your rapacious greed. You have destroyed our heritage, our culture, you have broken up our nation. That is your only achievement.

G. Boldt: Die Letzten Tage der Reichskanzlei (Reinbek 1964.)

Unfortunately that was not the Nazis' only achievement. It was not only the German nation they had broken up, nor was it only German youth who bled on the battlefields. Hitler and his brutal collaborators certainly had "sacrificed millions of lives"; the real total will never be known, but the blood of 30,000,000 is no more easily washed away than the blood of 40,000,000.

FAR EAST and PACIFIC

While the struggle for Okinawa continued all through the month, and dozens more Japanese pilots made their suicide flights, some efforts were being made to get peace in the East as well. These efforts brought to light an almost equal split in Japan's rulers between the "fight to the death" faction, and the seekers of negotiated peace. Difficult and mutually suspicious moves in Switzerland via Allen Dulles, OSS representative in Europe, produced nothing, and the suggestion that Russia should mediate was complicated by Russia's revocation of the Neutrality Pact.

Emperor Hirohito's Palace was threatened by fire in the fifth large-scale air raid on Tokyo (23rd). Over half of the city is now gutted, and millions are homeless. Sicknesses spread rapidly and there is less and less food. Eighty-five per cent of Yokohama was burnt in an air raid (27th), and practically the whole area between Tokyo and Yokohama is ruined.

At the end of the month, Stalin informed U.S. leaders that his troops would be ready for an attack on the Manchurian front on 8th August.

Burma has as good as passed into Allied hands after the recapture of Rangoon (3rd), though large numbers of "mopping up" operations have been in progress all month.

JUNE 1945

FAR EAST and PACIFIC

The bloody **battle for Okinawa has ended**. Large groups of civilians surrendered (20th) and the next day organised resistance petered out, though fanatical bands are still being hunted in cave complexes. The U.S. commander of the Okinawa campaign, Lt. Gen. Buckner, was killed while watching one of the last skirmishes (18th); the defender of the island, Lt. Gen. Ushijima, committed suicide with his Chief of Staff (22nd). One of the features of the Okinawa campaign was the large-scale use of *kamikaze*. From the first mass attack on 6th April to the end of the battle, more than 3,000 suicide-plane attacks were made by the Japanese; they sunk 21 naval craft and damaged over 60. The casualties on Okinawa were tragically high – only about 7,000 Japanese soldiers were taken prisoner, and the death toll was almost 100,000. Civilian deaths were extremely high – some 75,000 men, women and children were killed in the tumult of the battle between the armies. For the Americans too, losses were the heaviest yet in the Pacific – over 12,500 Marines, GIs and sailors are dead or missing.

Okinawa was the last place outside their homeland that the Japanese could expect to hold the American revenge, and its loss caused deep concern in Tokyo. Long before it was over, but when the outcome was in no doubt, peace moves via the Soviet Ambassador were dropped owing to the Japanese Supreme Command's insistence that the war should be fought to the end (6th). The non-military leaders were less anxious to condemn the Japanese nation to death, and Suzuki urged the need for peace before the senior houses of administration (13th). The Emperor's adviser, Marquis Kido, the Privy Seal, suggested to Hirohito that he, too, should bring up the question of peace, and on the 22nd the Emperor summoned the "Big Six" to an Imperial Presence Conference, and requested that they consider a way to end the war as quickly as possible.

It was not only the loss of Okinawa that caused these moves, for conditions in Japan itself have been getting rapidly worse. With Tokyo and Yokohama almost totally devastated, U.S. bombers turned their attention to Osaka and Kobe, and destroyed them too. Over 100 square miles of Japan's principle cities are now in ruins, and more than 13,000,000 people have lost their homes.

In America, different ways of ending the war quickly also occupied the minds of the leaders. The first atomic bomb is almost ready to be tested, and there has been much argument about how the bomb should be used – in a technical demonstration, or directly as a military weapon. The majority opinion was that a convincing, effective technical demonstration would be impossible. Truman called a major meeting of the Joint Chiefs of Staff and others (18th) to discuss the A bomb, and surrender terms. Some are in favour of scrapping "unconditional" surrender, or at least of giving some intimation that the Emperor would stay as the leader of the Japanese people. The fear that the Emperor might be executed, or imprisoned as a war criminal, is doing much to bolster support in Japan for the anti-surrender faction.

JULY 1945

FAR EAST and PACIFIC

New peace moves were made in Switzerland by the Japanese military attaché via Per Jacobsson, a banker and international negotiator of repute. The Allies tried to get through an assurance that unconditional surrender would not necessarily result in the Emperor's overthrow, but considered it impossible to put this into writing. The U.S. are by now well aware of the Japanese feelings, since they intercept and decode all messages between Tokyo and Moscow. Hirohito has tried to send former Prime Minister Konoye to Moscow, but their Ambassador had little encouragement from Stalin, and advised Tokyo that "unconditional" would probably have to be an accepted term. Moscow has still not mentioned to the U.S. that it has been approached by the Japanese to act as an intermediary.

Japanese "hard-line" militarists drew up plans for a final, suicidal defence of Japan which would muster well over 30,000,000 people – made up of 2½ million troops, 4 million employees in the Army and Navy, and a 28 million-strong civil militia. Intended arms would be every last gun on the island including muzzle-loaders, bows and arrows, and nearly 10,000 aeroplanes of all shapes and sizes still capable of flying. These fanatics seem quite prepared to call for the deaths of 30 million of their own people, and are confident their call will be answered.

In New Mexico the Allies' **first atomic bomb was successfully exploded** in a test at Alamogordo (16th), and Truman told Churchill about this at the Potsdam Conference. Churchill tried to dissuade Truman from insisting on unconditional surrender, but the success of the A-bomb strengthened U.S. resolve. On the 26th, the Potsdam Proclamation to the people of Japan was issued (27th in Tokyo); it made no mention of the A-bomb or of Hirohito's status, but threatened utter destruction. The Proclamation was drawn up by the U.S. and approved by Britain and China. It was not shown to Stalin – to his annoyance, but Russia was not then at war with Japan. In Japan the Proclamation met with a mixed reception. Togo and Adm. Suzuki supported it, Adm. Toyoda was fiercely opposed to it, and Japanese newspapers adopted an antagonistic line. Suzuki hoped to encourage another approach and perhaps even open a dialogue by using a "no comment" reaction, but this was taken by the U.S. as an official Japanese rejection (30th).

AUGUST 1945

FAR EAST and PACIFIC

The War is over. On the 14th, Japan surrendered unconditionally, and Emperor Hirohito announced to the Japanese people that he had accepted surrender. The 24 hours before capitulation was announced was a time

Above: Clipped-wing Spitfire VB and a pair of R.A.F. pilots on an airfield in the Mediterranean theatre (Photo: Imperial War Museum). Below: A group of Waffen-SS cavalrymen during the German advance into Russia during the summer of 1941.

of frenzied political activity in Tokyo, with the Big Six remaining divided between the "suicide" and the surrender factions. A military revolt was begun, plans were made to abduct the Emperor, minor militant bands sprang up, and it was probably only the direct order of the Emperor – a hitherto unknown step for a Japanese Emperor to take – that stopped the squabbling and stopped the war. The surrender was followed by a number of suicides, some officers committing ritual *hara-kiri*.

The first of three events which led to the Emperor's decision occurred on the 6th when, two days after leaflets were dropped to the 245,000 people still living in Hiroshima, a B-29 bomber dropped an **atomic bomb over the centre of Hiroshima**. At 8.15 a.m. it exploded about 2,000 feet above the ground, and within moments some 80,000 people were dead, and at least 100,000 were terribly injured, or tainted with deadly radiation. Almost 7 square miles of the city were turned into rubble. Fires broke out and flared up in high winds. Half an hour after the searing flash and the massive concussion, a fine black rain fell on the ruins from a cloudless sky.

The second event occurred on the 8th when **Russia declared war on Japan** (anxious to be in on the Japanese war and so have some say in post-war policies) and invaded a poorly-defended Mongolia. This sped up the surrender not so much because it meant another adversary (few in Japan believed she could last much longer against America) but because it finally cut the last tenuous line of communication and possible negotiation with the west.

The last event took place the following day (9th) when an **atomic bomb exploded over Nagasaki**. As with Hiroshima, estimates of numbers killed vary – 26,000? 35,000? 74,800? With atomic bombs, so many die the day after the explosion, and the next day, and the next . . .

SEPTEMBER 1945

FAR EAST and PACIFIC

On Sunday the 2nd, the **surrender of Japan and all Japanese forces was signed** before MacArthur on board the U.S. battleship *Missouri*. Over the following weeks, Japanese commanders on the various fronts surrendered.

Japan's ambitions in Asia and the Pacific, since its aggression on the mainland in 1937, had taken the lives of some 16,000,000 people, about 80% of them Chinese soldiers and civilians.

The Second World War was over. It had killed at least 50 million people, and scarred forever the minds and bodies of fifty times that number.

AFTERMATH

In this last great action of the Second World War we were given final proof that war is death. War in the 20th Century has grown steadily more barbarous, more destructive, more debased in all its aspects. The bombs dropped on Hiroshima and Nagasaki ended a war. They also made it wholly clear that we must never have another war.

Henry Stimson, United States Secretary for War

If mankind is never again subjected to global conflict, it will probably be thanks more to the technology which sacrificed tens of thousands of Japanese lives in two fateful days of 1945, than to the greater wisdom of politicians, leaders, and dictators. For just as The War to End Wars led to decisions which brought about the Second World War, the aftermath of these six years of barbarism once more saw premiers and dictators drawing lines on maps, clamping down iron rules, and shuffling the lives of millions into packs on which they staked their countries' futures.

Yalta and Teheran hardly followed the letter of the Atlantic Charter, even if Churchill and Roosevelt intended the spirit to follow rapidly. Churchill did have disturbing visions of Russia's future behaviour, but he was unable to interest others in his forecasts, and the seeds of new tension were sown long before prisoners of war had wearily reached home.

At the end of the European War Germany was divided up into American, British, French and Russian zones of administration. Berlin, deep in the Russian zone, was itself split into four sections as an "international city". Poland, Czechoslovakia, Hungary, Bulgaria, and the Baltic States were occupied by Russia, and then, as Churchill declared, an Iron Curtain was drawn across that part of Europe, and no-one west of the curtain knew what it hid. (Russian-occupied Austria was also governed by the four powers, but without tension, and in 1955 was given independence, neutrality and its old 1938 borders. Yugoslavia, having ousted the German invaders practically unaided, saw no point in falling under yet another dictator, and under Tito's inspired leadership kept itself free as a unique, non-aligned communist state.) Stalin had put his own meaning on the phrase "sphere of influence" which had guided the division of Europe before the war ended.

The Potsdam Conference (near Berlin) which began on 17th July 1945, was intended to settle the myriad problems facing the conquerors of Germany. For Churchill, it was to be the time to make a last stand on the tragic question of Poland, now no freer than it was after Hitler's invasion. He decided to leave it to the end, after dealing with the other matters facing the Conference. But in the elections of 25th July the British public – whom Churchill had hoped would bear him a reasonably grateful loyalty – voted in the Labour Party, and a new man,

Attlee, attended the rest of Potsdam. Whether Churchill would have been able to rescue some of Poland's independence can of course never be answered. Stalin was probably mildly amused at this peculiar result of democracy, but gave no indication of pleasure at having to deal with a Socialist instead of Churchill. Potsdam closed with the Iron Curtain still showing no chinks of light.

After Potsdam there emerged a fundamental difference between the Western Allies and Russia. Russia – who had, after all, suffered far more during the war than any of the Western Allies – was in no hurry to relieve Germany's misery. She demanded and extracted reparations, kept Hitler's virtually useless currency, and let the East Germans painfully reconstruct some form of life from their rubble. The West decided that West Germany would be less of a problem if she was able to stand on her own feet. America's enormous war production had made her a nation wealthy beyond compare, and from this emerged the humane, generous Marshall Plan which gave wealth and strength to the countries which had lost so much in the war.

These two entirely different approaches made the Iron Curtain even more impenetrable, alienated Russia from her former Allies, and began a new war – the Cold War. When the West introduced the British plan to reform Germany's currency by introducing the Deutschmark, it wiped out inflation, and at once opened up a huge gap in prosperity between East and West Germany. Russia retaliated by closing off the land corridor to West Berlin (she refrained from "occupying" West Berlin, potentially a simple act, perhaps out of respect for the West's then monopoly on nuclear bombs). To this the West replied with one of the greatest feats of determined humanitarianism – the Berlin Airlift. For almost a year, and through an exceptionally severe winter, thousands of aircrews from half a dozen of the leading Western Allies flew plane after plane into blockaded West Berlin, and supplied some 2,250,000 Berliners with food, fuel, clothing . . . even raw materials to keep their industries active. Eventually the Russians gave up and West Berlin and its corridor became a permanent feature on the map of Europe.

Since then, little has changed. The continued prosperity of West Berlin proved irresistable to East Germans and they began to flock across the border in their thousands – until in 1961 the puppet East German government built the Berlin Wall, a hideous monument to their own ineptitude. Hungary tried to escape the choking Russian yoke in 1956 and was bloodily smashed into submission. Czechoslovakia, surely with Poland one of Europe's most tragic countries, also drifted towards independent thought, but was eventually brought to heel by the overwhelming power of Russia.

So Germany is still not united; civilised, cultured people with long independent histories are still under compulsory rule of others. The mighty kings have at least put away War, and play instead the game of bluff and counterbluff. If they ever do bring out the old game, at least their doomed subjects will not have to play for longer than an hour or so.

The effects of the Japanese War were in many ways even more dramatic – and in fact brought freedom in its wake. MacArthur initially ruled Japan with a strange acceptance that this was his natural right, and the Americans sensibly did not meddle with the Emperor's status. Japan, too, received the benefits of Marshall aid, and she and her former partner in destruction, began economic recoveries that surpassed every other country, emphasising once more that to win the peace, it is not always necessary to win the war.

But the biggest change wrought by the war in the East was the end of colonialism. Lord Mountbatten, S.E.A.C.'s Supremo who accepted the surrender of the Japanese in S.E. Asia, was probably the first European leader to realise that the myth of European, and especially British invincibility was broken, and that, having been driven out by the Japanese, it would be impossible for the British, French and Dutch to simply walk back into their old colonies. Britain was not slow to begin dismembering her Empire, and Mountbatten himself, the last Viceroy of India, gave India its independence in August 1947. Burma was given hers five months later.

The Dutch ignored Mountbatten's warning at first, but soon quit the East Indies. France was much slower to learn, and only the bloody and humiliating lesson of Dien Bien Phu in 1954 drummed it home that colonial days had ended.

The pattern rapidly spread. The war that had put new shackles on Europe, the Old World, lifted the yoke of colonialism from the New World.

But what of the people who started it all? Hitler, Goebbels and Himmler had committed suicide. Hess, imprisoned in Britain since his mad flight to Scotland in 1941, joined a batch of the top Nazis and generals before an International Tribunal at Nuremberg, charged with war crimes. Hess, Raeder and Funk were imprisoned for life, Speer and von Schirach were sent to prison for 20 years, Neurath for 15, and Doenitz for 10. In his absence, Borman was sentenced to death, but was probably already dead.

Condemned to die were Goering, Ribbentrop, Rosenberg, Keitel, Jodl, Kaltenbrunner, Streicher, Seys-Inquart, Frank, Frich, and Sauckel. Late on the night of 15th October 1946, a few hours before he was to be hanged, Coering swallowed poison smuggled into his cell, and cheated the hangman. Early the next morning the executions began with Ribbentrop, and soon the bodies of the eleven leading war criminals were disposed of in some unknown, unmarked place.

Since then hundreds of Germans, from top industrialists (who grew rich on the manufacture of such diverse things as guns and gas ovens, and who boasted, in

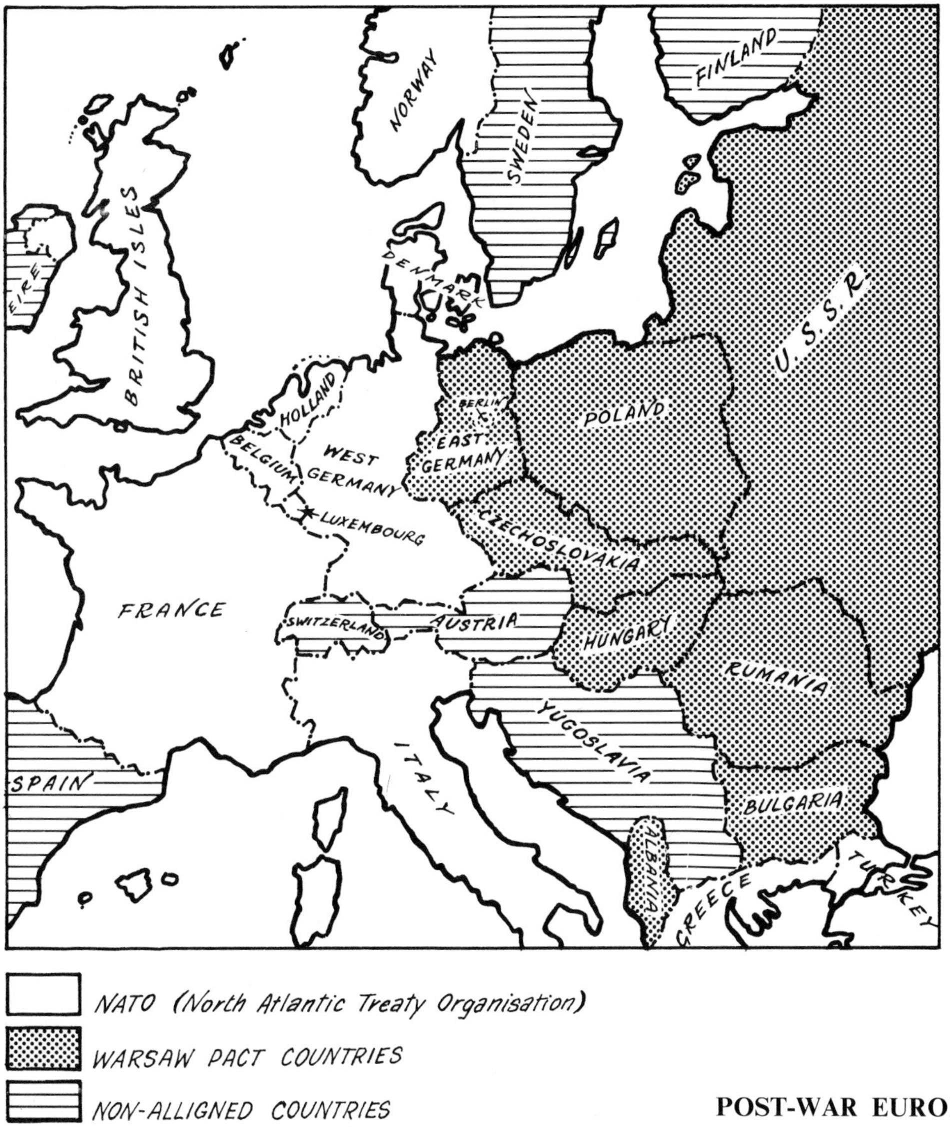

NORWAY
SWEDEN
FINLAND
BRITISH ISLES
EIRE
DENMARK
U.S.S.R.
HOLLAND
BERLIN
EAST GERMANY
POLAND
BELGIUM
WEST GERMANY
LUXEMBOURG
CZECHOSLOVAKIA
FRANCE
SWITZERLAND
AUSTRIA
HUNGARY
RUMANIA
YUGOSLAVIA
SPAIN
ITALY
BULGARIA
ALBANIA
GREECE
TURKEY

NATO (North Atlantic Treaty Organisation)
WARSAW PACT COUNTRIES
NON-ALLIGNED COUNTRIES

POST-WAR EUROPE

tenders for crematoria, of the high capacity of their firm's product) to half-witted SS guards (who methodically murdered "under orders") have been brought to trial. Some, like Adolf Eichmann (chief of the Gestapo's Jewish Office), have been found after years of painstaking search, and made to pay the ultimate penalty. Some have served a few years in prison on good rations and gone back to ordinary life. Some have escaped detection – yet the searches go on. On 23rd August 1973, for instance, two former members of the SS were sentenced in Berlin to life imprisonment for the murder of 45 Polish Jews near Cracow in 1941–42.

The tragedy of World War I is of those millions who died in battle; World War II has that tragedy too, but to it is added the horror of the millions of civilians who were killed in the clash of total war, or murdered in camps, on open fields, in sheltered woods, in locked and burning village churches, in the familiar surroundings of their own homes. And on top of these were the millions of prisoners of war – Russians taken by Germans, and Germans taken by Russians – who, faced with certain death in combat, surrendered, only to die far more slowly and agonisingly in prison. Some 5,000,000 Russian soldiers were taken prisoner by Germany and marched back to forced labour camps, where they were fed only if there was sufficient food once Germans had been fed. Fewer than one out of every five of those prisoners survived. When the tide of war turned, the Russians saw the barbarities that had been carried out in their conquered territory, and their treatment of their Axis prisoners reflected their own hatred of the invaders. From Stalingrad, 107,000 Germans marched into captivity. Fewer than 5,000 ever returned home. Only 12,000 of the 100,000 Italians captured in the Ukraine saw their sunny land once more. And there were many "Stalingrads" from which hundreds of thousands of Germans were driven to die over the years in Russia's vast wastes.

In Japan, on 19th November 1945, MacArthur ordered the arrest of eleven Japanese war leaders, for crimes dating back to the early 1930s, the invasion of Manchuria and the seizing of Nanking. Prince Konoye, three times Premier of Japan, committed *hara-kiri*. Gen. Tojo, the dictatorial war leader, shot himself within minutes of being arrested – but he was nursed back to health, tried, and hanged on 22nd December. On the fourth anniversary of Pearl Harbor, 7th December 1945, Gen. Yamashita (the "Tiger of Malaya") was hanged.

In January 1973 a Japanese sergeant was found hiding in the jungle of Guam, unaware that the war had been over for more than 27 years. As this book went to press a Japanese officer on Lubang Island was persuaded to surrender by his former C.O.

On 6th August 1973, 28 years after the atomic bomb exploded over Hiroshima, of the 3,660 who were within half a mile of the epicentre and survived the blast itself, only 53 were still alive.

---

2. THE DECISIVE CAMPAIGNS

1. BLITZKRIEG – The Crushing of Poland

1st–28th September 1939

A summary of other events during the period of each campaign precedes the descriptions.

Britain and France declared War; Athenia sunk (3rd). B.E.F. moved into France (4–9th). R.N. carrier Courageous sunk (17th). France made a brief, ineffectual move against Germany's Siegfried Line (17th). U-boats sank about 50 ships in the Atlantic.

For those commanders in the West who had not read Gen. Guderian's treatise on how armoured divisions could play a major rôle in future warfare, the German invasion and rapid defeat of Poland was a practical demonstration from which they should have learnt a great deal.

The *blitzkrieg* concept relied on a rapid assault, with as little warning as possible, which would cause surprise and confusion permitting armoured forces to smash through defensive lines. They would avoid getting bogged down against any determined resistance, and aim to penetrate behind the organised defences. The tanks, armoured personnel carriers, etc., would then make pincer movements, cutting communications and breaking up the opposing army into a number of isolated pockets which could then be dealt with at will by artillery, infantry, air attacks – or simply by leaving them surrounded. Sharing a key rôle with the armoured groups would be the air force, having the two objectives of eliminating the opposing air force (thus reducing the hazards faced by armour and infantry) and of using its bombing power to disrupt communications, and cause as much terror as possible among the victim population (who would take to the roads in a bid to escape the towns, and cause further chaos).

The crushing of Poland was a flawless execution of the *blitzkrieg* concept. About 60 German divisions, totalling some 1¼ million men, were moved to the front in readiness. Poland could have countered with 2 million, but was ill-prepared politically as well as militarily, and its ready force of about 600,000 had hardly doubled with called-up reservists before the whole battle was over.

In command of the invasion was General von Brauchitsch, C-in-C of the German High Command (OKH). He divided his forces into two army groups: Army Group North under General von Bock comprising the Fourth Army (with part of the XIX Panzer Korps) and the Third Army (with the rest of the XIX Panzer Korps); and Army Group South led by General von Rundstedt comprising three armies – the Eighth, the Tenth (with the XVI Panzer Korps), and the Fourteenth.

The crushing of Poland.

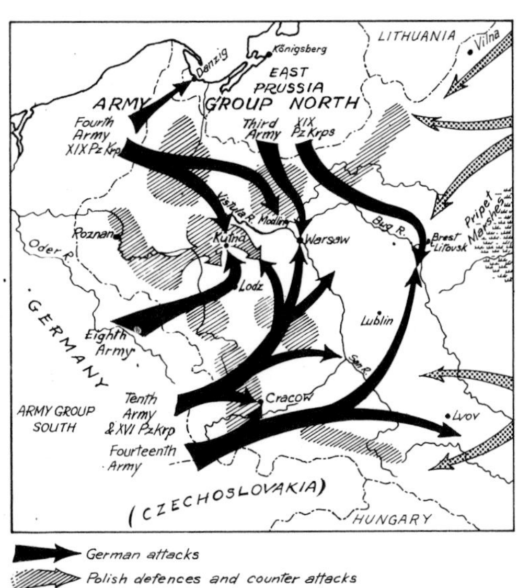

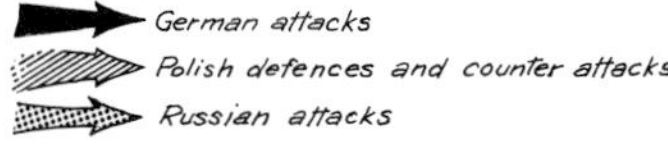

Before the battle even began, the Poles were virtually encircled: Germany bordered Poland along the West, the occupation of Czechoslovakia gave a south and south-west border, and East Prussia dug into Poland in the north. The attack was launched by the Luftwaffe using the terror bombing of its Stukas on the Poles' traditional defensive lines. Bombing smashed bridges and railways and prevented effective mobilisation of the Polish reserves. The Luftwaffe also destroyed most of Poland's 500 strong fighter air force – the major potential threat to the German offensive, for the planes and the pilots were of a high calibre. Few Polish planes even managed to get airborne, and the German attack on the ground went ahead under the Luftwaffe's protective umbrella.

The Polish defence was stubborn and heroic – but with Marshal Rydz's H.Q. constantly bombed, communications cut, and the Luftwaffe roaming freely, the defensive ring could not hold out for long. (The unequal struggle of the old meeting the new was emphasised when the Poles even tried cavalry charges in an effort to stem the Germans.) Gaps were soon found, or made, in the defence, and the armoured divisions roared through – none faster than Rundstedt's Tenth Army whose Panzer divisions led by General von Reichenau smashed their way to the outskirts of Warsaw by the 8th. One Polish group at Kutno had been completely by-passed between the flanks of Bock's and Rundstedt's Army Groups, and General Kutrzeba added nearby remnants to this group and launched a counter attack with 12 divisions against the German advance on Warsaw – but by the 19th this force too, had been defeated. The Polish Army around Modlin valiantly defended the Vistula and Warsaw's north, but on the 17th the giant pincer-movement by the eastern flanks of Army Groups North and South closed around Brest-Litovsk. With that, every Polish force was surrounded by Germans – and the final blow fell the same day when Russia swept in, almost unhindered, north and south of the Pripet Marshes.

Warsaw defended itself with a desperate heroism that it was to repeat twice more during the war, but on the 27th the city fell. The next day Germany and Russia divided the country roughly in half and began to take out of it what they wanted, and destroy what they did not – though it was 5th October before the last group of Poles capitulated.

The Fall of Western Europe
10th May–22nd June 1940

Churchill became Prime Minister of British Coalition Government (10th). British, French and Polish forces captured Narvik in attempt to counter German stronghold in Norway (27th). Allies evacuated Narvik (4th June). Norway capitulated (9th). Auschwitz concentration camp opened (14th). Russia invaded Lithuania, Latvia and Estonia (14–19th).

Apart from the rapid conquest of Denmark and the muddled goings on in Norway, there was surprisingly little surface action in Europe for the six months after the defeat of Poland (though Russia had expensively and temporarily defeated Finland). But nobody believed the "Sitzkrieg" would last forever, and the planners at least were busy. The French had the massive and virtually impregnable Maginot Line which bordered Germany, and they were busy trying to extend it along the Belgian border – or at least as far as Sedan. In spite of being confident that the Germans would not try to break through the Maginot Line (and that they would not succeed if they did try) the French still kept some 50 divisions along the German border. On the Belgian border, General Gamelin, France's aged C-in-C, had a total of 29 divisions, and the nine divisions of the British Expeditionary Force led by General Gort. Some divisions were motorised but whatever armour there was, was thinly spread-out and assigned to infantry groups.

In the suspicion (bred by World War I memories) that the Germans might come through the Low Countries, the Allies had a plan by which they would hinge on Sedan (protected by the natural terrain of the Ardennes, and east of the Ardennes, by the edge of the Maginot Line), and then sweep up to aid the Belgians and the Dutch. The Belgians and the Dutch meanwhile were so anxious to demonstrate to Hitler their neutrality that they did not even discuss defence with the Allies, and between them they only had about 26 divisions.

Germany's strategist, General von Manstein, correctly summed up the Allies' thoughts and expectations, and evolved a plan that was to lead to an even more spectacular victory than the swift conquest of Poland. To carry out Manstein's plan, OKH C-in-C Brauchitsch formed three Army Groups – Group B in the north, under Bock; Group C under Leeb in the south (a small group of 19 divisions spread along the double fortifications of the Maginot and Siegfried Lines); and the main Army Group A under Rundstedt in the centre, comprising over 45 divisions and the mass of the German armoured divisions.

The *blitzkrieg* on West Europe began before dawn on May 10th with the usual massive Luftwaffe attacks on Holland and Belgium. An added element was the dropping of German paratroops on Dutch airfields and bridges. This alone almost defeated Holland – their airforce was paralysed and their intentions to cut off the invaders by flooding the lowlands and blowing up the bridges were nullified by the rapid capture of key points by the paratroopers. Army Group B's Eighteenth Army swept into Holland and drove the Dutch back into a tight rectangle between Amsterdam and Rotterdam. The Queen and the Government left for England (13th), while three French Armies and the B.E.F. began their predicted move northwards to help. On the 14th the Luftwaffe smashed the centre of Rotterdam to rubble, causing over 30,000 civilian casualties. The Dutch could do nothing else but surrender.

Belgium fared little better. Their great hopes lay in the obstacle of the Albert Canal, and the "impregnable" fortress of Eben Emael near Liège. But on the 10th German gliders landed on top of the fortress, their troops attacked the air vents and turrets, and the next day the fortress surrendered. The dispirited Belgians fell back to join the B.E.F. between Antwerp and north of Brussels, but by the 16th these two cities had been abandoned to the invaders.

All this was exactly as Manstein had predicted it would be, and in fact it was a minor part of Germany's drive for her real objective, France. For while the French, British and Belgians thought they were fiercely defending France, Rundstedt's massive army ploughed through Luxembourg and southern Belgium, and approached France through the "impassable" Ardennes. The nucleus of this Army Group, on which the whole of Manstein's plan depended, was List's Twelfth Army, and specifically Lt. Gen. Kleist's Panzer Group, consisting of two Panzer Korps. Commanding the XIX Panzer Korps of three Panzer Divisions, was Guderian. By the 14th, the Meuse had been crossed on secure, unchallenged bridgeheads and there was a 50 mile gap in the thin French line between Sedan and Dinant/Namur, where Hoth's Panzer Korps had also crossed the Meuse. At Sedan, Guderian saw his chance to carry out Panzer warfare as he knew it could be waged. Kleist was anxious to consolidate in the more traditional manner, but with Rundstedt's backing, Guderian moved forward again. By the 18th, he had reached the old Somme battlefields near St. Quentin, well into France while the Allies were still falling back through Belgium.

Gamelin was replaced by the even more aged Weygand, de Gaulle tried counter attacks behind Guderian's leading groups, and the French and British attempted a link-up through the German lines west of St. Quentin on the

Exuberant German officers interrogate a Dutch officer. In only four days, almost a quarter of the Dutch army was killed or wounded. A large part of Rotterdam was wiped out by bombing on the day Holland surrendered.

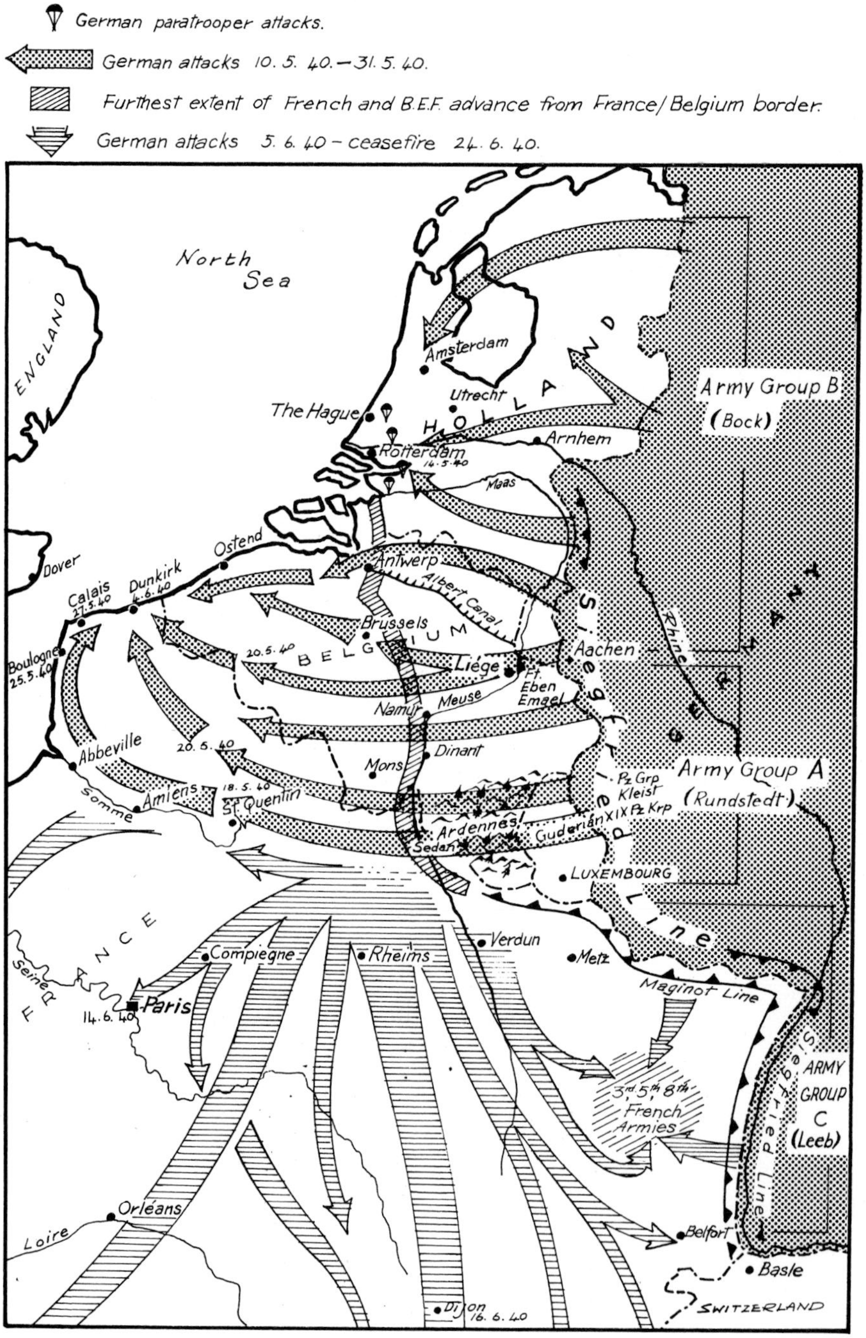

German paratrooper attacks.

German attacks 10. 5. 40.—31. 5. 40.

Furthest extent of French and B.E.F. advance from France/Belgium border.

German attacks 5. 6. 40 – ceasefire 24. 6. 40.

North Sea
ENGLAND
HOLLAND
Amsterdam
Utrecht
The Hague
Rotterdam 14. 5. 40
Arnhem
Maas
Army Group B (Bock)
Dover
Calais 27. 5. 40
Dunkirk 4. 6. 40
Ostend
Antwerp
Albert Canal
Brussels
BELGIUM
20. 5. 40
Boulogne 25. 5. 40
Liége
Ft. Eben Emael
Aachen
Rhine
Siegfried Line
GERMANY
Namur
Meuse
Dinant
Abbeville
20. 5. 40
Mons
Pz Grp Kleist
Army Group A (Rundstedt)
Amiens
18. 5. 40
St. Quentin
Somme
Ardennes
Guderian XIX Pz Krp
Sedan
LUXEMBOURG
FRANCE
Verdun
Metz
Compiegne
Rheims
Seine
Paris
14. 6. 40
Maginot Line
3rd, 5th, 8th French Armies
ARMY GROUP C (Leeb)
Orléans
Loire
Belfort
Basle
Dijon 16. 6. 40
SWITZERLAND

21st. By then Guderian had reached the English Channel, and the rest of the Panzer divisions in Army Group A had drawn a thick band of German armour across France from the Ardennes to the coast. Rundstedt halted the Panzers until OKH authorised further advances, but although Guderian's 2nd Panzer Division took Boulogne on the 25th, and the pocket of resistance at Calais fell to the 1st Panzer Division on the 27th, Rundstedt did not send his tanks further north along the coast. The first major stage in Hitler's conquest of Western Europe had almost ended. The German army began to consolidate its gains, and tighten the clamp around the French, the British and the Belgians caught between the Belgian border and the German armour north of the Somme.

The "squeezing" of the Allied forces against the Channel coast, instead of trying to encircle them, gave the French forces south of the Somme a breathing space; and it also enabled the British to rescue 338,226 of its best-trained soldiers from the beaches of Dunkirk. The British escape was a blot on Germany's perfect manoeuvring in Europe. It probably did not bother the war leaders that much, though they should have taken heed of the Luftwaffe's losses and its inability to disrupt the Dunkirk operation. Anyway, Belgium surrendered on the 28th, and no-one in the German H.Q. thought the rest of France would take long to give in.

It didn't. The French soldiers were demoralised and had scant faith in their ancient high-command. The remaining British and other Allies had little equipment and unity – those that could escape did, before Cherbourg fell, and the rest were soon captured. With Europe from the Somme to the North Cape in their hands, the German commanders prepared the final attack on France. Army Group C actually managed to get through the Maginot Line, by using imagination and daring, two forces against which Maginot had built no defence. Army Group B had Kleist leading a Panzer Group on the western flank, while in Army Group A, in the middle, Guderian had been given his own Panzer Group. Two and a half million confident, victorious Germans faced Weygand's one and a half million dejected French troops along a line from the mouth of the Somme to the Swiss border, only half of which was prepared for defence.

The German attack began on the 5th of June. For a few days the French held firm. Then the Panzers broke through near Rheims, and other holes were rapidly knocked through the French lines. Some of Guderian's Panzer Divisions raced for the Swiss border and trapped three whole French Armies against the Maginot Line and the advancing German Army Group C. The French Government declared Paris an open city on the 12th, and fled to Bordeaux. By the 14th, the Germans were in Paris. By the 19th, Cherbourg, Brest, Orleans, Nantes, Dijon, Nevers and Saumur were behind German lines.

With the defeat of France inevitable, Italy had declared war on France on the 10th. Churchill tried to persuade Reynaud's Government to escape France and form a union with England. But most French had lost their will to resist anymore, and led by Pétain and Laval, the pro-surrender faction held sway. Reynaud resigned, Italy made an ineffective attempt to break through French lines on the Alps, and on the 22nd France surrendered to Germany. The tame and obedient French Government ran southern France from Vichy after hostilities ended on the 24th, while Paris, the Channel coast and the northern half of France was occupied by Germany. The whole coast of Western Europe, from the Bay of Biscay to the North Cape, was in Germany's control, and Britain was only a few miles away across the Channel.

If the French commanders had been a little more imaginative, if there were fewer who had thought only of the standing, slamming, battering tactics of the Great War, the Ardennes might have been held. Its terrain would have made it easy to stop an armoured assault. But that would not have persuaded Hitler to abandon France, and what would have followed would simply have been a longer, harder, bloodier campaign which would have killed thousands more, and perhaps have resulted in heavy bombing of Paris. France's defeat was inevitable; but the terrible swiftness of it, the creation of the Vichy Government, and then the readiness of the French Navy to change allegiance, gave the fall of France a different kind of bitter sadness.

2. THE BATTLE OF BRITAIN
10th July–17th September 1940

Hitler disclosed to Army Chiefs his plans for 1941 invasion of Russia (31st). Italy invaded Somaliland (5th August). Russia annexed the Baltic States (3rd–6th). Italian troops entered Egypt, and massed on the Albania/Greece border (September).

The rapid fall of France, in Hitler's eyes, should have been enough to point out to "Churchill and the English" that some agreement would have to be reached with Germany. If that wasn't enough, an assurance that he would respect the British Empire should have allowed him, Hitler thought, a free hand in Europe. But Churchill made no such move, even if some Englishmen in high places were having conciliatory considerations; and so, to the dismay of his commanders, Hitler decided that Germany would have to invade and conquer Britain. The army commanders viewed the prospect with misgivings, for none of their troops had practised sea-borne invasions, and no-one had even considered such a gigantic undertaking – all German plans were for a Continental war. Admiral Raeder was alarmed at the thought of having to provide an invasion fleet and also keep the might of the whole Royal Navy at bay. Only the bombastic Goering offered little resistance – especially when Hitler declared that an invasion's success depended on control of the air. The Luftwaffe, Goering was eager to show, could lead Germany to victory over Britain.

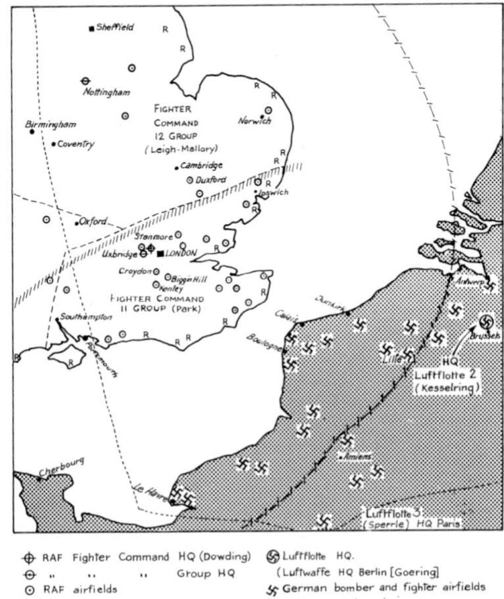

RAF Fighter Command HQ (Dowding)
" " " Group HQ
RAF airfields
R Radar stations —/—/—/ range
----- Command boundaries
Luftflotte HQ. (Luftwaffe HQ Berlin [Goering]
German bomber and fighter airfields
----- Command boundaries
///////// German fighter range

The army and navy leaders began preparations, somewhat relieved that everything now depended on the Luftwaffe.

All the same, it was the 10th of July before Hitler gave up hope of reaching agreement with Churchill, and then the Battle of Britain began with heavy bomber attacks on convoys in the English Channel. Even this was only a perfunctory start, designed to gauge the R.A.F.'s protective capacity. On the 16th of July, Hitler issued Directive No. 16 for Operation Sealion – the landing on and occupation of England. This called for preparations to be completed by mid-August – a hopeless task, considering that thousands of vessels had to be assembled from all over Europe and fitted out, and that troops had to be trained, strategy and plans worked out. Hitler agreed to put back Sealion by a couple of weeks, and it was really not until Directive No. 17 of the 1st of August that Germany's Supreme Commander ordered the intensification of air warfare against Britain to begin. August the 5th was to be the real start of the battle for supremacy of the air.

By that time, Goering had assembled over 2,800 aircraft for the task – a total numerical superiority over all England's planes, but since bombers could hardly defend Britain, the R.A.F. really had to face this vast Luftwaffe force with its 700 or so fighters. An important point, though, was that Britain was being rapidly geared into full-scale war economy, with production facilities assigned primarily towards military requirements. Although Germany had been spending heavily on armaments for many years, she had still not intensified war production to cope with losses. Until Speer arrived, German industry and the German economy was run on much the same lines as in the "peace" period of Hitler's rule. When losses on both sides became heavy, the difference in aircraft production capabilities was to prove extremely important.

A second vital factor helped redress the balance of power – this was radar, a British invention and one in which they were streets ahead of anyone else, to the extent that it is doubtful whether the German leaders even knew what sort of advantage it gave the defenders. Radar gave Britain warning of attacks, their approach direction, and the approximate size of the attacking force. The appropriate stations could then be alerted, and a defence planned in advance. There was therefore no need for the R.A.F. to fly search sorties, or to remain on tense stand-by for long, exhausting periods. Their fighters could be aloft for far longer sorties during the battle, and the pilots could have proper "rest and recovery" intervals between attacks. German fighters, on the other hand, were only able to be over the south of England for a very short time (10 minutes over London) if they were to have enough fuel to return to Calais. There was therefore far more planning involved in the German attacks, and so much hinged on everything going right if the flights of bombers were not to be left without fighter protection and devastated.

Intensive attacks on Channel convoys marked the first week of August in an attempt to draw out R.A.F. fighters, but the British simply stopped the convoys. Then on the 13th nearly 1,500 aircraft were sent over South East England with orders to destroy the R.A.F. fighter bases. The Battle of Britain was on in earnest. Radar ensured that the British fighters were in an attacking position before the Luftwaffe waves even reached their targets, and they lost 45 planes to the R.A.F.'s 13. But serious damage was caused to two fighter stations, and to a number of radar stations. Attacks continued that night, but one of the war's many lessons was being learnt – that it takes an enormous number of bombs to destroy something irreparably, and that when attacks stop, a great deal of repair work can be managed in a short time. When new flights of Luftwaffe bombers and fighters approached, there were always R.A.F. fighters waiting for them.

Goering had based his forecast of victory on simple arithmetic and even simpler predictions – he knew nothing of Air Marshal Sir Hugh Dowding, C-in-C of Fighter Command, or of the extremely effective team he had built up precisely to meet the armada being launched against England. The radar stations and groups of spotters were linked by highly efficient communications to the Fighter Command Group H.Q.s where decisions were taken to deploy fighter forces from stations in the threatened Group. The two Fighter Command Groups

The advanced use of radar enabled R.A.F. Fighter Command to "scramble" its Hurricanes (as here) and Spitfires in time for them to reach ideal attacking positions.

which bore the brunt of the attacks were 11 Group under Air Vice-Marshal Park, which had the vital south-east sector, and 12 Group under Air Vice-Marshal Leigh-Mallory covering East Anglia and central England. The close co-operation and understanding between these commanders, and the unobtrusive but reassuring presence of Dowding at Fighter Command H.Q. gave the whole of R.A.F. Fighter Command a dedication and an efficient flexibility which was never matched by the German air force.

So it was that when Goering threw a massive assault on the 15th, it still did not achieve its aims. Luftwaffe forces from Scandinavia to Cherbourg, totalling some 1,800 aircraft were sent to smash the fighter airfields. Goering figured that R.A.F. reinforcements would be sent south, opening the skies to his bombers from Norwegian airfields. The attack in the north did not succeed – the first wave lost 15 aircraft and caused little damage. A second attack by 50 bombers caused more damage, but 10 bombers were pursued and shot down on their way back to base. In the south, the sheer numbers of bombers almost swamped Fighter Command's controllers – but the numbers also confused the Luftwaffe, and co-ordination broke down, preventing the single massive attack which might have caused enormous damage. As it was, the R.A.F. was tested to the limit; many bases and radar installations were badly damaged, but the Southern Groups 11 and 10, reinforced by 12, accounted for over 50 planes. The R.A.F. lost 34 planes that day to the Luftwaffe's total of 76.

The next day, August the 16th, Goering once more sent out well over 1,000 planes, but made his first major mistake. Confidently believing his pilots' estimates of the number of planes they had shot down, Goering calculated that the R.A.F. must have almost run out of fighters. Never entirely sure of the role of the radar stations, he then assumed they would play even less of a role with "so few" fighters left. He decided not to divert bombers to the radar stations, but to concentrate on airfields. The constant fierce resistance surprised him and shocked his pilots. By the 26th, the Luftwaffe had lost 602 planes against nearly 260 lost by the R.A.F. (Both sides at this stage were buoyed by excessive estimates of the others' losses.) Another break in the pattern occurred after some German bombers had (accidentally, as it turned out) bombed London. On 25th August the R.A.F. retaliated by bombing Berlin. This infuriated Hitler, and he decided that London should be made a major target.

Towards the end of August, and early September, the Luftwaffe very nearly won the Battle. Losses were high on both sides, but Fighter Command was critically short of pilots, and almost running short of planes (though experienced pilots were always to be in far shorter supply). Between the 1st and the 5th of September, 11 major raids were made on Fighter Command airfields and on aircraft factories.

Then Hitler ordered the Blitz on London. With some relief, Goering's commanders agreed that this was a much better target. Goering accepted the change – convinced that little could remain of Fighter Command at this stage – and on the 7th of September the first major attack on London was launched. The attacks lasted most of the afternoon, and went on all night, guided by the fires of the burning East End. They continued on the 8th, . . . and again and again London shook beneath the Luftwaffe's bombs. Fighter Command, however, was freed – airfields were put back into fully operational condition, the radar network was brought back to maximum efficiency, and the aircraft factories began to turn out more and more Hurricanes and Spitfires.

On 15th September came the decisive, massive daylight raid on London. London suffered badly, but it was a sacrificial suffering. The R.A.F. shot down 56 planes, and the morale of the Luftwaffe pilots slumped as they realised the R.A.F. was very far from beaten. As if to rub it in, that night R.A.F. bombers carried out highly destructive raids on the tightly packed barges and small ships in harbours from Boulogne to Antwerp. On the 17th, Hitler realised that Goering had been humiliated, the Luftwaffe had lost, and an invasion would be suicidal. He ordered Sealion postponed indefinitely, and privately cancelled it altogether. The Battle of Britain was over, but the Blitz had begun and over the next months British cities were to suffer from repeated bombing attacks. As grim as that was, the grimmer prospect of invasion had been averted for good. It cost the Luftwaffe over 1,000 planes, to the R.A.F.'s 650. Three thousand Englishmen, Poles, Frenchmen, and young men from the Dominions, had saved Britain.

3. BARBAROSSA—Triumph and Travail in Russia 22.6.41–24.9.42

U.S.A., Britain and Holland placed embargo on oil supplies to Japan, and U.S.A. froze Japanese assets (26–28th July). Churchill and Roosevelt drew up

When Hitler ordered Goering to attack London, the Luftwaffe was unaware how close it had come to wearing down the R.A.F. The Blitz gave Fighter Command a vitally needed break, and the Battle of Britain was won.

Atlantic Charter (9th August). Gen. Tojo made Prime Minister of Japan (16th October). Strong Allied offensives in Libya (18–26th November). Japanese aircraft attacked U.S. Pacific Fleet in Pearl Harbor and launched offensives throughout Pacific and Far East, declaring war on U.S.A. and Britain (7th December). Germany declared war on U.S.A. (11th). Twenty-six countries signed the United Nations Pact, pledging defeat of the members of the Tripartite Pact (1st January 1942). German heavy surface fleet made successful Channel dash from Brest to Baltic (12th February). Singapore surrendered (15th). U.S. Army on Bataan surrendered (9th April). Malta awarded the George Cross. Battle of Coral Sea (3rd May). First "1,000 bomber raid" by R.A.F. over Germany hit Cologne (30th). U.S. beat Japan in sea Battle of Midway (4th June). Tobruk surrendered to Rommel (21st). U.S. Marines landed on Guadalcanal (7th August). Canadians and British made disastrous raid on Dieppe (19th). Rommel made unsuccessful attack on Montgomery's 8th Army in Battle of Alam Halfa (7th September).

Since neither Hitler nor Stalin were types to feel bound by their signatures on treaties of friendship and alliance, their Non-Aggression Pact of August 1939 was probably signed with as little honourable intent as any Pact in history. Both doubtless intended it to have short-term power, and this was made more certain by the simultaneous secret agreement to share the spoils of Poland's imminent defeat. Hitler had looked eastwards almost since he first had a political thought, for in the east lay the only possible land for Germany's "essential *lebensraum*". The lands of Poland were no less attractive than the endless storehouse of the Ukraine. Any scruples Hitler may have had about appropriating this land would have been easily swept away by his classification of Bolsheviks as only slightly less reprehensible than Polish Jews. His agreement with Russia was no more than a device to ensure his eastern border while he dealt with the inconvenient powers, France and Britain, which insisted on containing his eastern ambitions. The persistence shown by Britain necessitated the hasty, and probably hopeless, attempt to prepare an invasion. Even while this was being planned, Hitler was looking over his shoulder towards his real ambitions, and his comparatively mild reproaches over the Luftwaffe's failure to permit Operation Sealion to be launched mirrored his anxiety to grab the eastern lands before Russia built up a formidable military strength and made even greater demands from, or overtures towards Hungary, Rumania and Bulgaria – all, in Hitler's eyes, rightfully his own, despite the agreements of 1939.

Hitler's anxiety even made the Russian case an exception from his often-expressed "no two-front war", and his Directive No. 21 of 18th December 1940 emphasised that Russia might have to be crushed before the war against England was over. Strictly speaking, the war against England was, at that time, hardly a "front". There were no possibilities of an Allied landing, provided a few troops guarded the shores. Europe was conquered, and Hitler had a vast war machine "oiled and running". He decided, in Directive 21, to use it against Russia on 15th May 1941.

Hitler's objective, apart from simply destroying the Russian army, air force and navy, was "to erect a barrier against Asiatic Russia along the general line from the Volga to Archangel". Russian bombers would not then be able to reach into Germany itself, while the remaining Russian industry in the Urals could be wiped out by the Luftwaffe. First targets for the Army Groups (to be split into North and South on either side of the Pripet Marshes) were to be Leningrad and Kronstadt, and the Baltic area; and, south of the Marshes, the Ukraine west of the Dnieper. Second targets were Moscow for the North Group, and the Donetz Basin for the South.

But a number of loose ends had to be tied up before "Barbarossa" could be launched. Hitler's Russian aims hastened his **alliance with Japan**. Japan's own ambitions would keep pressure on Britain by the threat to her colonies. But Hitler foresaw that those ambitions could also involve America in the war – something he was anxious to avoid. Offsetting that potential disadvantage, was the realisation that a belligerent Japan would force Russia to keep large forces on her eastern borders, and already Russia and Japan had clashed a number of times on the easily-disputed Manchurian and Mongolian borders. In the end, however, disregarding Hitler's attempts to steer Japan differently, Japan "helped" in the downfall of Germany – her Pacific moves took pressure off Russia and even resulted in a pact between them. And it brought the U.S.A. into the European war.

Even more pressing, though, were the **Mediterranean and Balkan problems**. A strong British influence in the eastern Mediterranean would threaten Hitler's intended southern "Russian" frontier. More effort therefore had to go into driving Britain out of Africa (a task obviously well beyond the capabilities of the Italians). Then Mussolini had further complicated the position by invading Greece, and immediately suffering humiliating reversals back into Albania. Plainly a Balkan campaign had to precede the great attack on Russia, and in early 1941 five divisions (three of them armoured) were sent south. Pressure was successfully put on Hungary to join forces with Germany, and Yugoslavia also fell in line. But two days later Hitler's plans were knocked awry by the **Yugoslav coup** and rejection of Germany. In fury, Hitler ordered the destruction of Belgrade, and Yugoslavia joined Greece (her resistance stiffened by British troops from North Africa) on the list of Germany's targets.

Some have doubted the extent to which Mussolini's attack on Greece upset Hitler's invasion of Russia. Cer-

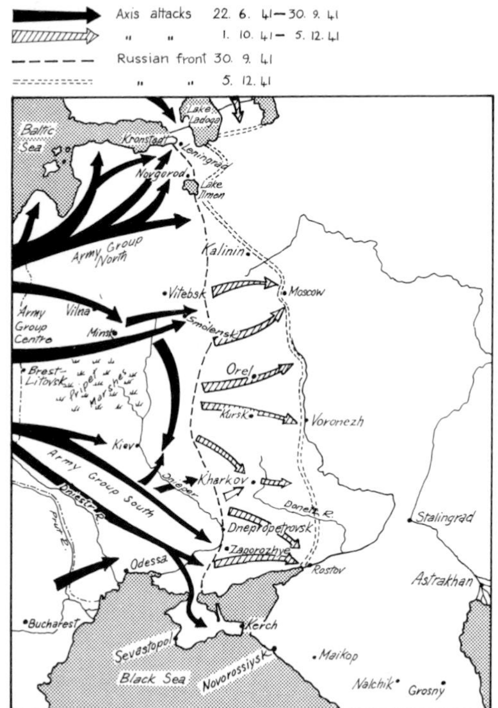

tainly it was more than likely that Germany would have become involved in some Balkan offensive before Barbarossa, regardless of Italy's timing. What is also certain, however, is that the unexpected and heroic resistance of Yugoslavia, and the desperate defence of Greece and then Crete by the Greeks, British and New Zealanders, caused considerable disruption to the German war machine, even if this machine did crush everything in its path. The five divisions originally allocated to the south in February, had by May grown to 25 – out of a total commitment in the east by then of 87. Such a distraction postponed Barbarossa four weeks, and then another week, as the Balkan divisions moved back to the Russian borders. The Balkan campaign, apart from the loss of a fair amount of equipment, and the almost total destruction in Crete of Germany's only highly trained paratroop division, had cost Hitler five weeks. Not much, perhaps, in a campaign that was only to reach a really decisive stage after 15 months; but seldom can five weeks have had such far reaching effects, for they meant that when winter came the German armies would be in positions that they should have passed through in autumn at the latest – and that was to make all the difference.

One of the strangest aspects of the development of Barbarossa was the Russian mood. Despite his own total lack of integrity, and all the evidence that pointed to a similar characteristic in Adolf Hitler, Stalin had extraordinary trust in the good faith of Germany and the Nazis (and in spite of the history of Nazi brutalities towards Communists). There was perhaps reason for some complacency in the Kremlin. Although his murderous purges of the 30s had left Stalin with a lack of experienced military and social leaders, the new order was rapidly finding its feet. The shameful showing against Finland had been avenged, Japan had been dealt a few very hard blows by Zhukov and the crack Russian mountain troops in the east, and the "imperialists and capitalists" of Western Europe, along with the "war-mongering" British, were being firmly put in their place. Russia had also gained over 70,000 useful square miles of former Polish territory, along with the very desirable former Baltic States. It also looked as if much of Rumania would be in the Kremlin's pocket.

But even these pleasant conditions should not have been enough to so totally blind Stalin to the obvious German preparations for attack. It is impossible to mass some 150 divisions and nearly 3,000 aircraft along a front, even a very long one, without a number of people noticing it. Many did, and the Kremlin was assuredly, reliably and honestly informed by its own intelligence sources, and by repeated warnings and explanations from Britain and America, that Germany was going to attack Russia. Stalin was even told the probable date. None of it seemed to make the least impression, except to cause Stalin to make scathing remarks about the imperialist countries who wanted to involve Russia in their wars. (One of the war's many bitter ironies is the speed with which Stalin changed his outbursts against the west into demands that the west should provide Russia with massive assistance of every sort, regardless of the cost in lives or materials.)

Apart from expressing concern to Berlin over the wide – "but obviously untrue" – rumours of a hostile German attitude, Russia did nothing to alert her 120 or so divisions near the western front (another 66 were in the east, and elsewhere). When Count Schulenburg delivered the declaration of war to Molotov on the morning of 22nd June 1941, Germany had already bombed ten Russian villages, and an artillery barrage had been in action for some hours. The Russians were caught hopelessly unprepared.

The attack was launched through three main thrusts, differing only slightly from Directive 21: Leeb's Army Group North (C) from East Prussia north-eastwards to the Baltic States, and towards Leningrad; Bock's Army Group Centre (B) from northern Poland past the Pripet Marshes towards Minsk and Smolensk; and, under Rundstedt, Army Group South (A) from southern Poland to the Ukraine and Kiev, and from Rumania towards Odessa. The Luftwaffe was as devastatingly efficient as the Army, and well over 1,000 Russian planes were knocked out of action within 24 hours – most of them while still on the ground. Armoured divisions penetrated up to 50 miles in the same 24 hours, and 10,000 Russians were taken prisoner.

These advances were maintained to the extent that by the end of July it seemed certain that the Germans would be celebrating Christmas in the capital. Huge numbers of Russians were taken prisoner when Minsk fell early in July to Bock's Army – which reached Smolensk less than a month later. The Finns swept down the Karelian isthmus and threatened Leningrad from the north, while Leeb's Army Group North attacked the city's approaches from the south. Rundstedt, in the south, was well into the Ukraine and approaching Kiev.

The mood of elation, however, did not persist throughout the army command, and already the Germans were facing bitter truths and making their first mistakes. Some of the truths arose from their mistakes. Hitler saw the Russian war, as he repeatedly told his commanders, as a clash of ideologies, as much as a quest for *lebensraum*. This induced a dedicated approach to annihilation, an approach made so much simpler for the Nazis by the fact that Russia was not a signatory of the international agreements governing the conduct of war, or the treatment of prisoners. On the 14th of June, Hitler had issued instructions that the war was to be conducted with "a ferocity previously unknown", and he emphasised that no-one should hesitate to use the harshest methods available in the rapid and total achievement of objectives. Special SS squads were set up to comb out all traces of Bolshevik leadership and followings, and to murder those that were found, or send them to the death camps. Russian prisoners of war were required for labour only, if at all, and their feeding was not something that was meant to unduly concern anyone, unless there were adequate food stocks remaining after Germanic people had been adequately fed.

Apart from the revolting barbarity of such attitudes (which most of the army fell in with, no matter what their later protestations were), they were also politically foolish. There were many hundreds of thousands of people of all types in former White Russia and the Ukraine who initially welcomed the Germans as an inevitably pleasant contrast from the harsh rule of Stalin.

In the summer of 1941 Germany launched its fourth massive attack on an unsuspecting country – this time Russia. And for the fourth time German soldiers, such as these Waffen SS troops, enjoyed the exhilaration of rapid conquest. But the cocky self-confidence was soon to ebb, and it would never reappear.

When they found that life under Hitler was even more brutal and precarious, their astonishment turned to fury. As word of the German atrocities spread to unconquered territories, resistance began to stiffen, while in the devastated, sacked areas behind the German lines, partisan groups of extraordinary daring sprang up and caused frequent supply disruptions. By their inhuman treatment of the Russians, the Germans also made it inevitable that when roles were reversed, they would suffer the same barbarities from the comrades of their victims.

In the north, the Germans also came up against the intense devotion of other Russians to their country – a devotion that made the most staggering hardships bearable. After the swift collapse of hundreds of thousands of soldiers and civilians in the west, the Germans were nonplussed by this fanatical, often suicidal resistance. Leningrad would simply not give in – even when it was finally entirely cut off by land from the rest of Russia by the fall of Schlusselburg, on the shore of Lake Ladoga, at the end of August.

By the time **Leningrad was entirely besieged** (but for the treacherous route across the lake) Hitler had made one of his bigger blunders of the war. The original Directive had put Moscow as a secondary aim, but the speed with which it was being approached made the generals consider going straight ahead and capturing it. The capture of Moscow could, after all, have hastened the collapse of the rest of Russia. Apart from its war industries, it was the major communications centre and it obviously had enormous psychological significance. Hitler, however, wanted to make sure of the Ukraine first . . . but Halder and Brauchitsch dreaded being caught, like Napoleon, outside Moscow in winter . . . the arguments went on until August the 21st, when Hitler, as usual, solved the problem by issuing his requests as orders. While Leeb kept hammering away at Leningrad, Bock had to send some of his armoured divisions south to form a pincer around Kiev with Rundstedt's left flank. The rest of Army Group Centre strengthened their supply lines, repaired equipment, and waited.

The pincer in the Ukraine was awesomely successful. It enclosed and captured around Kiev some 650,000 Russians. Hitler was ecstatic as this enormous force trudged westwards to their lingering deaths, while Bock's armour rejoined Army Group B and overhauled its tanks. Then Hitler at last came around to his generals' point of view, and in October the drive for Moscow resumed – along with the drive for the Crimea, the Donetz Basin, and the Caucasus.

October, however, was too late to take this decision. Halder had been depressed to note that while they reckoned there were 120 divisions facing Germany in June, over 350 had been identified since then. Set against the enormous manpower resources of Russia, the loss of the 650,000 soldiers at Kiev was insignificant. A foretaste of what might be expected at Moscow was given by the extraordinary resilience of Leningrad before the full weight of Army Group North's assault. Worst of all for Germany were two unknown developments: the pause before Moscow gave the Russians time to organise its defences, under the guidance of Zhukov (who had already turned Leningrad into a fortress); and an early winter was rapidly approaching.

The bite of winter made itself felt with early snow and rapidly falling temperatures – which showed up a fatal oversight caused by over-confidence. With a full Russian winter almost on them, and thousands of miles from home, the German army was without winter clothing or special equipment to deal with mud, snow, ice, and sub-zero temperatures. It is a testament to the extraordinary determination and hardiness of the German soldiers that in absolutely atrocious conditions, when often even tanks could hardly move, they managed to push closer and closer to Moscow, causing panic in the city and sending the Government fleeing. A pincer movement got half-way round; some Germans in the outskirts of the capital could see the distant spires of the Kremlin, and then the Russian resistance, and temperatures of below −30°C finally halted the German army. But five weeks earlier . . . ?

The army commanders knew they were in a very dangerous position, but they at least thought a short retreat would set them up for a renewed Spring offensive. Stalin, however, had received reports from his intelligence service that Japanese attentions had become firmly fixed on the Pacific, and that America and Britain, rather than Russia, were to be the victims. This time Stalin believed his reports and Zhukov immediately brought to Moscow superbly efficient forces, well-equipped and fresh, from the east. On the 6th December he flung this powerful, totally unexpected weapon at the Germans. It was the end of the German bid for Moscow.

The Russian winter offensive did not last very long, but it relieved Moscow, and the rest of winter gave the Russians adequate time to build up their line for a Spring attack. All the conditions and circumstances which helped Russia hindered Germany, whose armies were unaccustomed to Russian winters, whose supply lines were long and complex, and whose front-line, the further they advanced, grew longer and thinner. Russia's Spring counter-attack drove back the German army, especially in the north, though it was unable to shake the stranglehold on Leningrad where Küchler, replacing Leeb, had instructions to annihilate the city and its occupants. Thousands of Russian soldiers died trying to break the siege, where thousands of civilians were dying of hunger, cold and in the bombardments every week.

In the south, Russian counter-attacks were less destructive, though Kharkov was briefly taken. Attempts to relieve Sevastopol were fruitless, and cost 100,000 taken prisoner. Then the Germans launched their Spring offensive – 240,000 of Timoshenko's Kharkov army were captured – and the major **drive for the Caucasus** was on.

Right: map showing offensives in Russia, 1942.

The German lines north of about Kursk were put on the defensive, and Army Group South became the focus of attention. It was split into Groups A (furthest south) and B.

Initial advances were again rapid. The territory east of Kharkov was retaken and the German forces pushed towards Voronezh on the Don. Further south, Rostov fell to Army Group A where Kleist's I Panzer Army formed the spearhead. After Voronezh, Army Group B headed across the "Donetz Corridor" towards Stalingrad, with Paulus leading the 6th Army. On his left flank was Hoth's IV Panzer Army and the 2nd Army, mainly of Italian troops. As Group B neared Stalingrad, industrial giant of the south on the broad Volga, Hitler made an absurd move by ordering Hoth's Panzer Army south to form an east flank for Kleist's Panzer Army in its bid to capture the Caucasus oilfields and reach the Caspian Sea. This movement of a whole army across the front of another, advancing army (Paulus' 6th) caused considerable chaos and delay. Eventually Paulus reached the approach to Stalingrad – and then Hoth was ordered north again, this time as a right flank on the Stalingrad attack.

Army Group A, with the Crimean Kerch Peninsula captured, got as far as the foothills of the Caucasus Mountains, and almost made it as far east as Grozny (but the Maikop oilfields had been destroyed by the Russians). Army Group B almost cleared Stalingrad right to the Volga border . . .but this was **the end of Barbarossa**. Having still failed to take Leningrad, having so nearly got Moscow, Hitler resolved to get Stalingrad, a city whose name alone made it a priority target. In Paulus, Hitler had a commander with the right requirement of servile obedience to persist beyond the point of military necessity or sensibility; Hitler simply said "no retreat". But the German Army in Russia had lost its initiative, its strength, much of its will, and almost all its belief in the inferiority of the Russians – at any rate as combat troops. Paulus was in a sacrificial position against the immovable obstacle of Stalingrad. Further south, Kleist was too far away from home, too exhausted, and simply too wèak to make the final steps needed to break through over the Caucasus.

By the end of September 1942, the Germans had seen as much of Russia as they were going to – except on long marches as prisoners of war. The last person to admit this, or even consider it, was naturally Hitler, and his final denial of reason and truth came when he sacked Halder on the 24th September, in a rage against the Staff Chief's constant, accurate assessments and warnings. Halder's warnings conjured up the spectre of defeat before Hitler's eyes, a spectre Hitler could never tolerate. But the image was about to become the reality.

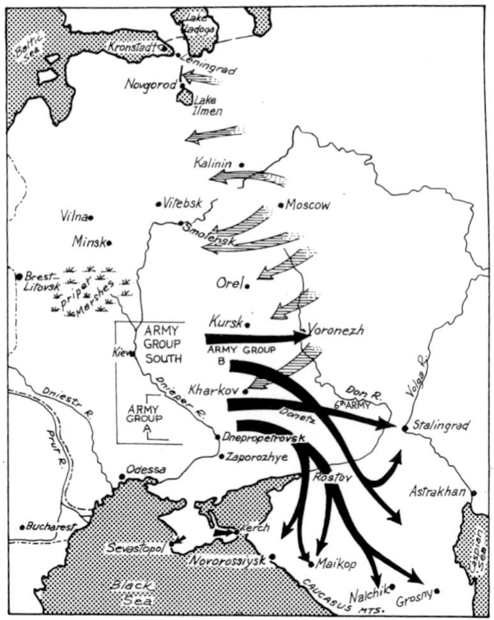

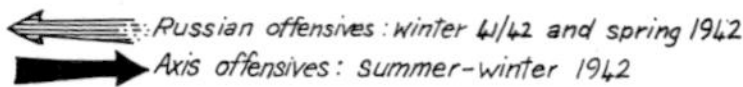

4. JAPAN'S COLONIAL AMBITIONS—
Pearl Harbor to Midway 7.12.41–7.6.42

Germans attempted final assault on Moscow, but were driven back by strong Russian counter-attack. (1st–6th December.) Allies drove Axis forces out of Cyrenaica and relieved Tobruk (2nd–9th). Germany declared war on U.S.A. (11th). Hitler took over as Commander-in-Chief of German Army from Brauchitsch (19th). Twenty-six countries signed the United Nations Pact (1st January 1942). German heavy fleet made successful Channel dash from Brest to Baltic (12th February). Malta awarded the George Cross (April). Germans captured Kerch Peninsula in Crimea (16th May). Russian counter-attack on Kharkov resulted in their defeat in a pincer trap (19th). Axis launched new attack across Gazala Line south of Tobruk (26th). 1,000 bomber raid on Cologne by R.A.F. (30th). Rommel's offensive in North Africa intensified (1st June).

Many of the elements which acted as catalysts to set off the Nazi explosion in Europe were also present in Japan at much the same time, and gave very similar results. The

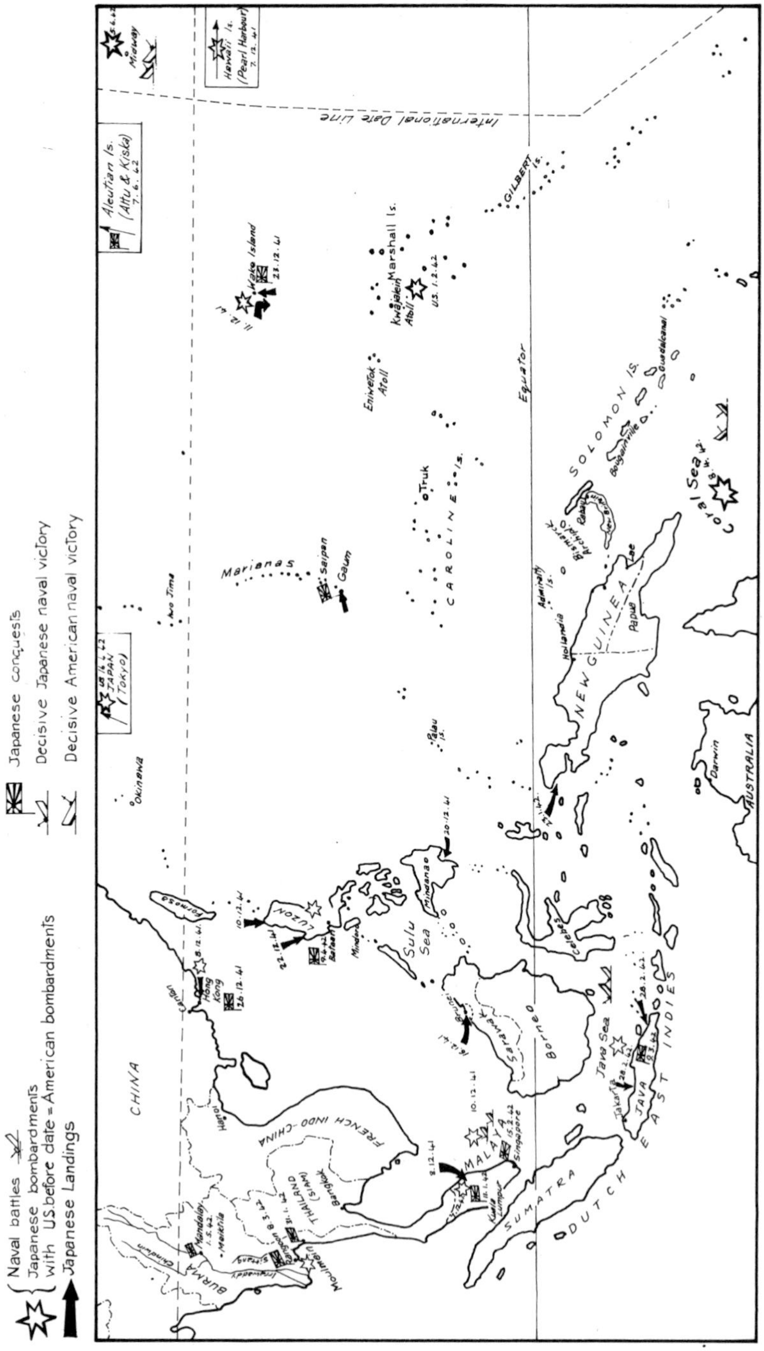
Naval battles
Japanese bombardments
with US. before date = American bombardments
Japanese Landings
Japanese conquests
Decisive Japanese naval victory
Decisive American naval victory
Midway
5.6.42
Hawaii Is.
(Pearl Harbour)
7.12.41
International Date Line
Aleutian Is.
(Attu & Kiska)
7.6.42
Wake Island
23.12.41
11.12.41
Marshall Is.
Kwajalein
Atoll
US 1.2.42
GILBERT IS.
Eniwetok
Atoll
Equator
SOLOMON IS.
Guadalcanal
Bougainville
Coral Sea
Marianas
Saipan
Guam
Iwo Jima
Truk
CAROLINE IS.
Admiralty Is.
Lae
NEW GUINEA
Papua
Hollandia
JAPAN
(Tokyo)
Palau Is.
Okinawa
Darwin
AUSTRALIA
Formosa
LUZON
10.12.41
22.12.41
Bataan
Mindoro
Mindanao
20.12.41
Sulu Sea
Celebes
Canton
Hong Kong
8.12.41
26.12.41
CHINA
Hanoi
FRENCH INDO-CHINA
THAILAND
(SIAM)
Bangkok
BURMA
Mandalay
Meiktila
Rangoon
Moulmein
Chindwin
Irrawaddy
MALAYA
8.12.41
Kuala Lumpur
Singapore
10.12.41
SUMATRA
DUTCH EAST INDIES
Borneo
Sarawak
Java Sea
JAVA
Jakarta

late 20s and early 30s saw Japan in much the same condition as pre-Hitler Germany . . . mass unemployment, unrest and dissatisfaction. Circumstances were ripe for strong military leadership, and a large number of militarists were ready to sieze the reins. Under an acquiescent Emperor, the military influence swept Japan, began a rejection of Western styles – replacing them with the older Japanese traditions – and put an emphasis on strength, dedication, loyalty and total sacrifice. With a populace burning at last with some unified purpose, the militarists could turn their attention to Japan's other pressing problem – which was their version of *lebensraum*, with a desperate requirement for raw materials. Just as Hitler looked to the open, rich lands of Asia, so Japan coveted the eastern end of the Asian Continent.

By moving into Manchuria in 1931 the Japanese brought themselves to the attention of America through China's appeals to the League of Nations. China had little real basis for complaint, however, since her contribution to Manchuria had been minimal at best. Japan stayed in Manchuria, and for a few years all was quiet. But Manchuria was to Japan only a front garden. What she wanted were the rich orchards – China herself. The hostilities which began the Sino-Japanese war in 1937 stung America as Hitler's annexation of Czechoslovakia was to sting Britain. America had a history of "special concern" for China, and had always advocated recognition of the country and insurance of her boundaries. America's Secretary of State condemned Japan's aggression, but there was little else that could be done. Concern for China was mainly felt by the few internationalists in power. The American people, after the experiences of World War I and the Depression wanted only to get on with their own affairs. To the huge isolationist majority, nothing could be further away than the fighting in the alien hills and plains of China.

The isolationists had their way over affairs nearer home too – Italy invaded Abyssinia, the Spanish Civil War broke out, Europe was threatened by Hitler's sabre-rattling. Yet the Americans (enormous numbers of whom came from countries becoming caught in the grip of fear and apprehension) still wanted to remain uninvolved, and politicians got away with mouthing platitudes.

Nothing could have pleased Japan more, and very soon she began to have even more grandiose designs – the creation of a Greater East Asia Co-Prosperity Sphere, of course with Japan at the centre of it. First, however, China had to be conquered, and the virtual impossibility of this task drove the Japanese to greater and greater barbarities. Chinese cities were bombed and burnt, hundreds of thousands of civilians died in the raids or were even, as in Nanking, deliberately killed. But no matter how much destruction the Japanese spread about them, the Chinese simply withdrew into their vast hinterland, and continued to resist.

Japan's increasing barbarity coincided with Hitler showing his true colours, and when Roosevelt won a third term as U.S. President he was at last able to gradually replace isolationism with internationalism. **America's attitude hardened towards Japan**. Hitler's invasion of Western Europe, and especially the fall of France woke America to the dangers she herself faced, and permitted Roosevelt to become more and more involved in the European war – a gradual escalation from favouring Britain with long-term credit, to the Lend-Lease Bill, to virtually undeclared war when U.S. warships escorted merchant vessels bound for Britain with war material.

Hitler's conquest of Western Europe had given impetus to Japan as well. Her ideas for the **Greater East Asia Co-Prosperity Sphere** (GEACPS) would be much easier to implement without the presence of France, Holland or Britain, all of whom had large colonies in the East, most of them rich in raw materials. The fall of France and the establishment of the puppet French regime paved the way for Japan's "peaceful" occupation of French Indo-China. Pacts were signed with Hitler and with Stalin. Holland was beaten in Europe and could do little against Japan. Only Britain and America kept obstacles erected against Japan's ambitions, and it looked as if Britain would soon be out of it as well. But to every request that America should acknowledge a Japanese "sphere of influence" in the east (as, Japan insisted, she acknowledged America's sphere of interest in South America and the West Indies), America held to her view that any talks or concessions were conditional upon Japan's withdrawal from China, and then also from French Indo-China.

But Japan needed China, and when America began to put sanctions on materials supplied to Japan, Japan needed China even more, and some of the East Indies as well. The oil fields of the Dutch East Indies appealed greatly to Japan and when demands were made for more and more oil and aviation fuel, the exiled Dutch Government appealed to Britain and America to help her resist the Japanese threat. America was still reluctant to take overt steps in any direction, and Britain had enough trouble simply trying to defend her own interests. Bravely, the Dutch made a stand on their own, and severely limited supplies to the Japanese – who were convinced this would only have been done with the guaranteed backing of America and Britain. The situation became increasingly strained as further embargoes were put on Japan, and the future war was guaranteed when an oil embargo was enforced.

Japan would not give up China. To stay in China, Japan needed oil. To get oil, Japan needed to occupy the Dutch East Indies. That could only be done if America and Britain agreed to it, which was highly unlikely, or if the Western powers were prevented from doing anything to stop occupation. This would mean war, and the relatively moderate Premier, Prince Konoye, decided to try to negotiate one last time. A respected and even pro-

The speed and ferocity of Japan's many attacks in December 1941 illuminated every Allied weakness. America's disaster was Pearl Harbor – for Britain it was the humiliation of Singapore. Lt. Gen. Percival (right foreground) surrendered the city and 85,000 captives to Gen. Yamashita (seated, first from left).

American special negotiator, Admiral Nomura, was sent to Washington to hold talks with Secretary of State Hull. But America was adamant on guaranteeing the integrity of the countries in the East. Further diplomatic talks became virtually pointless when America froze all Japan's assets in the U.S.A. and put a total ban on trade, but Nomura tried one last desperate appeal, by suggesting that Konoye himself should visit Washington. Hull squashed that idea by saying the visit would be pointless unless Japan first withdrew from the territories she had occupied.

Konoye's diplomatic approach had failed, and in October 1941 he was forced to resign. In his place came **Gen. Hideki Tojo**, a hard-as-nails militarist, but one who had the asset of being unquestionably loyal to the Emperor and powerful enough to keep the other militarists in check – which is why Marquis Kido had recommended him to Hirohito. Tojo's first act was to plan for war. It was obvious to the Japanese that they could not expect to conquer America – their war objectives were to firmly established the "GEACPS", which would guarantee Japan all her raw materials, and clear the Western powers out from the East. Once the major powers had recovered, they would, the Japanese figured, be faced with a huge unity of pro-Japanese countries, and then they would be able to do little. At that stage, Japan would willingly negotiate and grant concessions by pulling back from the outer limits of her conquests.

The geography of East Asia put an emphasis on sea power, and the only match for the formidable Japanese Fleet was the U.S. Pacific Fleet, based at Pearl Harbor near Honolulu in the Hawaiian Islands. The Pacific Fleet would have to go, and after that Japan would be able to attack the next two formidable obstacles – the American and Philippine garrisons on Luzon in the Philippines, and the British stronghold of Singapore – the Gibraltar of the East.

Japan's Washington negotiator, Nomura, was given the task of spinning out the already hopeless negotiations with Hull to give Japan time to get ready for war. Washington was quite prepared to go along with Nomura, for she, too, had preparations to make. The urgency of these was made clear by the enormous achievement of breaking the Japanese code (no less spectacular was their success in keeping knowledge of this achievement from the Japanese for so long), which showed war was brewing. Unfortunately the urgency did not spread everywhere it should have, due to a host of human weaknesses. The conviction that the Japanese would strike first at the British or the Dutch caused less anxiety than was sensible when the decoded messages told practically everything except where the blow would fall, and when. By the time "when" was made almost certain, the Americans began to suspect "where" – but it was too late, and there was an unintended irony and symbolism in the way the blows were struck as the sun rose on a lazy lackadaisical Sunday morning.

How and where the blows struck is detailed in the Chronology. The Japanese Navy's undetected approach so close to Pearl Harbor, and the frightening havoc of the first hour of the strike were remarkable feats that the Japanese echoed with attack after attack through the Far East in the few days early in December 1941. But they had immediately made two major blunders – Nomura, unaware of the import of the timing of the last message from Tokyo, delivered it an hour late, with the result that Japan attacked the U.S. Fleet before it declared war, earning the 7th of December the apt name "Day of Infamy", and uniting all Americans in hatred of Japan. And the attacking force left far too much undamaged at Pearl Harbor (port installations, oil storage tanks, etc.), an omission exaggerated by the absence from the port of the U.S. carriers on exercise. The presence of all the battleships, confirmed by Japan's spy in Honolulu, justified launching the attack, but subsequent events were to show that by missing the carriers, Japan was never to get a chance to prove the viability of her Co-Prosperity Sphere.

In December 1941, however, the outlook for the West was bleak, and it grew a lot worse as the months went by. The great bastion of Singapore was humiliatingly, shamefully defeated by bicycles, a few tanks, and a striking lack of imagination on the part of the British. Malaya, the Philippines, Solomons, New Guinea, Hong Kong, Burma. Country after country fell to the Japanese, and within 6 months the Greater East Asia Co-Prosperity Sphere was forged by brute force. But machinery cast and forged in a foundry needs to be carefully ground and

---

The course of the Pacific war would have been very different had the Japanese caught the U.S. carriers. Success depended increasingly on sea power, which was determined by aircraft flown from carriers. During the war America built 32 such vessels and only lost 5 heavy carriers, to 16 Japanese heavy and medium carriers lost.

polished before it will run smoothly, and the Japanese threw away golden opportunities, just as the Germans were doing in Russia.

In much of south-east Asia, the **Japanese were looked on virtually as liberators** – nowhere more so than **in Burma**, a country which the Japanese had long been courting. Their arrival was welcomed by many Burmese to whom the concept of the GEACPS was attractive – as it was to a number of countries. The Co-Prosperity Sphere offered independence, liberation – and anyone promising that, found an immediate ally. But, like Hitler in Russia and Poland (though they had no ambitions of genocide), the Japanese ill-treated the populations they had "liberated" from their European and British possessors. It was not only the pointless slaughter caused by the bombing of Rangoon or the dozens of other villages and towns in the Japanese path. Even after the last Europeans had been chased out of Burma or stuck away behind some stockade, the Japanese gave no indication that things were going to be any different.

In fact life in Burma and Malaya under the Japanese turned out to be infinitely more unpleasant than life under the benign if patronising and "superior" British. Things were no better in the Dutch East Indies, and in the Philippines the inhabitants suffered terribly. The Japanese were not liberators after all, but simply another foreign power whose motto seemed to be "exploitation at any price". GEACPS was a concept that promised prosperity (for Japan) and strife for the rest. By the time she had occupied the countries intended to fall under her net, Japan had lost a few tens of millions of potential allies, and added them to the few hundreds of millions of enemies she had made for herself in China, America, Britain and Holland. In May 1941, nationalistic resistance to Japanese occupation sprang up for the first time, led in French Indo-China by the **founder of the Viet Minh**, Ho Chi Minh. Over the next four years more and more "partisan" groups would be formed, armed and supplied by the Allies, in efforts to oust the invaders.

If the Japanese Cabinet was aware of its errors or even of Japan's unpopularity in the East, it did nothing to show it – perhaps the years of unbending militarist rule had totally erased sensitivity, emotion and humanitarian principles. But the war leaders did see that the U.S. Pacific Fleet, with new additions to the original left-overs of aircraft carriers and escorts, was still a major threat. They drew up a plan to forge a strong outer ring stretching from the Coral Sea to the Midway Islands, and then intended to lure the U.S. Pacific Fleet out towards the Aleutian Islands, and its final defeat. Thanks to knowledge of the Japanese Code, CINCPAC (Adm. Nimitz) was able to avoid being taken by surprise – initially in the Coral Sea, where the value of the carriers spared at Pearl Harbor was emphasised in the evenly matched, first-ever battle between ships at sea that was fought entirely by aircraft.

Clever use by Nimitz of the knowledge that Japan planned an invasion of Midway enabled him to meet the bigger force with superior tactics and inflict such severe damage that the invasion was called off. Germany had almost made it to Moscow, but thereafter faced minor victories in a hopeless future. Japan almost reached the security of Midway – but she too was thereafter only to know temporary achievement before final annihilation.

5. THE BATTLE OF THE ATLANTIC 3.9.39–31.5.43; and the War at Sea

Russia invaded Poland (17th September). Warsaw fell (27th). Russia attacked Finland (30th November). Treaty of Moscow signed by Russia and Finland (12th March 1940). Germany invaded Denmark and Norway (9th April). British landings in Norway (16–18th). Germany invaded Holland, Belgium and Luxembourg (10th May). Holland surrendered (14th). France invaded (14th). Belgium surrendered (25th). Evacuation of B.E.F. from Dunkirk began (26th). Norway surrendered (9th June). France surrendered (22nd). Battle of Britain began (10th July). Italy invaded Somaliland (5th August). Blitz on London began (7th September). Japan signed Tripartite Pact (27th). Axis invaded Greece (28th October). German and Italian troops began North Africa offensive (24th March 1941). Axis invaded Yugoslavia and Greece (6th April), which surrendered (17th and 27th). Abyssinia liberated (5th May). Germany invaded Russia (22nd June). Japan attacked U.S. Fleet at Pearl Harbor (7th December). Germany declared war on U.S.A. (11th). Singapore surrendered (15th February 1942). Philippines surrendered (9th April). Tobruk fell to Axis (21st June). U.S. landed on Guadalcanal (7th August). Disastrous Allied raid on Dieppe (19th). Battle of Alamein began (23rd October). Allies landed in North Africa (8th November). Germans defeated at Stalingrad (31st). Axis beaten in North Africa (13th May).

The shadow of the First World War hung over the Second in many ways apart from being the cause of it. Some obviously expected much strategy to be repeated, while many of the clearest lessons were forgotten. Perhaps mania over the imagined roles that aircraft would play made the Allied Generals forget the effectiveness of tanks and mobility, and the Admirals forget the terrible potential of submarine warfare. Doenitz, however, did not forget. He had been a submarine commander in the Great War, and knew exactly how submarines could be used in future wars. He even described "wolf-pack" techniques in a book published in 1939,

It was not until mid-1943 that ships crossing the Atlantic could do so without their crews being constantly aware of the danger from U-boats. For the crews who did survive torpedo explosions and the sinking of their ships, there were still the perils of survival at sea in small open boats. Lone ships were particularly vulnerable to U-boat attack, and the survivors sometimes faced weeks at sea before being rescued; thousands perished miserably.

though like *Mein Kampf*, it seems to have found few readers outside Germany.

Even those who had not forgotten that in World War I $12\frac{3}{4}$ million tons of merchant shipping were sunk – nearly all by submarines – had almost forgotten that the only effective defence was well-escorted convoys. It was therefore fortunate for the Allies that ex-corporal Hitler, Supreme Commander of the German Armed Forces, was a confirmed landlubber; that the Commander of the German Navy, Adm. Raeder, had none of Goering's pompous standing; and that the Navy's building programme was aimed at a war due to begin in 1944, not 1939. When war came, some collossi of the sea were being prepared – such as *Bismarck* and *Tirpitz* – while the ingenious "pocket battleships" (built to get around the disarmament regulations on the size of warships built in Germany) were immediately sent to sea. Submarines were low on the agenda and there were only 24 ready for service.

Britain was totally dependent on safe sea routes, and therefore had the largest merchant navy and practically the most powerful naval force in the world when war broke out. Hitler at least understood that he was unlikely to smash the Royal Navy, but he knew that if a sufficient number of merchant ships could be prevented from reaching British ports, Britain might be made ineffective by siege. Perhaps Hitler was simply caught unprepared by his own haste and over-reliance on British appeasement, for had he anticipated war with Britain, he might have put a greater emphasis on submarine production before September 1939. The presence of five times as many submarines in the Atlantic at the outbreak of war would have changed the course of history. As it was, the few submarines (even at the end of 1940, there were only 22 at large) caused greater havoc than they should have due to Britain's inability to enforce strict convoy systems. (There was a shortage of escort vessels at the beginning of the war, and finding warships "to spare" for escort duty was a consistent problem. But in the unlikelihood of there being naval engagements in the traditional sense, some came to believe that the warships' primary purpose was to escort the cargoships on which the life of Britain depended.)

While Western Europe lay in the strange calm of the Phoney War, the war at sea – as the Chronology clearly shows – was a harsh, frightening conflict that began hours after war was declared with the sinking of the liner *Athenia*. By the end of 1939, 106 ships had been sunk by

U-boats, and no merchant seaman sailed the Atlantic without an awareness of the cold shadows of sudden death that moved silently beneath the waves. But lessons were being rapidly learnt and memories revived. Of the 106 ships sunk, only four had been sunk while sailing in escorted convoys – all the rest were "loners". There were differences from the First War however, and they were soon discovered. Most important was the vastly increased range of the U-boats – the further out to sea the warships escorted or met the merchant ships, the further out went the U-boats, until it seemed that no matter where the white and red ensigns parted company, U-boats would begin to gather.

The first major escalation in the U-boat war came after **the fall of France** in June 1940. Whatever solace Britishers at sea derived from knowing that they were not alone in tasting war's bitterness, was cancelled by the increased U-boat capabilities resulting from access to French ports. Slipping out into the Atlantic from the Bay of Biscay was a lot easier than threading a way through the heavily mined waters of the North Sea, while the miles saved meant more miles and more days spent out on patrol. In October 1940 about 350,000 tons of shipping were sunk by U-boats, and the losses were felt all the more since aircraft were also taking a toll by bombing ships, as well as reporting on their movements – further advantages of the capture of Europe's west coast. (Nearly all the advantages the Germans gained would have been offset if the French Navy had gone over to Britain.)

U-boat construction soon began to receive its logical place in the priority list, and the moment he was able to, Doenitz put his "wolf-pack" theories into practice. The objective was to make convoys as vulnerable to U-boats as the independents were. On the approach of a convoy (reported by aircraft, by chance spotting, by radio intelligence, etc.) a group of U-boats would be directed to a specific area, where they would lie in wait for the convoy. A simultaneous attack on a convoy by five or six U-boats could cause enormous confusion, during which further strikes could be made or an escape effected. Despite these group attacks, the convoy was still the best defence, and the R.N. devoted itself to perfecting convoy formations and tactics. The American Lend-Lease Act which came into being in March 1941 greatly increased the R.N.'s stock of escort ships, and the establishment of a base in Iceland in April gave convoys on the Great Circle route to Canada even greater air and escort protection. The Germans began to suffer a number of reverses, and the sinking in March of *U47* with her brave and successful commander, Prien, was followed by the loss of *U99* and *U100*, two other submarines which had become legendary among the German people, and notorious among the British.

America became more and more involved in the European war, and when she divided the Atlantic into Western and Eastern Hemispheres, with a line running more or less south from Greenland, she assumed the right to patrol that area as being waters whose protection was in the American interest. The establishment of the American base in Greenland was followed by a practically overt act of antagonism when the U.S.A. moved onto Iceland, and relieved the hard-pressed Royal Navy. The U.S. Navy had formed escorted convoys for its own merchant ships which were carrying arms and materials for Britain, and these were still safe from U-boat attacks – until they undertook the second part of the voyage into the combat-area waters of the "Eastern Hemisphere". Gradually, however, more and more ships of other neutrals, and also of Britain, were let into the U.S. convoys, and with the Canadian Navy also playing a major role (though being subject to attack), losses in the second half of 1941 fell dramatically.

This was a calm before the storm that broke when Germany declared war on America on the 11th of December 1941. Immediately a whole new part of the Atlantic Ocean, and miles and miles of coastal waters became legitimate hunting grounds with hundreds more ships as targets. Sinkings by U-boats increased alarmingly: in January 1942, 31 were sunk off the coasts of America and Canada; in February it was 69; by the end of July 3 million tons had been sunk since America entered the war. Fourteen U-boats had been sent to the bottom, but only six of these in the far Western Atlantic. It was the worst time of the war for the Allies; not only were they short of warships, but Doenitz by late 1942 had some 200 submarines (at any one time, about one third of all submarines would be on patrol).

In the middle of the early disastrous period, the Royal Navy had an opportunity to repay some of Britain's enormous debt to America, and a group of R.N. corvettes and sub-hunter trawlers with highly experienced R.N. crews was lent to the U.S. Navy to help (and instruct) in the defence of America's east coast. As the enormous American industry swung into full war production, more and more convoys could be organised, and losses once more began to fall off – only to shoot up again in November 1942 when almost every available ship joined the 600-strong convoy that set off across the Atlantic in Operation Torch – the invasion of North Africa, America's first clash in the war with the German Army. In that month, U-boats sunk 117 ships, totalling some 700,000 tons.

1943 saw the beginning of the end of U-boat supremacy, as the Allies evolved effective machinery and strategy. A number of elements went into the final counter-measure. The extraordinarily seaworthy corvettes and the bigger frigates proved valuable escort ships that did not need large quantities of men or materials, and they were produced in great numbers. Experience taught the Allies to match wits and tactics with the U-boat commanders, and Asdic operators grew more and more adept at identifying and tracking the submarines. But the

Above: A wrecked Junkers Ju 52/3m transport aircraft on a desert airfield with a column of British trucks in the background (Photo: Imperial War Museum). Below: The U.S.S. *Arkansas* in February 1944 with a pair of floatplanes mounted above a gun turret (Photo: Properfoto Limited).

The Second World War

THE BATTLE FOR THE CONVOYS. The major shipping routes are indicated by **heavy black lines:** *the areas in which the greatest number of U-boat attacks took place are in* **vertical shading:** *the area of Luftwaffe dominance is* **diagonally shaded.** *Ship silhouettes show* **sinkings of capital ships** *(with turret)* **and carriers** *(without turret). National flash indicates nationality. Number key is as follows:–* **Germany 1** = *Scharnhorst* **2** = *Tirpitz* **3** = *Bismark* **4** = *Graf Spee* **5** = *Gneisenau** **6** = *Prinz Eugen** **7** = *Deutschland** **8** = *Adm. Scheer** **9** = *Adm. Hipper**. **Great Britain 1** = *Glorious* **2** = *Hood* **3** = *Royal Oak* **4** = *Courageous* **5** = *Eagle* **6** = *Ark Royal* **7** = *Barham.* **Italy 1** = *Littorio* **2** = *Duilio* **3** = *Cavour.* * = *vessels not sunk but unable to put to sea after 1942.* **Area of broken lines** *shows main hunting ground of Graf Spee and German surface raiders.*

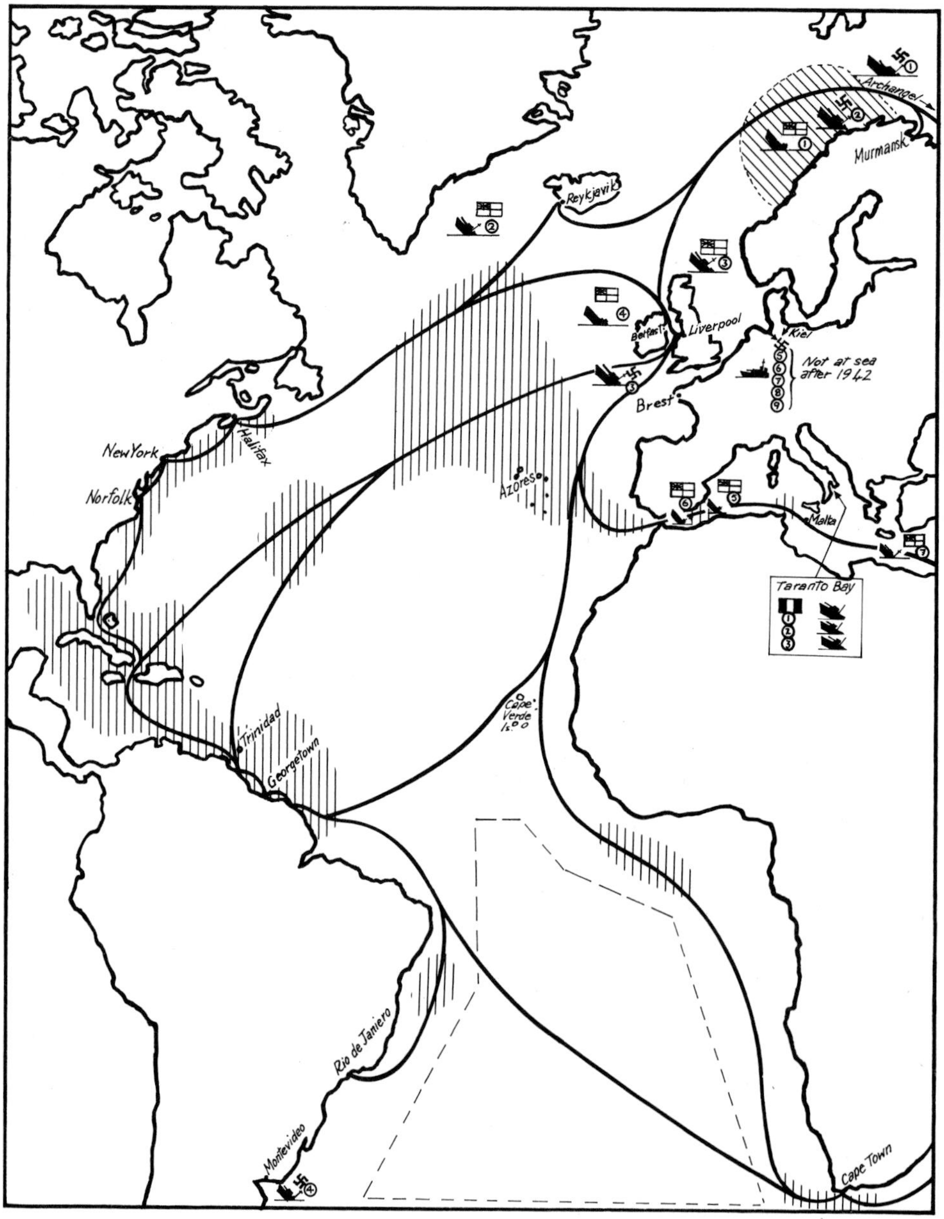

two most influential counter-measures were the **greater use of aircraft**, and the **development of "centimetric" radar**. The value of air support was well known during daylight, and the further that air cover could go, the more often U-boats would have to keep out of sight, and risk losing convoys because of slower underwater speed. For most of the war, U-boat commanders had been used to making surface attacks on convoys at night – this thwarted Allied reliance on Asdic which was not able to locate a submarine on or just below the surface, while the early forms of radar were unable to detect objects as small as a submarine's conning tower. Centimetric radar used impulses with a very short wave-length, and it did not need the enormously bulky systems previously used in concentrating radar beams sufficiently to positively locate small objects. The new radar could be fitted to the smallest warships and, most important of all, to aircraft.

At once, the U-boats lost the protection of night. They had to make their attacks from below the surface, and had to get below well before they were in a convoy's radar range. This slowed them up, and they often missed convoys altogether. Having to remain underwater for the attack made them prone to detection by Asdic. Worst of all for the U-boats, lone patrolling aircraft far out at sea could locate them running on the surface at night, forcing them to dive. Frequent night dives prevented the submarines from fully charging their batteries while running on diesel engines, and from using their higher surface speeds to reach interception areas in time.

Combined with these developments was the availability of far more warships released after the Axis defeat in North Africa and the consequent lifting of the siege on Malta. Even more warships were released as a result of the destruction, by early 1943, of the majority of the German surface fleet. At the same time shipyards in America were turning out new ships at a fantastic rate, and the British shipyards were being harassed less and less by the Luftwaffe. The Allied navies formed close-support escort groups which could undertake U-boat hunts directed by aircraft spotting – this tactic left the convoy's escort intact. Distant-support groups formed an emergency source of help in the event of massed U-boat attacks, or of strong surface attacks by marauding raiders, as happened twice in the Arctic Sea. When some merchant ships were converted into "escort carriers", the already increased range of R.A.F. Coastal Command and the U.S. Coast Guard planes was supplemented by a convoy's ability to provide its own aerial escort. (Much disputed at the time was the decision taken in accordance with Harris' urgent pleading not to put a large number of long range bombers under the control of Coastal Command. It is quite likely that their accomplishments would have been far more effective by helping convoys get through than by bombing Germany.)

Against all this, the U-boats were almost powerless. March 1943 was the last very bad month for Allied shipping – 108 ships of 627,000 tons were sunk by U-boats in all oceans. After that, sinkings dropped as dramatically as the destruction of U-boats increased. In May, 40 U-boats were destroyed (30% of those at sea) and Doenitz was forced to admit defeat and call them back to their base ports. In July, 37 were sunk – mostly by planes, and half of them in the Bay of Biscay. By November only about 80,000 tons of merchant shipping was lost in a month. Like Goering, Doenitz had to admit he was unable to break Britain's defences, and the "total economic warfare" against the country was brought to a halt. U-boat production continued, however, and the development of the *schnorkel*, which allowed submarines to use a periscope-depth breathing tube for their diesel engines; and the preparation of a brand-new type of fast submarine, gave some Germans desperate hope that they would once more return to the attack. But although there were nearly 50 out at sea on the day Germany surrendered, U-boats never formed a real threat after May 1943.

The ending of the Battle of the Atlantic brought a welcome relief from the three years of tension and suffering so heroically endured by merchant seamen, particularly those in the British Merchant Navy, though the especially grim torments of the Arctic convoys were not yet over. Voyages were filled with danger – the usual perils of the North Atlantic, plus the lethal danger of Doenitz's submarines. Attack was sudden, devastation enormous and rapid. The anxious nightly waiting for the U-boats found some relief when the first explosion was heard – but then anxiety only began again, in wondering whose ship the next torpedo would find. On the tanker and ammunition ships the danger was extremely great, yet for voyage after voyage they came back – if they could. Surviving an explosion and the ship's sinking brought the further hazards of the icy seas, of perhaps being run down, of not being seen and left to die. The crews of lone ships sunk before a message could be sent out often faced many weeks in open lifeboats, before they were rescued or simply died. In the whole of the war, over 32,000 British merchant seamen died. Over the whole European war period, their casualty rate was higher than in any of the armed services – only the Fleet Air Arm, in the early years of the war, were more dangerously occupied.

The Battle of the Atlantic, or the whole U-boat war, was only a part of the struggle for supremacy of the sea, and merchant ships and warships had much else to worry about besides silent torpedoes. Mines, fast torpedo boats, midget submarines, and above all, aircraft, were effective weapons of the war at sea – apart from warships themselves and some of their spectacular developments (which are covered in the section "The Armed Forces"). But Hitler's attitude towards the navy, and the Allied success in preventing Germany from getting adequate oil, gave the European war at sea a peculiar slant.

Enormous expenditure went on awesome giants that eventually fired few shots in anger; and other, extremely effective ships, such as the disguised merchant raiders, were recalled early and never used again. Except for a few isolated engagements – such as the Battle of the River Plate in December 1939, the sinking of *Hood* and *Bismarck* in May 1941, the daring escape from Brest by *Scharnhorst*, *Gneisenau* and *Prinz Eugen* in February 1942, the humiliation of the German surface navy when an Arctic convoy's escorts chased away *Hipper* and *Lützow* (leading to Raeder's replacement by Doenitz), and the sinking of *Scharnhorst* in December 1943 – except for these, most of the war between the Allied and German navies took place "through" the water, rather than along it or above it. In the Mediterranean, the Allied navies and the Italian navy clashed in more conventional manner, though here British submarines were highly active during the Axis occupation of North Africa. The Mediterranean theatre became noted for heralding (though obviously unsuspected at the time) the Japanese attack on Pearl Harbor. The Japanese recollected in 1941 with great interest and optimism the daring and successful raid by torpedo-carrying planes off an R.N. aircraft carrier, on the Italian Fleet in the shallow waters of Taranto Bay in November 1940.

In the Pacific, roles were reversed. Japan was an island dependent on being supplied by sea, and United States Navy submarines caused enormous losses which eventually reduced essential food and other supplies in Japan to little more than survival proportions. The island-hopping war placed tremendous emphasis on naval power, but it was in the Pacific, even more than in the Atlantic, that it was demonstrated to what degree sea-power depended on air-power. Japanese aircraft smashed in a few hours four mighty battleships of the U.S. Pacific Fleet, and two days later they sank two of Britain's formidable capital ships – the last fortresses in the East. And then within a few years, Japan's own very powerful fleet was destroyed, very largely because the U.S. Pacific Fleet's aircraft carriers happened to be out of port on the morning of 7th December 1941.

* * *

The Japanese fleet was completely destroyed in the war. Eleven of her battleships were sunk, against 2 U.S. (only 2 of the battleships that were attacked at Pearl Harbor did not eventually get back into service). They lost 16 aircraft carriers, against 5 American, and 39 heavy and light cruisers against 10 American. The Japanese fleet also lost nearly 140 destroyers and 150 submarines.

In the European war, 5,150 merchant ships were sunk, totalling 21,570,720 tons. Over half of this shipping belonged to the British merchant navy, which thus lost some 54% of the tonnage it had when war broke out. Of the 5,150 merchant ships sunk, over 2,800 were sunk by submarines, more than 800 by aircraft, and some 540 by mines. In the Arctic, 91 merchant ships were sent to the bottom and 830 merchant seamen died in these waters – but over 1,800 Royal Navy men died in the desperate conditions of the Arctic convoys. The Germans paid heavily, though. Excluding small craft, over 1,300 German navy ships were destroyed – 785 of them being U-boats. (Almost equal numbers were destroyed by aircraft as by warships.)

---

6. THE STRUGGLE FOR NORTH AFRICA
10.6.40–15.5.43

France surrendered (22nd June 1940). Russia occupied Bessarabia (26th). Battle of Britain began (10th July). Blitz of London began (7th September). Japan signed Tripartite Pact (27th). Germany occupied Rumania (7th October). Greece invaded by Italians (28th). Battle of Taranto Bay (11th November). Great Fire of City of London (29th). Allies began conquest of Italian occupied Abyssinia and Somaliland (January 1941). Germany invaded and conquered Yugoslavia and Greece (17th and 24th April). Japan signed neutrality treaty with Russia (13th). Haile Selassie returned to liberated Abyssinia (5th May). Germans won Crete (20–28th). Hood *and* Bismarck *sunk (24th and 27th). Germany and Turkey signed treaty of friendship (18th June). Germany invaded Russia (22nd). Churchill and Roosevelt signed Atlantic Charter (12th August). First Arctic convoy sailed to Russia (21st). Russians launched counter-attack at Moscow (6th December). Japan attacked U.S. Fleet at Pearl Harbor (7th). Germany declared war on America (11th). Singapore surrendered to Japanese (15th February 1942). Rangoon surrendered (8th March). Japanese occupied Java (9th). U.S. Army on Bataan in Philippines surrendered (9th April). Burma passed into Japanese hands (20th May). Battle of Midway in Pacific – U.S. naval victory (4th June). Sevastopol fell to Germans in Crimea (1st July). Convoy PQ17 destroyed in Arctic (4–10th). U.S. Marines landed on Guadalcanal (7th August). Allied raid on Dieppe failed (19th). German armies attacked Stalingrad and Caucasus (September). Germans surrendered at Stalingrad (31st January 1943). Warsaw ghetto uprising began (19th April). Battle of Atlantic resulted in U-boat withdrawals (May).*

Mussolini – "Il Duce" of Italy – enjoyed a notoriety as Europe's primary fascist dictator well before Hitler or

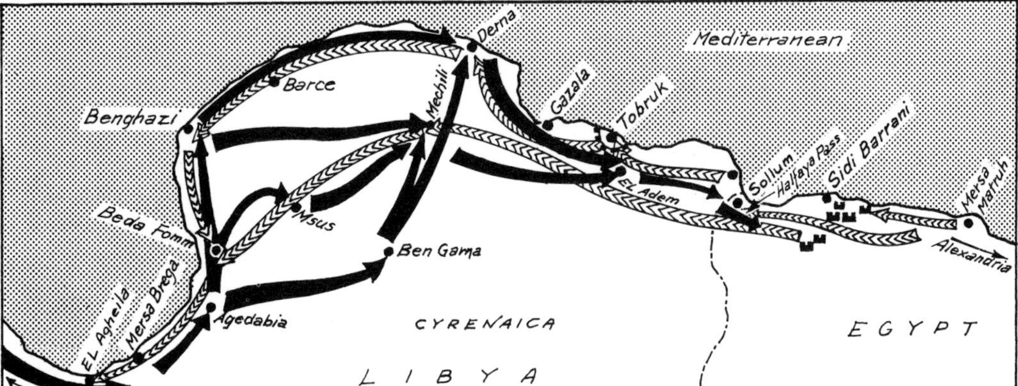

First Allied advance and retreat in North Africa.

Franco established themselves, and he doubtless took considerable delight in putting on a typically strutting performance, in his black military uniform, before the shabby-looking Hitler when they first met in 1934. But if his wardrobe and theatrics were superior to Hitler's, his (realistic) ambitions were far more mundane, though once again Hitler must have cast an interested and envious glance south when the Italians rampaged into Abyssinia in 1935, even if there was a fundamental difference in the policies of colonialism and acquisition of *lebensraum.* (What particularly encouraged Hitler was the lack of world reaction to Italy's aggression, apart from indignant squawking at the League of Nations.) Playing the "grand strong-man of Fascism" Mussolini helped Franco in the Spanish Civil War and nurtured Hitler, who for a few years at least, maintained a discreet respect for Italian ambitions. (Later the two dictators simultaneously sensed the moment when the baton of supremacy passed from the ex-school teacher to the ex-corporal.)

Although the Rome–Berlin Axis had been in operation for three years, Italy refrained from being too closely identified with Hitler when the war in Europe broke out in 1939. Correctly assessing the fighting ability of his army, he sat and watched while the Nazi monster tore through Denmark, Norway, Holland, Belgium, half of France, and swept Britain's expeditionary Force off the coast of Europe. Then, with the renewed German offensive crashing towards Paris, Mussolini judged the time right and declared war on the Allies on 10th June 1940. Even then, he was almost too early, and his troops were unable to knock a way into crumbling France, which surrendered to Hitler 12 days later.

If Europe scarcely felt a ripple on Italy's declaration, a deeper rumble of concern was noticeable in the Mediterranean and in North Africa. The boot of Italy and rocky Sicily effectively divided the Mediterranean in half; and directly south, in their colony of Libya, was a garrison of some 500,000 Italians. Between the two masses lay tiny Malta, another "Gibraltar" to the British on the sea route to the East, the Dominions, to oil, Suez – and Egypt, where Gen. Wavell commanded a garrison one tenth the size of the Italian force in Libya.

Later on in the Desert War another General, on the Axis side, would repeatedly demonstrate that "attack is the best method of defence", and it was prophetic that the first shots in the North Africa campaign were loosed by this maxim. Four days after Italy's declaration, Wavell began a series of raids into Libya which eventually caused over 3,000 Italian casualties against some 150 British – and an air raid on Tobruk killed the Italian Supreme Commander, who was then replaced by Marshal Graziani. In September, under pressure from Mussolini, Graziani launched an attack across the border into Egypt, seemingly headed for Mersa Matruh, an important port-town on the coastal road. But he stopped at Sidi Barrani and constructed several fortresses whose placement gave them doubtful value.

Reinforcements eventually arrived for Wavell (traffic between Britain and Egypt had to follow the long Cape Town route, or chance the hostile Mediterranean; but Australian, New Zealand, South African and Indian troops had no distance added to their journeys), and a counter-attack was launched under Gen. O'Connor. The Italians outnumbered the Allied forces by far more than two to one, but they were overcome with startling ease.

Tobruk passed into Allied hands early in 1941, and some 125,000 Italians had by then been taken prisoner. Such rapid success was unexpected and the Allies, not equipped for rapid advances, paused awhile before relaunching the offensive. Air reconnaissance indicated that the Italians were preparing to pull out of Benghazi; O'Connor took a calculated risk and cut across the Benghazi bulge, making a trap at Beda Fomm into which marched tens of thousands of Italians while other Allied troops moved rapidly along the coast-road.

With the Italians cleared out of Egypt and even out of Cyrenaica (and Graziani out of Africa in disgrace), O'Connor was understandably keen to push them out of Tripolitania as well, and despite his rapidly lengthening supply lines, there is good reason to suppose that this could have been done and that the war for North Africa could have ended within a year of its beginning. Two events, however, changed the immediate plans and the course of the war.

Italy's invasion of Greece had turned into an Italian defence of Albania (their "annexed" territory) and it was obvious that Hitler would soon go to the aid of his luckless fellow dictator. Churchill saw that the fall of the Balkans to Germany would give the Nazis a route to the Middle East and to India. Accordingly he made the controversial decision to take troops away from North Africa and send them to aid the defence of the Balkans. The British presence there perhaps influenced the Yugoslav rebellion, and together with the battles for Greece and Crete certainly helped add at least five weeks to the Axis defeat of the Balkans – which in turn delayed Barbarossa five weeks and so appeared to save Moscow from capitulation.

However it is as equally likely that the transfer of the North African troops lengthened the North African Campaign by over two years – for while British troops were going to Greece, **German troops were on their way to Tripolitania, under the command of Gen. Rommel**. Although officially subordinate to Mussolini and the Italian High Command, and with a German force tiny in comparison to the Italian force, Rommel's mastery of tactics rapidly put him unofficially in command of the Axis, and he wasted no time in preparing an offensive. In March the Axis attacked the very depleted Allied front being held by Gen. Neame V.C. The Axis breakthrough was rapid, and from Agedabia they split into three groups to sweep across the Benghazi bulge. By April the 11th, the Allies were back in Egypt – except for the beleaguered garrison of Tobruk, which was determined to hang on.

Tobruk was a thorn in Rommel's side, but no matter how many times he tried, he could not remove it. The Royal Navy had sufficient power in Adm. Cunningham's Mediterranean Fleet to keep the besieged garrison supplied, and the troops were kept fresh by being "turned over" via troop convoys of about 6,000 at a time. Rommel desperately wanted to penetrate deeper into Egypt (doing that would have solved the problem of Tobruk as well), and he begged Hitler for additional troops. At that time, however, the German Command was preparing for the invasion of Russia, and that took priority over North Africa in Hitler's eyes. The British, on the other hand, were only too keen to reinforce Egypt (and they were not fighting anywhere else at that time) so a large convoy was risked through the Mediterranean. Learning it was well on its way, Wavell again took the offensive, with Gott in command, aiming to relieve Tobruk.

This was the **first British offensive against Rommel**, and his immediate response by counter-attacking confused the Allies and drove them back until the Halfaya Pass, on the Egypt/Libya border, was firmly under Axis control. The arrival of the convoy, virtually intact, spurred Wavell to another attack, but Rommel again counter-attacked, destroyed a large amount of the brand new armour, and firmly secured the Halfaya Pass. Wavell had been in control of an enormous sphere of operations since the war began, and Churchill felt he had more than earned relief. On the 21st of June 1941 Gen. Auchinleck relieved Wavell, and Lt. Gen. Cunningham, fresh from the rapid liberation of Somaliland and Abyssinia, was put in command of the newly formed 8th Army.

Auchinleck was able to resist Churchill's insistence on an early offensive until he had built up a considerable superiority in men and equipment. The Desert Air Force outnumbered the Axis by some three to one, and Auchinleck had twice as many tanks as Rommel. The 8th Army attacked in November, but Auchinleck and Cunningham wasted their superiority by spreading out and staggering their attacks. Rommel was able to deal with each attack in turn, and eventually prevented the 8th Army linking up with Tobruk by occupying Sidi Rezegh, south-east of the port. Every Allied thrust had been met and repelled and then Rommel – who was meant to be defending his position – made a rapid and powerful push for the border, cutting through the Allied lines, causing enormous confusion, and very nearly breaking through into Egypt. Auchinleck at this stage (25th November) replaced Cunningham with Ritchie while the Allies sorted themselves out and regrouped. Two days later Rommel was back south of Tobruk, and Allied contact had been made with the garrison. Rommel tried an offensive yet again, and again cut off Tobruk . . . but his supplies had run low, and his troops were severely depleted. In December the **Axis reluctantly abandoned the siege of Tobruk** and began a headlong retreat back to Tripolitania, many thousands of Italians being caught on the march (there was neither enough transport nor fuel for all). The Long Range Desert Group (LRDG) and the SAS Desert Raiders were particularly effective at this stage, and constantly harassed Rommel's columns, as well as carrying out destructive raids on airfields and supply dumps. Throughout the war they were invaluable to the Allies, and irritating to the Axis, in supplying vital

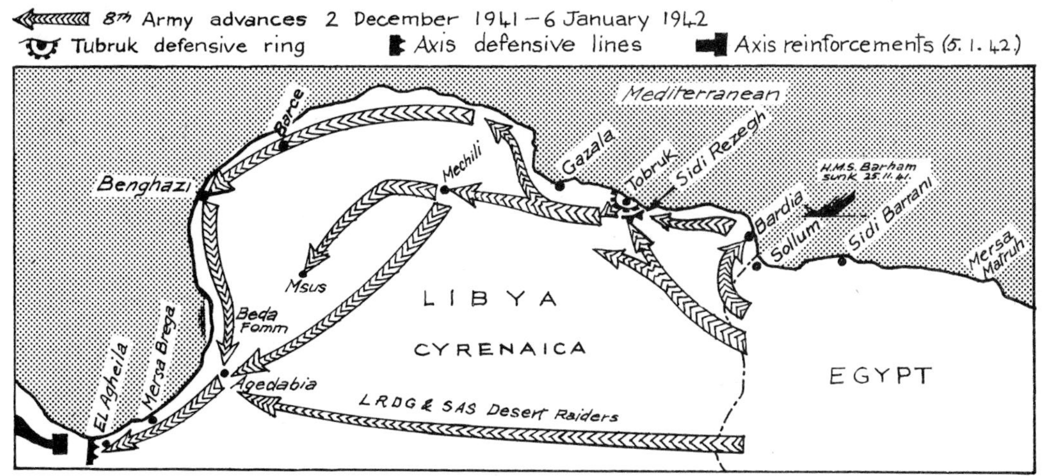

Second Allied advance in North Africa.

information and in causing considerable destruction.

Early in January 1942 Rommel received reinforcements at his defensive line west of Mersa Brega, and he wasted no time in preparing a new offensive. The Italians were less than enthusiastic about another offensive, but Rommel listened to no-one and by January the 25th Benghazi had been retaken – this time together with enormous quantities of supplies. For the second time, the **Allies were on their way back to Egypt**, with the Axis close behind. The last opportunity for a stand before Tobruk was at Gazala, and the Allies prepared a line while Rommel waited for his tailenders and reinforcements to catch up, and while Auchinleck resisted Churchill's plea for a counter-attack.

On 26th May 1942 Rommel relied on another favourite tactic. He made feint attacks on the Gazala Line proper and then launched his main attack at the southern tip, turning the line and heading north-east towards Tobruk. The move ran Rommel right into a British armoured division with new, very effective Grant tanks. Trapped in a self-made defensive ring christened "The Cauldron", Rommel's position was extremely precarious, but instead of steadily squeezing his position tighter, the Allied ground forces attempted to soften up the Axis concentration with aerial attacks. These were not nearly as effective as a massed armour, artillery and infantry attack would have been, and on the 13th of June Rommel broke out of the Cauldron and in a daring arc swept south and east, immediately changing roles from "the trapped" to "the trapper".

The Allies managed to break away to the east, leaving once more a powerful, well-supplied garrison in Tobruk. This time, Rommel was not to be defeated. The Allied outer defence at this stage of the Desert War relied largely on the system of "boxes", which were fortified positions comprising dugouts inside rings of artillery surrounded by wide minefields. These "open forts" contained a brigade or a regiment and while they were open to artillery or aerial bombardment, they could form a strong defensive ring. However, not being large, self-sufficient and well-prepared positions, they were highly dependent on regular supplies of ammunition. Once communication links were cut, the boxes had to surrender fairly soon. This was the fate of many at Gazala, and was to be the fate of more on the perimeter at Tobruk.

The Axis attacked Tobruk from the south-east, which was as much "behind" as was possible against the stronghold. The Allies in their trenches were subjected to a tremendous artillery barrage accompanied by repeated Stuka dive-bombing raids, and while Tobruk itself had a vast total supply of ammunition and artillery, most of it was of little use to the troops facing the direct Axis onslaught. After hours of bombardment, and without having the boost of seeing any of their own aircraft, the Allied lines broke up before the rapid approach of the Panzers. The German armoured sections drove straight into the heart of Tobruk, whose name then joined Singapore's in the British Army's chapter of humiliation when Gen. Klopper, commanding the 2nd South African Division, **surrendered Tobruk and the garrison of 33,000 men**.

The rest of the 8th Army was in full retreat towards Egypt, and after the Italian High Command was overruled by the Germans, Rommel (created Field Marshal for his exploits) went in pursuit. The 8th Army began to regroup at Mersa Matruh, but Auchinleck took over direct command from Ritchie. He decided to pull further back and drew up at El Alamein. Alamein offered numerous advantages: it was far closer to the Allied supply bases; it was within easy range of the Desert Air Force fighters; and it was possible to form a far stronger, conventional line of defence (instead of the box fortifications) in the narrow gap between the coast and the Qattara Depression.

The closer the Allies were to their supply dumps, the further Rommel was from his, and while the Allies were hard pushed to keep Malta alive (let alone get beyond Malta except by the Cape route), the R.N. Mediterranean surface fleet and its very effective submarines were making it equally difficult for the Axis to supply Rommel's columns. When they confronted the 8th Army at Alamein, the Afrika Korps and the Italian divisions were at the furthest stretch of a taut supply line. Every day that he delayed, his position worsened in relation to the Allies, and so Rommel launched an offensive on the 1st of July (1942). The attack caused sufficient consternation in Alexandria, only some 60 miles away, for official files to be burnt (it was, fittingly, Ash Wednesday) and the Fleet put to sea. The Axis attack was repulsed, however, and Auchinleck's choice of Alamein was vindicated.

Auchinleck, however, came under relentless pressure from Churchill and the War Cabinet to launch a counter-attack, and after insisting that he should be allowed to build up a stronger force, he was replaced by Gen. Alexander after Churchill, C.I.G.S. (Brooke), and Smuts had flown to Cairo. The three appointed Gott to lead the 8th Army, but within 24 hours he was killed in an air

Second Axis advance in North Africa after the capture of Tobruk.

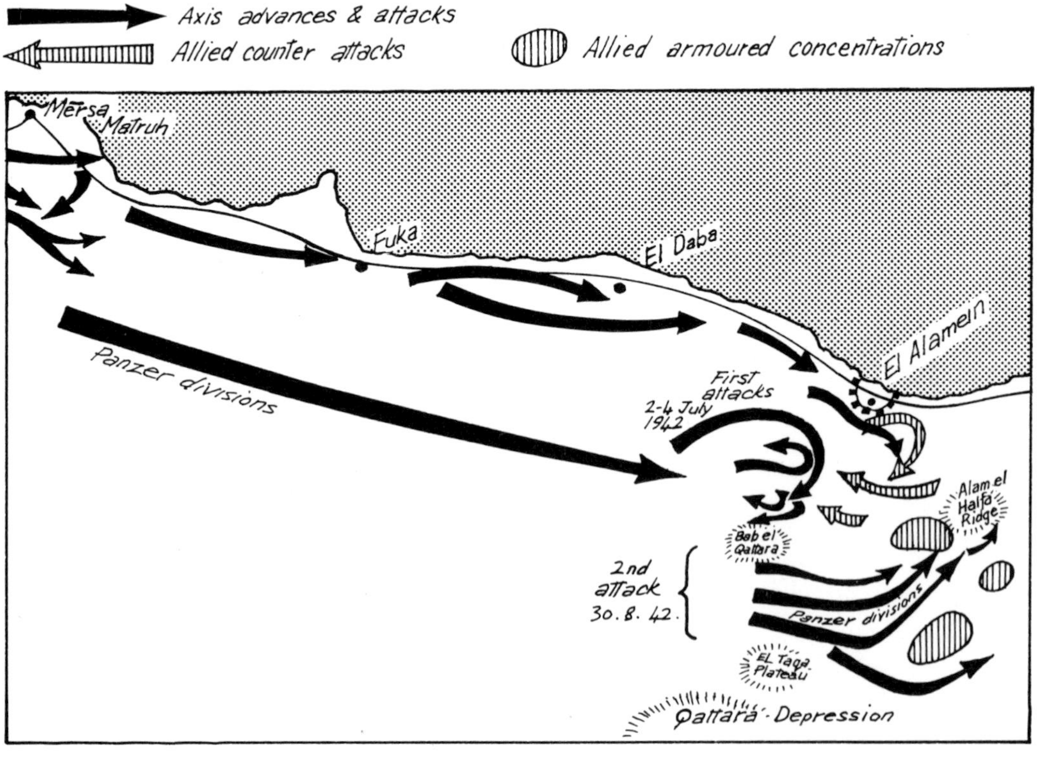

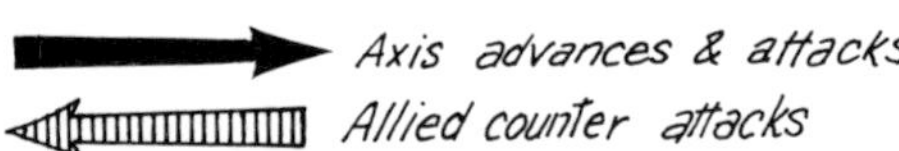

attack on his plane. Gen. Montgomery was brought in, having just begun work as Eisenhower's deputy for the projected Anglo–American invasion of North Africa (Operation Torch). If anything, Alexander, and especially Montgomery were even more determined to resist a precipitate attack, and the British war planners had to grind their teeth in frustration in the face of Montgomery's solid obstinacy – soon to be a feature of Allied campaigns against Germany.

Within a fortnight of Montgomery's arrival, Rommel launched another attack on the Allies – again feinting in the north and centre, and then thrusting strongly in the far south towards the command positions on the Alam Halfa ridge. But this time his move was anticipated. He was forced to take a more northerly approach by the presence of strong British armour far to the south, and that concentrated him up against very strong defences. Simultaneously his fuel supply became critical (even for a retreat to be possible), and again Rommel had to pull back from the Alamein line. Montgomery then began to build up the 8th Army until it had an unprecedented superiority over the Axis forces.

The 8th Army attack at Alamein was launched in October, when Rommel, fortuitously, was on sick leave in Germany. The Chronology recounts the progress of the battle – Rommel held the Allies and even attempted counter-attacks, while Hitler forbade retreat. But by the end of the month Rommel's 90 tanks were opposed by over 1,000 Allied tanks, and the R.A.F. commanded the skies. It is a measure of the defence put up by the Axis (yet again aided by the enormously effective use of their 88 mm anti-aircraft guns as anti-tank guns) that they were not simply trampled into the dust. In November, **the Axis began to fall back** in earnest.

One of the issues in the struggle for North Africa that will always be argued is whether Montgomery should have pursued Rommel with greater daring. Allied losses had already been heavy before the pursuit began and Montgomery had both the foresight to realise that long campaigns were still ahead, and the iron determination not to be defeated at any time. There was nothing that justified chance-taking. But the Axis columns were in considerable disarray, and unable to form a defensive line. Tens of thousands of tail-enders – mainly Italians deprived of transport – fell into Allied hands, and one or two bold strokes could well have netted the majority of the Afrika Korps – and perhaps the "Desert Fox" as well.

At any rate, Rommel's retreat scarcely paused until he reached the bottleneck at El Agheila, where he drew up and halted the 8th Army's advance for two weeks at the end of November (1943). In the meantime Operation Torch had been launched – Casablanca, Algiers and Oran had fallen by the 11th November, and the Vichy Commander, Adm. Darlan had surrendered. Tunis had become the Axis stronghold and the Allies' target. In a leapfrog action eastwards along the coast, commandos and paratroopers took Bône on the 12th. Tripoli fell to Montgomery in January 1943 but hold-ups were caused by heavy rain and the Axis' Mareth Line of defence. Rommel was given supreme command of all Axis troops in North Africa and tried to cut off the Allied advance on Tunis with a break through the Kasserine Pass and towards the coast. The hard fighting – the first fierce clash between Americans and Germans in the war – stopped when Rommel swung back to try to halt the 8th Army which had turned the Mareth Line. But by March Rommel was very ill and left the continent for home. Events moved rapidly as the Axis forces were squeezed against the coast – where the Royal Navy ruled out any German "Dunkirk". On the 13th May von Arnim surrendered almost a quarter of a million Germans and Italians. Their efforts to control North Africa had cost the Axis powers some 1 million killed or taken prisoner. As the dusty columns of men trudged into captivity, the Allies prepared to cross the gap to Sicily – and from there to Italy, where the first of the Axis powers would soon surrender.

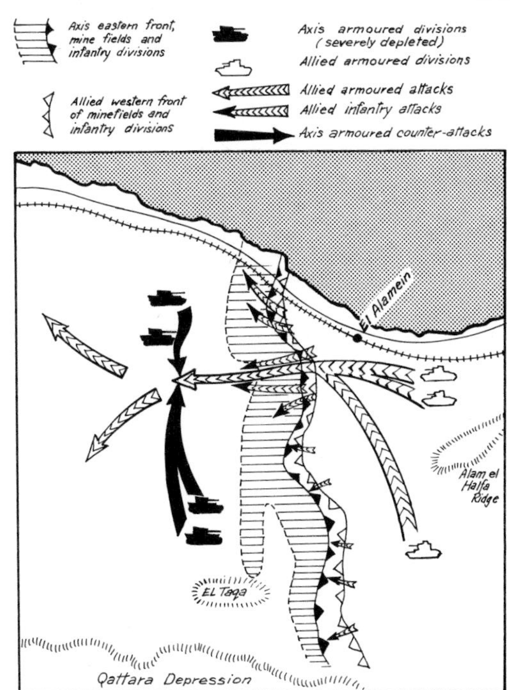

The breakthrough at Alamein.

Above: a divisional HQ of the Afrika Korps, the most powerful force on either side in North Africa. Below: the final defeat of the Axis in Africa.

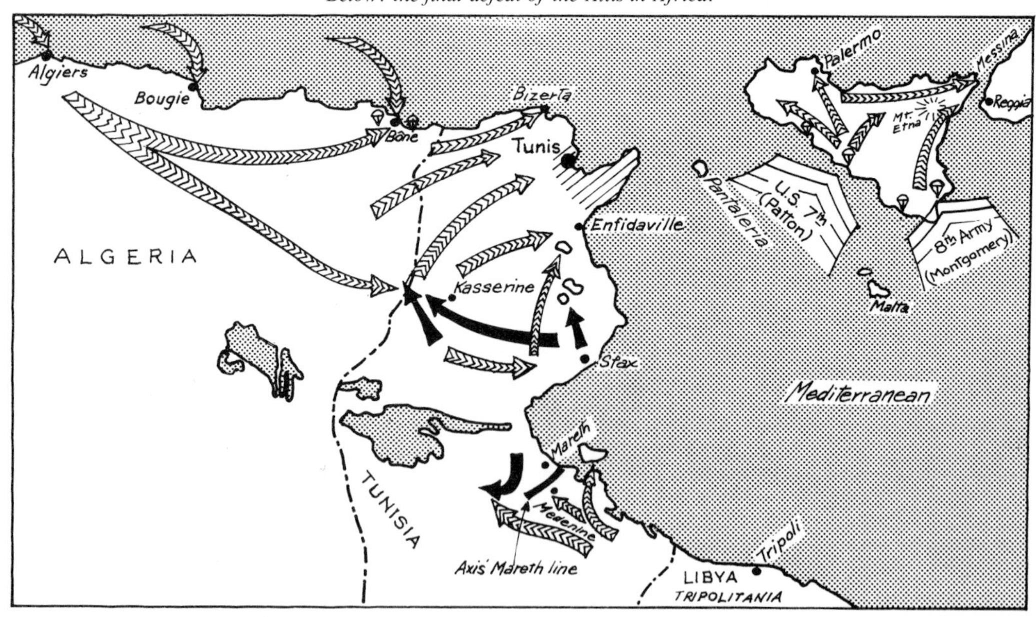

Allied attacks and Operation "Torch" landings by U.S. & U.K. troops.
Axis counterattacks.
Area of Axis entrapment
Allied paratroop landings

7. RETREAT AND RETRIBUTION IN RUSSIA
1.12.42–3.5.45

Japanese evacuated Guadalcanal (7th February 1943). Adm. Yamamoto killed in air ambush (18th April). Warsaw ghetto uprising began (19th). Axis surrendered in North Africa (13th May). Allies invaded Sicily (10th July). Allies invaded Italy (3rd September). Armistice signed by Italy (8th). Italy declared war on Germany (13th October). Bougainville invaded by U.S. (1st November). Rome occupied by Allies (4th June 1944). Allies invaded Normandy (6th). Japanese siege of Imphal ended (4th July). U.S. captured Saipan (9th). Unsuccessful attempt on Hitler's life (20th). Allies invaded southern France (15th August). Paris surrendered by Germans (25th). Civil war began in Athens (6th October). Germans counterattacked in Ardennes (16th December). U.S. began invasion of Iwo Jima (19th February 1945). Luzon, and Mandalay captured (March). Massive Tokyo air raids (9th). U.S. invaded Okinawa (1st April). Roosevelt died. Truman became President of U.S. (12th). Germans in Italy surrendered (29th). Rangoon liberated (3rd May).

Although the Third Reich was to last for two and a half years longer, the end of 1942 marked the zenith of its ascendancy. Hitler had given up all hope of ever invading Britain, or even of capturing Gibraltar. Rommel, his invincible Field Marshal, was on the run from the massive British 8th Army and heading into the advancing U.S., British and Free French forces from Operation Torch. On the Russian front, Moscow had repulsed Germany's greatest efforts while Leningrad still refused to give in. And now, on top of Kleist's Panzers being unable to break through the Caucasus Mountains, Paulus wanted to withdraw his Sixth Army from Stalingrad. To everyone but Hitler, it was clear that the Sixth Army was in a perilous position, but Hitler could not face the thought of letting yet another Russian city slip from his grasp when it was so nearly his – and particularly one named after the Bolshevik leader himself.

The Russian blow inevitably fell, and Marshal Zhukov directed a sweep through Paulus's left flank, capturing hundreds of thousands of Italians and Rumanians. When the encirclement was almost complete, Hitler still forbade a retreat. Even attempts at a breakout were forbidden long after the army was fully encircled, and long after it was obvious that the soldiers were all doomed anyway. It is unlikely that Hitler had much of an idea of the aching, dismal horror that Stalingrad had become. Luftwaffe reports told him how many supply planes were despatched each day for the besieged army – not how many actually reached the Stalingrad airfield. Paulus was far too much in awe of his leader to be elaborate in his reports, and the intermediaries too wary to pass on messages likely to unleash their leader's illtemper. Thus when Hitler should have understood that Paulus's men were reduced to half starved, exhausted, nervous wrecks, likely to be slaughtered by the first major Russian offensive, all he heard was that the Stalingrad situation was "grave" or "serious".

Hitler's command to Paulus to hang on at all cost – while a hopeless attempt was made to force a path through to him – possessed at least an inkling of military sense, for while the Sixth Army was dying and preparing for greater death, it was acknowledged that Army Group A was not going to reach its Caucasus objectives. That meant it should be withdrawn as soon as possible, for when the Sixth Army collapsed, the whole Russian front would automatically surge forward. (There is little to suggest that the Russians could not have left a minor force to contain the Sixth Army, and made a concerted attempt to trap Army Group A in the Caucasus. Paulus's tanks and trucks had fuel for no more than 20 miles, there was little ammunition and practically no food or medicines. And the Luftwaffe was losing transport planes by the score.) As it was, Paulus held out until Manstein had got the last troops past Rostov – and then the Caucasus, and the Sixth Army, were wiped from the maps of the German High Command.

Hitler had much else to worry about. With the onset of winter, the Arctic convoys had begun again, and apart from Russia's own phenomenally increased industrial output, tens of thousands of tons of arms and supplies were finding their way to Murmansk and Archangel (instead of using the slow summer route via the Persian Gulf). The German surface fleet – or a part of it still remaining undamaged – had been ignominously turned away from an attack on one of these convoys and Hitler had hysterically threatened to scrap every ship. Instead he scrapped Raeder and put Doenitz in his place. But the convoys still got through, and Russia, early in 1943, had become immensely powerful. Before the mass of arms, and the seemingly endless millions of soldiers, the weary Germans were only able to retreat.

Kursk, Kharkov and Rostov fell in the south – then Kharkov was re-occupied, and this left the Russians filling a deep bulge into the German line, around Kursk. It was a perfect formation on which to make an attack – so perfect and obvious, that the Germans should have left it alone, for the Russians could see exactly what was going to happen, and they began to prepare for it. But the Germans could never resist an attack, and in July Manstein began what was to be the biggest tank battle of the war. Despite the Russian's vast numerical superiority in artillery, the German Tiger and Panther tanks proved

Hitler's obsession with capturing Stalingrad led to the slaughter and capture of practically the whole 6th Army, and marked the end of German advances in Russia. Paulus, for long totally subservient to his leader's commands, finally surrendered his starving, exhausted troops on the day Hitler made him a Field Marshal.

---

highly formidable, and achieved almost a two to one destructive rate over the Russians. For every Russian tank destroyed, however, there was another to take its place, which was not the case with the Germans.

Once again Hitler had to taste the bitterness of defeat and authorise a withdrawal, but once again he displayed his lack of military ability by insisting on a limited, fighting withdrawal, whereas Manstein wanted to fall right back to the Dnieper and draw up a strong defence. When the Russians began their offensive, pushing up towards Orel, and in the south once more freeing Kharkov, the Germans were forced back right beyond the Dnieper; and in October 1943 the Russians poured across in pursuit. By the end of the month, the Germans in the Crimea were cut off, and Manstein's forces had shrunk by some 100,000, though on paper he kept the same number of divisions.

When the Allied bomber offensive switched from Hamburg to Berlin in November, Hitler turned away from the miserable picture in the east, to new problems in the west – chiefly the prospect of being invaded. (In 1941 he had turned with relief from the problem of having to attempt an invasion of Britain, to the excitement of Barbarossa.) But someone still had to fight the Russians, though Hitler spared only enough of his attention to keep disallowing retreats, strategic or otherwise – and so lost tens of thousands taken prisoner in a Russian encirclement at Kiev.

It was clear to Stalin that, while his war was by no means won, it was not going to be lost. His forces now outnumbered Hitler's by nearly two to one; the Arctic route was providing more and more American and British war supplies, aided by longer ranging fighter cover and the sinking of *Scharnhorst*; and he knew that within about six months a major second front would be launched (a third front really, now that Germany was the only Axis force facing the Americans and British in Italy). Not unexpectedly – though he could hardly complain of lack of *lebensraum* – Stalin's eyes began to slither across the map of East Europe, and Churchill's suspicions of what Russia's postwar attitudes would be were confirmed at the Teheran Conference in November and December, when Stalin resisted Churchill's attempts to come to a firm understanding on Poland's future.

After a brief respite in December, the Russian offensive began again in January 1944 – thus exploiting their greater ability to wage winter warfare, a move that brought exultation in the **relief of the 890-day seige of Leningrad** – though with it, numbing sadness over almost one million civilian lives claimed by cold, hunger and the endless German bombardment. The recovery of Leningrad, and its tragedy, fired the Russian spirit to pursue the German armies remorselessly – a determination that gained in intensity with every account of the occupation's hardships, and with the uncovering of every barbarous atrocity committed against civilians and prisoners of war.

On no front did Hitler ever change orders or generals with greater regularity than he did on the Russian front, and in February Manstein was replaced by Model – though not before Manstein had commanded a spirited battle to avoid a crippling encirclement. Nevertheless, the Germans had fallen back into Rumania by the time Model took over. Hitler did allow a strategic withdrawal in the north, to Estonia, and this halted the Russians. In April, the North and Centre Army Groups held the Russians, but in the south Odessa was liberated, and positions were reversed in the Crimea where the Germans were cornered, and then captured, in Sevastopol.

On the third anniversary of Barbarossa, the Russians launched an offensive on a 450 mile front with the main concentration, in Belorussia, coinciding with extensive partisan attacks. Hitler's stupid obstinacy over withdrawals led to almost the whole of Army Group Centre – some 350,000 soldiers – being deducted from the German strength, removing forever the last vague hope of ever stemming the Russian tide. In July, at Minsk, there were 100,000 German casualties in yet another hopeless stand, and with that the one force (in Estonia) that was holding the Russians became isolated from the rest of the German Army.

Then, on August the 1st, as the Russian line halted almost within sight of Warsaw, the **Polish resistance movement sprang into action** and began a revengeful battle against their oppressors, certain that the Russians would soon arrive to prevent German reinforcements being sent in. But the Russians stayed where they were, and once again, for the third time, the Germans began a vicious rampage of slaughter and destruction in the Polish capital. It is just possible that Marshal Rokossovsky was apprehensive about committing his forces in yet another attack, on what was a fairly strong German position. His supply lines were strained, and his army had been advancing steadily for weeks. Yet it is difficult to believe that he was unable to do anything to help the people of Warsaw while their radio messages pleaded for aid. Eventually the Russians did drop a few supplies over odd parts of Warsaw – but even a conviction that Rokossovsky's actions, or lack of them, were militarily correct, does not explain why the Russians refused to let Britain and American use Russian landing grounds to enable them to attack the Germans, and drop equipment to the Polish partisans. Besides, the decision to do nothing would either have come from, or been agreed to by Stalin, and there was no doubt that a Poland in which the dominant nationalist elements had been subdued would be a Poland far more easily shaped to fit Stalin's future ambitions. So the Poles in Warsaw died in their thousands, the city was virtually razed, and only in the south did the Russians move forward.

There, in August, the Rumanians switched sides, and that helped in achieving more massive German losses. Finland sought an Armistice . . . September came and Bulgaria was overrun . . . Estonia and Latvia found themselves freed of the Germans but once again under Stalin's heel . . . and still the line east of Warsaw stood still. In October Churchill met Stalin, and the degree of interest that each country would have in the future affairs of other lesser countries was argued over and agreed on – except for Poland. Britain had gone to war because Poland was violated, and five years later, after all the misery and bloodshed, the future of that country's independence looked as bleak as it did in the most dismal days of 1939.

The Russians facing battered Warsaw (beyond which lay Berlin) continued to build up their strength while Churchill and Stalin talked, and while the Germans accepted the surrender of the Polish patriots and began to despatch the survivors to various forms of incarceration or extermination. In December the Germans, recklessly depleting their eastern forces, launched their pointless counterattack in the Ardennes. Now it was the West's turn to ask for a diversionary offensive, and the Russians duly began theirs on the 12th of January, 1945. Five days later they took control of the remains of Warsaw, and had little trouble in also taking East Prussia and Danzig. Auschwitz concentration camp revealed its horrible spectacle to the Russians, but however much it may have moved Stalin, it was not enough to make him show diminished self-interest over Poland at the Yalta Conference in February.

In Silesia the hardened Russian troops – men from the harsh steppes, from the Ukraine, from beyond the Urals, from Mongolia – found themselves fighting increasing numbers of teenage boys and very old men, but everything was swallowed up in the massive machinery of total war.

At last, in April, Zhukov directed **the final battle for Berlin**, which mainly consisted of gigantic artillery barrages reducing everything to rubble, over which the Russian tanks and infantry could follow, wiping out anyone still living. The boys defending Berlin were even younger than those in Silesia, and nearly all of them were killed – although some the Russians did not have to shoot, since they had already been hanged from lampposts by youthful members of the SS for the crime of turning their backs on the senseless carnage.

In Berlin itself, conditions were atrocious. The shells and bombs rained down incessantly. For days there was no water and the inhabitants developed a horrible thirst amidst the dust and acrid smoke. Beneath a hot April sun, the people lived like terrified starving rats, huddling

Axis retreat in Russia, December 1942–June 1944.

The Russian conquest of Eastern Germany.

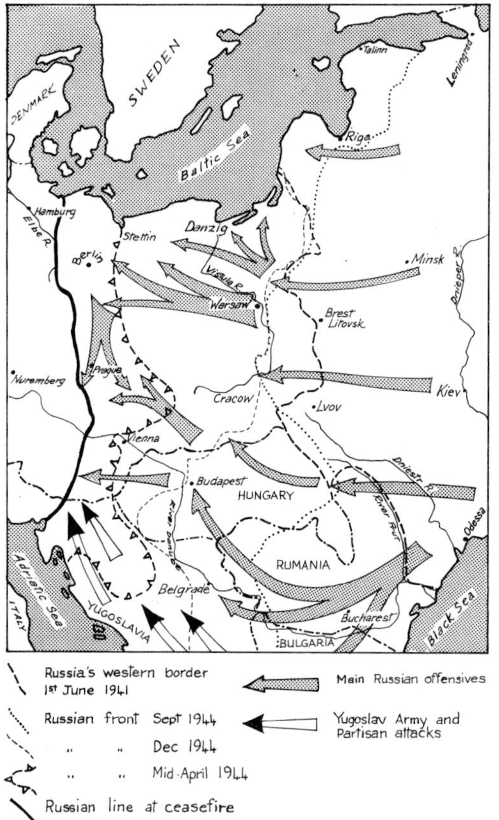

in cellars and hovels, while below the ground, in his elaborate warren, Adolf Hitler pulled the disintegrating strings of his monstrous puppet with increasingly erratic jerks. By April the 25th Berlin was surrounded by Russians, and covered in smoke, fear, and the stench of explosives and death. On the 27th, perturbed by visions of Russians suddenly appearing from below the ground, Hitler ordered the flooding of the Berlin underground railway tunnels, despite the fact that they were being used as a refuge from the shelling by hundreds of civilians and soldiers. But at last Hitler blew out his brains, and Russian shells scattered his ashes among the ruins of his capital city.

Incredibly, many still wished to keep up the fight, but the commander of Berlin's defence, Gen. Weidling, surrendered the city to Chuikov on the 2nd May, and the Marshal ordered the fighting to stop. On the next day, as thousands still tried to flee from the Russians (for rumours of their revenge had thrown half of Germany into panic), there were desperate attempts to get across the Havel Bridge, at Spandau. Hundreds were forced off the sides of the bridge, and tanks and lorries had to push through the swarms of people, till the bridge ran red with blood.

8. THE ALLIED BOMBER OFFENSIVE OVER EUROPE 27.1.43–30.4.45

Doenitz replaced Raeder as C-in-C German navy (30th January). German Sixth Army surrendered at Stalingrad (31st). Japanese withdrew from Guadalcanal (9th February). Axis surrendered North Africa (13th May). U-boat groups withdrawn from Atlantic (30th). Tank battle at Kursk (5th July). Allies invaded Sicily (10th). Allies invaded Italy; Italian Armistice signed (3rd; 8th September). Russians crossed Dnieper (October). Italy declared war on Germany (13th). U.S. invaded Bougainville (1st November). Leningrad siege broken (19th January 1944). Battle of Monte Cassino (March). Rome occupied by Allies (4th June). Allies invaded Normandy (6th). Siege of Imphal broken (4th July). U.S. captured Saipan (9th). Unsuccessful attempt made to assassinate Hitler (20th). Allies invaded southern France (15th August). Germans surrendered Paris (25th). Civil war in Greece (6th October). German counterattack in Ardennes (16th December). Final Russian offensive began (12th January 1945). U.S. invaded Iwo Jima (19th February). Luzon, and Mandalay fell to Allies (March). Devastating air raids on Tokyo (9th). U.S. invaded Okinawa (1st April). Roosevelt died and Truman became U.S. President (12th). Germans in Italy surrendered (29th). Hitler committed suicide (29th).

Although the co-ordinated and concentrated bombing offensive of Germany and German-occupied territories did not begin in earnest until the Battle of the Ruhr in March 1943, it is important to trace the stages leading to the campaign that shattered so much of Germany. The alarming experiences of World War I when airships and aircraft bombed cities many miles from the battlefronts, and inflicted death and destruction on civilians caused radical rethinking among war experts. Gen. Smuts vigorously emphasised the importance of carrying the war to an enemy's cities, and was supported by Trenchard – so laying the foundation for an independent air fighting force. The early thinking was decidedly slanted towards counter-attack, or counter-destruction, since no-one believed that there was any effective method of defence against aeroplanes. The simple multiplication of the effects of the few bombs dropped in the First World War (and later seemingly corroborated by the Spanish Civil War) produced the terrifying but "unmistakable" picture of aircraft being able to wipe out whole cities in a matter of days. So countries began to build up air forces, in some cases as a branch of the army, in others as separate entities. In many ways, however, the first steps were taken in the dark – very little attention was given to the problems of navigation, for instance, or of bomb-aiming. But delays, confusion, argument and strict economies in Britain between the wars resulted in the situation where an air force born to bomb found itself without the bombers that would be needed, and that forced attention on defence rather than counter-attack. Thus R.A.F. Fighter Command was formed (and eventually, the Battle of Britain won through it and other defence-motivated techniques and technology).

The Allied strategic offensive in fact began well before the first heavy raids on southern England, for on the day Holland surrendered, Air Marshal Portal, C-in-C of Bomber Command, ordered an attack on oil and railway targets in the Ruhr. A number of years and endless arguments were to pass before oil refineries and railways again became primary targets, but in this instance they were chosen by simple logic – oil installations were "self-destructive", and railway marshalling yards were easy to see, even at night, when they were frequently lit.

After Dunkirk and the successful conclusion of the Battle of Britain, the London Blitz began, and more and more cities in England were bombed. At that time practically the only way to hit back at Germany was by bombing (although the Royal Navy was constantly involved on its own "front"). The destruction of the centre of Coventry in November 1940 induced Portal, by then Chief of Air Staff, to pursue bombing missions which simply aimed at the middle of cities, although oil installations and communications were still primary targets.

There were many calls on the services of the R.A.F., and in March 1941 much attention was diverted by the Battle of the Atlantic towards bombing the German capital ships in Brest. After another period of "blitz" or "area bombing" (as opposed to the "strategic" bombing of targets specifically linked to war-effort) the conclusion was reached – in July – that on average two thirds of all bombs dropped landed more than five miles away from the target centre. This result was not at all encouraging to the proponents of strategic bombing – or even of area bombing – and after a period of high aircraft-losses towards the end of 1941 the bombing offensive slackened off.

In February 1942, coinciding with the **appointment to the head of Bomber Command of Air Marshal Harris**, raids recommenced, assisted by the rudimentary radar navigational aid known as "Gee". Harris decreed that bombers should aim at built-up areas in general, a decision made less questionable through the pronouncement by Lord Cherwell, Churchill's Scientific Adviser, that area bombing could destroy one third of Germany's dwellings by the summer of 1943. This doom-laden prophecy seemed true after a devastating raid on Lübeck. But that was only one instance – many things could make a raid by an equal number of bombers a total failure. Weather conditions, the location of the target, the strength of the AA defence, all influenced the outcome of a raid.

There were also the German night fighters to worry about, and they were building up a deadly proficiency. By the autumn of 1942, Bomber Command losses climbed to the unacceptable rate of 5·3%. Figuring that the fighters could only shoot down a certain number in each attack, the R.A.F. reduced the loss rate by increasing the number of aircraft taking part in a raid. That meant better navigation was needed, which, with training-time a precious commodity, resulted in a logical "follow-my-leader" approach using the highly skilled Pathfinder Force to locate and mark the target.

Meanwhile the **U.S. Army 8th Air Force**, with Lt.-Gen. Arnold as commander of the U.S. Air Staff, was getting prepared to play its part – unfortunately amid some acrimony between Portal and Arnold. The U.S.A.A.F. decided it would do daylight strategic bombing, and that by using sufficient numbers of their B17 "Flying Fortress" bombers (which bristled with guns) they would create their own air cover and could therefore manage without fighter protection. Portal foresaw disaster, and said so, but the first U.S. raid over German territory (Wilhelmshaven, in January 1943) commanded by Gen. Ira Eaker, was fairly successful.

Technology had developed two new night navigational aids. With "Oboe" an aircraft equipped with a receiver flew along on the end of a predetermined beam sent out by one transmitter (as a model plane flies in an arc at the end of a wire), until it met the point at which a pre-calculated and pre-aimed "straight" signal intercepted the curved flight-path beam. At that point the plane was over the target. H2S provided a rather fuzzy radar map of the ground, could show up the shape of towns, and was most suitable for towns on the edges of lakes or seas.

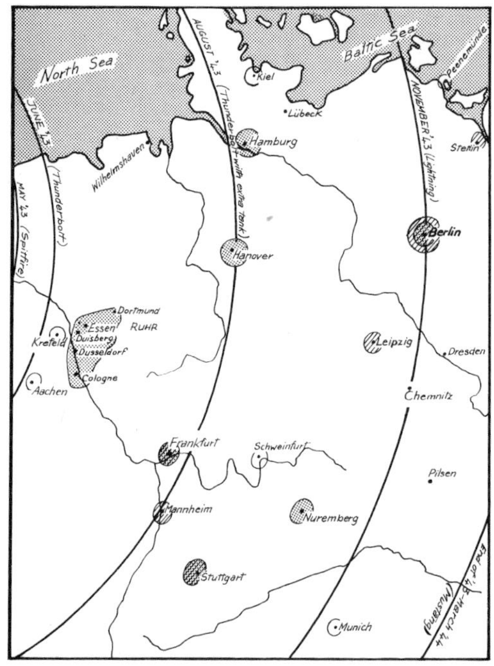

THE ALLIED BOMBER OFFENSIVE: radii show maximum range of Allied escort fighters before establishment of airfields on the continent of Europe. Cities marked to indicate number of sorties flown against them in period March 1943–March 1944: **circled** *= up to 1,000 sorties:* **hatched** *= up to 2,000 sorties:* **dotted** *= up to 3,000 sorties:* **hatched and dotted** *= over 3,000 sorties – in case of Berlin, approx. 10,000.*

The Pathfinders grew adept at using both these systems.

The Germans had also developed their radar, and their night fighters were better able to intercept allied bombers. The stage was thus set for the combined Allied air offensive to begin.

It began on the 5th March 1943 with **the Battle of the Ruhr**, when a group of Mosquito fighter bombers equipped with Oboe accurately dropped red target-indicator bombs on Essen. They were followed almost simultaneously by Pathfinder bombers which dropped green markers for the more than 400 Lancasters and other heavy bombers which streamed behind in the night sky. Most of the markers had been accurately dropped (some bombers actually arrived before the Pathfinders, and effectively increased the red glow of the Mosquitoes' markers), and the mixture of incendiary and high explosive bombs fell on the city with sufficient accuracy for a reconnaissance flight the following day to report a very great amount of damage.

For the next couple of months the Ruhr took frequent poundings, while assorted attacks all over German-occupied Europe ensured that the Germans did not concentrate their defences. But the Ruhr was the main target and received 43 main attacks, involving some 18,500 sorties. Bomber Command lost 872 planes above German territory, while over 2,000 crashed in England or arrived back badly damaged. The devastation in the Ruhr complex was extensive, and the Germans had to redistribute a great number of their manufacturing processes to less damaged areas.

Strategic bombing also forged ahead dramatically in this period, when No. 617 Squadron carried out an extremely difficult attack on the Ruhr dams. The end result – although the raid itself was successful – was not as destructive as had been hoped. Hundreds of workers were killed and many factories damaged, and so on, but the consequences of the raid were overcome in a short period. Perhaps more important was the development of the Squadron itself, with its nucleus of teams of extremely competent bomber crews whose special qualities were later to be used in attacks on U-boat pens, on *Tirpitz*, viaducts and other targets requiring total accuracy, and in making them the marker-bombers at the head of large formations in area bombing raids.

The Battle of Hamburg followed that of the Ruhr, and in four main attacks in July and August, 3,095 sorties dropped 9,000 tons of bombs on the city – half of which were incendiaries. Hamburg's position gave a very clear H2S pattern, the bombing was accurate, Allied bomber casualties were light, and the mixture of high explosives and incendiaries as deadly a combination as ever. The raids were horribly effective. In those four nights Hamburg took the shattering of more explosives than the whole of Britain received during the entire war. The citizens, the air raid workers, the firemen never had a chance. Fifty thousand Germans were killed – practically all of them civilians. Over half the houses and apartments in the city were completely destroyed, and more than 1 million people fled from the holocaust, causing incredible confusion on the roadways.

Not unnaturally, the Hamburg raids greatly perturbed the German war planners. Speer predicted that another six such raids could cripple the country – but they never came. The Hamburg result, however, was not easily duplicated by the Allies. Apart from the unusually good H2S reading giving greater accuracy, the R.A.F. were troubled less than was usual on the Hamburg raid owing to the use of a method of confusing ground radar stations, known as "Window", in which clouds of thin metallic strips released by the planes produced misleading radar readings. Consequently the Luftwaffe night fighters did not know exactly where to go, and many AA batteries were not prepared for an attack. Simultaneously with the

Battle of Hamburg, Hanover also received over 3,000 sorties, but destruction in this inland city was far less extensive. And again defences were kept widespread by many other raids – on the Ruhr again, on Frankfurt, Mannheim, Stuttgart, Berlin, Leipzig, Nuremberg, and many others.

The U.S.A.A.F. in the meantime had been building up its strength, and began to urge concentrated attacks on the German aircraft industry. Arnold, unlike Portal, believed to a fair degree in the existence of a panacea, and consequently in August 1943, 376 B17s left to bomb the ball-bearing factories at Schweinfurt and Regensburg, under the theoretically correct assumption that if the supply of ball-bearings in Germany was stopped, then there could be no new German machinery of any kind, from bicycles to battleships. The U.S. planes were also trying-out for the first time their theory of deep-penetration daylight raids in close formation without fighter escorts, relying on the screen of fire that the formation itself could put up (each plane had up to thirteen half-inch machine-guns, with at least five gunners). But the raid did not work to plan, and there was a devastating 16% loss.

In that summer, the Luftwaffe reached its maximum strength, with over 1,500 fighters. When the B17s of the 8th Air Force tried Schweinfurt again in October, they had fighter-escort for as far as possible and were met on their return. But Allied fighters could only go about half-way to the target – and the German fighter planes waited a little beyond half-way. Of the 291 Flying Fortresses that took off for Schweinfurt, no less than 198 were lost or badly damaged. To add insult to considerable injury, the manufacture of ball-bearings was soon deployed from the quite badly damaged factories, and actual production was only temporarily affected.

While the U.S. Air Staff rethought policy, 444 bombers of R.A.F. Bomber Command began **the first Battle of Berlin** on the 18th of November – carrying on with 15 more major raids until March 1944 which altogether amounted to over 9,000 sorties. Almost 500 planes were brought down over Germany, and once again minor

U.S. 8th Air Force B-17 "Flying Fortresses" being escorted on their way to Germany. The American daylight raids did not become really effective until they were able to enjoy fighter cover all the way. While the B-17s were not able to carry such heavy individual loads as the R.A.F. night bombers, such as the Lancaster, the U.S.A.A.F. far surpassed the R.A.F. in total tonnage of bombs dropped on Germany.

raids by small groups of Mosquitoes – sometimes by only a single plane – made dozens of "alert" attacks on many other German cities. Towards the end the U.S. B17s joined in, for by this time major developments had resulted in increased fighter cover ranges. By November 1943 the U.S. Lightnings could just reach Berlin, but then came the P51 Mustangs and they could give excellent high-speed, high-altitude fighter cover beyond Berlin and Schweinfurt. So on the 6th of March 600 B17s reached Berlin; 500 arrived two days later, and on the 22nd another 600 dropped their bomb loads. Between the 18th of November 1943 and the 31st of March 1944 over 20,200 sorties were flown to Berlin. The German defences (mainly night fighters) claimed 1,047 bombers over Germany.

These enormous raids on Berlin were proportionately not nearly as damaging as the Hamburg raids, and a sense of frustration and disappointment among the Allies was heightened when the R.A.F. made a disastrous raid on Nuremberg at the end of March in which 108 planes out of 795 were shot down, killing more members of the R.A.F. than died in the whole Battle of Britain.

Of course very extensive damage was done to Berlin – some 75,000 people were killed, and 3 million were without homes. Life in the German capital was hellish, but it was going to get worse – a fact which began to plague a few consciences among the Allies. By the end of this Battle of Berlin, the Allies had managed to build up a formidable force of heavy bombers – some 1,200 by April 1944. To this could be added the presence in Italy of the U.S. 15th Air Force, which was able to attack southern Germany and occupied territories in eastern Europe. The 15th and 8th Air Forces were formed into the U.S. Strategic Air Forces in Europe (U.S.S.T.A.F.) under the command of Gen. Spaatz.

Area bombing was called-off in the Spring of 1944, as all forces were being directed towards the forthcoming Operation Overlord. Air Marshal Leigh-Mallory, in charge of air operations, had the difficult task of getting Harris and Spaatz to co-operate on what he, and Eisenhower, thought best. That meant getting Harris away from thinking about area bombing, and Spaatz away from thinking about oil refineries, to the concentrated effort of bombing all railway marshalling yards and railway communications which would affect the Normandy landings. Trial bombings showed encouraging results and in the end this policy proved extremely effective, producing by June a complete railway standstill in Northern France.

After the invasion, **strategic bombing attacks on oil wells and synthetic oil plants** by Bomber Command and by

Allied bomber attacks on the German oil industry.

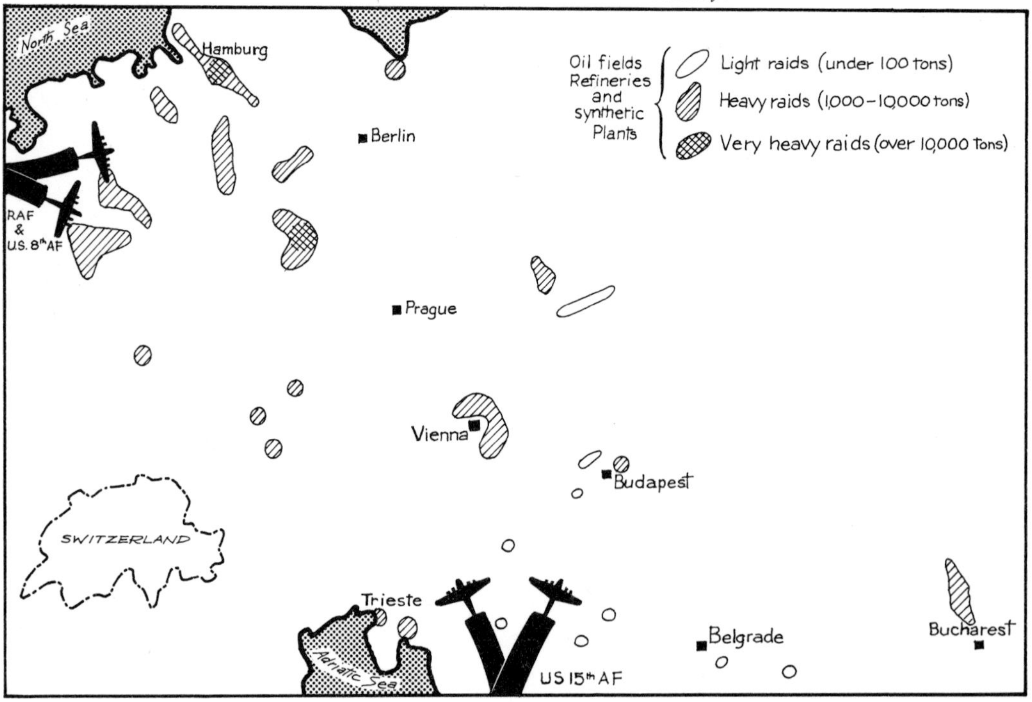

Right up to the last days of the war, the Allies were justifiably apprehensive about German technical developments – flying bombs, rockets, schnorkel submarines and atomic research forbade complacency. The formidable Me 262 jet fighter was potentially very dangerous to the Allies, but a combination of Hitler's scepticism and relentless airfield bombing prevented significant numbers becoming operational.

U.S.S.T.A.F. proved extremely effective. From an average total oil availability in May 1944 of 662,000 tons, bombing halved this by December, and by March 1945 it was down to 80,000 tons. The shortage of fuel had always been a major reason for keeping the German surface fleet inactive – now it began to affect submarines, tanks, and the Luftwaffe as well. As the Allies pushed further into Europe, their air superiority increased. Even short range fighters could be used as escorts for the Allied bombers, while the increasing fuel shortage meant fewer and fewer fighters were able to fly against them.

Even so, there seemed to be something about the whole bombing offensive that left a sense of frustration. Synthetic oil production was virtually stopped. What still came from wells and storage dumps had to travel on hopelessly disrupted railways. Whole cities were pounded day and night. In one 24 hour period the medium-sized town of Duisberg was hit with as many bombs as fell on London in five years. The Allies had a superiority in the air of five to one, and by March 1945, 120,000 Luftwaffe personnel had been transferred to the Army. What fighters there were had no fuel, or if they had, their airfields were badly damaged. But still Germany fought on, and the air commanders, able to bomb what they liked, when they liked, with as much explosive as they wanted, simply could not get the result they were after – which was victory.

Communications were totally smashed, cities crumbled in ruins. The Russians asked for some effort to aid them in the east, and so for a day and a night the communications centre of Dresden was bombed by the R.A.F. and the U.S.A.A.F., turning it into a raging holocaust, the funeral pyre of tens of thousands. In March and April bombs fell almost incessantly on Berlin. German soldiers, civilians, refugees, foreign workers, young and old, jailers and jailed were blown up, burnt, covered in rubble, choked by dust and smoke, deafened, driven insane by the constant blasting – and yet victory only came with the ground defeat of the German armies. There seems to be nothing among German military records which shows that the German war leaders considered whether the desperate plight of the civilians did not make it advisable to surrender. London swore never to give in, Leningrad stood firm while one third of her population died, the Berliners, the citizens of Hamburg, Dresden, Nuremberg, Frankfurt, Cologne, Essen, Duisberg . . . they were blown to pieces in their thousands, but the surrender when it came was not from them. Besides, how does a civilian population in war stop another country bombing it? How do civilians surrender?

During the war, some 130 major towns in Germany were subjected to heavy air raids. Nearly 30 major raids were made on Berlin. Brunswick received 21, the Mannheim/Ludwigshafen complex had 40, Cologne 18, Munich and Hamburg 16 each. How many people these raids killed is not exactly known, but it was certainly over 590,000. Obviously if bombing results in the death of everyone capable of working in a factory, their army will be overrun when it has no more guns, petrol or ammunition. But the area bombing of Germany showed that it takes a lot of time and explosives to try to kill every factory worker, and that bombs do not seem to break down morale or make an enemy well-disposed towards its would-be conquerors. The U.S. Air Forces, originally determined to execute strategic bombing but forced to abandon it mainly due to lack of command of the air, undertook area bombing on a massive scale in Germany, and to an even greater extent in Japan – even when their planes could roam the skies at will. In doing so, it brought the world from the stage of area bombing of little effect, to the stage of total destruction of immense areas. By carrying their concept to its most horrendous extremity – the instant obliteration of complete cities and the immediate death of all the people in them – the proponents of area bombing have shown that they have at last found a way to destroy an enemy, even if, in some way, their final goal of victory still eludes them.

9. THE LIBERATION OF EUROPE, AND THE DEFEAT OF GERMANY 6.6.44–7.5.45

V1 attacks began on England (13th June). Battle of the Philippine Sea (19th). Siege of Imphal broken (4th July). U.S. captured Saipan (9th). Assassination

The battle for Normandy.

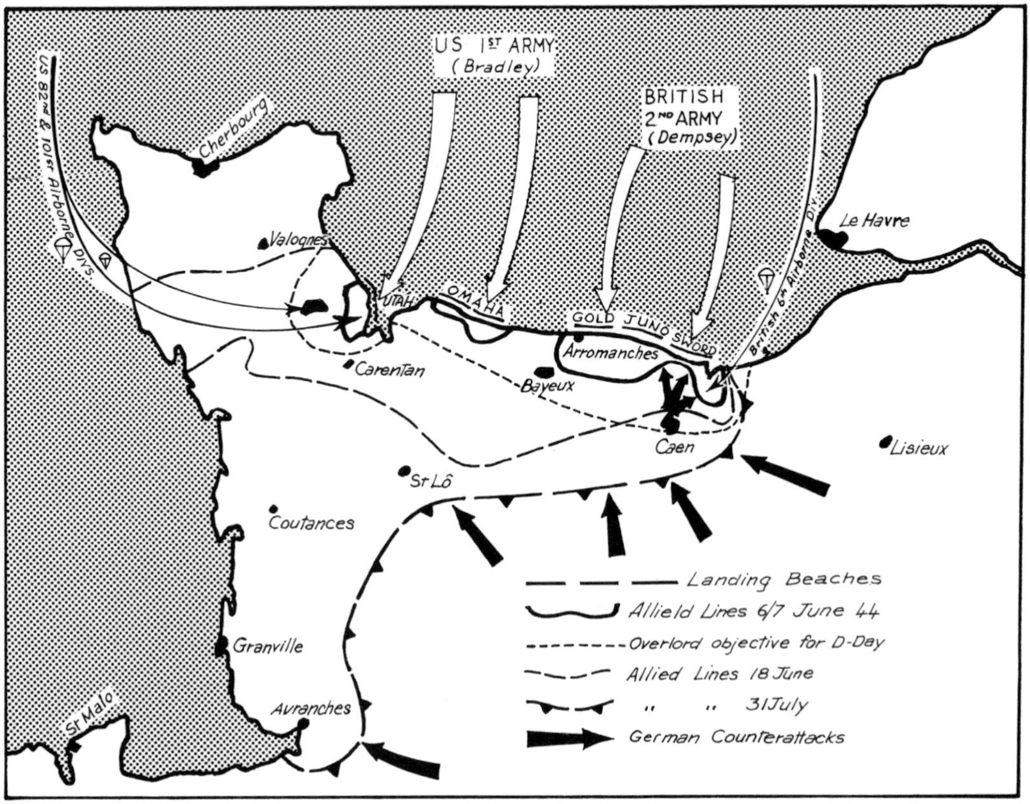

attempt on Hitler failed (20th). Warsaw uprising quelled (2nd October). Civil war broke out in Athens (6th). Russians began last major offensive (12th January 1945). Dresden bombed (13th February). U.S. invaded Iwo Jima (19th). Mandalay, and Luzon captured by Allies (March). Heavy air raid on Tokyo (9th). U.S. invaded Okinawa (1st April). Roosevelt died; Truman became U.S. President (12th). Germans in Italy surrendered (29th). Rangoon retaken by British (3rd May).

Even as the last boat from Dunkirk reached the safety of England in the summer of 1940, it was practically certain that there would have to be a return to occupied Europe if the Third Reich was ever to be brought down. The arrogance and barbarity shown by Germany even at that stage made it extremely unlikely that there would be any easy compromise resulting in an Armistice with Britain – certainly not while Churchill was Prime Minister. Once the threat of invasion by Germany had passed, and Britain was on full-scale war production, thoughts began to turn to the problems of hitting back – and getting back. No-one imagined it would be easy, but no-one at that stage realised just how difficult it would be.

The rest of 1940 and the first half of 1941 were occupied by the campaigns in North Africa, Abyssinia and Somaliland, and by the vain attempt to save Greece. Then Germany's war against Russia began, and the prospect of attacking a Germany already heavily committed on another front a thousand miles away looked a good deal less formidable. But any premature surges of optimism were dashed by the debacle of the Dieppe raid, when even the strictly limited objectives were only reached by a fraction of the whole force. Whatever the faults and mistakes of Dieppe, it did provide a dramatic preview of invasion problems, and did a lot towards preventing a far greater disaster later on.

The entry of America into the war, and the agreement by the Combined Chiefs of Staff to first concentrate on defeating Germany changed conditions greatly, but despite pleas by Stalin for a second front in Europe, and despite early optimistic forecasts by the Allies, the first joint invasion by U.S. and British forces took place in North Africa – and then only in November 1942. Even at that stage it was hoped the invasion of Europe might follow in 1943, but that was soon seen to be totally unrealistic. However, with the Axis cleared out of North Africa, and the Russians fighting for their lives, it was obviously impossible – as Churchill above all realised – for the Allies to do nothing, even for six months. After considerable argument, the decision was taken to invade Sicily, and possibly to follow that with an invasion of Italy – which in fact happened. That solution gave the Allied leaders considerable experience in joint operations, in sea- and air-borne invasions, and at the same time kept a large number of Germans (and Italians) away from the Russian front.

In Germany, the turn of his fortunes had brought home to Hitler the very real danger of an Allied invasion of occupied Europe. It would certainly be mounted from England, but where it would strike was so unpredictable that Hitler had no recourse but to instruct Rundstedt to prepare a very large tract of the coast. Two spots were considered the most likely right from the start – the Calais area, and the Normandy coast. At first Hitler actually suspected it would be the Normandy coast, but he was easily persuaded by Rundstedt and others that the Calais area, being closer, was a more likely spot. The Allies did their best to give credence to the Calais theory with reports from double agents, dummy camps in East Anglia, and even radio messages between the "make-believe" army there and Command H.Q. in London. (British deception methods early in 1943 had already misled the Germans into expecting an invasion of Greece, and possibly Sardinia, when in fact Sicily was the target.) At the same time Hitler could not forget the British attempts to invade Norway in 1940, and he strengthened the already very large garrison there.

When June 1944 came, therefore, the Germans were facing the increasingly forceful Russians in the East, the U.S. 5th Army and the British 8th Army in Italy, and maintaining a strong defence garrison from Norway to the Bay of Biscay. On the northern French coast – where the main preparations were in progress – the German efforts were hindered by the lack of well-trained troops, and by the generally lethargic local labour gangs. To Rundstedt and his deputy, Rommel, the defences looked far from satisfactory, even at Calais. Further acrimony was caused by argument over the placing of reserves. The German plan allowed for no fallback line of defence (until the Siegfried Line), and relied entirely on preventing any invasion from even making a toe-hold on the coast. Rommel therefore wanted the mobile Panzer divisions kept close to the beaches, while Rundstedt wanted them kept well back until it was clear where they were needed. With Hitler's intervention, they were left halfway in-between – probably a reasonable compromise, since they would have been poorly placed to counter-attack Overlord if Rommel had them right in the Calais area. In the end though, their waiting-point scarcely mattered, for Rundstedt held them back too long for them to mount a counter-attack against the much larger Allied forces.

At the same time as Overlord, it had been intended to land a diversionary force, which would become a supporting force, on the French Mediterranean coast, in Operation Anvil. The Anzio landings, and then the primary need for maximum resources for Overlord, forced Anvil to be put back so far that from fear of security leaks its name was changed to Dragoon. When the invasion did take place (in August), the Allies swept north through France with such ease that the operation's value was debatable, especially since it had deprived the

THE LIBERATION OF N.W. EUROPE

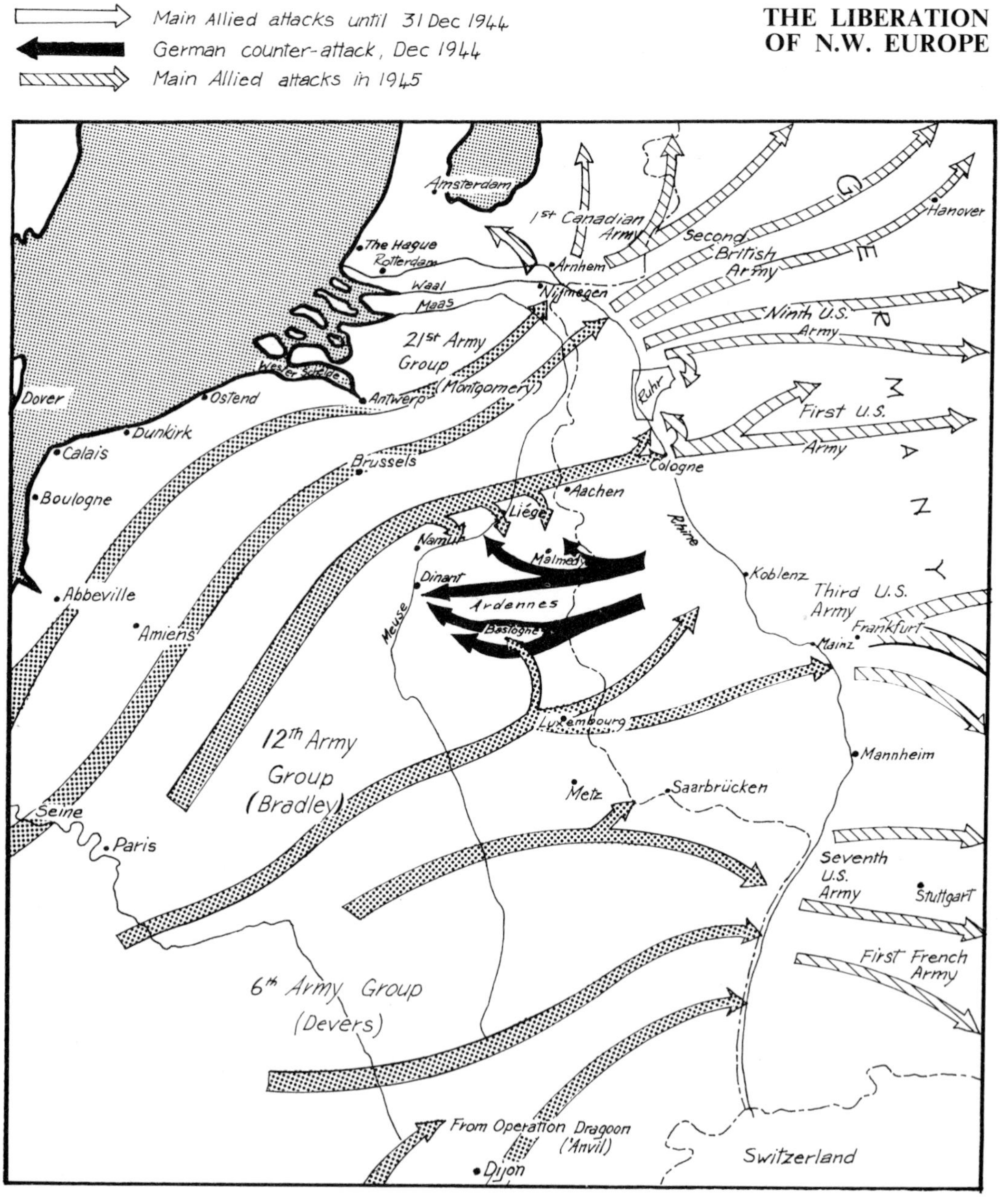

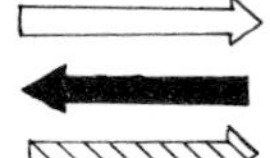
Main Allied attacks until 31 Dec 1944
German counter-attack, Dec 1944
Main Allied attacks in 1945

Allies in Italy of so many of their desperately needed men. Overlord was originally planned for May 1944, but that proved too optimistic a date, especially for the provision of sufficient landing craft, and the invasion was postponed until June, in the face of increasing Russian demands for a second front. The date for the landings – between the 5th and 7th of June – was determined by the need for moonlight to aid the essential paratrooper and glider landings which were to precede the invasion; for a low tide to allow the landing craft to avoid the underwater obstacles; and for the Navy (commanded by Adm. Ramsey) to make a night approach yet still have an opportunity to bombard the defences for at least an hour in daylight. The combined air forces – under the direction of Air Marshal Leigh-Mallory – would also be assisted by daylight for their attacks on German airfields, roads and railways (the strategic bombing of railway marshalling yards in Northern France had already been going on for some weeks, with great success).

The landing – postponed from the 5th to the 6th by poor weather – is described in the Chronology. The invasion force was the largest, most powerful armada that ever sailed, and the fact that the first day's objectives were not attained, and that the landings on Omaha came perilously close to disaster, indicate that a catastrophe would have been inevitable had an invasion been attempted in 1943, or had it been prepared on anything less than colossal scale – or, indeed, had the invasion been launched against a very well-prepared coast line. By the end of the 6th of June, however, the ground forces of Bradley (U.S.) and Dempsey (British and Canadian) under the command of Montgomery had all gained a firm footing on the European shore.

Initially Rundstedt took little action apart from the obvious step of sending the nearest German forces to counter the invasion (most powerful were the Panzers of the German 15th Army under Gen. Salmuth, around Caen). The poor weather of early June had relaxed German vigilance, and Rommel had even gone home for a few days leave. Reports in the early hours of the 6th of paratroopers landing aroused little anxiety, and even the scale of the D-Day landings themselves were not enough to convince Rundstedt that this was "the real thing". Instead of rushing in reinforcements he waited and scanned the seas off Calais for the main attack. Hitler, too, was convinced that the Normandy landings were only a feint, and two weeks were to pass before every available German force was flung against the Allies. By then it was much too late.

In August **the south of France landings** were virtually unopposed, and the U.S., French, and British forces moved ahead rapidly in typical *blitzkrieg* fashion, leaving isolated areas of resistance to be dealt with by the rear-guard. Encouraged by the fast approach of the Allies, the French Resistance captured Paris, Gen. Choltitz fortunately deciding to disobey Hitler and neither fight to the last man nor raze the city. The easy Allied progress continued through Belgium in early September, and by the time Antwerp was taken, some 700,000 Germans were killed, taken prisoner, or surrounded far behind Allied lines. The remainder of the German armies fell back to the Siegfried line, the only significant barrier, with the Rhine, before the heart of Germany.

An **attempt to by-pass the Siegried line** by going round it in the north required fast mobility across the canals and rivers of northern Belgium and Holland. This called for airborne landings to capture vital bridges – and so the tragic disaster of Arnhem was launched, for the British and Canadian paratroopers landed in a prepared, heavily defended area, while their relief forces were seriously delayed. Some 6,000 highly-trained airborne troops were killed or captured, and the Allied advance came to its first major slowdown.

After the consolidation of the Allied forces on French soil, Eisenhower (still with Air Marshal Tedder as his deputy) had assumed supreme command of the Allied forces, while the British and Canadian units of the 21st Army group which had carried out the Overlord landings took the northern route towards Belgium and Germany under Montgomery (together with Simpson's U.S. 9th Army). Gen. Bradley formed the 12th Army Group out of his D-Day U.S. 1st Army (under Hodges) and Patton's 3rd Army. Pushing up from southern France to join Patton's right flank was the 6th Army Group (Gen. Devers). The major forces were Montgomery's and Bradley's, and inevitably a dispute arose between them as to whether or not one Group should get the bulk of the supplies and make a strong push through to Germany. Montgomery naturally thought that he should be allowed to smash through in the north and head straight for Berlin, and no doubt he could have managed that. Bradley felt that a two pronged attack – especially with Patton's powerful 3rd Army in the south – would achieve better results. Montgomery's plan would have called for a considerable diversion of fuel and materials from the 12th Army Group, and though Eisenhower told Montgomery that he agreed with him on the importance of Berlin, he was reluctant to commit himself to the rather risky capture of a specific target, when he saw his task rather as the systematic defeat of the German Armed Forces. So Eisenhower rejected Montgomery's plan, and instead of pushing into Germany, the 21st Army Group consolidated, cleared the approaches to Antwerp, and isolated large German contingents in Holland (where the civilian population was desperately short of food).

Meanwhile Hitler had decided to launch **a major counter-attack on the Allies**, and he recalled Rundstedt to direct it. Once again the Allies had a complacent attitude towards the Ardennes – though obviously they did not expect any sort of counter-attack anywhere at all. Consequently the Allied line across the Ardennes was the thinnest of the whole front, manned either by fresh

British and Canadian troops formed the northernmost flank of the Allied front, liberated much of Belgium, and were the first Allies into Hamburg. Close-range fighting among the rubble of war characterised many stages of the advance; here three British infantrymen dash for cover during a house-to-house battle.

troops or resting "veterans". Intelligence reports about nearby Panzer movements and troop concentrations were considered to indicate a possible thrust with limited "holding" objectives at some point, but not at the "natural obstacle" of the Ardennes. Exactly what Hitler thought he would achieve is not clear. He took valuable units and tanks away from the Russian front, gathered the last remnants of the Luftwaffe's aircraft, assembled about 250,000 troops, and argued his generals (purged and acquiescent after the 20th July Plot) into accepting his plan to try to recapture Antwerp – though no-one questioned him too far on what he intended to do with the port, nor on how long he thought he would be able to hold such a long corridor between the powerful Allies. Nevertheless, he made his attack and was initially successful; but the pointless stupidity of it was soon apparent, and within two months the attack might as well never have happened – except for the extra tens of thousands from both sides dead and injured.

The Germans' Ardennes offensive – the Battle of the Bulge – caused another disruption among the Allies, for when the German front approached Dinant, Eisenhower saw that Bradley's 12th Army was in danger of being divided. He therefore put Montgomery in command of Hodges's U.S. 1st Army in the north, leaving Bradley with Patton's 3rd Army. But nine tenths of the fighting was done by American troops, and Montgomery's diplomatic Chief of Staff, Maj. Gen. de Guigand, smoothed the hackles raised by Montgomery making too great an issue of his new, temporary role.

In the middle of January, with the German advance in the Ardennes more than blunted, the **Russians in the east renewed their offensive** along the Polish sector, and soon the massive Allied vice began to close again on the dwindling resistance of the Third Reich. In February Patton cleared the Saar-Moselle area and the whole west bank of the Rhine, and in March the jubilant U.S. 1st Army captured an intact bridge across the Rhine, at Remagen near Cologne (the German officers responsible for its defence or destruction were executed on Hitler's orders), and the Allies began to pour across. Rundstedt was replaced by Kesselring in a bid to hold back the Allies, but further crossings of the Rhine followed, and from Montgomery in the north to Patton in the south, the last obstruction was in Allied hands.

Late in March the Allies were clearly in a position to make a concentrated push into Germany and capture Berlin well before the Russians could have got there. But without conferring with the Combined Chiefs of Staff, or discussing it with Churchill or Montgomery, Eisenhower decided to aim for Leipzig instead, and telegraphed Stalin of his intention. Eisenhower's intention (as he explained to an angry and disappointed Montgomery, as well as to himself and Stalin) was to cut Germany in half, after which he could concentrate his powerful forces on the

"National Redoubt" and the formidable resistance in the south.

The "National Redoubt" was a spectre which haunted not only Eisenhower. Unaware of Hitler's exact whereabouts and fed by rumour, a number of Allied leaders were convinced that far from being a mountain retreat, Hitler's Berchtesgaden was to be the centre of a desperate last stand by the top Nazis and a powerful army of loyal troops, fighting from extremely well-prepared defences in an awkward, mountainous area. It is surprising that great efforts were not made to exactly locate and formulate the defences of the Redoubt – the Allied network of agents was not insignificant – steps which would have quickly shown that it did not exist at all. Thus an extremely important decision, and one whose consequences marked the future of Europe, was taken partly on assumption rather than on knowledge. Berlin, acknowledged by Eisenhower as recently as the previous September as being the primary target, became merely another German city without any special significance, and it was not even mentioned in his telegram to Stalin. (The division of Germany, and the "shared" future of Berlin, had already been agreed with Stalin. But the Russians gained enormous negotiating power through actually capturing Berlin, and many of the postwar years would quite likely have been far less tense had this power not existed. Even more important, the early capture of Berlin, and the capture or death of Hitler, would have meant an earlier end to the war, and the saving of thousands of lives.)

Leaving Berlin to the Russians, the U.S. completed a pincer movement around the Ruhr where Model was conducting, as ordered, a last-ditch stand with the German Army Group B. With the capture of that complete army (and Model's suicide), little difficulty lay before the Allies in the west. U.S. and Russian troops met for the

---

Hitler's unexpected offensive in the poorly defended Ardennes temporarily halted the Allied advance on the Rhine – but it disastrously weakened both German fronts, and only contributed further misery and bloodshed. Pictured at the height of the German advances is Col. Jochen Peiper of the 1st SS Panzer Division, whose combat group committed the atrocity at Malmédy when over 70 American prisoners were shot in cold blood.

first time in the south, but amidst the relief came the confirmations of the real and terrifying barbarity of the "master race". U.S. forces liberated Buchenwald on the 13th of April, and two days later the British opened the gates of Belsen to find 10,000 unburied corpses and 40,000 living prisoners – though some 13,000 of these died before anything could be done to save them. From the east came columns or cattletrains of living-dead, escorted by their SS guards, from Ravensbruck and Auschwitz, and on the 29th of April, Dachau was discovered.

The end was only days away, and four days after Hitler's suicide, Adm. Friedeburg, Doenitz's emissary, surrendered the German forces in Northern Germany, Holland and Denmark to Montgomery. Other surrenders rapidly followed: Army Group H at Wageningen to General Foulkes and Prince Bernhard of the Netherlands; Army Group G to Gen. Devers at Haar, near Munich; the Norwegian garrison to the Norwegian Resistance; then the capitulation of all Germany by Jodl at Eisenhower's Rheims H.Q., followed the next day, the 9th of May, by the formal unconditional surrender in Berlin by Friedeburg, Keitel and Stumpf, before Tedder and Zhukov. The Third Reich had come to an end.

10. THE WAR OF THE ISLANDS, AND THE DEFEAT OF JAPAN 9.2.43–2.9.45

Warsaw ghetto uprising (19th April). Axis capitulated in North Africa (13th May). U-boat packs withdrawn from Atlantic (30th May). Allies invaded Sicily (10th July). Allied air raids began on Hamburg (24th). Allies invaded Italy; armistice signed (3rd; 8th September). Italy declared war on Germany (13th October). Siege of Leningrad broken (19th January 1944). Battle of Monte Cassino (March). Allies invaded Normandy (6th June). V1 attacks began on Britain (13th). Attempt to assassinate Hitler failed (20th July). Allies landed in southern France (15th August). Germans surrendered Paris (25th). Civil war broke out in Greece (6th October). Germans counter-attacked in Ardennes (16th December). Dresden bombed (13th February 1945). Roosevelt died, and Truman became U.S. President (12th April). Hitler committed suicide (30th April). Germany surrendered unconditionally at Rheims (7th May). Potsdam Conference began (17th July).

U.S. landings around the Rabaul stronghold.

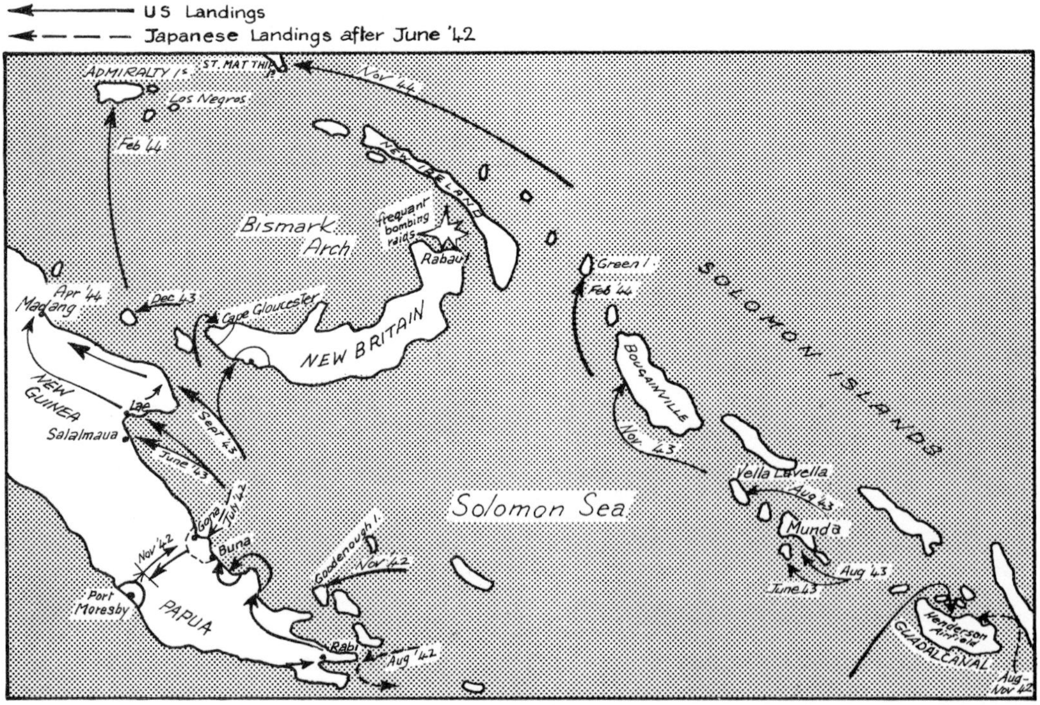

US Landings
Japanese Landings after June '42

Churchill replaced as British Prime Minister by Attlee after elections (26th).

The mutual respect and confidences between Churchill and Roosevelt ensured that little time was lost after Pearl Harbor in preparing the joint campaign against the Axis. The two leaders formed the Combined Chiefs of Staff whose duties were to work out and approve the plans of war in Europe and the Pacific. (The Combined Chiefs of Staff were formed by representatives from the U.S. Joint Chiefs of Staff, and the British Chiefs of Staff Committee.) The decision was immediately taken to concentrate first on the destruction of Germany, and then of Japan – though there were many voices in America raised in protest against this sequence, largely out of a simple desire for revenge. But Germany presented the greatest threat to the world's future, was causing far greater destruction, and was more likely to affect America herself. Another decisive point was that it would be relatively simple to contain the Japanese expansion until it could be effectively dealt with, while it was impossible to "hold" the German position.

Nevertheless, some actions in the Pacific and Far East had to be planned, and it was decided to divide the Japanese war into two main areas of responsibility. The Pacific Ocean area would be the responsibility of the U.S. Joint Chiefs of Staff, while the Indian Ocean area, with Burma, Malaya and Sumatra would come under the direct control of the British Chiefs of Staff. The U.S. in turn divided the Pacific into two principal areas: the South-West Pacific, comprising Australia, New Guinea, the Dutch East Indies and the Philippines, being commanded by Gen. MacArthur with American and Australian forces; and the remainder of the Pacific under the command of Adm. Nimitz, with American forces. The objectives given to Nimitz and MacArthur were to stop any further expansion of the Japanese Empire and to carry-out whatever counter-attacks were possible until larger numbers of men and materials were made available by the conquest of Germany.

(Much the same was demanded of Adm. Lord Mountbatten by the British Chiefs of Staff when they appointed him Supremo of the newly formed South East Asia Command (S.E.A.C.), which was comprised of highly heterogeneous forces – Mountbatten's Deputy was Gen. Wheeler (U.S.). Within S.E.A.C. jurisdiction came the difficult dealings with China, and the attempts to re-establish ground links and maintain air contact with the Chinese Army.

The following pages concentrate on the Pacific war of the islands, which did not directly involve S.E.A.C. – but that does not mean that S.E.A.C. did not play a major role in the defeat of Japan. Its 14th British Army – mainly of British, Australian, Indian and Gurkha troops – was responsible for the greatest land victories of the Japanese war, under extremely arduous conditions; and, with the Chinese Army, S.E.A.C. prevented Japan from establishing a powerful position on the Asian mainland. China and S.E.A.C., as late as June 1945, kept some 1,600,000 Japanese troops occupied on the Asian mainland, while another 650,000 were in Manchuria and about 1½ million in Japan. About 780,000 were still in the Pacific theatre. The activities of S.E.A.C. and the Chinese Army therefore prevented vast strengthening of the Japanese positions in the Pacific.

After the U.S. victory at Midway in June 1942, Nimitz was understandably keen to begin an offensive. In this he was supported by Adm. King, C-in-C of the U.S. Fleet who had little sympathy for Roosevelt's "Europe first" policy (perhaps since the Pacific was obviously going to be very much a Navy affair, while the German war would mainly involve ground troops, and the Royal Navy). MacArthur was anxious to avenge the defeat of his army in the Philippines and also hungered for some form of offensive. Consequently the Joint Chiefs of Staff proposed a combined, compromise operation (both MacArthur and King/Nimitz wanting to have priority themselves) which required Nimitz to attack the East Solomons – Tulagi and Guadalcanal – and MacArthur to complete the occupation of the Solomons, invade New Guinea and then move on Rabaul in New Britain. Early reports of a Japanese build-up on Guadalcanal (a stage in their new, post-Midway outer defence ring) prompted an early start (August) to Nimitz's campaign. Constant U.S. reinforcement of Guadalcanal, and the sea battles of Santa Cruz and Guadalcanal, led to its evacuation by Japan in January 1943; by which time MacArthur's Australians had repulsed an attack on Port Moresby, and captured Gona and Buna on the north coast of Papua.

Neither Nimitz's nor MacArthur's campaigns had been at all easy, and the Joint Chiefs realised that their original plan would take far longer than expected. A pattern of the Pacific war was then established – that of having a final objective, but maintaining flexibility in deciding on the stages and methods needed to reach the objective. A new plan therefore created the South Pacific Area, under Adm. Halsey, and his force was made responsible for taking the New Georgia group in the Solomons prior to invading Bougainville, from where Rabaul could be attacked. MacArthur, meanwhile, would continue his New Guinea campaign and gain control of the Dampier Strait between New Britain and New Guinea by invading the southern end of New Britain. Nimitz would move north to gain control of the Marshall and the Gilbert Islands.

Once again, however, the ferocity of the Japanese defences forced rethinking – (Halsey in particular encountered extremely strong resistance in New Georgia) for it was apparent that if an island's defenders were prepared to fight virtually to the last man – in one case

Above: American paratroopers (not in battle kit) grouped around a Douglas C-47 transport aircraft (Photo: Properfoto Limited). Below: A Cassino landscape with a wrecked Sherman tank and Bailey bridge in the foreground (Photo: Imperial War Museum).

literally that – it would take many months, and many thousands of lives to systematically clear every island in order to gradually tighten a noose around the Japanese Empire.

This frightening prospect produced the simple solution (and, with hindsight, the logical one), of employing what was virtually a marine version of *blitzkrieg*. That is, strikes would be made towards strategic positions and any occupied position which was not required for its own sake and had no strategic value would simply be "leap-frogged", or by-passed. The principle relied, of course, on strong sea power to carry the assaults forward without being destroyed on the way; on strong air power for the same reason and to be able to bombard intended invasion points; and on there being sufficient naval reserves and submarines to blockade the ignored strongholds, and to prevent them from being used as bases from which attacks behind the front could be launched. This strategy was tried on a minor scale, but its feasibility was so obvious that it was enthusiastically adopted. Adm. Spruance's 5th Fleet had had a decisive victory over a Japanese task force between Rabaul and Bougainville, and it was clear that the U.S. Pacific Fleet would soon gain supremacy of the sea – and with that would come air supremacy. With relief and the enthusiasm of the "free" advance gained, the Joint Chiefs decided to leap-frog Rabaul's large garrison.

At the same time that this solved one set of problems, however, it raised another set. The Allies hoped that Japan could be defeated within a year of the surrender of Germany, but how this was to be done had still to be decided. Japan could be blockaded by sea until it "starved" to surrender; bombardment from the air could produce a collapse; or an invasion might be necessary – and if so, from where? . . . overland from S.E. Asia? . . . from the Philippines? . . . from Formosa and the "home islands"? . . . perhaps from the north Pacific, and first to Hokkaido?

The S.E. Asia and China approach was ruled out by the intended withdrawal – for Overlord – of many amphibious craft from the Indian Ocean area, and by Russia's expressed intention to declare war on Japan after the defeat of Germany. This made Russia potentially the most powerful force on the mainland, and it also contributed to ruling out the northern approach to Japan. Beyond those decisions, no long term plans were made late in 1943 – except to follow the "wait and see" policy which had already altered a number of plans. It was simply decided that locations in the northern Philippines, Formosa or China areas should be reached from which Japan could be blockaded, bombed, or invaded. Immediate objectives were the destruction of the Japanese fleet and the Japanese lines of communications, the mounting of air attacks on Japanese industry, and the maintaining of S.E. Asian operations in order to keep China in the war.

Leaving the door open to opportunism had its advantages in the Pacific theatre, but it also led to some confusion and rivalry. What it basically came down to was whether the U.S. should advance through the Central Pacific to Formosa, by way of the Marshall, Caroline and Marianas Islands – as advocated by Adm. King, and largely supported by Nimitz; or whether the final attack should be launched from Luzon in the Philippines, which would be reached after capturing New Guinea and then Mindanao – which was MacArthur's plan.

One of the first stages in the Pacific War after the tide turned at Midway was the re-conquest of the Solomon Islands. The largest island was Bougainville, and many of the Marines on patrol here would have been veterans of Guadalcanal.

Once again the unpredictable Far East prevented any premature decision. Nimitz overran the Marshalls far quicker than expected, took Eniwetok two months ahead of schedule, and saw that Truk could be by-passed. By June 1944 he would be able to attack either the Palaus (to support MacArthur's Mindanao approach) or the Marianas. MacArthur also leap-frogged and took the Admiralties in March, while Halsey saw possibilities of faster jumps as well. From these developments the joint Chiefs decided in March 1944 that Nimitz should isolate Truk, move into the Marianas in June, and the Palaus in September. MacArthur was to leap-frog in New Guinea to Hollandia in April, using some of Nimitz's naval forces, and then move into a position to assist the Palaus

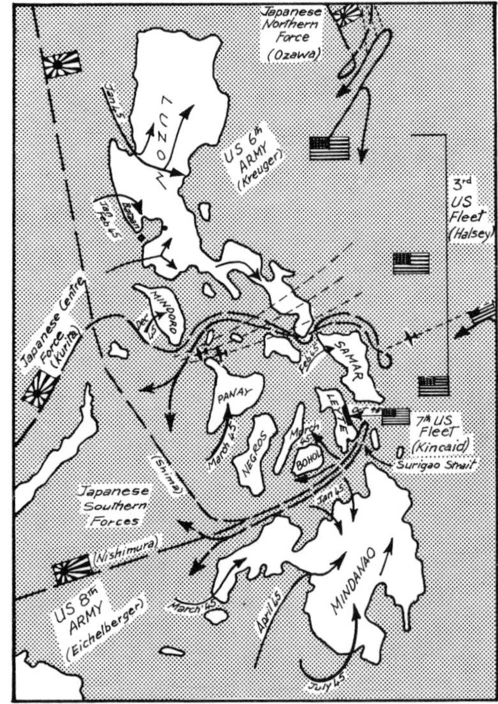

The battle for Iwo Jima was one of the hardest of the war. A long period of bombing raids made the U.S. intentions clear, and enabled the Japanese to dig in behind formidable fortifications. The tenacious defenders had to be located and wiped out one by one – here a Sherman tank helps U.S. Marines inch forward over the devastated landscape.

---

campaign, preparatory to his invasion of Mindanao – for which the Pacific Fleet would again be used. The Joint Chiefs therefore favoured both approaches, but envisaged using the one main naval force to support a two-pronged attack. Seaborne invasions were consequently to be in the order of Hollandia (MacArthur); Marianas and Palaus (Nimitz); Mindanao (MacArthur). After these stages had been achieved the alternative of Formosa or Luzon would be decided on, though it was clear that the Joint Chiefs had some preference for Formosa.

Events closely followed the plans for the middle of 1944, and in addition the Battle of the Philippine Sea caused severe losses to the Japanese aircraft-carrier strength. But through it all King and MacArthur remained at loggerheads, each convinced in the strength and logic of his own strategy, and they were both singularly strong-willed men. Nimitz still basically supported King, though he valued the prospect of a covering force in the Philippines if he was to launch an attack on Formosa (the Japanese still controlled the Chinese mainland ports, though their navy was steadily being destroyed). In one instance the three commanders "on the spot" – MacArthur, Nimitz and Halsey – immediately and unanimously disagreed with the Washington planners, who had suggested that both Luzon and Formosa be by-passed and a move made directly against Kyushu.

Once again, however, events altered intentions. With most of the army units assigned to MacArthur, Nimitz realised that his Marines alone would not give him the strength to take Formosa; and MacArthur decided that instead of completely occupying Mindanao, he would establish his Philippines base on the island of Leyte, north of Mindanao, which had a better harbour. Under Gen. Marshall's urging in September, MacArthur was told to go ahead with this plan. But within two weeks the situation changed yet again. Adm. Halsey launched carrier attacks on the Philippines, and considered that Japanese strength was less formidable than expected. He therefore suggested that the Leyte landings should begin as soon as possible, by-passing the intermediate stages. So the order to invade Leyte in October went out, and that advanced MacArthur's plans for Luzon by two months as well – a speed-up which King could not match for Formosa.

With Formosa ruled out, Nimitz then suggested that the Central Pacific attack should go north from the Marianas to Iwo Jima, and then to Okinawa to provide advance air bases. This was accepted, so the proposed invasions were then: Luzon (MacArthur) December 20th; Iwo Jima (Nimitz) January 1945; Okinawa (Nimitz) early March.

At last strategy as far as Japan's doorstep was decided on, though no decision was taken on what would happen after the Philippines had been freed and Iwo Jima and Okinawa won. Luzon and the two smaller islands would enable the U.S. to mount airborne attacks on any part of Japan, and also to prepare a sea-borne invasion of Japan. And then there was Russia's role to consider, and the availability of British forces released after Germany's imminent defeat.

As scheduled, the U.S. began to attack Okinawa in March, and the first landings on the island itself were made on the 1st of April. But it was the 20th of June before the defenders of the 70 mile long island were finally subdued – at a cost of some 170,000 Japanese lives (with only about 7,000 taken prisoner). The U.S. Navy suffered its heaviest losses, and the American dead numbered about 12,500. The battle for Iwo Jima was scarcely less vicious and these two battles had been typical of nearly all the island battles. It could have been with nothing other than dread that MacArthur, Nimitz and the Joint Chiefs drew up plans for the invasion of Japan. It was a very real possibility that even a complete destruction of all the Japanese mainland forces by the Russians, and a total blockade of Japan itself, would still not end defiance. The Japanese had shown a tragic tendency to commit suicide rather than surrender. Nevertheless it was

In the Japanese Empire's closing days the decade of blind militarism and the revival of ancient traditions produced thousands of pilots willing (and sometimes compelled) to make suicide attacks on Allied ships – their only form of attack after the destruction of their Navy. Here a *kamikaze* plane dives on a Royal Navy aircraft carrier.

planned to invade Kyushu in November, in Operation Olympic, and Honshu in Operation Coronet in March 1946.

At this stage, Japan was in extensive ruin, and the Chronology tells of the enormously destructive U.S. air raids that were carried out practically at will. The majority of the population was on mere subsistence rations, the country had virtually no navy left, and the remains of its air force were being rapidly used up in *kamikaze* attacks. If the invasions had been attempted, however, the loss of life on the Allied side would have been extremely high, for many Japanese leaders were prepared to sacrifice over 2 million troops and many more civilians.

It is no wonder that the "miracle cure" presented by the atomic bomb was taken with eagerness. Surrender without invasion and without something drastic like the atomic bomb then seemed a comparatively remote possibility. Even though the majority of Japanese must have known that they could never hope for victory, the alternative to them was not defeat but either a fight to death, or suicide. If sergeants and lieutenants on remote, foreign islands preferred death to surrender, could it reasonably be doubted that their leaders, on the very soil of Japan, would choose differently? Even the overtures for peace came only from a minority of those who wielded power, and, so long as no guarantee was being made by the victors about the future structure of Japan's leadership, the minority was unlikely to win over the majority. By August 1945, the world had seen and suffered six years of the purgatory created by the dictatorships of two countries. Whatever alternatives can be suggested with hindsight, at the time the atomic bomb – to the millions of opponents and victims of the Axis – was a gift promising merciful relief. For many hundreds of thousands, for dying prisoners of war, for those who would have died in an invasion or even in a long drawn-out blockade (whether they were Japanese or American), the bomb was a life-saver. For far fewer it did bring death and long suffering. For the whole world it brought a horrible warning – and momentary peace.

3. SECOND WORLD WAR BIOGRAPHIES

(Any rank given is that held at the end of the war, or at death. The biographical details do not normally go beyond the end of the conflict.)

ALEXANDER, Field Marshal Sir Harold. b. 1891. Alexander was one of the war's outstanding commanders, and played a prominent part in practically every major Allied operation involving British troops. As a General, he led the 1st Division of the B.E.F. into Europe in the first days of the war, and commanded the last corps to leave the beaches of Dunkirk. The urgent task of training the new British Army was given to him when he took over Southern Command in the U.K. After the Japanese invasion of Burma he conducted the highly successful strategic withdrawal of the British forces to Assam, which greatly facilitated the eventual conquest of the Japanese in Burma.

In the most difficult stage of the North African campaign, when Rommel threatened Egypt, Alexander was again summoned, and as C-in-C Middle East, with Montgomery commanding the 8th Army, he directed the pursuit of the Axis to Tunisia. The Casablanca Conference following Operation Torch made him deputy to Eisenhower (the Supreme Allied Commander) in which capacity he commanded all Allied land forces. After the surrender of the Axis in North Africa (May 1943), Alexander commanded the invasion of Sicily, and then of Italy. The Italian campaign was one of considerable frustration – although the Italians themselves had surrendered, there was a powerful German contingent under Kesselring, and Alexander had to put up with continual depletion of the British and U.S. forces for both the Greek emergency, and, even more, for Overlord and Dragoon (Anvil). In December 1944 he was made Supreme Allied Commander Mediterranean, and in 1945 he launched the final Allied offensive in the Po Valley resulting in the surrender of German forces in Italy at his H.Q. on 29th April – the first unconditional surrender signed by Germany. Alexander had a reputation of the highest integrity, and was unreservedly respected by fellow Allied commanders as well as by all under his command. (He later became Earl Alexander of Tunis.)

AMERY, Leopold. b. 1873. An early political supporter of Churchill, Amery argued frequently in Parliament for the rapid arming of Britain in the face of the German

Field Marshal Sir Harold Alexander was one of the war's most respected, liked, and successful commanders – a rare combination. Few commanders could have maintained such a strong grip over the extraordinarily heterogeneous 8th Army in Italy, and had his troops not been constantly depleted for campaigns in southern France and Greece, Italy would doubtless have been cleared of Germans well before April 1945.

arms build-up. He made a forceful attack on Chamberlain and helped pave the way for Churchill to become P.M. – who appointed him Secretary of State for India and Burma.

ANAMI, General Korechika. Japanese War Minister and former military aide to the Emperor. An ardent militarist member of the Big Six group that governed Japan. Although well aware of the inevitable Allied victory, he was one of the fanatics who advocated a last, massive confrontation, or at best favoured suing for peace only after inflicting massive losses on U.S. forces. He committed a particularly painful type of *hara-kiri* at dawn on the 15th August 1945, and his death ended numerous attempts at coups, plots and counterplots in the last days of the Empire.

ANDERSON, Sir John. b. 1882. As Home Secretary and Minister of Home Security, Sir John gave his name to the inexpensive Anderson shelter used extensively throughout Britain, and which saved thousands of lives in the Blitz. From 1940–43 he was Chairman of the committee co-ordinating economic policy, and was jointly responsible with Bevin for the Manpower Committee. In August 1942 he became the Cabinet representative on "Tube Alloys" – the project for the development of the atomic bomb. From 1943–45, he was Chancellor of the Exchequer.

ANDERSON, General Sir Kenneth. b. 1891. Commanded the 11th Infantry Brigade to France in 1939, and the 3rd Division at Dunkirk. In Operation Torch Anderson led the British 1st Army, and his forces in the advance on Tunisia included large numbers of untried U.S. and British troops. The campaign was halted by bad weather, during which the Germans built up a larger force. The resumption of the campaign led to many brushes with Rommel's forces and some temporary setbacks, but the Axis eventually capitulated in May 1943. Anderson then commanded the 2nd Army in the U.K., was made G.O.C. Eastern Command, and later G.O.C.-in-C, East Africa.

AOSTA, Duke of. 1898–1942. In 1939 the Duke of Aosta, cousin of the King of Italy, was Governor-General of Italian East Africa and Viceroy of Abyssinia (captured by the Italians in 1937). He was also C-in-C of the Italian forces in the territories, and led the invasion of British Somaliland in August 1940, which was subsequently liberated by the Allies in January 1941. He commanded one of the last large Italian forces in Abyssinia, and on his surrender was accorded the privilege of the "honours of war", being highly respected by the Allies for the chivalrous conduct of his campaigns. He died in Nairobi, while a prisoner of war.

ARNOLD, General Henry. b. 1886. General Arnold was the commander of the U.S. Army Air Forces in all theatres, and he arrived in Britain soon after the entry of America into the war to set up the 8th Air Force – which eventually dominated the Allied air offensive over Europe. He was a member of the U.S. Joint Chiefs of Staff, and of the Combined Chiefs of Staff Committee. Arnold was an early supporter of U.S. assistance to Britain, and from 1938 had vigorously built up U.S. air power, emulating the beliefs of Smuts and Trenchard.

ATTLEE, Clement. b. 1883. The leader of the British Labour Party was Deputy Prime Minister in the Coalition Government which ran Britain from 1940 to 1945. As Deputy, Attlee performed an invaluable service in taking over many of the duties of Prime Minister, not only during Churchill's frequent trips abroad but while Churchill was in the U.K. as well, thus enabling him to also act as Minister of Defence and head of the War Cabinet. Attlee was instrumental in minimising industrial problems during the war. He became Prime Minister when the Labour Party was elected in July 1945, and replaced Churchill in the middle of the vital Potsdam Conference on the future of Europe, an extremely difficult task, since he did not have Churchill's experience in negotiating with Stalin.

AUCHINLECK, Field Marshal Sir Claude. b. 1884. Auchinleck was one of the British generals who had the misfortune to be in crucial command positions at times when Allied forces were not sufficiently large or well-trained to counter the efficient Axis machine. In 1940 he was C-in-C of the unsuccessful British operations in northern Norway, became G.O.C. Southern Command, and in 1941, C-in-C India. In May that year he despatched an Indian division in support of Wavell's troops in Iraq, thwarting Axis attempts to bring Iraq and Syria into the Axis sphere, which would have had disastrous effects on the Allies in Africa as well as the East. In June 1941 Auchinleck relieved Wavell as C-in-C Middle East, and after the initially unsuccessful attempts to break Rommel's hold on Tobruk and the Halfaya Pass, he replaced Cunningham with Ritchie as commander of the newly formed 8th Army. The Allied offensive eventually broke through the Axis lines, relieved the siege on Tobruk and pushed Rommel back to Tripolitania, capturing Benghazi on the way. Auchinleck's lines of communication had by then become over-extended, while Rommel had received considerable reinforcements of men and equipment. In January 1942 the 8th Army was sent into retreat and lost Benghazi, and then Tobruk. It was only when Auchinleck himself took command of the 8th Army that the retreat was halted, Auchinleck falling back to form a strong defensive line at El Alamein. Churchill then replaced him with Alexander, and Auchinleck returned to India where he took command of the training of troops for S.E.A.C., which eventually drove the Japanese out of Burma.

BADER, Squadron Leader Douglas. b. 1910. A legendary hero of the war, Bader lost both his legs in a pre-war flying accident, but rejoined the R.A.F. in 1939. In the Battle of Britain he was a fully operational pilot credited with over 20 "kills" while commanding No. 242 Squadron in 12 Group. In 1941 his plane was brought down over occupied France, and after one escape he spent the rest of the war in prison.

BADOGLIO, General Pietre. b. 1871. Italian Chief of Staff who resigned after the Greeks had driven the Italian invaders back into Albania in December 1940. Badoglio was an Anti-Fascist and became Premier in July 1943 after Mussolini was deposed. He signed an Armistice with the Allies after the invasion of Italy in September 1943, and in October declared war on Germany. He resigned as Premier in June 1944.

BALBO, Italo. 1896–1940. The popularity of this ardent anti-Fascist angered Mussolini. He was openly critical of Germany, and tried to persuade Mussolini to keep Italy out of the European war (Balbo was then Governor of Libya). Returning to Libya shortly after Italy declared war, Balbo's plane was "mistakenly" shot down by the Italians, and he was killed.

BARUCH, Bernard. b. 1870. An adviser on economics to the U.S. Government, long a friend of Churchill, and a life-long opponent of Nazi Germany. Baruch played an important part in mobilising America's massive war industry and became a special adviser to Byrnes, the Director of Economic Stabilisation, and later Director of War Mobilisation.

BEAVERBROOK, Lord. b. 1879. (Maxwell Aitken.) A remarkably efficient and energetic organiser and formidable adversary, Beaverbrook, as Minister for Aircraft Production, achieved dramatic increase in output of aircraft. He led the Anglo-American mission to Moscow which agreed the supply of war material to Russia, worked closely and effectively with the Americans, especially on Lend-Lease administration, and was a member of the British War Cabinet. He encouraged a spirit of great national co-operation as Minister of Supply (1941–42), and was Lord Privy Seal from 1943–45. One of the colourful personalities of the war, Beaverbrook was highly respected for his competence – even by those whose schemes he thwarted.

BECK, General Ludwig. 1880–1944. Beck played a prominent role in the rebuilding of the German Army after 1933, and was made Chief of the General Staff in 1938. He was, however, one of the "old school" of army generals who was not taken in by ex-corporal Hitler, and resigned his post in protest at the increasing power of the SS. He was also against the invasion of Czechoslovakia (though mainly because he thought it was militarily premature) and steadily became more and more opposed to Hitler. Beck considered Hitler's ambitions for large scale conflict to be well beyond the reach of the army's preparedness, and deplored the grandiose ambitions of the Nazis. He was one of the first members of the anti-Nazi "Wednesday Club" and was constantly seeking a way to get rid of Hitler. Beck was therefore a prominent member of the 20th July Plot, and was to be the head of the military arm after its conclusion. Knowing he faced certain execution after the plot failed, Beck took his own life.

BEDELL SMITH, General Walter. b. 1895. Bedell Smith held one of the key staff positions in the joint U.S.–U.K. war effort, but before the war was Secretary to the War Department General Staff. In February 1942 he became Secretary of the Joint Chiefs of Staff, and U.S. Secretary of the Combined Chiefs of Staff Committee. As Eisenhower's Chief of Staff from 1942 to the end of the war, he was involved in all major Allied operations in Europe. He conducted the Armistice negotiations with the Italian envoys in Lisbon, and during the liberation of Europe was greatly responsible, with de Guigand (Montgomery's Chief of Staff), for maintaining a smoothly-operating combined offensive against Germany. Bedell Smith signed the unconditional surrender of Germany with Jodl at Eisenhower's Rheims H.Q. on 7th May 1945.

BENEŠ, Eduard. b. 1884. The principal founder of present-day Czechoslovakia, Beneš was also the country's pre-war President, but resigned and went to the West as a result of constant pressure from Hitler in 1938. He was largely instrumental in founding the Czech National Committee after Germany invaded the country in March 1939. The Czech Government-in-exile, with Beneš as its President, was recognised by Britain in 1940. The Czech army and air force, built up from refugees, formed a brigade in the British Army, and provided a number of pilots for the Battle of Britain. By the end of 1942 the Beneš Government was recognised by all the Allies, and he persuaded Britain and Free France to renounce the Munich agreement. After Molotov's assurance of support from Russia, a Czech brigade was also formed in the Red Army. Beneš paid state visits to Canada and America, and in Moscow signed a treaty of mutual assistance with Stalin. In April 1945 the Czech Government made its temporary seat in Kosice, Slovakia, and on the 16th May 1945 Beneš re-entered Prague.

BENNETT, Air Vice-Marshal Donald. b. 1910. The founder of the famous R.A.F. Pathfinders whose superb navigation, and frequent daring, proved invaluable in accurately marking bombing targets during the Allied air offensive over Europe. Bennett, an Australian, supervised the "Atlantic Ferry" of Canadian and American aircraft to Britain and was later the

Commander of 77 Squadron, Bomber Command, and then 10 Squadron. He was shot down leading the Trondheim attack on *Tirpitz* but escaped to Sweden, from where, after a brief internment, he returned to Britain. The R.A.F. Pathfinders Force began operations under his command in January 1943, and he led it until the end of the war.

BERNADOTTE, Count Folke. 1895–1948. Count Bernadotte played an important humanitarian role in the war, as President of the Swedish Red Cross. During 1943 and 1944 he arranged two exchanges of disabled and seriously-ill prisoners of war between the Allies and the Germans (excluding Russian prisoners). As virtually the only person of high repute known to the Allies and the Nazi leaders alike he was Himmler's choice as mediator in the latter days of the war when the SS leader tried to arrange a surrender to Britain and America (without Hitler's knowledge and to his total fury). Since Himmler intended war against the Russians to continue, Bernadotte informed him of the rejection of his approach on 27th April. (The Count was assassinated in Palestine in 1948.)

BERNHARD, Prince. b. 1911. Two days before her country's defeat in May 1940, Queen Wilhelmina of the Netherlands fled to London together with members of the Dutch Government and of the Royal Family, including the heiress Princess Juliana and her husband Prince Bernhard. Bernhard became a pilot in the R.A.F., and using information gathered from people escaping from Holland to Britain, he reorganised the Dutch Intelligence Service into one of the most efficient in the occupied countries. He made a secret trip to the Dutch East Indies while it was under Japanese occupation, and also went to America and Canada. In 1944 Prince Bernhard was made C-in-C of the Dutch Armed Forces and returned secretly to Holland where he integrated the highly efficient Dutch resistance groups, to whom most of the Germans in Holland surrendered after Doenitz's capitulation.

BEVAN, Aneurin. b. 1897. A prominent member of the British Labour Party, Bevan's voice was frequently raised in lone opposition to Churchill in the Houses of Parliament. He held no public office during the war, but was active in the Trade Union movement.

BEVIN, Ernest. b. 1881. One of the ablest members of the British Labour Party, as well as of the Coalition Government in which he was Minister of Labour and National Service, and a full Cabinet member. Within nine days of taking office Bevin presented the Emergency Powers Bill by which Britain's entire industrial resources would be mobilised for the war effort. He used his considerable debating and negotiating skills to get tremendous voluntary co-operation between employers and unions, and brought in a number of regulations protecting the status and handling of essential workers who had to remain in the country. The Female Conscription Act of 1941 released thousands of men for the fighting forces. Bevin also drafted – well in advance – plans which led to Britain's comparatively smooth demobilisation in 1945.

BLAMEY, General Sir Thomas. b. 1884. In 1939 Blamey was Chairman of the Australian Manpower Committee, and rose rapidly through a number of Army posts to head of the Anzac Corps in Greece in 1941. He organised the preparations for the Allied evacuation of Greece, as deputy to Auchinleck. Not long after the outbreak of the Japanese war Blamey returned to Australia, and became C-in-C of the Australian military forces. As Commander of Allied Land Forces he supervised the first attacks on the Japanese in New Guinea, and commanded the fierce fighting which led to the recapture of Papua. Until the battlefront moved further north, Blamey generally took personal command in the field. He retained until the end of the war his post as C-in-C Allied Land Forces, South-West Pacific.

BLEICHER, Sergeant Hugo. b. 1899. One of Germany's most successful counter-intelligence agents, also known as "Colonel Henri" and "Monsieur Jean". Bleicher was a Hamburg businessman and linguist recruited in 1939 who went to Holland, and then France, in 1940. His first success was in arresting the leader of the first major French Resistance network, after which he was attached to the *Abwehr*, the Intelligence department of the German Armed Forces. He then infiltrated the Franco-British network controlled from London, and arrested Peter Churchill and Odette Sansom. He was also responsible for the arrest of Henri Frager, a leading French Resistance organiser. Bleicher was arrested by Dutch Police in Amsterdam after the war, and imprisoned by the Allies.

BLUM, Leon. b. 1872. The French Socialist statesman who, while reservedly supporting the Munich agreement, was fiercely opposed to any compromise with the Germans after the defeat of France. Although in obvious danger as a Jewish intellectual Socialist, Blum refused to leave France after the invasion, and travelled to Vichy in an attempt to lead the socialists against Laval. He was arrested by the Vichy Government, but used his trial for an outstanding and embarrassing attack on the Vichy French – as a result of which the Germans ordered the trial stopped. Blum spent from 1943 to 1945 in Buchenwald concentration camp, and returned to political life after liberation.

BOCK, Field Marshal Fedor von. One of the German generals who played an active part in the German conquests, but was dropped altogether once the tide turned. Bock commanded Army Group North in the invasion of Poland and Army Group B in the west during the "Phoney War" and in the conquest of Western Europe.

From there he went to command Army Group Centre in the preparations for Barbarossa, and in the attack itself, until the deadlock in December 1941. In January 1942 he was put in command of Army Group South, but was sacked by Hitler in July 1942 for not moving fast enough into the Caucasus. Bock was killed in one of the last air-raids, three days before the end of the war.

BOISSON, Pierre. b. 1898. Governor General of the French Colonies in North West Africa, who, although he urged France to continue the war from her colonies, immediately complied with the Vichy order that the Armistice was also to apply to French possessions. His loyalty to Vichy-France made him resist de Gaulle's attempts to gain control, and it was only after the German occupation of Vichy-France in November 1942 that Boisson supported Darlan's attempts to reach agreement with the Allies. He was appointed a member of the "Imperial Council" but lost this post, and his Governorship, when de Gaulle became head of the provisional "French National Committee". On top of that he was tried as a collaborator, and imprisoned from the end of 1943 until the end of the war.

BONHOEFFER, Pastor Dietrich. 1906–1945. Although the Nazis had forbidden this prominent theologian from publishing or public speaking, Bonhoeffer was given a post in Adm. Canaris's *Abwehr* in 1940. Amidst his church duties, he secretly worked with the plotters against Hitler, and sought support outside Germany. Eventually, however, he was arrested and imprisoned at Tegel. In September 1943 he was charged with plotting the "Destruction of Germany's Fighting Power", but the failure of the 20th July Plot exposed his full activities. His prominent position and wide reputation were no longer sufficient protection against normal Nazi tactics, and he was imprisoned by the Gestapo. Unlike others, however, in April 1945 he was given the formality of a court-martial, at Flossenburg, and hanged. Within two weeks of his death his brother and two brothers-in-law were shot by the Gestapo in Berlin.

BORGHESE, Commander Prince Valerio. b. 1912. Prince Borghese was principally responsible for the unparalleled success of the Italian navy in making daring raids on ships in harbour, using miniature submarines. A submarine commander from 1939, his vessel ferried two "human torpedoes" to an attack on Gibraltar in September 1940 – the first of a series of such assaults there. In 1941 he took command of this type of operation, which also included an extremely successful and perilous attack on Royal Navy ships in Alexandria Harbour. He received Italy's highest military decoration, and until the Italian Armistice was engaged on a plan to attack ships in New York harbour.

BORIS III. 1894–1943. With the evidence of Czechoslovakia, Austria and Poland before him, King Boris of Bulgaria tried his best to keep his country out of the conflict, and was not at all sympathetic to the Nazis. However he signed an Alliance with Hitler in December 1941 to prevent the occupation of Bulgaria, and declared war on the Allies – a move which he later confessed to have been his most mistaken; the large degree of pro-Russian sentiment in his country prevented him from declaring war on Russia. However Hitler made increasing demands on Bulgaria to provide forces for the whole German offensive, and after a stormy meeting with Hitler on the 28th August 1943, King Boris died – possibly from a heart attack, though murder has not been unsuspected.

BORMANN, Martin. 1900–1945(?). An early confidant and adviser of Hitler's, Bormann became the Nazi Party Chief after Hess flew to Scotland in 1941, in which position he was theoretically second only to Hitler (though in fact Himmler was considerably more powerful). A devious and skilled self-promoter, Bormann jealously guarded his position and exercised considerable power by monitoring all information reaching Hitler, and frequently determining who could see him. He was thus disliked by most other members of the Nazi Party, and even more by the Generals. Considerable mystery still surrounds Bormann – it has been suggested that he was the source of the accurate and very high-level information which reached Russian intelligence via their agent in Switzerland. Bormann remained with Hitler in the bunker, and did not protest at Hitler's command that he should not commit suicide with him, but that he should further the cause of the Nazi Party. When the bunker was evacuated, Bormann was seen running towards the encircling Russian lines (as others were, in hope of slipping through), and was thought to have been killed by a shell which burst not far from him. His death has not yet been authenticated and "he" has repeatedly been reported seen, initially in South Africa, and then in South America. He was sentenced to death *in absentia* at the Nuremberg trials, but it is generally believed that he did die in Berlin.

BOSE, Subhas Chandra. 1897–1945. A leading Nationalist revolutionary in India who was imprisoned in July 1940 for his propaganda attempts to create an uprising in India, using Britain's preoccupation with the war as an opportunity to gain independence. He escaped in January 1941, went to Berlin via Afghanistan, and organised the nucleus of an Indian National Army. He then went to Japan to organise further troops among prisoners of war. His attempts to stage an uprising at the time the Japanese had forced the British out of Burma into Assam failed. Bose was killed in an air crash in Formosa.

BRACKEN, Brendan. b. 1901. A prominent British newspaper publisher, Bracken became one of Churchill's closest advisers and associates, and was his Parliamentary Private Secretary from 1940 to 1941, when he became Minister of Information (which included propaganda), and a Member of the Emergency Housing Committee in 1944. He briefly held the post, in the 1945 Caretaker Government, of First Lord of the Admiralty.

BRADLEY, General Omar. b. 1893. One of America's most outstanding commanders, and a highly respected leader who worked well with other commanders in the joint Allied offensives. He took part in the campaign in Tunisia as commander of the 2nd Corps, and in May 1943 captured Bizerta. He led the U.S. forces in the invasion of Sicily, and was commander of the U.S. 1st Army (all the American forces) in the D-Day landings on Normandy. This army was later joined by Patton's 3rd Army to form the 12th Army Group – with 1,300,000 ground troops the largest army ever commanded by a U.S. general. The German's Ardennes offensive drove a deep bulge into Bradley's Army Group, and Eisenhower temporarily gave part of Bradley's command to Montgomery because of a possible communications breakdown across the bulge. After restoration of the Allied front, Bradley's Group was first across the Rhine at the captured bridge at Remagen, drove across Germany, and first met the Russians on the 25th of April 1945.

BRAUCHITSCH, Field Marshal Walter von. Commander in Chief of the German Army from February 1938 until 19th December 1941. Brauchitsch did not have the strength of character nor the mental abilities needed to cope with the difficulties of leading an army which was never "allowed" a defeat. Before the war and in the early stages he was frequently approached to support anti-Hitler factions, but he was always completely dominated by Hitler. The victories over Poland and Western Europe, and over Russia in the first stage of Barbarossa gave him some prestige, but this evaporated when, with Halder, he tried to persuade Hitler to go all out for Moscow in Autumn of 1941, instead of making the digressionary attack towards Kiev. By the time Hitler acquiesced to Brauchitsch's arguments and ordered the Moscow assault, it was too late and the offensive ground to a halt in the Russian winter. Foreseeing this, Brauchitsch's health suffered badly and he had a number of minor heart attacks. After repeated requests, Hitler accepted his resignation, and took over the post of Army C-in-C himself. Brauchitsch was imprisoned after the war, and died in British captivity in 1948.

BRAUN, Eva. 1912–1945. Hitler's almost-constant companion from 1932, who lived at Berchtesgaden from 1936. She joined Hitler in his Berlin bunker in the last days of the war, and they were married early in the morning of 29th April 1945. On the afternoon of the following day she took poison moments before Hitler shot himself, and her body was burnt with his. She took no part – or even interest – in Hitler's political affairs, and remains an enigma from his private world.

BRAUN, Wernher von. b. 1912. The technical director of the rocket research centre at Peenemunde, who was responsible for the design and development of the V2 rocket. Hitler was not persuaded about its potential until 1943, otherwise large numbers could have been in use before the summer of 1944. Himmler attempted to take over control of the project, and von Braun was briefly imprisoned until Hitler ordered his release. Some 3,600 V2 rockets were launched over a period of about nine months. Von Braun fled west from Peenemunde as the Russians advanced, gave himself up to the British, and was eventually released to continue research in America.

BRERETON, General Lewis. b. 1890. In 1941 Brereton was in command of the U.S. Army Far East Air Force, which suffered great damage in the sudden and widespread Japanese attacks. He subsequently held commands in India and then the Middle East, where the U.S. units operated with R.A.F. squadrons. As commander from late 1943 of the U.S. 9th Air Force in Britain, he organised many raids on German communications before "Overlord". In August 1944 he was put in command of the 1st Allied Airborne Army, units of which fought in the crucial and tragic battles at Nijmegen and Arnhem.

BROOKE, Field Marshal Sir Alan. b. 1883. General Brooke went to France as the commander of 2nd Corps B.E.F., and advised on, and then covered, the withdrawal from Dunkirk. He was made C-in-C Home Forces with the responsibility of reorganising the British army to resist invasion. In 1941 Brooke was appointed Chief of the Imperial General Staff (C.I.G.S.), with a seat on the Combined Chiefs of Staff Committee. In June 1942 he became Chairman of the British Chiefs of Staff Committee, and held this post, and C.I.G.S., for the rest of the war. He was highly trusted and respected by Churchill, with whom he was in almost daily contact, by the Americans, and – after an initial disagreement – by Stalin as well. An excellent strategist, he was assured of the command of the invasion of Europe as early as 1943, a decision Churchill later changed in view of the larger part that would be played by American troops, although this was naturally a great disappointment to Brooke. He later became Viscount Alanbrooke.

BROOKE-POPHAM, Air Marshal Sir Robert. b. 1878. With the unenviable position of being in charge of the air defence of British territories in the Far East, being ordered to avoid war with Japan, and with Far East requirements running a hopeless second to those of Egypt, Brooke-Popham was powerless to prevent the overwhelming Japanese superiority from flooding over British territories. He was relieved of his command at the end of 1941, although none of his actions and efforts could really be faulted.

BROSSOLETTE, Pierre. 1903–1944. One of the first French Resistance leaders. He went to England in 1942 and became a political adviser to de Gaulle, and a deputy to the head of the Free French Central Bureau of Intelligence and Action, which was involved in sabotage and espionage. He worked closely with the French Section of S.O.E., and parachuted into France a number of times. He played an important part in ensuring close co-operation between all anti-German groups, among whom there was often rivalry, and this led to the very successful Resistance operations which coincided with Overlord. On a mission to France in 1944 Brossolette was betrayed and arrested. Doubting his ability to withhold information while under torture, he committed suicide, jumping from a fifth floor window of the Gestapo H.Q. in Paris.

BROWNING, Lieutenant General Frederick. b. 1896. Browning was transferred from the Guards armoured training unit in 1941 after Churchill had ordered the formation of a force of parachutists. In the face of considerable Air Ministry opposition, Browning formed an airborne division of parachute and glider troops, by 1943 comprising three parachute brigades and a glider-borne brigade. The Parachute Regiment eventually comprised 17 battalions, and in 1942 it was given its famous emblem, the red beret – which led to the nickname of the "Red Devils". Browning was Brereton's deputy, and commanded the 1st Airborne Corps at Arnhem. Brooke praised Browning's formation of the highly effective and respected Parachute Regiment, and towards the end of the Japanese war, he was appointed Chief of Staff to Mountbatten.

BRUCE, Viscount Stanley. b. 1883. Viscount Bruce was the Australian High Commissioner in London throughout the war, and from 1942 to 1945 Australia's representative on the British War Cabinet. He was a former Prime Minister of Australia, and was largely responsible for the pre-war Dominions' training schemes for pilots which provided so many for the R.A.F., especially from Australia and Canada. He was also a former president of the Council of the League of Nations, and while constantly supporting Britain in the war, disagreed with Churchill on a number of issues – none more than on the post-war treatment of Germany, having clearly seen the consequences of the Treaty of Versailles.

BUCKMASTER, Maurice. b. 1910. The head of the French Section of S.O.E. from September 1941, Buckmaster built up a force of several hundred agents in France who carried out innumerable acts of sabotage, from minor disruptions in factories to delaying the movement of whole German divisions. (The S.O.E. was independent of de Gaulle and the Free French, who had a similar operation.)

BUCKNER, General Simon. 1886–1945. Having spent most of the war in command of U.S. Defence Forces in Alaska, Buckner was appointed commander of the U.S. 10th Army in 1945. He thus directed Okinawa, one of the last and bloodiest battles of the Pacific War. He was killed when a Japanese shell scored a direct hit on his forward observation post, only two days before the island fell to the Americans.

BUDENNY, Marshal Semyon. b. 1883. C-in-C of Russian armies in the Ukraine and Bessarabia after the German invasion of June 1941. The lack of preparedness of the Russians, and the greater abilities of the German generals resulted in Budenny's forces, although far more numerous, being quite easily routed. Within less than a month, his two major forces (at Kiev and Uman) comprising almost half the Russian soldiers on the front, had been cut from each other. Most of the Uman forces were encircled and captured, while Budenny, withdrawing across the Dnieper, carried out the scorched-earth policy decreed by Stalin. With his commissar, Kruschev, he saw to the destruction of the huge Dnieper dam at Zaporozhe. When Hitler saw the chance to encircle the remainder of Budenny's troops at Kiev and took the opportunity (against his generals' advice) Budenny destroyed Kiev too, but he had by then been responsible for two tremendous defeats – over 1½ million Russian soldiers killed or captured. He was not given another command post during the war.

BURKE, Admiral Arleigh. b. 1901. A very successful U.S. naval commander and destroyer expert whose Destroyer Squadron 23 provided the escort for the U.S. landings on Bougainville, the largest of the Solomon Islands. Burke's squadron was involved in more than 20 engagements against the Japanese, before he became Chief of Staff to Adm. Mitscher, the commander of Fast Carrier Task Force 58 which decisively won the Battle of the Philippine Sea, took part in the Iwo Jima and Okinawa campaigns, and sank the *Yamato*.

BYRNES, James. b. 1879. A former member of the U.S. Senate Foreign Relations Committee, Byrnes became Director of the Office of Economic Stabilization after Pearl Harbor, with the special tasks of preventing inflation and achieving full war-time production. From May 1943 he was Director of War Mobilisation, and in 1944 went to Yalta with Roosevelt as his special adviser on shipping, Lend-Lease, and Home Affairs. He resigned shortly before the President's death, but returned at Truman's invitation and in July 1945 was appointed Secretary of State. He strongly urged the enforcement of unconditional surrender on Japan, advocated the dropping of the atomic bomb, and played a major role at Potsdam.

CALLAGHAN, Admiral Daniel. 1892–1942. After being Roosevelt's Naval aide for three years, Callaghan was in command of the cruiser *San Francisco* in Pearl Harbor when the Japanese struck. He became Chief of Staff to the commander of the U.S. naval forces in the South Pacific, but was killed in an extraordinary and courageous encounter in November 1942 when *San Francisco* led a spearhead attack at night on a large Japanese force which had entered American positions in the Solomons. Callaghan took his ship right through the far larger Japanese group, sank one ship and disabled two others. The cruiser also tackled a Japanese battleship, silenced its guns, and damaged it so severely that it was later easily sunk by torpedoes. *San Francisco* suffered many casualties and Callaghan himself was killed, though the ship was taken safely back to port where it became one of the first U.S.N. ships to win an outstanding service decoration.

CALVERT, Brigadier Michael. b. 1913. Known as "Mad Mike", Calvert was a leading figure in the tough, unconventional area of the war – the commandoes and special forces. After taking part in the Norway campaign, Calvert trained commandos in Britain and then in Australia and New Zealand. In 1941 he was put in charge of the "school" of jungle warfare in Burma, and became an obvious choice for Wingate's Chindits. In 1943 he led a Chindit column behind enemy lines, and when the army expanded Calvert commanded 77 Brigade. In 1944 he returned to Britain to lecture on the Burma war. He was then transferred to the SAS, which he led through Belgium and Holland, and across the Rhine. At the end of the war, he returned to Norway and assisted in its return to liberation.

CAMERON, Lieutenant Donald. b. 1919. Together with Lt. Godfrey Place, responsible for putting *Tirpitz* out of action for many months – in fact ensuring she never effectively put to sea again. In the midget-submarines *X6* and *X7* respectively, Cameron and Place and their crews were the only two of the original six teams that managed to penetrate all the defences in Altenfjord where *Tirpitz* was anchored. *X6* accidentally surfaced briefly before Cameron dropped his explosives beneath the battleship, and when the craft became unmaneouvrable Cameron and his crew surfaced and surrendered. Place did so as well a short while later, when his submarine went out of control and sank – though only Place and one of his crew managed to escape. Both explosives went off, and caused enormous damage to *Tirpitz*. Cameron and Place each received the V.C.

CANARIS, Admiral Wilhelm. 1888–1945. An intriguing figure among the German commanders, Canaris was head of the *Abwehr* – the Intelligence unit of the Armed Forces. He was a comparatively outspoken anti-Nazi who argued against Germany's more aggressive policies. Canaris has been the subject of considerable conjecture – among other things, that he purposely let the Allies get hold of top secret information, especially about invasion plans in the early part of the war. Canaris did not take a part in the early plots against Hitler, though he advised the conspirators and was sympathetic towards them. Himmler and he were arch enemies, Himmler believing that all Intelligence should be under the SS. The defection of numerous *Abwehr* agents to the British gave Himmler a chance to oust Canaris in February 1944, when Hitler united Intelligence matters under Kaltenbrunner. Canaris was removed, and he then actively supported the 20th July plotters. After its failure he was among the first to be arrested. The SS hanged Canaris in Flossenburg concentration camp in April 1945.

CARRÉ, Mathilde. b. 1910. (Known as "the Cat".) Initially a nurse on the French eastern front, who then helped to form the first powerful intelligence network – the "Interallié". She obtained a great deal of important information from conversation with German officers and was a valuable agent; but when Sergeant Bleicher uncovered the Interallié leaders, she saved her life by giving away the names of some colleagues, and by agreeing to work as a double agent. A member of S.O.E. French Section discovered her complicity, and she then briefly had to play a precarious double-double role. In 1942 she was sent to Britain, where she was promptly imprisoned. After the liberation of France she was tried for treason, and sentenced to life imprisonment.

CAVALLERO, Count Ugo. 1880–1943. Marshal of Italy and Chief of the Italian General Staff who replaced Badoglio after the Greek fiasco, and imposed a new, iron rule in the army – though his position made him subordinate to the Germans. Cavallero had considerable industrial experience, and created some order out of the chaos of Italy's war production. As Italian fortunes declined in 1942, his reputation fell; and when he tried to prevent what he imagined to be a Fascist move to take over the army and the police and depose the king, many others thought he was trying to take over Mussolini's own position. The dictator had him imprisoned for a short while early in 1943, but when Cavallero realised that his anti-Fascist motives were bound to be known sooner or later, he committed suicide.

CHADWICK, Roy. b. 1893. The British aircraft designer whose radical design for the Manchester heavy bomber was developed into the four-engined (Rolls Royce Merlin) Lancaster. This was the most famous bomber of R.A.F. Bomber Command, and could carry heavier loads than any of the American B-17s. Lancasters dominated the night-bombing attacks of the Allied air offensive, and were used in many special operations, being the only plane able to carry 10 ton bombs. Chadwick also designed the Anson, York, and Lincoln planes during the war.

CHAMBERLAIN, Neville. 1869–1940. British Prime Minister from May 1937 who saw appeasement and conciliation as the only way to avoid the catastrophe of a second war. He was persuaded to permit a certain amount of re-arming in Britain, but signed away the rights of Czechoslovakia in the Munich agreement of 1938, when Britain was in fact considerably less strong than Germany. Chamberlain had no concept of the degree of Hitler's treachery and self-interest, and allowed himself to be easily persuaded by the Nazi leader. Yet at that time there was certainly little to suppose that a tougher line would have had the desired effect on Hitler, or have been anything but extremely unpopular in Britain. Once war became inevitable, however, Chamberlain lost his authority and determination, and the Coalition Government became inevitable. He remained as Lord President, had a seat in the War Cabinet and was still leader of the Conservative Party. After serious illness, he died in November 1940.

CHENNAULT, Major General Claire. b. 1898. An extremely talented American pilot who, before the entry of the U.S. into the war, organised a group of American volunteer pilots to fight on the side of the Chinese against Japan. In July 1942 the "Flying Tigers" were incorporated into the U.S.A.A.F. and, although never numbering more than 250, the group shot down over 300 Japanese planes in six months over the S.E. Asia mainland. In May 1943 he went to Washington for the Conference on Far Eastern strategy, and within two more months his forces had won undisputed air supremacy all over China. Chennault resigned in July 1945, rather than disband the joint Chinese-American wing of the Chinese air force.

CHERWELL, Lord (Frederick Lindemann). b. 1886. The British physicist who was a friend of Churchill, his chief scientific adviser, and the only scientist in the War Cabinet, having the post of Paymaster-General. His report on the probable effects of area bombing proved to be wildly optimistic, but he did make a large number of significant contributions to the war.

CHESHIRE, Group Captain Leonard. b. 1917. Cheshire was one of R.A.F. Bomber Command's most outstanding pilots, and was eventually appointed to command 617 Squadron – the "Dambusters" – in succession to Gibson. He made a number of hazardous and highly successful raids with the squadron, and his target-marking techniques – often in a lone Mosquito flying dangerously low through curtains of flak – led to very accurate strategic bombing raids. For his constant gallantry he was awarded the V.C. In 1944 he went to H.Q. Eastern Air Command, South East Asia, and in 1945 joined the British Joint Staff Mission in Washington. Cheshire was the official British observer at the dropping of the atomic bomb on Nagasaki.

CHIANG KAI-SHEK, Generalissimo. b. 1887. With China having been at war with Japan since 1937, Chiang was the West's symbol of resistance to Japan. He therefore benefitted greatly when Japan attacked Pearl Harbor, being able to count on American backing to enforce his own position. But he was difficult to work with, and the Americans, once apprehensive about the growing Communist powers in China, sought to maximise their own strength in China, rather than greatly strengthen China herself. Chiang refused to allow Chinese forces to be unified under American command, and that led to the recall of Stilwell, the commander of Chinese and American forces in the China-Burma theatre who was aptly nicknamed "Vinegar Joe". Although Chiang attended the November 1943 Cairo Conference, the Allies were never too certain that he would be the head of the fourth great power after the war.

CHURCHILL, Peter. b. 1909. The highly competent member of the French Section of S.O.E. who made numerous trips to France, initially leading groups of agents in and out of France by submarine. In January 1942 he landed with instructions for a group of agents at Lyons, and returned to Britain via the Pyrenees, Madrid and Gibraltar. In August he parachuted into France and acted as the principal liaison officer between a French Resistance group and London, though he never carried out sabotage himself. In April 1943 he was arrested by "Colonel Henri" – Sergeant Bleicher – and spent the rest of the war in prison and concentration camps.

CHURCHILL, Winston Spencer. b. 1874. Churchill had for long warned about the dangers facing Europe from Hitler, and Chamberlain appointed him to the War Cabinet as First Lord of the Admiralty on the day that Hitler invaded Poland. He soon became the popular symbol of British determination, and was the natural successor to Chamberlain when the Coalition Government was formed on the 11th May 1940. A brilliant orator, Churchill rallied Britain as probably no-one else could have, and taking on the post of Minister of Defence as well, he was a tireless source of strength. His American associations and close friendship with Roosevelt were to prove invaluable during the early stages of the war, and this, together with Churchill's own visits to America, paved the way for the enormous amount of American aid to Britain. The two leaders worked closely after the entry of America into the war, and rarely disagreed over major issues. Churchill never made concessions in his dislike and distrust of Communism, but did not hesitate to offer assistance to Russia when she, too, was attacked by

Germany. His relationship with Stalin was successful, Churchill having more than enough strength to stand up to the Russian dictator – a quality Stalin respected.

Churchill's conduct of the war never went unchallenged, but on the only occasion that opposition to his "dictatorial" rule of the war went as far as a Vote of Censure, he emerged with an overwhelming majority in his favour. From his mistrust of Communism and his knowledge of Stalin, Churchill began to warn against the potential danger from Russia, but was ignored as he was about Hitler almost ten years before. The loss of the election to the Labour Party not two months after the end of the war was a bitter personal blow to Churchill, who reasonably expected a vote of gratitude, though he did little to judge the mood of the people. The disappointment of the loss of Premiership was made all the more acute by his being unable to complete the Potsdam talks, in which he was determined to win for Poland a measure of the independence over which Britain had gone to war.

CIANO, Count Galeazzo. 1903–1944. As Italian Foreign Minister from 1936–43, Ciano left the world, in his extensive diaries, a valuable record of Fascist meetings. He was Mussolini's son-in-law, but this did not save him from being executed on Mussolini's orders after he had been captured by the Germans and held in captivity in Verona. Ciano met Hitler and Ribbentrop at Berchtesgaden in August 1939, and only then realised – to his considerable horror – that a world war was imminent. He tried to counter Hitler's enormous influence on Mussolini, and keep Italy out of the conflict. After Italy declared war on the Allies Ciano was put in command of a bomber squadron, and flew on some missions. Italy's military ineffectiveness reduced Ciano's role, and being frequently very argumentative with Mussolini, he was dismissed in February 1943, becoming Ambassador to the Holy See. He attended the meeting of the Fascist Grand Council that deposed Mussolini, and recommended that Italy sign a separate peace with the Allies. He left Rome after Mussolini was overthrown, and was then captured by the Germans. After they had rescued Mussolini, Ciano was given a mock trial before his "traitors" death – being shot in the back, while tied to a chair.

"CICERO." The alias used by an Albanian named Elias Basna, who could have been one of Germany's best sources of intelligence. In October 1943 he called at the German Embassy in Ankara and was interviewed by the Intelligence attaché. Basna offered photographs of secret British documents for £10,000. As valet to the British Ambassador in Turkey, he supplied the Germans with over 400 photographs of secret documents from the British Embassy, for a total of £300,000, over a period of six months. All these photographs were sent on to Berlin, and although they were all genuine copies, they were virtually ignored – yet many were of secret Allied war plans that could have been vitally important to the Germans. After the war, Basna built a hotel with his substantial earnings – but was imprisoned before he could start to run it, for it turned out the Germans had always paid him counterfeit money.

CLARK, General Mark. b. 1896. One of the most respected and successful U.S. commanders in the German war, as Eisenhower's second-in-command in 1942 he commanded all the U.S. ground forces in Europe. In October 1942 Clark travelled by submarine for a secret meeting with French officers near Algiers to co-ordinate movements sympathetic to the Operation Torch landings scheduled for November. After the landings he took Darlan into protective custody and arranged the cease-fire. In September 1943 he commanded the successful Salerno landings and entered Naples the following month. He took command of the Anzio landing after it had lost its initial purpose under Lucas's hesitancy, and later reluctantly decided on the bombing of the Cassino Monastery. Two days before D-Day, Mark Clark had entered Rome and after Alexander became Supreme Commander of the Mediterranean, Clark commanded the Allied armies in Italy – the 15th Army Group. Despite the constant drain on his forces for the European and Greek areas, he and Alexander eventually overpowered the considerable German forces in northern Italy.

CLAY, General Lucius. b. 1897. A brilliant organiser, in 1942 Clay was in charge of the Army Procurement programme and later contributed largely to the setting up of a smooth logistics system for Normandy. In April 1945, as Deputy Director of the Office of War Mobilisation and Reconversion, he acted as Eisenhower's deputy for the government of Germany. Clay believed firmly in the rapid reconstruction of Germany, rather than in retribution, and with an eye to the future when a civil government should take over from the military government, he kept his office and operations entirely separate from the military machine. Clay's contribution to the restoration of order to Germany was very great.

COCKCROFT, John. b. 1897. Appointed Assistant Director of Research, Ministry of Supply in 1939, and from 1941 to 1944 Chief Superintendent of Air Defence Research and Development. Cockcroft, a nuclear physicist, played an important part in the highly successful use of radar in the aerial defence of Britain. In 1944 he was appointed Director of the Atomic Energy Division of the National Research Council of Canada.

COHEN, Morris. b. 1889. A son of an immigrant Jewish couple from the East End of London, who ended up as a legendary figure in Chinese revolutionary history, and was made a Chinese Republican General. As an arms-dealer, he was introduced to agents of the Chinese

Republican Army and eventually became dedicated to their cause. Before the war he went on their behalf to Hong Kong to try to elicit guarantees of assistance from the garrison commander in the event of a Japanese attack on the island, and to maintain contact with the Chinese "fifth column". He was arrested by the Japanese when Hong Kong fell on Boxing Day 1941, beaten up and tortured, and imprisoned.

COLLINS, General Joseph. b. 1896. From the command of the U.S. 25th Infantry Division on Guadalcanal, Collins commanded the 7th Army Corps in the Normandy invasion, landed at Utah beach and captured Cherbourg. He was a hard, uncompromising general, but an enthusiastic and frank leader who was well-liked by his troops. After Cherbourg, he led the breakout from Normandy, crossed the Siegfried Line, captured Aachen and Cologne and eventually met the Russians on the Elbe. Not surprisingly, he was nicknamed "Lightning Joe".

CONINGHAM, Air Marshal Arthur. b. 1895. Coningham, in 1941, commanded the Desert Air Force which supported the 8th Army, and after the capture of Tripoli he went to Algeria to command the 1st Allied (North African) Tactical Air Force. The air operations against Pantellaria and in support of the Sicily invasion were under his command. In 1944 he went to England to command the Second Tactical Air Force, moving to Normandy in July and eventually being in charge of 1,800 planes and some 100,000 men belonging to the air forces of seven nations, from the Baltic to the Mediterranean.

COOPER, Alfred Duff. b. 1890. An ardent Francophile who worked tirelessly for Anglo–French co-operation. A former Secretary of State for War in the British Government, and First Lord of the Admiralty, Cooper resigned over Chamberlain's Munich settlement and remained a back-bencher until Churchill became Premier. He undertook a lecture tour of America and from 1940–41 was Minister of Information. In August 1941 he went to Singapore to investigate Far East conditions, and stayed on to form a war council with himself as Resident Cabinet Minister, returning to Britain after Wavell's appointment as Supreme Commander. In October 1942 he became the British representative on the French Committee of Liberation, and was a constant advocate of de Gaulle as the best future French leader. He was accredited to de Gaulle in September 1944 and worked hard against strong odds and sentiments to forge Anglo–French unity, achieving at last the 1947 Treaty of Dunkirk. With de Gaulle, Cooper must share much of the credit for France's rapid rise from humiliation.

CREASY, Admiral George. b. 1895. From commanding the 1st Destroyer Flotilla in the Mediterranean, Creasy took part in the Norwegian campaign and was then briefly Chief of Staff to the First Sea Lord. From September 1940–42 Creasy was Director of Anti-Submarine Warfare in the Admiralty, and then took command of the battleship *Duke of York*. He headed the naval section which planned Overlord and was Chief of Staff to Ramsey, the Allied Naval C-in-C for the invasion.

CRERAR, General Henry. b. 1888. The planner of Canada's militia between the wars who came to England in 1939 to organise the Canadian Military H.Q. He aimed at building up a mobile Canadian force based in Britain, favouring offensive rather than defensive roles. In 1941 he resigned and dropped his rank, returning to England as acting-G.O.C. 1st Canadian Corps, which he led in Italy. In 1944 he was appointed C-in-C of the 1st Canadian Army and his troops fought hard and brilliant campaigns up the west coast, clearing the heavily defended Pas de Calais and eventually freeing Antwerp. In February 1945 he led the offensive south east of Nijmegen, and isolated the Germans in the Netherlands.

CRIPPS, Sir Stafford. b. 1889. An ardent Socialist of the British Labour Party who Churchill sent to Russia as a special envoy in May 1940. A year later he had effectively become an ambassador there, and was appointed a Privy Councillor. In February 1942 he was made Lord Privy Seal and Leader of the House of Commons. He visited India to explain ways in which the War Cabinet was prepared to aid Indian self-government, but this draft was rejected by the two leading Indian factions. His ideas of planning for peace clashed with the general tone of the War Cabinet at that time, and in 1942 he accepted the non-Cabinet post of Minister of Aircraft Production, which position he filled most competently.

CUNNINGHAM, General Sir Alan. b. 1897. The G.O.C. East African Forces who led the rapid and very successful liberation from the Italians of the Somalilands and Abyssinia. In August 1941 he briefly led the nucleus of the British 8th Army under Auchinleck, in the General's first bid to break beyond the Halfaya Pass to Tobruk. Auchinleck felt that Cunningham was too hesitant, and too "defence-minded" and replaced him with Ritchie. Cunningham returned to England and held a number of staff commands. From 1944 to 1945 he was G.O.C. Eastern Command, and at the end of the war became the last British High Commissioner of Palestine. He was the brother of Admiral Cunningham.

CUNNINGHAM, Admiral Sir Andrew. b. 1883. Probably Britain's foremost naval commander, Cunningham began the war in the crucial role of C-in-C of the Mediterranean Fleet. He succeeded in the bloodless immobilisation of the French Fleet in Alexandria, and won decisive and daring victories over the numerically superior Italian Fleet. The command of the whole Northern Mediterranean by the Axis – in fact at times the only

Allied naval bases were Gibraltar, Malta, Alexandria and a few miles of Egyptian coast – made the Mediterranean Fleet indispensible in keeping Malta alive and aiding and supplying the British 8th Army, though warship losses were heavy. He was for six months the British representative in Washington to the Combined Chiefs of Staff Committee, but, being essentially a "man of action" returned in 1942 as Allied Naval C-in-C. In September 1943 he received the surrender of the Italian Fleet at Malta, and after Pound's death became First Sea Lord.

CUNNINGHAM, Group Captain John. b. 1915. One of the most famous R.A.F. night-fighter pilots, who flew with 604 Squadron in the Battle of Britain in Blenheims, and later with 604 and 85 Squadrons, flying Beaufighters and Mosquitos. He was credited with 20 victories, 19 of which were at night. In one engagement his brilliant maneouvring reputedly led to a Heinkel III crashing, without a shot being fired by Cunningham.

DALADIER, Édouard. b. 1884. Premier of France from 1938, Daladier seemed to comprehend the true extent of Hitler's ambitions, but he always followed Chamberlain's example and vacillation was one of his trade-marks. He waited until Chamberlain declared war, after Germany invaded Poland, and then dissolved the Communist Party after Russia also invaded Poland. He became War Minister when Reynaud's Government replaced his own in March 1940, and then Minister for Foreign Affairs in June. While attempting to aid resistance in Casablanca, Daladier was arrested by Vichy officials and tried in February 1942 for "leading France into war unprepared". He embarrassed his accusers with a courageous defence and his trial was suspended – after which he was interned, and then imprisoned in Germany until the end of the war.

DARLAN, Admiral Jean. 1881–1942. The C-in-C of the French Fleet, who had once assured Churchill that the French Navy would not fall into German hands. But when France capitulated, he declined appeals to sail his Navy to Britain, America or a neutral port, and this led to the tragic clash between the French Navy and the Royal Navy. Darlan was made Minister of Marine in the Vichy Government, and in 1941 became Vice-Premier. He met Hitler in May and agreed to German requests for the use of French African ports – an agreement vetoed by the Vichy Government. After Laval returned to power, Darlan lost his ministerial posts, but was put in command of all French forces. He was by accident actually in Algiers (where he was High Commissioner) when the Allies invaded North-West Africa, and decided to cooperate – especially when Germany occupied the remainder of France. Darlan acted on behalf of the Allies, but on Christmas Eve 1942 he was assassinated by a French monarchist.

DARNAND, Joseph. 1897–1945. The French soldier who became head of the Milice (virtually a Vichy-French Gestapo), an enthusiastic supporter of Darlan, and the most-hated collaborator in France. He fought openly for the Germans, was responsible for numerous barbarities and for the inhuman detention conditions in North Africa. He was the first French minister to swear allegiance to Hitler, and to wear a German uniform. After the liberation of Paris he fled to Germany and became a member of the "French Government" of Sigmaringen. Darnand was tried by the French in 1945, and shot for treason.

DE GAULLE, General Charles. b. 1890. One of the few far-sighted French commanders, but much younger than the ruling groups, de Gaulle advocated mobile armoured warfare, as did Liddell-Hart and Guderian. When France was invaded, he was a tank brigade colonel in Alsace, but was soon made Brig. Gen. in command of an armoured division. In June 1940 Reynaud made him Under Secretary of State for War, but when Pétain sought an Armistice after Reynaud's resignation, de Gaulle fled to London, from where he made his famous radio appeal to the people of France. He was recognised as the head of the Free French, but was to prove both a reassuring source of future assistance and a tiresome ally to Churchill. He won allegiance from many French colonies in Africa, formed the Defence Council of the Empire, and renamed the Free French the Fighting French. Although virtually powerless, he acted as if he led a large nation, and bitterly resented the superior positions of Darlan and his successor Giraud, after the invasion of North Africa (to which he was not invited). Giraud was eventually forced to step down, and by 1943 de Gaulle led all former French colonies, except for Japanese-occupied French Indo-China. De Gaulle and Leclerc entered Paris in August 1944, and he was immediately accepted as the leader of France. Stalin remained indifferent to France's claims to any of the benefits of the war, and de Gaulle was not invited to Yalta or Potsdam. He was formally made President in 1945, but immediately led his country into a disastrous war when he tried to bring Indo-China under France's control again.

DE GUINGAND, General Francis. b. 1900. Began the war as military assistant to the Secretary of State for War and while Director of Military Intelligence in the Middle East in 1942 took up the duties of Chief of the Staff of the 8th Army, remaining with the 8th Army until 1944. He stayed with Montgomery, becoming Chief of Staff of the 21st Army Group, and apart from his military ability, he played an invaluable role in the Allied conquests through his great skill as a diplomat. Eisenhower had a very high regard for de Guingand, as did Montgomery and other Allied leaders, and he helped still many troubled waters.

DE VALERA, Eamon. b. 1882. The President of Eire,

which remained neutral throughout the war. Not many years before the war Britain had given up her rights to two Irish ports, which would have been invaluable during the war. De Valera banned all British ships and planes from the Irish Republic, but kept on both the German and the Japanese ambassadors throughout the war. There were rumours of U-boats entering Irish ports, and Churchill stopped civilian traffic between the two countries.

DEMPSEY, General Miles. b. 1896. Dempsey gained invasion experience in commanding 13th Corps in the invasions of Sicily and Italy. On D-Day he commanded the landing of the 2nd Army on Juno, Sword and Gold beaches, as the advance part of Montgomery's 21st Army Group. He had the very difficult job of holding back the concentrations of powerful German armoured troops at Caen while the Allied west flank moved round to push into France. Dempsey commanded the spectacularly-fast advance to Brussels, and he was always near the front of the push into Germany.

DEVERS, General Jacob. b. 1887. After commanding U.S. forces in Britain, Devers went as Deputy to Maitland Wilson in the Mediterranean and then commanded the Allied invasion of southern France (Operation Dragoon) in August 1944. He took the bold decision, on meeting only isolated pockets of strong resistance, to advance as fast as possible up the Rhône Valley, leaving his rearguard to surround German units which did not surrender. He met the main body of the Allies in September 1944, and was in command of the forces which captured Munich and Berchtesgaden.

General Charles de Gaulle (left, with U.S. Chief of Staff Gen. Marshall) was both a hindrance and an asset to the Allies. He was by far the most able and forward-thinking French army leader, but was constantly frustrated by the old order. The arrogant self-appointed leader of the Free French gave an indication of the role France could have played in the war had it had different leaders at the outset.

DILL, Field Marshal Sir John. 1881–1944. Appointed vice-C.I.G.S. in April 1940 and in May reported from France on the German attack. He succeeded Ironside as C.I.G.S. and was a highly respected and trusted man. However there was little that Britain was able to do at that stage, and his policy of restraint was felt by Churchill to be one of obstruction. Amidst the tremendous pressures of those days of the war, and after his wife's death, Dill's health suffered. He went to the Mediterranean with Eden, and strongly advised against sending troops to Greece – though he was, to his everlasting regret, persuaded to change his mind. Later events showed his might have been the wiser step. At the end of 1941, Brooke succeeded Dill, who then accompanied Churchill to Washington where he remained as head of the British Joint Staff Mission and became a close friend of George Marshall, the American Chief of Staff. Dill had tremendous prestige in official circles in Washington, being particularly highly regarded by Roosevelt. But his health never fully recovered, and he died in 1944.

Grand Admiral Karl Doenitz, architect of Germany's U-boat strategy, succeeded Raeder after a series of defeats suffered by the German surface fleet. After being named as his successor by Hitler, Doenitz made a futile attempt to head a German government after the surrender, but he and his government were arrested on 23rd May 1945.

DOBBIE, General Sir William. b. 1879. As Governor of the island of Malta and C-in-C of its military bases from 1940–42, Dobbie saw Malta through its desperate and heroic siege. Constantly pounded by German and Italian bombs, and with its supplies almost cut off by Axis air and sea forces, the tiny island managed to keep going, largely thanks to the abilities and zeal of its Governor. The task of keeping up civilian morale, defending the island, and feeding all its inhabitants was a gruelling one, but he won such co-operation that Malta was awarded the George Cross on 15th April 1942. That was the island's most crucial month, and after the Defence Committee in Britain decided that Dobbie deserved and needed a rest, he was replaced by Gort on 7th May.

DOENITZ, Admiral Karl. b. 1891. A U-boat commander in the First World War, whose concept of the "wolf pack" technique of submarine warfare caused tremendous destruction, even against convoys, in World War II. He constantly urged Hitler and Raeder to concentrate on more and more U-boats instead of a large surface fleet, and Hitler at last wished he had done so when he sacked Raeder in January 1943, making Doenitz C-in-C of the German Navy. Doenitz's ambitions could not be fulfilled, however – partly due to constant bombing of U-boat construction areas, partly due to rapidly diminishing oil supplies, and partly due to the significant aid given to submarine-hunting by centimetric (microwave) radar. In May 1943 most U-boats were recalled, and they never again achieved the disastrous sinkings of the first years. Hitler nominated Doenitz as his successor on 30th April 1945, and it was Doenitz who negotiated the surrender of Germany – having first attempted to make peace with Britain, America and France and continue to fight the Russians. He and his "Government" were arrested on 23rd May, and he was sentenced to 10 years imprisonment at the Nuremberg trials.

DONOVAN, William. b. 1883. An American internationalist who was Roosevelt's special envoy to Europe in 1940–41, and urged U.S. help for Britain, which he visited many times. With America in the war, in June 1942 Donovan explained the workings of the American Secret Service to British chiefs of staff. He was co-ordinator of Information and then the head of the American OSS – the forerunner of the CIA – which played a considerable role in the organisation and supply of Resistance groups in occupied Europe.

DOOLITTLE, Lieutenant General James. b. 1896. In April 1942 Doolittle conceived, planned and led the daring first air-raid on Tokyo, taking off from an aircraft carrier and landing in China. While the raid was not big enough to cause great damage, it had tremendous (and opposite) repercussions on morale in Japan and America, and Doolittle received the Congressional Medal of Honour. He led the 12th Air Force in Operation Torch, and commanded the Strategic Air Forces in long-range raids on Italy, including a devastating daylight raid on Rome in August 1943. He led the U.S. 8th Air Force against Germany, and destroyed many rocket launching sites. King George VI made him an honorary K.C.B. He then led the 8th Air Force against Japan for the remainder of the war. Aggressive and "bigger-than-life", he easily won the appreciation and support of men under his command.

DOUGLAS, Air Marshal Sir William Sholto. b. 1893. In November 1940 succeeded Dowding as commander of R.A.F. Fighter Command, when its role began to turn from defensive to offensive with strong air attacks over France. In 1943 he commanded the R.A.F. in the Middle East, and in 1944 became commander of Coastal Command, playing an important role in the preparations and planning of the D-Day invasions.

DOWDING, Air Chief Marshal Hugh. b. 1882. Practically as responsible as any one person could be for a major victory, Dowding called well before the war for a defence network based on early-warning radar, and urged the development of single-engined fighters. While the Germans were smashing their way through the Low Countries and France, Dowding insisted on rescuing a significant portion of the R.A.F. fighters to defend Britain in the event of France's collapse. His brilliant organisation – and ability to delegate properly – in the weeks before the Battle of Britain led to the destruction of the Luftwaffe's ambitions and Hitler's plans for the invasion of Britain. He was relieved by Sholto Douglas after the Battle of Britain, and retired in 1942 after doing special duty for the Ministry of Aircraft Production in America. He later became Lord Dowding.

DULLES, Allen. b. 1893. President Roosevelt's special envoy in Switzerland and a leading member of the OSS. He held numerous discussions with German emissaries, to whom he emphasised the unacceptability of any post-war German Government including Hitler – which satisfied ambitious, if unrealistic Nazis like Himmler. Dulles apparently had a number of contacts in the SS, including Kaltenbrunner. He was instrumental in arranging the early surrender of the German troops in Italy, but a number of Japanese approaches from May onwards led to nothing.

EAKER, Lieutenant General Ira. b. 1898. The commander of the U.S. Army Strategic Air Force in Europe and leader of the first U.S. bomber attack on Western Europe. He attended the Casablanca Conference as the commander of the U.S. 8th Air Force and urged the trial of daylight bombing, which led to the Allied air offensive in which the U.S.A.A.F. bombed by day, and the R.A.F. by night. He was the Air C-in-C of the Allied Air Forces in Operation Dragoon – the invasion of Southern France – and led numerous accurate raids on German communications networks.

EDEN, Anthony. b. 1897. The British Foreign Secretary for most of the war, who accompanied Churchill to practically every major conference and was closely involved in the whole conduct of the war. Churchill had tremendous respect for Eden, and valued his judgements and opinions. They had long been politically on the same paths, and Eden had earlier resigned as Foreign Secretary over the Munich Agreement. He had shown the same regard for observation of a country's rights in strongly denouncing Italian aggression in Africa, and had tried to get France to act in the German invasion of the Rhineland in 1936. Eden was also highly thought of by the Americans, and he negotiated very successfully with the Russians.

EICHMANN, Adolf. b. 1906. The SS officer appointed head of the R.S.H.A. department of Jewish affairs. Heydrich entrusted him with the execution of the "Final Solution", which Eichmann followed through with high efficiency until it was abandoned in 1944. He introduced gas chambers, and his total devotion to Hitler made him "sabotage" many of Himmler's more moderate orders towards the end of the war. He himself had Jewish relatives, and maintained he did not hate Jews. He disappeared in 1945. (In 1960 he was discovered in Argentina, tried in Israel, and executed in 1961.)

EISENHOWER, General Dwight. b. 1890. From Chief of Operations in Washington, America's most famous soldier came to Britain in 1942 as commander of U.S. forces in Europe. He was appointed commander of the Allied Forces for Operation Torch – the landings in N.W. Africa – and in February 1943 became Supreme Allied Commander, North Africa. The part that would be played by U.S. forces in the invasion of Europe compelled Churchill to decide that it should be led by an American rather than by a Britisher as originally planned, and in December 1944 Eisenhower was made Supreme Commander of the Allied Expeditionary Forces. He began the preparations for Overlord in January 1944 and on 6th June launched the operation with 176,000 troops, 1,100 planes, 600 warships and 4,000 landing craft. He took command of the Allied forces in Europe (S.H.A.E.F.) when the invasion force was well established, and it is doubtful whether any other general had his extraordinary ability to gain the maximum co-operation from many different personalities and nationalities. He was unreservedly respected, though many did criticise his decision not to make a determined bid to reach Berlin early in 1945.

ELIZABETH, Queen. n. 1900. The popular wife of King George VI of Britain who did much to encourage all levels of people in the most difficult days of the war. She constantly visited bombed areas, and gave great attention to the women whose homes had been destroyed – while in September 1940 Buckingham Palace itself received a direct hit. She acted as Counsellor of State when the King visited North Africa in June 1943.

EMBRY, Acting Air Vice Marshal Basil. b. 1902. With a distinguished pre-war flying record, Embry continued a heroic career both in Bomber Command and Fighter Command. He was shot down and captured, and eventually reached Britain after escaping and being recaptured twice. He was "honoured" by the Germans by having a price put on his head, and in Bomber Command led three of the war's most daring low-level, pinpoint bombing raids – including the one on the Copenhagen Gestapo H.Q. where a part of the building was accurately hit to allow the escape of important Danish Resistance members.

ESMONDE, Lieutenant Commander Eugene. 1909–1942. A pilot with the Royal Navy Fleet Air Arm who escaped when *Courageous* was sunk in 1939. He flew the sturdy but slow Swordfish torpedo bombers in the strike which crippled *Bismarck* in 1941. In February 1942 he led six Swordfishes of 825 Squadron in a suicidal attack on *Scharnhorst*, *Gneisenau*, and *Prinz Eugen* in their daylight dash through the Channel. All six planes were destroyed in the barrage of hundreds of guns. Esmonde was posthumously awarded the V.C.

FALKENHAUSEN, General Alexander von. b. 1886. The C-in-C of German troops in Belgium and Northern France from 1940–44, who initially demonstrated the worst aspects of Nazidom, including the taking and shooting of hostages as reprisals or to enforce orders. In 1942, however, Falkenhausen became more and more involved in anti-Nazi movements, and inevitably became one of the plotters for the 20th July attempt on Hitler's life. With Stülpnagel he persuaded Rommel to give his support, but when the plot failed he was arrested. Imprisoned, eventually in concentration camps, Falkenhausen was highly respected by other inmates, and even by the SS guards who admired his dominant character (he had won Germany's highest award for bravery in the First War). He was doubtless marked for execution, but was freed by the Americans in a South Tyrol camp on 4th May 1945. (He was eventually tried as a war criminal by the Belgians after four years awaiting trial, but served only 2 weeks of a 12 year sentence.)

FALKENHORST, General Nikolaus von. After H.M.S. *Cossack* raided the German supply ship *Altmark* in Norwegian waters in February 1940, Hitler was determined to go ahead with his plans to invade Norway before England did, but almost forgot to appoint a commander. Falkenhorst was suggested to him and he prepared the basis for invasion in a few hours using a Baedeker guide to Norway. It eventually turned out – when Falkenhorst went to ask for troops – that Hitler had not even bothered to tell Brauchitsch of his plans. Falkenhorst remained C-in-C of the considerable forces in Norway until the end of 1944. He was responsible for using hostage terror tactics, and in 1946 was condemned to death for the execution of British commandos, but eventually he was released in 1953.

FAROUK, King of Egypt. b. 1920. The 1936 Anglo-Egyptian treaty which called for the gradual withdrawal of British troops from Egypt was stopped in 1940, and Farouk was therefore theoretically an ally of the British. He was pro-Nazi, and with a considerable following wished for the German victory which he imagined would lead quickly to independence. The tension between the British and the Egyptians increased when the British rejected Farouk's choice of a pro-Nazi Prime Minister.

FLEISCHER, General Carl. 1883–1942. The Norwegian commander of their 6th Division which was near Narvik when Germany invaded Norway. Unable to save Narvik, he at least held the Germans from moving further north, and when the British landed he assisted in the recapture of the town. However the Allies soon withdrew, and Fleischer was evacuated to England with the King of Norway and the Government, where he became C-in-C of the Norwegian army abroad. Differences of opinion with his Government led to him missing the post of Chief of Defence Forces, and he went to Ottawa as Military Attaché in the same year that he died.

FORRESTAL, James. b. 1892. One of President Roosevelt's assistants who became Secretary for the U.S. Navy in 1944. In 1941 he went to London to establish co-operation with the Admiralty. He watched the invasion of southern France, and twice went to the Pacific, being present at the Iwo Jima attack.

FRANCO, General Francisco. b. 1892. Despite the strong urging from his fellow dictators, Hitler and Mussolini, and despite the help he had received from them in winning the Spanish Civil War, Franco refused to be drawn into the war. The "price" he demanded in return for an Axis attack on Gibraltar and Spain's Atlantic islands was too high for Hitler, and when Hitler again tried persuasion, Franco was more or less certain that Britain would be the victor.

FRANK, Anne. 1929–1945. The young Jewish girl whose diary of the 25 months she hid with seven relatives and friends in a secret room in Amsterdam has done so much to show the world the inhumanity of racial persecution. The fugitives were discovered in August 1944 and in September they were sent to Auschwitz, in the last movement of Jews from Holland. The family was split up, and they began to die. Anne was moved to Belsen, where she caught typhus and died two months before the camp was liberated. Only her father, and her diary, survived.

FRANK, Hans. 1900–1946. Highly schooled in law, this Nazi became the despotic ruler of Poland – or what was left of it after Russian annexation and German "recovery". With vicious efficiency he squeezed the life out of the country, turned her ordinary folk into slaves for the Third Reich, and murdered her intelligentia and her Jews. He enthusiastically supported the Jewish extermination aims of the SS, saw the ghetto system as an ideal intermediate step in dealing with the "problem", and arranged the despatch of hundreds of thousands of Jews to Auschwitz, Treblinka, and other camps. There is some evidence that the enormity of his crimes eventually penetrated even his mind; he tried a number of times to resign his post, and "attempted" suicide more than once – but not even the Polish Resistance was able to put an end to him. He left Cracow in 1944 and at the Nuremberg trials admitted some of his crimes (having since "discovered God"). He was hanged with the other leading Nazis early on the morning of 16th October 1946.

FRANK, Karl Hermann. A vicious Sudeten thug used by the Nazis to stir up pro-German feelings in the Sudeten area of Czechoslovakia before the war. When the country was invaded by Germany, Hitler proclaimed the Protectorate of Bohemia and Moravia, and Frank was made Secretary of State. Himmler appointed him chief of police and the senior SS officer, thus also getting a hold on the "Protectorate". After Heydrich died of his assassination wounds in June 1942, Frank authorised the horrifying reprisal in which the town of Lidice was obliterated and practically all its inhabitants murdered. Sentenced by a Czech court after the war, Frank was publicly hanged near Prague on 22nd May 1946.

FRASER, Admiral Sir Bruce. b. 1888. After being responsible for the expansion of the Royal Navy as Third Sea Lord, Fraser became C-in-C of the Home Fleet from 1943–44, when his main responsibility was the protection of the Russian convoys. In September 1943 he refused the post of First Sea Lord, recommending that Cunningham was better suited. Three months later, in his flagship *Duke of York*, he directed the night engagement against *Scharnhorst* near Bear Island, and crippled the German raider with his guns before she was sunk by torpedoes. In 1944 he became C-in-C Eastern Fleet in S.E.A.C., and then C-in-C of the British Pacific Fleet. As the British representative, he signed the Japanese surrender documents on board U.S.S. *Missouri* in September 1945.

FREYBERG, General Sir Bernard. b. 1889. The highly competent and respected commander of New Zealand forces in the Mediterranean who was frequently chosen for some of the toughest assignments. After delaying the German invasion of Greece, Freyberg was put in command of the defence of Crete, which the Allies knew must eventually fall to the Germans. Freyberg's troops inflicted extremely heavy casualties on the invaders, however, and nearly paralysed Germany's crack parachute division. After the evacuation of Crete Freyberg saw action in North Africa and the Middle East, and led some outstanding New Zealand attacks in the battles against Rommel. In November 1943 he went to Italy and in February 1944 led the second offensive in the Battle of Monte Cassino, where so many New Zealanders died. In May 1945 Freyberg took the surrender of the German garrison in Trieste.

FRICK, Wilhelm. 1877–1946. An ardent Nazi and one of the manipulators who engineered political advantages for Hitler's party in the Reichstag before total domination had been secured. As Minister of the Interior, Frick was well aware of all the plans for total war, and although the police were nominally under his control, he was in fact dominated by Himmler. He was appointed Protector of Moravia and Bohemia. At the Nuremberg trials it became clear that he had full knowledge of Nazi atrocities, and he was hanged on the morning of 16th October 1945.

FROMM, General Friedrich. As C-in-C of the Replacement Army (*Ersatzheer*), roughly equivalent to the British Home Forces, Fromm was frequently wooed by the anti-Hitler plotters, for a military take-over by the troops in Germany was an important ingredient of any coup. In the early years Fromm refused to co-operate with Halder or Brauchitsch, as he did not believe the average German soldier would march against Hitler, no matter what his commanding officer might say. He was well aware of the 20th July plot in 1944, but would not commit himself to the cause (though he did not betray the plotters). His refusal to act purely on Stauffenberg's word that Hitler was dead, and alert the replacement Army, seriously disrupted the plotters' plans, and they arrested him. When it was evident the attempt on Hitler's life had failed, Fromm managed to turn the tables on his jailers, organised a counter-revolt, and captured the ringleaders. Mindful of his own precarious position – since he had known of the plot all along – he had Stauffenberg and three others executed immediately, permitted Beck two suicide attempts and then had him shot, and imprisoned many remaining suspects. However he himself was arrested the following day by Himmler, who took over the Replacement Army. In February 1945 the People's Court tried him on charges of "cowardice", and he was executed on 19th March 1945 by firing squad.

FUCHIDA, Commander Mitsuo. The highly experienced pilot chosen to co-ordinate and lead the preparation and training of aircraft carrier pilots who attacked Pearl Harbor on 7th December 1941. Fuchida was the observer of the attack itself, reporting back on the success of the raid, and directing the incoming waves. On returning to the carrier striking force Fuchida begged Adms. Nagumo and Kusaka to launch another attack, this time on the oil reserves and dockyard installations. This would undoubtedly have succeeded, but Kusaka decided to retire as planned, also turning down the suggestion to search for the American carriers. Fuchida was summoned to report to the Emperor on his return. Appendicitis prevented him from also leading the Midway attack from the same carrier, the flagship *Akagi*, one of the four Japanese carriers sunk by Nimitz's U.S. Pacific Fleet at Midway.

FUJIMURA, Commander Yoshiro. The Japanese naval attaché in Switzerland, who tried unsuccessfully to persuade his superiors in Japan to negotiate for peace through him and his contact with Allen Dulles, the OSS representative in Europe.

FYFE, Sir David Maxwell. b. 1900. The British Solicitor-General who began preparatory work on war crimes as early as 1942. Churchill appointed him Attorney General in the Caretaker Government in May 1945, and he was the Chairman of the four Allies' War Criminals' Conference. After the change of Government in July 1945 he remained as Deputy Chief Prosecutor, and effectually continued as head of the British prosecutors. He worked tirelessly to unite the principles of prosecution of the Allies, and stood firm against the Russian approach that the top Nazis' guilt was a foregone decision. Fyfe's cross examination won wide admiration, and he managed to maintain a high degree of impartiality in the proceedings, which lasted – for the top 22 Nazis – some 10 months.

GALE, General Sir Humfrey. b. 1890. The British Deputy Chief of Staff, and Chief Administrative Officer to Eisenhower for Operation Overlord, who had to master the biggest logistics problem ever confronting an army group, and at the same time co-ordinate the bewildering mass of administrative details involving hundreds of thousands of men from many armies, forces and countries. He and his highly proficient team had the background of the extremely successful multi-national invasions in North West Africa, Sicily and Italy. Officers with the talents and abilities of Gale's were little-known to the public or to the general forces, yet were absolutely vital to any campaign.

GALLAND, Lieutenant General Adolf. b. 1912. One of the war's most successful Luftwaffe pilots, with over 100 confirmed victories. In April 1940 he moved from a staff post to lead a fighter wing from France in the Battle of Britain. He was made General of Fighters when Mölders died, but was relieved, mainly as a result of his disagreements with Hitler and other superiors, in January 1944. Towards the end of the war, he led the elite jet fighter squadron. *JV44*.

GAMELIN, General Maurice. b. 1872. The C-in-C of the Allied armies in France after the declaration of war, and organiser of the pathetically ineffective defences against Germany. Apart from a brief excursion into German territory, his strategy was to wait for the Germans to strike, but unfortunately he waited in the wrong places, and seemed to expect the First World War all over again. On 19th May 1940 Pétain replaced him with Weygand. After the fall of France, Gamelin was arrested by the Vichy French and tried at Riom in February 1942, together with Daladier, Reynaud and others, as being responsible for the French collapse. Gamelin refused to defend his actions and a judicial inquiry was scheduled, but then Germany occupied Vichy France and Gamelin was sent to Buchenwald, and later to a Tyrol prison camp, where he was released by the Americans in May 1945.

GANDHI, Mahatma. b. 1869. The Leader of the Indian Congress Party who embarked on a long campaign to win independence for India. Gandhi refused Cripps's promise of postwar independence and did nothing to mend the split between Muslim and Hindu. He advocated sabotage by passive disobedience, and was placed in prison from August 1942 until May 1944.

GEORGE II, King of Greece. b. 1889. In October 1940 caused considerable Axis disruption by driving out the Italian invaders of his country and occupying half of Albania. The Germans eventually came to Italy's assistance and King George took on the duties of Prime Minister after the successive deaths of two Prime Ministers. Greece fell in April 1941, and the King carried on the Government – in-exile first from Crete, then from Cairo, and from London after September. He negotiated a Lend-Lease Agreement with America in 1943, and returned to Cairo when the liberation of his country was imminent. The liberation was, however, followed by a brief Civil War, and the King agreed not to go back to Greece until summoned by a stable, democratically-elected Government. He returned as King in 1946.

GEORGE VI, King of Gt. Britain and the British Empire. b. 1895. Together with Queen Elizabeth, King George won the respect, admiration and great loyalty of the British people, and even of many people of other nations in and out of the British Empire. This was a sign of success of the King's self-set task, which was to represent a Christian country fighting for the continuation of Christian values against the tyranny and barbarity of extreme Fascism. His understanding of the problems of other monarchs and heads of state was instrumental in making London the refuge of so many, and of many Governments-in-exile. The King and Queen made extensive visits to bomb-damaged areas, and never left London during the worst period of the Blitz, though Buckingham Palace itself was badly damaged by direct hits in one raid. The King took every opportunity to visit his troops, in England and abroad, and was not easily dissuaded from witnessing the D-Day invasion. Throughout the war he kept himself fully informed on every development of the conflict and enjoyed a particularly harmonious relationship with Churchill, who lunched informally with the King practically every week of the war and greatly valued his counsel and encouragement. Anglo–American relations were another sphere in which King George, likeable, humble and unassuming, played an important part.

GIBSON, Wing Commander Guy. 1918–1944. The leader of one of the war's most spectacular and daring aerial attacks – the breaking of the Ruhr dams in May 1943. A special squadron, No. 617, was formed to drop Barnes Wallis's special bombs on the surface of the dams in a manner that called for brilliant flying, and the talents of the squadron were repeatedly used for bombing which called for total accuracy. Gibson was awarded the V.C. for leading the "Dam Busters", but was killed in September 1944 on the way back to England in a Mosquito after being the marker bomber in a raid on Rheydt.

GIRAUD, General Henri. b. 1879. The commander of the French 9th Army who was taken prisoner by the Germans on 18th May 1940. He escaped in April 1942, and eventually reached North Africa in November 1942. He put himself in opposition to de Gaulle for the leadership of the Free French, but de Gaulle had a two-year start on him. However the Allies were not hasty in choosing de Gaulle, and the Americans favoured Giraud. When Darlan was assassinated, Giraud took his place as High Commissioner of French North and West Africa. Despite Allied attempts to reconcile the two generals, de Gaulle refused to accept Giraud as leader of the Fighting French. A joint-leadership only lasted five months, and by April 1944 de Gaulle and his supporters had forced Giraud to resign as C-in-C of French forces in Africa.

GOEBBELS, Joseph. 1897–1945. An incongruous figure in the Nazi hierarchy for many years before the war, for then he was an intellectual among a bunch of thugs and misfits. During the war only Speer had similar intellectual qualities, and yet Goebbels – almost from the moment he saw Hitler – practically venerated the Nazi leader. He became Head of the Propaganda Ministry, and was certainly extremely competent in this role. He retained a bitter revulsion of Jews throughout, an attitude of superiority hardly mitigated by his own small stature and his slightly crippled left leg. His rapid assessment and management of the situation after the failure of the 20th July Plot in 1944 stopped the revolt almost as it began, and he rapidly identified and isolated the main plotters. Scrupulously faithful to his "beloved leader" until the very end, he remained in Hitler's bunker with his strikingly attractive wife and six children (aged twelve and under, and all having names beginning with H). Goebbels witnessed the burning of the bodies of Hitler and Eva Braun. On the evening of 1st May 1945 he instructed a doctor in the bunker to give lethal injections to his six children, and a little while later, at their request, Dr. Goebbels and his wife were shot in the back of the head by an SS officer, and doused with petrol. Their bodies were only charred, however, and were easily identified by the Russians when they arrived at the bunker garden the following day.

Adolf Galland, photographed while visiting one of his fighter units in Russia, was a most able young commander whose realism and loyalty to the men of the fighting squadrons eventually led to his dismissal.

GOERDELER, Karl. 1884–1945. A determined anti-Nazi civil servant who constantly planned for the day when Hitler might be got rid of. He drew up a new constitution and even composed a speech he would broadcast when he took over as Chancellor. However he was indiscreet as well as over-optimistic, and after the

20th July plot, the Gestapo had little difficulty in finding evidence of his intentions. He was hanged in February 1945.

GOERING, Reich Marshal Hermann. 1893–1946. One of the first members of Hitler's party (1922), he was welcomed by the shabby ex-Viennese layabout, for Goering was one of the air-ace heroes of the First World War. He was made leader of the stormtroopers, and in Hitler's first Cabinet was Minister of the Interior for Prussia. As the organiser of the Gestapo, he also set up the first concentration camps for enemies of the Reich. In the mid-1930s he was put in charge of aviation, and began to build up the German air force with a massive programme of "civil aviation" training. When the pretence over re-armament was dropped, Goering became C-in-C of the Luftwaffe. A bombastic, gross, vain man of no great intelligence, Goering enjoyed the pomp and ceremony of the pre-war years and probably found the actual command of war well beyond his capabilities. After he lost the Battle of Britain his prestige among the other rulers declined considerably, and gradually his Luftwaffe grew less and less powerful. Goering practically lost interest in the war itself and devoted most of his energies to stripping wealth in every form from occupied countries. He built up a vast hoard of art treasures from all parts of Europe, and in the last days of the Third Reich sent a telegram to Hitler's bunker in Berlin to the effect that he intended to take over as leader of the Reich once Hitler was dead or no longer able to command. By that stage Hitler cared little for Goering, whose Luftwaffe had repeatedly proved inadequate, and promptly expelled him from the Nazi Party. Bormann had him arrested, but soon after he was captured by American troops. At the Nuremberg trials he was pompous, arrogant and unrepentant. Sentenced to death, he cheated the hangman by a couple of hours, committing suicide by taking poison smuggled into his cell.

Marshal Graziani, seen here in Allied hands in 1944, was the commander of the large Italian army decisively defeated by Generals Wavell and O'Connor in December 1940.

GORT, Field Marshal Viscount. b. 1886. Much decorated in the First World War (V.C., D.S.O. and two bars, M.C., eight mentions) Gort was C-in-C of the British Expeditionary Force that went to France within a few days of war being declared. The surprise German offensive through the Ardennes, and their rapid advance south through Belgium left 10 divisions of the B.E.F. hopelessly caught and gradually squeezed during the last days of May 1940 onto the beaches of Dunkirk. But almost 500,000 men escaped to England from there and from Cherbourg and other ports. In Britain Lord Gort was Inspector General to the Forces for Training and in 1941 was appointed Governor of Gibraltar. On 7th May 1942 he relieved Dobbie as Governor General and C-in-C of Malta, which at that time was at the peak of its struggle to stay alive.

GRAZIANI, Marshal Rodolfo. b. 1882. When Italy declared war on Britain in May 1940, Graziani was Governor of the Italian colony of Libya, and C-in-C of Italian forces in North Africa. Stung by the damaging raids made by Wavell's troops from Egypt, and anxious to add that country and the Suez canal to his African possessions, Mussolini constantly urged an invasion of Egypt. Graziani eventually obliged, the British fell back, but Graziani pushed no further than Sidi Barrani where he built a number of fortresses whose positioning and purpose seemed obscure at best. When the Allied troops in Egypt struck on 9th December 1940, led by General O'Connor, Graziani's Italians were routed and fled all the way back through Cyrenaica to Tripolitania, losing over 100,000 men and vast quantities of equipment. Only the Greek crisis, which took Allied troops away from

O'Connor, seems to have prevented the Italians from being pushed right out of Africa. Graziani relinquished command in February 1941 and was censured by a court of inquiry for his direction of the campaign. In September 1943, after his rescue by German commandos, Mussolini formed a republic in northern Italy with Graziani as its Minister of Defence. He was entirely loyal to the Germans who effectively ran the republic. Graziani was captured by the Allies when he moved south to rejoin his troops after spending some time with Mussolini at his Lake Como retreat. The Italian Government tried Graziani for collaborating with Germany after the Armistice, and he was sentenced to 19 years imprisonment.

GRIGG, James. b. 1890. A former private secretary to Churchill, and later Permanent Under Secretary of State for War, Grigg was an extraordinarily efficient and accomplished administrator. His administrative reforms cleared the way for greater flexibility and in February 1942 he was appointed Secretary of State for War, standing for election to become a Minister in the House of Commons. He directed his formidable expertise to creating and equipping a modern army, and by the time of the Allied invasion of Europe in 1944 Montgomery was able to describe the British Army as one of the best ever created for its tasks. Brooke, the C.I.G.S., was another professional soldier who had very high regard for Grigg.

GROVES, General Leslie. b. 1898. The U.S. General appointed in 1942 as Director of the Manhattan Project – the construction of an atomic weapon. He assembled the scientific and management team from various Allied countries and was responsible for a budget of £150 m per year. The Project employed 125,000 people, and the first successful explosion of an atomic bomb took place on 16th July 1945, in New Mexico.

GUDERIAN, General Heinz. b. 1888. The German Panzer specialist who had been greatly influenced by Liddell Hart, and who more than other German officers saw the tremendous potential of armoured warfare and *blitzkrieg* attacks which also relied on air power. Guderian's insistence on breaking through to Sedan, and then going ahead with his Panzers to the English Channel cut the Allied forces in Europe in two in May 1940, and was the single most decisive action that brought about the collapse of Western Europe. Guderian repeated these phenomenal advances on the Russian front in 1941, but lost favour when he made a strategic withdrawal against orders. Later in the war he temporarily joined Speer, charged with rationalising the different tanks being developed but not yet produced. When Heusinger was injured in the 20th July bomb plot of 1944, Guderian was made Chief of the Army General Staff and was a member of the "Court of Honour" which heard Gestapo evidence against fellow officers (the officers were not able to give counter evidence). Guderian went so far as to reaffirm a pledge to Hitler that the Army was loyal and devoted to its leader, and would remove any "undesirable elements". He was replaced as Chief of Army General Staff at the end of March by Krebs, when his Russian-front reports grew too factual. Guderian advocated making peace with the west but continuing the conflict against Russia. He finally fell out of select circles in March 1945 when his pessimistic appraisal of the outcome in the east so greatly depressed Hitler.

GUÉRISSE, Albert. b. 1911. Guérisse became known as Lieutenant Commander Patrick O'Leary, R.N., having trained as an agent after escaping from occupied Belgium. His Q ship (disguised raider) was arrested on the south coast of France, but "O'Leary" escaped to Marseilles from his Toulon prison. He then became an assistant to Garrow, an agent who had planned an escape route for Allies via Spain (these were generally escaping air crews). In 1941 Garrow was arrested and Guérisse took over, greatly enlarging the escape network to cover Belgium, Italy and Spain, and making use of 250 agents. The network produced forged documents and papers, and by the end of the war had smuggled over 600 men back to England. In March 1943, however, Guérisse was arrested. Despite brutal torture he refused to reveal the names of his agents, and he eventually landed up at Dachau concentration camp. Here again he organised an "escape" system, by substituting corpses for living inmates. In this way, though none escaped the camps, he and his helpers saved 5,000 inmates of the camps from the death convoys. "Pat O'Leary" was freed on the 29th April when the U.S. 7th Army liberated Dachau. He was awarded the G.C.

HAAKON VII, King of Norway. b. 1872. The former Prince of Denmark who was fiercely opposed to the Germans and led a Resistance Government from Trondheim after Quisling's Nazi Government was formed in April 1940. When the Allies withdrew, Haakon also left Norway but remained the symbol of Norwegian Resistance. He led the Government-in-exile in London, and established particularly good relations with neutral Sweden. The Norwegians assisted the Russians in a northern attack from Finland in late 1944. Haakon returned to liberated Oslo in June 1945.

HAILE SELASSIE, Emperor of Abyssinia. b. 1891. Deposed and driven out in 1936 by the Italian occupation of Abyssinia, Haile Selassie was both the first monarch to lose his throne to Fascism, and the first to regain it when the British conquered the Italians in East Africa by the end of 1941. Haile Selassie managed to get an unstable country back to shaky independence largely through an agreement with Britain in January 1942.

Above: A stick of British paratroopers in full equipment aboard a C-47 aircraft (Photo: Imperial War Museum). Below: The D-Day commanders, left to right: Bradley, Ramsay, Tedder, Eisenhower, Montgomery, Leigh Mallory and Bedell-Smith (Photo: Imperial War Museum).

HALDER, General Franz. b. 1884. The Chief of the Army General Staff from November 1938 to 24th September 1942, who disliked and mistrusted Hitler, but in common with many others never actually achieved anything besides carrying out his orders. Halder almost persuaded enough people to join him in a coup before world war broke out, but in the end it was Halder who did most of the organisation for the invasion of Poland – and later of Russia. He was one of the strongest opponents of Hitler's decision not to strike directly at Moscow in late summer 1941. Hitler only gave in to Halder when it was too late, and then dismissed him when the attempt failed. After the July 1944 plot, Halder was under suspicion, and kept in Dachau until released by the Americans.

HALIFAX, Earl of. b. 1881. The British Foreign Secretary from 1938–40, and deeply sympathetic with Chamberlain on the policy of appeasement – so much so that he was Chamberlain's choice for his successor in May 1940, when some were making peace overtures towards the Axis. Receiving little support, he stood down before Churchill's popularity. Churchill chose him as Ambassador to America in 1940 – scarcely an advancement for a Foreign Secretary, but a measure of Churchill's dependence on American understanding. Halifax remained a Member of the War Cabinet as well, and was enormously successful in his role in America, winning the respect of all and a close friendship with Roosevelt.

HALSEY, Admiral William. b. 1882. One of the American admirals who played a decisive role in the defeat of Japan. In October 1942 Halsey was appointed to command the newly-divided South Pacific area, and to take over the Solomons campaign – notably Bougainville. The carrier task forces in his 3rd Fleet made numerous successful attacks, and his suggestion that the landings on Leyte be advanced by leap-frogging Mindanao brought forward the Japanese defeat. Halsey was one of the most able tacticians in the new type of naval war, which relied so heavily on air power.

HARDING, General Sir John. b. 1896. Played a significant role in the North African campaign, planning the victory over the Italians at Sidi Barrani and their pursuit. When Rommel pushed the Allies back for the first time, Harding successfully implemented the holding of Tobruk. In the Spring of 1942 Auchinleck made him Director of Military Training. He was Deputy C.G.S. at Alamein, and in January 1944 became Chief of Staff to Alexander in Italy. Harding advocated a pause in the Italian campaign, with a massive new offensive to coincide with Overlord, distracting German attention. Had so many troops not been taken away for the South of France landings, this offensive might have carried on without pause to the borders of Italy. Harding eventually commanded 13th Corp in the 8th Army, and was a highly respected officer.

General Heinz Guderian, seen here with Panzer officers in France in 1940, was perhaps more responsible than anyone else for Germany's rapid victory over Western Europe. He applied the full potential of fast armoured warfare, long advocated by Liddell-Hart in England. Only the vastness of Russia and the drawn-out destructive war there ended his dominance in strategy. Unlike most generals in the field, he remained a comparatively loyal Nazi until the end of the war.

HARRIMAN, Averell. b. 1891. One of the successful U.S. businessmen who became attached to the American Government during the war for their negotiating and analysing skills. As a representative of Roosevelt's in London in 1940 he helped smooth the way for the Lend-Lease programme and later headed its administration in London. In August 1941 he accompanied Beaverbrook to Moscow to arrange assistance and co-operation. In 1943 Roosevelt gave him the tough task of Ambassador to Moscow, and he had regular monthly meetings with Stalin. Harriman was a member of the three-power commission which organised the provisional government of Poland.

HARRIS, Air Marshal Sir Arthur. b. 1892. The commander of No. 5 Bomber Group at the beginning of the war who became C-in-C of Bomber Command from February 1942 until the end of the war. While he had advocated, as Deputy Chief of Air Staff, the concentrated bombing of limited enemy targets, Harris was eventually persuaded by the difficulties in accurate aiming to concentrate on "area" bombing. To this direction he brought tremendous energy, and was the driving force behind the massive R.A.F. bombing offensive over Germany. The destructive force at Harris's command realised its potential in 1943 when the R.A.F. began to concentrate on night attacks (using latest radar equipment, and techniques such as target-marking by the Pathfinders, or by a Master Bomber) in conjunction with the U.S.A.A.F. daylight raids. Towards the end of the war, increasing numbers of people (and pilots) began to doubt the military, let alone the moral justification of area bombing.

HASSELL, Ulrich von. 1881–1944. His outspoken criticism of the Nazis, made while he was the German Ambassador to Fascist Italy, naturally led to his dismissal in February 1938, and after that he was a leader of the anti-Hitler conspiracies. He strongly urged sympathetic generals to stage a coup, but they felt Hitler commanded too much loyalty among the people (Hassell hoped for the restoration of the Hohenzollern monarchy). The Gestapo were always suspicious of him and his was an early arrest after the July Plot failed in 1944. After a short spell in Ravensbrück, he died agonisingly by being hanged on a loop of piano wire, two hours after being sentenced to death by the People's Court on 8th September – these "trials" and executions were filmed by Goebbels's men, and totalled some 30 miles of film.

HENDERSON, Sir Nevile. 1882–1942. The unfortunate diplomat whose lot it was to be British Ambassador to Germany's Third Reich from 1937–39. Henderson made the prevention of war his destiny, and he always felt that Hitler, and especially the German people would change their attitudes. The outbreak of war he saw as his own failure – he had tried desperately for appeasement even after nothing on earth could have prevented conflict – and then devoted his energies to aiding British war refugees. But his health declined rapidly after the tense Berlin years and his own disillusionment, and he died in December 1942.

HESS, Rudolf. b. 1896. One of the original Nazi leaders and an old confidant of Hitler's (from 1920) who was theoretically second only to Hitler in the Nazi hierarchy though he had few qualities of leadership. By no means over-endowed with intelligence, Hess waxed enthusiastically on endless concepts, with little regard for their sense or value. Hitler found him an ideal companion, for not only was he totally devoted, but also seemed without ambition – until one day in May 1941 he appropriated a Messerschmitt and crash landed in Scotland, intending to talk to the Duke of Hamilton, whom he had once met. His purpose, he said, was to arrange a peace, for he was convinced the British knew they were beaten. His departure was an extreme embarrassment for Hitler, who tried to cover it with the inference – not far from the truth – that Hess had lost his senses. In Britain Hess was, to his total chagrin, virtually ignored, locked up in various establishments and then sentenced to life imprisonment at the Nuremberg trials. At the time of writing, he is the only one of the top two dozen Nazis judged at Nuremberg who is still imprisoned.

HEWITT, Admiral Kent. b. 1887. An American expert on amphibious operations who commanded part of the Casablanca landings in Operation Torch in November 1942, and greatly assisted in the simultaneous capture of Morocco and Algeria. Hewitt was given command of the U.S. 8th Fleet based in North West Africa early in 1943, and in the Sicily invasion he commanded the Western Task Force, following up this operation with the Salerno landings. In August 1944 Hewitt commanded the naval operations in the Allied invasion of southern France.

HEYDRICH, Reinhard. 1904–1942. One of Nazi Germany's most sinister and vicious individuals, who was an early protegé of Himmler in the SS. Possessing the desired Aryan physical attributes and gifted with more intelligence than most of those involved in the barbarities of the SS and the Gestapo, Heydrich carried enormous authority at a very early age. He greatly strengthened Himmler's SS and his hatred of the Churches and detestation of Jews made him go well beyond the original excesses envisaged even by Himmler. His Action Groups (*Einsatzgruppen*) murdered on the spot over 700,000 people in the early days of the Russian campaign, and on Goering's orders he drafted the outlines for the "Final Solution" to Jewry. There is no doubt that this creature would have superceded Himmler to become a dominant figure in the Third Reich, for he was desperately ambitious. But in May 1942 Czech agents ambushed his car in the Prague region and he died within a few days. Had he lived, he would doubtless have murdered millions who lived to see the end of Nazi tyranny – yet even in his death his name brought terror and death, for reprisals, executions and deaths during "investigations" within a month had killed nearly 2,500 people, and led to the obliteration of the village of Lidice and all but a few of its inhabitants. (Hitler was so angered at the assassination of the *Obergruppenführer* and Protector of Bohemia and Moravia, that he ordered the execution of 30,000 Czechs – an order Frank argued should not be carried out as it would severely deplete the labour force.)

HIMMLER, Heinrich. 1900–1945. After Hitler, only Himmler had as much power and authority, a position he had systematically worked towards since the days long before the war when he joined the Hitler clique of Goebbels, Goering, Hess, etc. The SS was made responsible only to Himmler, and Himmler was, as head of the SS, responsible only to Hitler. Thus when Himmler was also put in charge of all Intelligence services, security offices, the Gestapo, and in 1943 became Minister of Interior as well with authority over the uniformed police, Hitler and he had built up a total dictatorship and police state. A fanatical racist who efficiently built up the system of terror and extermination that dragged Europe into a new dark age, he was nevertheless quite sickened when he actually witnessed the shootings of hundreds of Jews. Perhaps that influenced the decision to make greater use of gas chambers, though with ammunition needed on the fronts there were economical reasons as well. He also authorised the many barbaric medical experiments carried out on concentration camp inmates and through its "appropriation" of Jewish firms and personal wealth he made the SS an enormously wealthy organisation. Himmler had considerable ambition and frequently saw himself as the successor to Hitler. His moves – without Hitler's knowledge – to make peace overtures when it was obvious that Germany would lose the war were the first stages of trying to establish himself as head of a new Germany fighting with the west against the Russians. But when these came to nothing, and Hitler expelled him in the last few days of the war, Himmler tried to pass himself off as an ordinary soldier and was duly captured. After eventually identifying himself to his British captors, he was given a brief interrogation, but then he bit into a secreted vial of poison, and died despite frantic efforts to save him for trial.

HIROHITO, Emperor of Japan. b. 1901. Hirohito had few means to rule his country or even influence its rule, and his assent was traditionally given to the decisions of the top governing committee of the Cabinet – popularly known as the Big Six. Nevertheless the majority of the Japanese and the war-hungry Tojo venerated him in the traditional manner. With his country getting nearer and nearer war, Hirohito did urge caution and diplomacy, but was powerless to influence events. It was only in the last days of the war that Hirohito, with Kido's urging, decided it was necessary to attempt to assert authority, and in an unprecedented step virtually commanded the Cabinet to surrender. The Allies never went so far as to guarantee the Emperor's safety or position after the war, and many suggest this prolonged the war – but in the last days there were groups in Japan who drew up plans to kidnap or kill the Emperor, as he seemed to be willing to surrender; and most Japanese felt just as strong a loyalty to Japan as to their Emperor. Nevertheless MacArthur's respect for Hirohito, and the way in which he took no step to interfere in his position, greatly assisted relations between the American occupying force and the Japanese people.

HITLER, Adolf. 1889–1945. The Prelude and the Chronology in this book virtually encompass the life of Hitler. He was born on 20th April, the third son of the third marriage of an illegitimate Austrian customs

Air Marshal Sir Arthur Harris – known affectionately and otherwise as "Bomber Harris" – directed the R.A.F.'s air offensive over Germany from 1942. He was a forceful and effective leader, but was considered by many to be far too singlemindedly committed to "area bombing", which caused hundreds of thousands of civilian deaths with doubtful military effect.

official, who for many years had used his mother's name of Schicklgruber. Hitler's mother was a second cousin of his father. The name Hitler in numerous variants – Hiedler, Huetler, Huettler – occurred in both his paternal and maternal ancestry. Hitler's paternal grandfather (Heidler) only admitted to being the father of Alois Schicklgruber when he was 84, and consequently Hitler's father's name was changed in 1876. Early journalistic mockery of Adolf Schicklgruber was therefore fanciful, though many have been intrigued by wondering whether world history was not changed the day Johann Hiedler admitted his illegitimate son. (Not only was Hitler thankful not to be called Schicklgruber, but he even expressed a much greater liking for "Hitler" than for the softer "Hiedler" of his grandfather.) The young Hitler resisted his father's attempts to have him well educated for the role of a civil servant, and was instead set on an artistic career, for which he was only moderately suited. After his father's death when Hitler was 13, the future warlord spent a number of contented years with his mother, who had not lived with his father. He did practically no work of any sort from 16 to 19, and seemed to have had only one friend. He showed an early interest in politics, but even more in art and was distressed by his failure to get into art schools. When his mother died at the end of 1908 Hitler entered the lowest point of his life (in his judgement), living as little more than a vagabond in Vienna – doing occasional manual work, living in charity hostels, eating at soup kitchens, selling his mediocre drawings for a little money. His hair long and dirty, wearing a shabby raincoat and a soiled hat, Hitler – teetotal, a non-smoker and vegetarian – lived like (and sometimes with) the sewer rats of Vienna, dreamed of destiny, and began to loathe the people who seemed so successful and wealthy while he was a penniless failure. When he began to read voraciously, and to attend political meetings, his life began to change. From then onwards ambition seemed to prod him on, with the First World War arriving in the nick of time and giving him a chance to attain dignity – and become a German rather than an Austrian. After that war, his story is the story of the Third Reich.

HO CHI MINH. b. 1890. The leader of the first nationalistic group of rebels in South East Asia to rise against the Japanese. He persuaded the Allies to supply him with arms (S.E.A.C. tried to foster nationalist uprisings) and his forces in northern French Indo-China became very powerful. The Vichy French had not been at all popular, as virtual collaborators of the Japanese, and when France tried to return to its former colony Ho proclaimed the Republic of Viet Nam, run by a Nationalist coalition called the Viet Minh.

HODGES, General Courtney. b. 1887. The commander of the U.S. 1st Army in England during the preparation for Overlord, and on D-Day itself he was immediately below Bradley. When the advance through Europe began, Hodges took command of the 1st Army, forming the left flank of Bradley's 12th Army Group (with Patton's 3rd Army on the right). Hodges' advance took his army across the Seine, to Mons and Liège. It liberated Luxembourg and captured Aachen, and held the northern line of the German offensive in the Battle of the Bulge (when Hodges was temporarily placed under Montgomery's command). His 1st Army captured the bridge across the Rhine at Remagen, his troops were first to cross the river and they went on to help encircle the Ruhr. After the liberation of Europe, Hodges went to the Pacific and took part in the Okinawa battle. Far more reserved than many of his contemporaries, his achievements surpassed most.

HOEPNER, General Erich. 1886–1944. One of Germany's Panzer specialists who took part in all the *blitzkrieg* attacks. He was one of the few to get within sight of Moscow in December 1941, leading the 4th Armoured Group. The Russian counter-attack against his pitifully ill-equipped army sent him into retreat – and public disgrace. Always a member of anti-Nazi plots, he was to have replaced Fromm as C-in-C of the Replacement Army (the Home Forces) after the July 1944 attempt. Its failure led to his arrest and he was brutally treated by the Gestapo. He was offered suicide or a trial, chose a trial, but had been so thoroughly wrecked by the Gestapo that he was unable to make his hoped-for impression at the trial. He was hanged in Ploetzensee prison in August 1944 – like all the plotters, gradually, on a loop of wire suspended from a meathook.

HOESS, Rudolf Franz. 1900–1947. A convicted murderer long before he began to murder on a gigantic scale, Hoess served six years before finding his niche in the Nazi Party – who had considerable use for people of his talents and personality. In June 1940 he was made the SS commandant of Auschwitz concentration camp, having gained experience as a corporal at Dachau and adjutant at Sachsenhausen. His devotion and efficiency earned him high praise from his superiors, and soon Auschwitz was managing to kill and burn more people in a day than most of the other camps combined. In 1943 he was rewarded by being made inspector of concentration camps, and did his best to bring some Auschwitz efficiency to them all, though it upset him that his advanced methods could not be incorporated in all the camps. At Nuremberg he unrepentantly gave evidence that he had superintended the purposeful "extermination" of about 2,500,000 people, and that about another 500,000 had died of starvation under his control. It is quite possible these were low estimates. In April 1947 the Polish People's Court sentenced Hoess to death, and he was hanged, fittingly, at Auschwitz.

HOMMA, General Masaharu. 1888–1946. The Japanese General who led the surprise attack and invasion of

Luzon in the Philippines on 10th December 1941. He resolutely forced the U.S. and Philippino troops onto the Bataan peninsula, where 76,000 (35,000 U.S. soldiers) eventually surrendered in April 1942 (the island garrison on Corregidor lasted out a little longer). While the Japanese were totally unprepared for such a massive surrender, they did little to attempt to alleviate the prisoners' terrible conditions. In fierce heat, for five days with scarcely any water and no food, the captives endured the infamous Bataan Death March. Some 10,000 died before they reached a camp – of starvation, illness, beatings, by being shot for falling out of line, by suffocation in a packed railway train that they reached on the ninth day of the march. In September 1945 Homma was arrested by U.S. forces in Tokyo, taken to Manila on trial for other atrocities as well as the Death March, and executed by firing squad in April 1946.

HOPKINS, Harry. 1890–1945. Roosevelt's trusted and admired personal envoy, and former Secretary of Commerce. Throughout the war he played a leading role in its direction and strategy, and was Chairman of the Munitions Assignment Board. He frequently met Churchill, and they both got on extremely well. Hopkins made two journeys to England, and accompanied Roosevelt to Teheran and Yalta. After Roosevelt's death, and with his own health failing, he was Truman's envoy on a mission to Moscow, but was unable to attend the Potsdam Conference in Berlin. Hopkins died not long after that conference ended.

HORE-BELISHA, Leslie. b. 1893. As the British Secretary of State for War, he did not have an enviable record of preparation when hostilities began in earnest, and he had a number of conflicts with Gort and Ironside. He supported the immediate declaration of war after Poland's invasion, and also wanted stronger defences between France and Belgium. But constant criticism from the generals resulted in his dismissal (Grigg taking over), and Hore-Belisha did not again hold Government office. He was one of the few supporters of the Vote of Censure against Churchill in June 1942.

HORROCKS, General Brian. b. 1895. A British specialist in armoured warfare who achieved considerable success in North Africa, where Montgomery took note of his talents. Horrocks took part in Alamein, and in the attack on Tunis in May 1943. He commanded 30th Corps of the British 2nd Army in north west Europe after the invasion, and was largely responsible for the extremely rapid advance through Belgium. His force battled through against powerful opposition to relieve the besieged paratroopers in the tragic battle of Arnhem.

HORTHY, Admiral Miklos, Regent of Hungary. b. 1868. A leader who was one of those placed in the impossible position of trying to keep conflict from his country. Hitler's anti-communism appealed to Horthy, but little else did, and he had to be threatened with invasion before he would allow the use of Hungarian troops, even against Russia. Under Gestapo pressure he was forced to give up his protests over the deportation of Hungarian Jews. In October 1944 he offered an Armistice to Russia and sought peace with the Allies. He was deported and imprisoned by the Germans in Austria, and freed by U.S. troops in May 1945.

HULL, Cordell. b. 1871. The U.S. Secretary of State from 1933 to 1944, when he resigned due to ill-health. He had conducted the frustrating and futile negotiations with the Japanese envoys for months prior to Pearl Harbor, trying to keep them going as long as possible to give America time to prepare herself for the war that seemed increasingly inevitable. Hull received the declaration from the Japanese 80 minutes late due to their difficulties in decoding the long message from Japan – but Hull already knew its contents and that Japan had already attacked Pearl Harbor. Hull attended the Moscow Conference of Foreign Ministers in October 1943.

IRONSIDE, Field Marshal Lord. b. 1880. In 1939 he replaced Gort as C.I.G.S., but General Ironside also found Hore-Belisha difficult to get on with. In May 1940 he visited Gort (leading the B.E.F.) ostensibly to order a southwards breakthrough, but agreed that this was not feasible, and backed the decision to evacuate the B.E.F. from Dunkirk. Later that month Dill succeeded him as C.I.G.S., and Ironside became C-in-C of Home Forces drawing up plans for the defence of Britain against invasion, which basically found full approval. He was relieved by Brooke in July 1940.

ISMAY, General Sir Hastings. b. 1887. After heading the Secretariat of the Committee of Imperial Defence, Ismay became Churchill's Chief of Staff in May 1940, and was the main communication link between Churchill and the whole machinery of war with which Churchill was so involved as Prime Minister and Minister of Defence. He was a member of the Chiefs of Staff Committee, and did much valuable work in the Committee's contact with Churchill. He was respected for his tact and patience, both of which were greatly needed on the Anglo–American delegation to Moscow in September 1941. Ismay returned to Moscow for the Foreign Secretaries' Conference in 1943, and at the Potsdam Conference Admiral King paid a warm tribute to Ismay's contribution to the Allied victory.

JAMES, Lieutenant Clifton. b. 1897. A British actor whose strong resemblance to Montgomery led him into an elaborate ruse when, shortly before D-Day, he went to Gibraltar as "Montgomery" and was ceremonially greeted by the Governor. A Spanish agent reported "Montgomery's" presence in Gibraltar to Berlin (and he was later "on show" in Algiers). This deception contributed to the general lack of preparedness of the Germans when D-Day came, for it was known to them that Montgomery was to command the actual landing.

JODL, General Alfred. 1890–1945. The Chief of the Armed Forces Operational Staff for the duration of the war, and immediate deputy to Keitel. One of the more competent generals, and the main prop without which Keitel would have crumbled. Except for the second half of the Russian campaign, Jodl effectively directed all the others, but he did cause some faulty decisions on the Russian front which resulted in great losses. He also miscalculated the conditions of the Western front in late 1944 and thus let the Ardennes offensive go ahead, which despite its initial rapid success, was a final disaster for the German Army. Jodl signed Germany's unconditional surrender at Eisenhower's Rheims H.Q. on 7th May 1945. His diaries revealed his approbation of the killing of hostages and of other atrocities the Army eventually condoned – especially in Russia – and he was tried with the top Nazis at Nuremberg. Jodl was hanged on 16th October 1946.

Field Marshal Wilhelm Keitel, Chief of OKW for the duration of the war, was a man of extraordinarily limited intelligence for this high military position (which was only below that of Hitler, the Supreme Commander). His crawling subservience to Hitler, and the real capabilities of his Chief of Staff, Jodl, made him useful to the Nazis, however; and he was not above issuing Nazi-style orders. Keitel was hanged after the Nuremberg trials.

JOHNSON, Group Captain James. b. 1916. "Johnnie" Johnson was officially top of the British and Commonwealth fighter pilots with a score of 38 planes shot down. Although he fought in the Battle of Britain, he only had his first victory in May 1941. He flew an enormous number of operations, generally escorting bomber squadrons, and was frequently with Canadian wings.

JONES, Frederick. b. 1884. The New Zealand Minister of Defence who, from an army of 1,000 at the outbreak of war, had by the end of 1943 mobilised, equipped and trained 80,000 men and 10,000 women in New Zealand. New Zealanders fought with great distinction in North Africa and the Mediterranean in the early years of the war, and later in Italy and the Solomons in the Pacific, by which time a third of New Zealanders of military age were serving abroad.

JONGH, Andrée de. b. 1916. The Belgian girl who became a Resistance leader and established an escape route for Allied prisoners of war and aircrews. In three years over 800 escaped via her "Comet-line". She was interrogated by the Gestapo in 1942, and her father – a wanted man with a high price on his head – was captured and executed. Andrée de Jongh moved to France but was arrested in January 1943, and spent the rest of the war in prison and in a concentration camp. The Gestapo never realised her leading role in "Comet", for over 20 in the organisation were executed.

JOYCE, William. 1906–1946. The British Fascist who went to Germany just before war broke out and became the notorious "Lord Haw-Haw", making propaganda radio broadcasts against Britain – to which the British listened with considerable enjoyment and little apprehension. Joyce was discovered in Germany after the war and returned to Britain where he was hanged for treason.

KAISER, Henry. b. 1882. An American industrialist who developed methods of shipbuilding using prefabrication which resulted in a very rapid output of the simple, standardised merchant ships known as "Liberty" ships. About one third of the thousands built by America came from Kaiser's shipyards.

KALTENBRUNNER, Ernst. 1902–1946. The head of the SS in Austria at the time of *Anschluss*, and possessor of such a barbaric nature that he was Hitler's automatic choice to replace the ghastly Heydrich, whose monstrous inhumanity was even excelled by Kaltenbrunner. He was responsible for Reich security, and after the murder or arrest of all the anti-Hitlerists also headed Military Intelligence (*Abwehr*). Although Himmler was officially the holder of these positions, and Kaltenbrunner's superior, even he is reputed to have feared the Austrian, who enjoyed a good deal of favouritism from Hitler. Kaltenbrunner stepped up the already horrifying rate of Nazi atrocities, ruthlessly murdering opponents to Hitler, witnesses of atrocities, and anyone who seemed to seek peace. He was responsible for the murder of many prisoners of war, apart from the "normal" extermination of political prisoners and Jews. The blood of millions never seemed to affect him in the slightest, and at Nuremberg he simply denied everything in a monstrous, ox-like manner, even in the face of totally irrefutable evidence. He was the third of the ten Nazis hanged on the morning of 16th October 1946.

KEITEL, Field Marshal Wilhelm. 1882–1946. Preceded Kaltenbrunner up the steps of the gallows in Nuremberg on 16th October. For the duration of the war Keitel was Chief of the High Command of the Armed Forces (Chef. OKW), though he had limited ability and was little more than a puppet dancing as Hitler pulled the strings. His chief of staff, Jodl, carried out most of the functions that Keitel was credited with, but it suited Hitler to have at the head of the OKW someone who would not query his decisions or argue with him. Keitel refused to listen to criticism of Hitler's conduct of the war, and only later maintained he had shared the doubts of the critics. By agreeing to Hitler's order that the conquest of Russia should be carried out with "unprecedented viciousness", and by excusing German officers from criminal acts, Keitel smeared the image of the German Army with guilt. He signed the second, formal declaration of surrender in Berlin on 8th May 1945.

Field Marshal Albrecht Kesselring was one of Germany's most highly talented generals – in the opinion of the Allies as well, who came up against him in North Africa, the Battle of Britain, Italy, and after D-Day. Kesselring resisted all attempts to influence him against Hitler, and only gave up belief in Germany's victory after Hitler's suicide.

KENNEDY, Joseph. b. 1888. U.S. ambassador to Britain, his pessimistic reports on British morale and strength created considerable ill-feeling and misunderstanding. On returning to America in 1941, Kennedy urged isolationism but supported Lend-Lease, although he remained sceptical of British ability to remain unconquered. After America entered the war, his political influence declined.

KESSELRING, Field Marshal Albrecht. b. 1885. During the war General Kesselring took part in practically every major operation. He commanded the Luftwaffe in the invasions of Poland and of the Low Countries and thus was responsible for the destruction of much of Warsaw, the Rotterdam terror attack, and considerable damage and death by the bombing of the Dunkirk evacuation. He directed major forces taking part in the Battle of Britain. In December 1941 he became C-in-C Armed Forces South (Mediterranean) and shared the direction of Rommel's African campaign. In 1943 he was put in command of the German forces in Italy, and conducted a brilliant defence against powerful Allied forces. He was brought in briefly to stop the advance of the Allies through Europe in March 1945. His military skill was respected by the Allies, but only the suicide of Hitler made him query the whole Nazi cause. A British court sentenced Kesselring to death in May 1947, but this was commuted to life imprisonment (and he was pardoned and freed in October 1952).

KEYES, Lieutenant Colonel Geoffrey. 1917–1941. Awarded a posthumous V.C. for a number of commando attacks and mainly for the hazardous attempt to kill or capture Rommel. Keyes and his group were landed at night by submarine near Apollonia in November 1941, and they raided the house where Rommel was believed to be. They killed a large number of soldiers and officers in the house, but Rommel had not stayed there for some time. Keyes was killed during the raid.

KHAN, Noor Inayat. 1914–1944. A British S.O.E. agent who was landed in France (where she lived before the war) in June 1943, with the task of ensuring radio contact between London and a local ring of Resistance workers. Soon after there were mass arrests, but "Madeleine" refused to abandon the rest of the group, though the Germans knew her code name and her description. In July she and some colleagues were ambushed but escaped, killing some of the Germans. In October she was betrayed and taken to the Gestapo H.Q. in Paris. She was interrogated for several weeks and suffered brutal treatment, but gave no information. After two unsuccessful escape attempts "Madeleine" was sent to Germany, and then on 12th September 1944 to Dachau, where she was shot on arrival.

KIDO, Marquis Koichi. The Japanese Privy Seal and confidential adviser to Emperor Hirohito, who was able to wield a fair amount of influence on Japanese affairs. He was largely responsible for the Emperor's appointment of Tojo as Premier, a shrewd move, for although Kido disliked Tojo's intense militarism, he knew him to be utterly loyal to Hirohito and to be strong enough to keep other militants in check. Kido played an important part in persuading some of the members of the Big Six to accept the inevitability of defeat, and advised Hirohito to speak out against those who wanted to continue the war.

KIMMEL, Admiral Husband. b. 1882. As C-in-C of the U.S. Pacific Fleet in 1941, his was the head that had to roll after the disaster of Pearl Harbor. He was dropped from his post almost immediately and criticised harshly for not taking better precautions. But it was also true that he had received very unclear and inadequate warnings, and for some of the mistakes – such as the planes parked in tight rows on the airfields – he was not responsible.

KING, Admiral Ernest. b. 1878. The C-in-C of the U.S. Fleet who in 1942 became Chief of Naval Operations and a Member of the Combined Chiefs of Staff Committee. King had little time for the war in Europe, regarding it almost as a sideshow against the main conflict against Japan. This caused considerable friction, especially as King was a blunt, determined and strong-willed man. Although some energy was wasted in the Pacific War by the arguments between the strategies of MacArthur and King, King's Navy undoubtedly brought about the defeat of Japan. The mobilisation of America's resources gave King a huge fleet, and he brilliantly co-ordinated vast operations, overcame supply difficulties across thousands of miles of ocean, and remorselessly established naval and air superiority over Japan. In 1944 he was made Fleet Admiral.

KING, William Mackenzie. b. 1874. Prime Minister of Canada who, while originally an isolationist, led Canada into a tremendous war effort. The Canadian contributions in convoy escorts were soon relied on, and great quantities of supplies came from Canada to Britain. King was determined not to introduce conscription, and only had to do so in 1945. Despite this, Canadian troops were invaluable in the Allied war effort. From their tragedy at Dieppe, the Canadians triumphantly swept through Europe after D-Day. King acted as an intermediary between Roosevelt and Churchill, and Quebec was twice the scene of informal meetings between the two leaders.

KLEIST, General Paul von. b. 1885. The Panzer commander who led the attack through the Ardennes which smashed Western Europe in May 1940, though much credit was due to Guderian's corps under Kleist. Kleist led similar rapid armoured attacks in Russia, and was put in command of the German attempt to capture the Caucasus. This effort, however, came to a halt before the mountains could be crossed, and all the oil-fields within occupied territory were destroyed before Kleist's arrival. He also lost much of his strength in an abortive attempt to save the German 6th Army at Stalingrad.

KLUGE, General Günther von. 1882–1944. A successful German commander who particularly distinguished himself with the Army Group Centre in the east during the defensive battles against the Russians in 1942–43. Kluge replaced Rundstedt in July 1944 in France after the latter's pessimistic (but realistic) assessment of the position once the Allies had firmly established themselves in Normandy. Kluge knew little of the conditions, and tried to follow Hitler's orders not to fall back. All this ensured was that he was never able to make a strategic retreat, and his dispatches to Hitler frankly expressed his feeling that Germany should surrender. On 17th August Model took over from him. Kluge realised the war was lost, and while he had not taken part in the plot on Hitler's life, he knew his despatches and his known contacts and talks with the conspirators put him in jeopardy. Distressed also by his inability to hold back the Allies, Kluge took a fatal dose of poison the day after he was relieved of his command.

KNOX, Jean. b. 1908. Succeeded the Director of the A.T.S. in Britain in July 1941, in time to face the critical manpower shortage in 1942. The controversial solution was the introduction of conscription for women, and Mrs. Knox had to deal with enormous welfare and organisational problems. However A.T.S. women took over more than 100 army trades that were previously reserved for men, releasing thousands for active service.

KOENIG, General Pierre. b. 1898. The French captain who fled to England with the fall of France, and in

November 1940 captured Libreville, which became a base for Free French Forces. He commanded French Forces in the desert war in 1941, and later in France in 1944. After the liberation of Paris Koenig was made the military governor and brought back law and order – though not without difficulty, as de Gaulle was not universally accepted.

KOGA, Admiral Mineichi. 1882–1944. Succeeded Yamamoto (after his assassination) as C-in-C of the Japanese Combined Fleet. But there was nothing Koga could do to stop the decline of Japan's naval fortunes against the rapidly increasing size of the U.S. Fleet. He went to Singapore to prepare a final confrontation, but was killed in an air crash before he could develop his plans.

KONOYE, Prince Fumimaro. 1891–1945. Twice Prime Minister of Japan, who initially resigned in 1939 over his inability to stop the militarists waging war in China. In July 1940 he was recalled, and then concluded the Tripartite Pact with Germany and Italy. The inability to reach an agreement with America drove him to resign again, leaving the outbreak of war to Tojo. In July 1945 he went to Moscow as a peace envoy vainly seeking Russia's help in stopping the war. In the post-war Cabinet he was Vice-President, but was then listed to be tried as a war criminal. He committed suicide, and was posthumously condemned by a war crimes tribunal.

KRAMER, Josef. 1906–1945. In contemporary newspapers called the "Beast of Belsen", Kramer was a blindly obedient SS official who led a gruesomely successful career in the concentration camp service. At Natzweiler camp he supervised the erection of a gas chamber and was personally responsible for killing 80 people in it. In May 1944 he went to take charge of part of Auschwitz, and in November arrived at Belsen. Till then more of an exchange camp where Jews were swopped for extradited Germans, Belsen was also made a depository for sick prisoners from other camps. Conditions at the camp deteriorated rapidly, until it held over 40,000 people living in accommodation and on rations which were originally intended to be barely adequate for 15,000 inmates. When the camp was liberated by the British, 10,000 unburied corpses were found, and another 13,000 prisoners died before they could be saved. Kramer was hanged for war crimes in November 1945.

KRETSCHMER, Captain Otto. b. 1912. The most efficient German U-boat commander whose second command, *U99*, became well known in Germany and Britain for her captain's daring exploits, in which he used to penetrate a convoy and carry out a surface attack within it. He was credited with sinking some 350,000 tons of Allied shipping. *U99* and *U100* (another successful submarine) were trapped in March 1941 by two British destroyers, and after scuttling their craft Kretschmer and his crew were taken prisoner.

KRUPP von BOHLEN, Alfred. b. 1907. One of the three directors of the vast Krupp empire which had supplied so much of Germany's armament. Alfred Krupp was in charge of Armaments and Mining and was responsible for incorporating many industries in occupied countries into the Krupp concern. Whole factories were transported after his inspection – even from as far away as the Ukraine – and rebuilt in Germany. Krupp agreed to the use of 45,000 Russian civilian prisoners in his steel works while his coal mines used 120,000 prisoners of war, and another 6,000 Russian civilians – even though they were far weaker than the workers an average factory would find desirable. Krupp also installed factories close to concentration camps – for example, a shell factory near Auschwitz. He was highly decorated by the Nazis, and was a central figure of their war plans. Most of the Krupp factories were destroyed in the Allied bomber offensive, and Krupp himself was arrested in 1944, tried as a war criminal, his property was confiscated and he was sentenced to 12 years imprisonment – though he eventually received compensation and served only a few years.

KURIBAYASHI, General Tadamichi. 1885–1945. Conducted the fanatical suicidal defence of Iwo Jima, in which over 21,000 Japanese died after a month of bitter fighting from February to March 1945.

LACEY, Squadron Leader James. b. 1917. The highest-scoring N.C.O. in the R.A.F. during the Battle of Britain, in which he shot down 15 aircraft. In common with many pilots during the hectic months of the Battle, "Ginger" Lacey often flew from four to eight combats in one day. He was commissioned in 1941, and commanded squadrons in S.E. Asia.

LANGSDORFF, Captain Hans. 1890–1939. The captain of the German pocket-battleship *Graf Spee* which sailed for the South Atlantic before war was declared, and sank nine merchant ships totalling 50,000 tons. In December 1939 she was sighted by three R.N. cruisers off the mouth of the River Plate, and although they were outgunned they managed to harass and damage Langsdorff's ship sufficiently for it to put into Montevideo, a neutral port. The authorities would not give permission for repairs, and expecting to meet a large British force, Langsdorff scuttled the *Graf Spee* in the estuary. His crew were interned, but, ashamed at the early loss of his ship, Langsdorff shot himself on 20th December.

LARSEN, Lief. b. 1906. Norwegian fisherman who became one of the most decorated and heroic Resistance men in the war. He worked with S.O.E. and organised the escape of many Norwegians from occupied Norway, most of whom were volunteers for training in Britain. He played an active part in running the "Shetland bus service", laid mines from a fleet of whalers and torpedo boats, and took part in the raids on the Lofoten Islands and on Vaagso. He was the guide for the underwater "Chariots" which first attempted to reach *Tirpitz* in Altenfjord.

LATTRE de TASSIGNY, General Jean de. b. 1889. At the outbreak of war he headed the French 14th Division at Aine, and was Chief of Staff to the 5th Army. Loyal to the army and to its superiors, Lattre de Tassigny was put in command of Tunisia by the Vichy regime, but recalled when they were suspicious about his sympathies with the Allies. At the end of 1942 he denounced the German occupation of Vichy-France, and was sentenced to 10 years imprisonment. He escaped and was flown to England. Put in command of Free French troops in North Africa, he played a significant role in the rapid advance of the Allies from southern France up the Rhône and across the Rhine. He signed the unconditional surrender of Germany to France in Berlin on 9th May 1945.

LAVAL, Pierre. 1883–1945. The virtual head of Vichy-France, who convened the Assembly that appointed Pétain head of State of the Vichy Government, Laval convinced the Assembly that Germany would defeat Britain, so it was best to be on the right side. Initially Secretary and Pétain's deputy, he was dismissed in December 1940, but recalled in April 1942. A toady of the Germans, Laval acted strongly against his countrymen in the Resistance, but eventually became unpopular with the Germans as well. With the German defeat inevitable, he tried to form a National Assembly in Paris, but was forced by the Germans to form a Government-in-exile in Germany. Laval escaped to Switzerland but was captured and tried for treason. After an unsuccessful suicide attempt, he was executed by a firing squad.

LAYCOCK, Major General Robert. b. 1907. An officer in the Horse Guards who formed one of the first commando units. In 1941 "Layforce" operated with Wavell's army in North Africa, making raids deep behind enemy lines. Laycock commanded the unsuccessful raid on Rommel's H.Q. in which Keyes won the V.C., and with only one companion survived several weeks in the desert after the raid. He led the Royal Marine Commando battalion in the Sicily and Italy invasions in 1943, and was subsequently made Chief of Combined Operations, playing a major role in the co-ordinating of D-Day forces.

LEAHY, Admiral William. b. 1895. The former U.S. Ambassador to Vichy-France who became Roosevelt's Personal Chief of Staff, and took part in practically all major decisions during the war, attending also the international conferences. He was made Fleet Admiral in 1944 and was also Personal Chief of Staff to Truman. Leahy was also highly successful as Chairman of the American Joint Chiefs of Staff, but his dislike of de Gaulle led him to advocate greater trust in the Vichy Government.

LECLERC, General Jacques Philippe. b. 1902. After being captured twice, and escaping twice, Leclerc joined de Gaulle in England in 1940, became the military governor of Chad and Cameroun, and the G.O.C. for French Equatorial Africa. In December 1942 he led a Free French force from Chad to join the British 8th Army 1,500 miles across the desert in Libya, attacking Italian positions *en route*. In 1944 he commanded the 2nd French Armoured Division into Normandy, and in August entered Paris and took its formal surrender. After taking part in the remainder of the Allied advance across France, Leclerc went with French Forces to Indo-China.

LEESE, General Sir Oliver. b. 1894. Distinguished in the command of 30th Corps of the 8th Army at Alamein, he later led the spearhead of the British landings on Sicily. He became the popular and successful C-in-C of the 8th Army during its Italian campaign against Kesselring's German forces, and was finally appointed C-in-C of Allied land forces in S.E. Asia.

LEIGH-MALLORY, Air Chief Marshal Sir Trafford. 1892–1944. As commander of No. 12 Fighter Group Leigh-Mallory shared with Park the burden of the Battle of Britain, the Midlands and all east coast shipping coming under his cover. In December 1940 he took over Park's No. 11 Group, and began Fighter Command's changeover from a defensive to an offensive role. In November 1942 he headed Fighter Command, and in 1944 was C-in-C of Allied Air Forces for the invasion of Europe – commanding some 9,000 R.A.F. and U.S.A.A.F. aircraft. His defences were so good that no German aircraft managed to bomb the D-Day forces, a factor which helped the invasion enormously. In November 1944 he was appointed Air C-in-C for South East Asia, but he and his wife were killed in an air crash on the way to his new post.

Le MAY, General Curtis. b. 1906. A successful air commander who contributed greatly to new bombing tactics both in Europe and Japan. After commanding units of B-17 Flying Fortresses over Europe, Le May took command of the U.S. 21st Bomber Command in the Marianas in the Pacific, and then of the 20th Air Force on Guam.

LEOPOLD III, King of Belgium. b. 1901. Leopold took command of the Belgian Army on the invasion of the Low Countries on 10th May 1940, and large numbers of French and British troops moved into Belgium. However on 28th May Leopold felt that continued resistance would be pointless, and ordered a surrender. The Government was opposed to capitulation, declared the surrender illegal, suspended allegiance to the Crown, and urged the army to continue its resistance. But all that took time, and little effective action could be taken. King Leopold was taken prisoner by the Germans, and kept at the Palace of Laeken. At the time Leopold's capitulation was greatly criticised, in that it led to the rapid defeat of France. Yet the breakthrough into France had little to do with Belgium's defence, and the Belgian armed forces were no match at all for the Nazi war machine. Leopold was moved to Germany after the Allied invasion and released by U.S. forces in 1945. (But only in 1950, after a commission had examined his conduct of the war, was Leopold permitted to return to Belgium.)

LEY, Robert. 1890–1945. An early follower of Hitler who retained his close friendship and received many favours. From 1933 onwards Ley was the head of the Nazi Labour Front, supervising the use of foreign and German manpower for the war effort. However he was a poor organiser and drank excessively, leaving major tasks to subordinates. While awaiting trial as a war criminal in October 1945, Ley hanged himself (many of the slave labour conditions and policies would have been blamed on him).

LIDDELL HART, Basil. b. 1895. The British military theorist and historian who after the First World War predicted the far greater mobility of future wars, and the importance of tanks and aircraft. The Germans proved more willing listeners than the British, and many *blitzkrieg* tactics had their roots in his writings. He held no official appointment during the war.

LIST, Field Marshal Wilhelm. Commanded the 14th Army in the attack on Poland, and achieved even greater success in the offensive against Western Europe, when his 12th Army, including Guderian in Kleist's Panzer Group, cut a devastating path through northern France. In February 1941 List concluded an agreement with the Bulgarian General Staff which gave his 12th Army access through Bulgaria to smash Greece. He then took part in the Russian campaign, and in the summer of 1942 was C-in-C of Army Group A, commanding the armies in the Caucasus. His army's inability to break through the Caucasus barrier led to his sacking by Hitler in September 1941. List was condemned to life imprisonment at Nuremberg in 1948, but was pardoned and released almost five years later.

LOTHIAN, Lord. 1882–1940. The British Ambassador in Washington, who despite having had no political or diplomatic training and experience successfully influenced American attitudes in the crucial early stages of the war, and laid the foundation on which such beneficial relations between the two countries were built.

LOVAT, Brigadier Lord. b. 1911. A Guards officer who in 1939 commanded the Lovat Scouts (raised by his father in the Boer War). In 1942 Churchill suggested that they should be made into a commando unit, and Lovat became one of the war's most successful commando leaders. His group replaced the original "Layforce" in the Middle East, and in August 1942 Lovat led No. 4 Commando in the tragic assault on Dieppe – the only attacking force that achieved its objective and withdrew without being decimated. In the Normandy invasion of June 1944 he was wounded while commanding the 1st Special Service Brigade, and had to withdraw from active service. His personality impressed Stalin when he accompanied Laycock to Moscow to exchange information on river-crossing techniques with the Russians. From May to July 1945 Lovat was Joint Under-Secretary at the Foreign Office in the caretaker government.

MacARTHUR, General Douglas. b. 1880. In 1941 MacArthur was recalled to the U.S. Army from his position as military adviser to the Philippine Government, and became Commanding General of the U.S. Forces in the Far East. The Massive Japanese invasion of Luzon forced MacArthur to lead a retreat onto the Bataan Peninsula and he was eventually ordered to leave his troops and set up his H.Q. in Australia. From then on he fought with single-minded purpose for a triumphant return to the Philippines. This led to some conflict with Admiral King over priorities in the war, but eventually a two-pronged offensive led to the recapture of the Philippines. MacArthur's tremendous determination and considerable talent were a major contribution to the defeat of Japan, first in New Guinea, and then in the Philippines. In April 1945 he was put in command of all ground troops in the Pacific, and he was chief Allied signatory at the Japanese surrender on board U.S.S. *Missouri* on 2nd September. As the military governor of Japan, MacArthur carried enormous power and responsibility, but his tactful handling of the Emperor helped to establish co-operation.

McINDOE, Archibald. b. 1900. The New Zealand-born surgeon whose revolutionary methods of after-care and brilliant skill in plastic surgery contributed so much to the lives of many disfigured in the war. The Battle of Britain gave him his first opportunity to bring about radical changes in rehabilitation procedure, apart from putting his surgical skills to the test with badly burned and injured pilots.

MACLEAN, Brigadier Fitzroy. b. 1911. Explorer, and former member of the British Foreign Office who joined the SAS in Cairo, took part in two raids on Benghazi, and then served in Iran where he organised the kidnapping of General Zahidi. In September 1943 he parachuted into German-occupied Yugoslavia as leader of the British Military Mission accredited to Tito, who controlled some 150,000 partisans. In November 1943, reporting to Eden in Cairo, he recommended greater support for Tito, and together with a partisan delegation, met Churchill in December. Maclean's suggestions were accepted – he took part in the uprising which led to the liberation of Belgrade and established Tito as the head of Yugoslavia.

MACMILLAN, Harold. b. 1894. A close supporter of Eden, and for two years the Parliamentary Secretary for the Ministry of Supply. Macmillan later became Resident Minister at Allied H.Q., North West Africa, where a highly complex political situation was so diplomatically handled that he won favour from both the Americans and the French. He took part in the Casablanca Conference, and in the Italian Armistice negotiations in September 1943. Two months later Macmillan was appointed British High Commissioner for Italy, and in November 1944 he was made Head of the Allied Commission in Italy. Macmillan contributed to reforming the Italian government, and played an important role in the Yugoslav and Greek settlements.

McNARNEY, General Joseph. b. 1893. In March 1942 was appointed Chairman of the U.S. War Department Reorganisation Committee, applying his great administrative talents to simplifying the command structure of the U.S. Army, which gave it far greater efficiency. He was subsequently appointed Deputy Chief of Staff in the U.S. Army, but only got a command in October 1944 when he was made Acting Supreme Allied Commander, Mediterranean. (In December 1945, he took over from Eisenhower as C-in-C of the U.S. occupation forces in Germany.)

MAISKY, Ivan. The Russian Ambassador in London until he was recalled to Moscow in 1943 and made Deputy Commissar for Foreign Affairs. His task was difficult after Russia signed the pact with Germany, but he advised Stalin that the British would stand firm even when France fell. In June 1941 he personally took to Stalin the information that Germany was about to attack Russia, but this was not acted on. After "Barbarossa" he was constantly urged by Stalin to badger the British about the "Second Front". Maisky negotiated with the Polish and Czech governments-in-exile and did much to persuade Hopkins to visit Stalin.

MALAN, Group Captain "Sailor". b. 1910. South African-born R.A.F. fighter pilot who shot down five planes over Dunkirk and won a wide reputation for his "score" of 18 during the Battle of Britain, when he led No. 74 Squadron. His final war total was 32 aircraft shot down which placed him third among the R.A.F. pilots – but this tally stood for nearly three years. Malan commanded Biggin Hill fighter station, lectured in America, trained fighter wings for the invasion of Europe, and in July 1944 took command of the advanced gunnery school at Catford.

MANSTEIN, Field Marshal Erich von. b. 1887. General Manstein was Chief of Staff to Rundstedt in 1939, and gained an early reputation as one of Germany's most brilliant tacticians, for it was his plan of a surprise attack through the Ardennes which appealed to Hitler, and which so rapidly defeated France. In 1941 Manstein commanded the 56th Panzer Corps in East Prussia, and advanced rapidly towards Leningrad before being given command of an Army Group in September 1941. He defeated the numerically superior Russians in the Crimea and finally captured Sebastopol. He was then promoted and given command of Army Group Don in November 1942. Manstein was charged with relieving the 6th Army at Stalingrad but was unable to get his forces close enough. In February 1943 he commanded Army Group South, but was not permitted to make strategic withdrawals. Hitler eventually tired of his continuous requests to withdraw (the eventual but inevitable failure of the Kursk offensive also counted against him), and he was dismissed in March 1944. (A British court sentenced Manstein to 18 years imprisonment in 1950, but he was freed in May 1953.)

MARSHALL, General George. b. 1880. Appointed Chief of Staff of the U.S. Army on the day Poland was invaded, when the American Army totalled fewer than 200,000 men. With America neutral, but Roosevelt aware of the likelihood of war, Marshall had the task of building up the Army's strength, equipping and training it, until it totalled some 5 million men. After Japan's declaration Marshall urgently advocated the unification of Allied commands, and became Chairman of the Combined Chiefs of Staff Committee. Marshall wanted an early invasion of Europe and was impatient with Churchill's caution. He was initially expected to head Overlord, but Roosevelt preferred to keep Marshall in Washington; he was thus able to give advice on a far wider range of issues, and attend numerous conferences.

MASARYK, Jan. b. 1886. A leading Czech statesman and Ambassador in London at the time of Munich. When war began, Masaryk broadcast daily to his compatriots, and he acted as the mediatory between Beneš and the British Government. Masaryk was Foreign Minister in the Beneš Government-in-exile formed in July 1940.

MATHEWS, Vera Laughton. b. 1900. Appointed Director of the W.R.N.S. in 1939, she turned it into a highly efficient body. Consisting entirely of volunteers, the Wrens carried out a large number of vital shore jobs and freed men for service at sea. After the war the Service was made a permanent part of the Royal Navy.

MENZIES, Robert. b. 1894. Prime Minister of Australia at the outbreak of the war until political differences led to his resignation in August 1941. Menzies took immediate constructive action to get Australia on a war footing, and troops and supplies were quickly on their way to Britain and the Mediterranean. Menzies himself went to London in January 1941 to discuss the defence of Singapore and Australia, and was perturbed by the absence of definite policy on Japan. After his return, the war measures had become increasingly unpopular and his suggestion for an All-party Government was turned down. His immediate successor only lasted about one week, then Curtin became Prime Minister for the rest of the war.

MERRILL, General Frank. b. 1903. The leader of a group of tough U.S. volunteers, "Merrill's Marauders" – part of Stilwell's forces – left Ledo in Assam in February 1944 and travelled hundreds of miles through enemy-held northern Burma, living off the land and attacking isolated Japanese units and supply dumps. Eventually they joined up with a Chinese Army group and captured Myitkyina airport, which brought about the joining of the Ledo and Burma roads. Merrill eventually became Chief of Staff of the U.S. 10th Army.

MESSE, General Giovanni. b. 1883. After experience in the invasion of Abyssinia, Messe was with the forces that occupied Albania and later took part in the invasion of Greece. One of Italy's ablest commanders, he went to the Russian front commanding the Italian Expeditionary Corps, but was recalled after disagreements with German High Command. In 1943 he was appointed C-in-C of the Italian 1st Army in Tunisia, but by the time he arrived there was little to salvage between the jaws of the two groups of Allied armies. In May Messe was instructed by his superiors in Rome to surrender.

MIHAJLOVIĆ, Draza. 1893–1946. The leader of the Serbian Četnik Resistance group in Yugoslavia formed in opposition to Tito's Communist Partisans. Although the two groups sometimes fought together in the early stages of occupation, Mihajlović was in favour of more cautious resistance due to the fatal reprisals on innocent hostages. Eventually he felt there was little to choose between the Nazis and the Communists, and he began talks with both the British and the Germans. He was appointed War Minister by the Yugoslav Government-in-exile, but the British eventually favoured Tito's larger force, and Mihajlović was deposed. In March 1946 he was captured by the Communists, tried and executed.

MITCHELL, Reginald. 1895–1937. Although he died more than two years before the war started, Mitchell played a considerable part in its outcome, for he designed the Spitfire fighter plane. He only saw the prototype fly before he died.

MITSCHER, Admiral Marc Andrew. b. 1887. The commander of the carrier *Hornet* whose planes under Doolittle flew the first air raid over Japan in April 1942. "Mich" Mitscher also played a central role at Midway, and for a number of months in 1943 commanded all air forces in the Solomon Islands. From January to October 1944 he commanded the famous Task Force 58 which destroyed or damaged over 4,400 Japanese planes and nearly 800 ships. Task Force 58 supported the Okinawa invasion in April and May 1945.

MODEL, Field Marshal Walther. 1891–1945. Model took part in the Polish campaign, and the invasion of France. In the invasion of Russia he led the drive across the Dnieper, and in 1942 took command of the 9th Army, playing a leading role in the Kursk offensive. Despite its eventual failure, Model retained Hitler's favour and was changed from one command to another on the Russian front. He was then sent by Hitler as a "saviour" to the western front after the Allied invasion, and on 17th August 1944 became Supreme Commander of Armed Forces in the West. This only lasted until 4th September, when Rundstedt replaced him to plan and direct the Ardennes offensive in December. In charge of Army Group B, Model launched the offensive with Rundstedt, but by early 1945 he had retired to the Ruhr pocket. The whole of the Ruhr was surrounded by the Allies, and the complete Army Group B was disbanded and surrendered. A few days later, Model shot himself rather than face capture.

MOELDERS, Colonel Werner. 1913–1941. Leading and very influential German fighter pilot who commanded a group in the Battle of France and the Battle of Britain. In the summer of 1941 he went to the Russian front, where he destroyed a very high number of Russian aircraft. In November 1941, shortly before he was due to be made a general, Moelders left the Crimea for the funeral of a colleague, Udet. His plane developed engine trouble and he crashed and died while landing at Breslau. He had 115 confirmed air victories, and possibly shot down many more.

MOLOTOV, Vyacheslav. b. 1890. The totally dedicated Russian Foreign Minister who worked tirelessly at Russia's various aims (by July 1941 Russia had signed, at some stage, pacts with Germany, Japan, and Britain). He was a member of the State Defence Committee, with Stalin, Voroshilov, Beria, and Malenkov. Molotov took on a great deal of Stalin's functions in connection with the Allies, and his diligence impressed foreign leaders and diplomats.

MONTGOMERY, Field Marshal Bernard. b. 1887. Having led the 3rd Division of the B.E.F. in France, Montgomery became known for the toughness of his training methods in the Army in south east England. Gott's death in Egypt led him from being Eisenhower's deputy for Operation Torch to commander of the 8th

Army. Under Alexander, Montgomery began to build up an enormous superiority in men and equipment over the Axis, in the meantime repelling an attack on the Alam Halfa H.Q. The Alamein offensive was launched at night on 23rd October 1942, and, after some critical moments, it finally broke the Axis line. Montgomery was criticised for the caution with which he chased the retreating Axis, and a bolder offensive might well have cut-off and captured the whole of Rommel's army long before it reached the reinforcements in Tunisia, and before many managed to leave Africa altogether. But Montgomery never took risks, and the conservation of his troops and equipment was always uppermost in his mind. He was aware of the dangers of an over-extended supply column, and the ease with which a retreating force could turn and inflict considerable casualties on the vanguard of the pursuers.

After taking Tripoli, the 8th Army's offensive became involved with the Allied campaign following Operation Torch, with Eisenhower the Supreme Commander. Montgomery led the British contingent in the attack on Sicily and took the 8th Army on into Italy. In January 1944 he went to England to plan the invasion of Normandy, being commander of the landing itself. After the beachheads were secured, Montgomery took command of the 21st Army Group, fought a tough battle at Caen, and then headed north through the Low Countries. He urged Eisenhower to give him priority of materials to launch a fast drive towards Berlin, with the aim of reaching it long before the Russians, and bringing the war to an early end. Being overruled on this was perhaps his greatest disappointment of the war. Montgomery's forces liberated Hamburg and on 4th May he took the surrender at Lüneberg Heath H.Q. of German forces in Holland, Denmark and North West Germany.

Montgomery's ardent belief in "set piece" warfare ensured he never acted until he was confident of his superiority, but this caution often aggravated other commanders. But some tacticians have stated that his greatest ability was to assess changing conditions and immediately alter his own plans to take advantage of them; and that it was his insistence that what happened was only what he expected to happen that prevented people from fully appreciating this. A rigid disciplinarian and hard task-master, he was nevertheless liked by his troops; with fellow commanders, however, relations were frequently strained, and it was only the diplomacy of de Guingand that overcame many awkward moments in the Allied conquest of Europe.

MORGAN, General Sir Frederick. b. 1894. The little known British "architect" of the successful Allied invasion of Normandy, for it was Morgan who drew up the first sketchy plans for the D-Day landings when he was appointed Chief of Staff to the Supreme Allied Commander (COSSAC) long before there even was a Supreme Allied Commander. Morgan's plans were accepted at the Largs Conference called by Mountbatten in the summer of 1943, and the later appointment of Eisenhower as Commander helped in the allocation of landing craft etc. The whole enormous plan was worked out in detail under Morgan's supervision from the end of the Largs Conference till D-Day, almost a year later. Morgan was one of many who recognised the enormous value of the lessons learnt at Dieppe.

MORRISON, Herbert. b. 1888. Leading member of the British Labour party, and largely responsible for the motion of no confidence which led to Chamberlain's resignation. Morrison became Home Secretary and Minister of Home Security in October 1940, and like his predecessor Anderson, he gave his name to a shelter – an indoor one which resembled a large, mesh-sided rabbit hutch. Morrison inaugurated the National Fire Service and set up the fire-watchers, being also responsible for Civil Defence and the Home Guard. In January 1945 he drafted the Labour Party's declaration which resulted in Churchill's defeat in July. Churchill objected, early in the year, to the political nature of Morrison's speeches during war-time, but would not accept Morrison's offer to resign.

MOUNTBATTEN, Lady Louis. b. 1901. A tireless worker on behalf of social services, she became superintendent-in-chief of the St. John's Ambulance Brigade in 1942. When Lord Mountbatten was made S.E.A.C. Supremo, Lady Mountbatten visited hospitals all over S.E. Asia, India and China and proved a highly effective organiser as well as winning the admiration and affection of an enormous number of people of every class and creed. When Japan surrendered and the existence and state of the many prisoner of war camps became known, she travelled from one to another organising medical relief, and set up the Recovery of Allied Prisoners of War and Internees (R.A.P.W.I.), which cleared 90,000 men and women from Japanese camps within its first six weeks.

MOUNTBATTEN, Admiral Lord Louis. b. 1900. Commanded the 5th Destroyer Flotilla and took part in the evacuation of troops from Norway, after which the flotilla went to the Mediterranean. His ship, *Kelly*, was sunk during the great naval engagement off Crete in May 1941. Mountbatten was appointed commander of the carrier *Illustrious* (then under repair in America) and lectured at Pearl Harbor on sea warfare. He was recalled by Churchill and made Chief of Combined Operations, with the responsibility of planning an eventual invasion of Europe, and of planning other raids which would use the large number of troops in Britain and also damage German power. As overall commander of commando operations, Mountbatten was responsible for the highly successful raid on St. Nazaire in March 1942 (when he was also appointed to the Chiefs of Staff Committee), and the unsuccessful, but eventually important, raid on Dieppe. He also took part in planning Operation Torch, and attended the Casablanca and Quebec Conferences of 1943. He was directly responsible for the concept of the "Mulberry" artificial harbours which were highly effective in the Normandy landings.

Lord Mountbatten was then made Supreme Allied Commander of South East Asia Command (S.E.A.C.) and brought about a tremendous uplift of morale and effectiveness among the Allied forces. He was unable to get landing craft or ships for the operations he wanted, so conceived a land-based offensive. His ability to adopt unconventional tactics led to a successful operation, and his forces inflicted the heaviest land defeat suffered by the Japanese. Mountbatten was one of the few leaders who was able to achieve total co-operation between commanders of different forces and nationalities, and his flamboyant personality, personal courage and great ability made him one of the war's most successful Allied commanders. His assessment of wider issues helped determine the political future of Britain's colonies.

MÜLLER, Heinrich. b. 1896. The head of the Gestapo from 1936, and a senior SS leader (known as "Gestapo Müller") who effectively stopped most anti-Nazi plots from gathering force by his spy system which gave everyone the impression they were constantly under surveillance (as many of them in fact were). Müller was a highly efficient administrator, and since he saw the extermination of Jews, Russians and Poles as essentially an administrative and organisational problem, he was also a highly efficient murderer. Eichmann was one of his subordinates, and it was Müller's decree which resulted in the slaughter of hundreds of thousands of Russian prisoners of war. Apparently a mild-mannered and polite person, his system spread terror throughout occupied countries, and the very name of his organisation still evokes dread. Although he was in Hitler's bunker at the end of April 1945 (to interrogate and condemn Fegelein on trumped-up charges of treason), Müller vanished at the end of the war, and has not been seen or heard of since.

MURPHY, Lieutenant Audie. b. 1924. With 21 medals, including the Congressional Medal of Honour, Murphy was America's most-decorated war hero. He first saw action in the invasion of Sicily, and he also took part at Palermo and Messina, and in the Salerno landings. He went to Anzio and by the time his company had reached Rome he was a sergeant with numerous daring attacks behind him. In the landings in the South of France in August 1944 a close friend was killed and in a blaze of temper Murphy killed the whole German gun crew responsible. He saw a great deal of action in Europe, received a serious wound but returned to the conflict, becoming involved in some of the heaviest fighting. By the war's end he was credited with having single-handedly caused nearly 250 casualties. He was modest and comradely, and even when he was a liaison officer went into a perilous position in the Siegfried Line to lead out a group of his trapped men.

Admiral Lord Louis Mountbatten (right) played an adventurous, varied and distinguished role in the war, and was one of the Allies' ablest leaders – sharing with Eisenhower the invaluable talent of getting co-operation, liking and respect from highly talented people of different temperaments and nationalities. Of all his key positions, that of Supremo, S.E.A.C., proved to have a great effect on the post-war world.

MUSSOLINI, Benito. 1883–1945. Appointed Prime Minister of Italy in 1922, he became "*Il Duce*" – the leader – a Fascist dictator whose megalomania far surpassed his own or his country's abilities. He flaunted his power by ignoring the League of Nations' condemnation of his invasion of Abyssinia in 1935, and gave considerable support to Gen. Franco in the Spanish Civil War. In May 1939 Italy signed the "Pact of Steel", a military alliance with Germany, but Hitler's war aims initially seemed a frightening reality to Mussolini, who preferred day dreams. Hitler's easy conquest of Poland and Western Europe made Mussolini think that warfare might not be so unpleasant after all, and he declared war on Britain and France just before the fall of France. But it soon turned out that his earlier apprehensions were correct (he had not expected real war until 1942 at the earliest), and from then on the Germans had to drag the Italians out of difficulties – in North Africa and in Greece. Despite his awe of Hitler's massive power, Mussolini never set up any of the barbarous offshoots that so characterised the German dictatorship.

Germany's invasion of Russia depressed Mussolini even more, and the necessity to declare war on America as well put him in a perilous position, for the Italians were by then tired of war. Mussolini tried to persuade Hitler to come to an agreement with Russia, but this only alerted Hitler to Mussolini's diminishing enthusiasm for conflict. He emphasised the German control of Axis matters and made it clear that any weakening of Italy would result in German occupation. On 24th July 1943 the Fascist Grand Council deposed Mussolini, who was arrested and imprisoned in the Abruzzi Mountains. In September Italy surrendered to the Allies, but Mussolini was taken from his prison in a daring German raid and set up a puppet Government for the Germans in northern Italy. With few forces and practically no power (though he succeeded in arranging the arrest, trial and execution of some of his opponents, including Ciano) Mussolini remained in northern Italy as the Allies steadily advanced. When the German defence collapsed, Mussolini tried to go further north, to Como, accompanied by his mistress Clara Petacci. But on 26th April a communist partisan group discovered them, and they were shot two days later. Their bodies were hung upside down in a Milan square for public ridicule.

NAGUMO, Vice Admiral Chuichi. The small and slight commander of the Carrier Strike Force *Kido Butai* which attacked Pearl Harbor on 7th December 1941. Nagumo, on the flagship carrier *Akagi*, was worried throughout the approach by the chance of meeting elements of the U.S. Pacific Fleet or of being sighted. After the successful attack Nagumo readily agreed with Kusaka (Chief of Staff of the 1st Air Fleet) not to carry out a second raid, and returned to Japan where he gave a graphic account to the Emperor. He commanded the same force to Midway in June 1942 where *Akagi* was sunk, Nagumo transferring to a cruiser. He hoped the American ships would remain until nightfall, allowing him a conventional naval engagement; but Spruance prudently withdrew and Nagumo was ordered by Yamamoto to break off the Midway invasion. *Kido Butai* was also involved in the Battle of the Eastern Solomons, and in Guadalcanal, where Nagumo again lost his flagship. He went to Saipan and assisted in organising its defence with naval personnel. In the last moments of the desperate battle on 6th July 1944 Nagumo carried out the first stage of *hara kiri* by *seppuka* (cutting open one's stomach) and was then shot in the back of the head by an aide.

NEURATH, Konstantin von. b. 1873. Former German Foreign Minister who was appointed Protector of Bohemia and Moravia after the invasion of Czechoslovakia. Hitler felt that Neurath did not carry out the subjugation of intellectuals, the churches, and opposition members strongly enough, and replaced him with "Hangman" Heydrich in 1941. Neurath was a sympathiser with the anti-Hitler plotters, but was not suspected by the Gestapo.

NIMITZ, Admiral Chester. b. 1885. Appointed C-in-C of the Pacific Fleet (CINCPAC) and Commander of the Pacific Ocean and Central Pacific areas shortly after Pearl Harbor, and thus in charge of Marine as well as Navy forces. Initially war was conducted mainly by submarine and naval bombardment, but in May 1942 the U.S. Navy engaged the Japanese in the "air battle" of the Coral Sea. Partial knowledge of Japan's naval code enabled Nimitz to deploy his forces to engage the Japanese Fleet when they attempted to capture the Midway Islands, and the losses inflicted there proved the turning point in the Pacific war – a stage confirmed after the Americans had forced the Japanese off the island of Guadalcanal. Inevitably Nimitz was drawn into the controversy between King and MacArthur, and in general favoured King's navy-dominated strategy. However, Nimitz was able to assess and appreciate advantages in MacArthur's plans, and his quiet, strong, and very able leadership was put to the best use in the numerous changes of tactics in the Pacific theatre. His conduct of the vast American naval forces had almost completely destroyed the Japanese fleet before the end of June 1945.

NOMURA, Admiral Kichisaburo. The retired Admiral, good natured, honest and with many friends in America (including Roosevelt) who was sent as Ambassador to Washington, and used by the war leaders to spin out negotiations with Cordell Hull while preparations for the conflict went on in Japan. Nomura's mission got off to an unfortunate start over a Draft Declaration when both Hull and he made errors of interpretation and presumption, but Nomura genuinely tried to find common ground. He had no knowledge of the significance of the final message he was to deliver at 1 p.m. on 7th December 1941, and when he arrived 80 minutes late at Hull's office, he did not know its complete text, or that his country had already begun to attack Pearl Harbor. Genuinely grieved by the deception, Nomura was later placed under escort and returned to Japan.

NYE, General Archibald. b. 1895. A brigade commander at the outbreak of war, Nye became Director of Staff Duties in 1940. He was one of the possible successors to Dill as C.I.G.S., but was made deputy C.I.G.S. to Brooke. The partnership lasted throughout the war and was extremely successful, Brooke having a very high estimate of his deputy. Nye accompanied Eden to

Moscow, and went to Cairo with Cripps to confer with Auchinleck when Churchill was impatient for an Allied offensive.

O'CONNOR, General Sir Richard. b. 1889. The highly successful desert commander who, under Wavell, launched the offensive against the Italians in Libya in December 1940, captured Tobruk within six weeks, and had taken the whole of Cyrenaica by February 1941. O'Connor's daring diagonal attack across the "Benghazi Bulge" captured vast numbers of Italian troops and material. O'Connor was made G.O.C. of British troops in Egypt, with General Neame in Cyrenaica, but when Wavell had to deplete his forces to aid the Greeks, Rommel and the newly-arrived German divisions attacked the skeleton British forces on the Tripolitania border. O'Connor and Neame were captured and sent to captivity in Italy. They escaped in December 1943 after the Italian capitulation. In Normandy in June 1944 O'Connor commanded the 8th Corps, and directed tank operations. The abilities he displayed in the desert war could have drastically changed the conflict in North Africa had he not been captured.

ODETTE, see **SANSOM.**

OLBRICHT, General Friedrich. 1886–1944. The personal deputy to General Fromm, C-in-C of the Replacement Army in Germany. By February 1943 he had been persuaded to assist the anti-Hitler plotters, since the co-operation of the Home Army was essential and Fromm was evasive. When Stauffenberg planned "Operation Valkyrie" Olbricht gave the alert and began to move troops to Berlin on 15th July 1944 before he could be told that the attempt scheduled for that day had not come off. He explained the moves to Fromm as an "exercise". When Stauffenberg's bomb exploded on 20th July, Olbricht again gave the signal, and arrested Fromm.

Admiral Chester Nimitz (left, with Admiral Halsey), the quiet but strong-willed CINCPAC whose ideas for the defeat of Japan frequently clashed with those of the equally strong-willed but less quiet Gen. MacArthur. Nimitz scored his first great success with the defeat of the Japanese Fleet at Midway.

But too many already knew that Hitler had in fact lived, and the coup broke down. Olbricht was one of those, with Stauffenberg, whom Fromm ordered to be shot immediately.

ONISHI, Vice Admiral Takijiro. With his highly talented subordinate Commander Genda, Onishi carried out the first feasibility study of Yamamoto's concept to attack Pearl Harbor, and it was on this basis that final plans were drawn up. In October 1944 Onishi took command of the Fifth Base Air Force on Luzon, directed to support Admiral Kurita's attack on the U.S. Leyte-invasion force. Finding only one hundred operational planes at his command, Onishi established the *Kamikaze* Special Attack Corps (various spontaneous *kamikaze* attacks had already taken place). This corps was to inflict considerable damage on Allied ships, but for every *kamikaze* plane that struck its target more than ten were shot down. Volunteers eventually grew fewer, and forced recruitment began. More than 3,000 Japanese pilots – *Kamikaze* and escorts – died in these attacks. In the last days of the war Onishi begged Togo and other Cabinet members to lead Japan in one last struggle and produced a plan calling for the sacrifice of millions of Japanese soldiers and civilians. After the Emperor's decision to surrender, Onishi committed *hara kiri* by cutting open his abdomen and stabbing himself in the throat and chest. He took several hours to die, and refused the aid of his friends.

OPPENHEIMER, Robert. b. 1904. Established the most notable school of theoretical physics at the University of California, where a number of scientist refugees from Nazi Germany gathered. Oppenheimer was made director of the Los Alamos laboratory in New Mexico, charged with the design and construction of an atomic weapon. It was known that Germany was working along similar lines, but their progress had been disrupted by Allied bombing and by sabotage. The Allied bomb was perfected in time for use against Japan.

PAPAGOS, General Alexander. b. 1883. The C-in-C of Greek forces when Greece was invaded by Italy in October 1940. To the Italians' embarrassment, Papagos drove them back into Albania. Wavell was ordered to send British troops to assist Greece, but eventually Germany decided on the capture of the Balkan States; in April 1941 they invaded Yugoslavia and Greece and Papagos was captured. In 1943 he was taken as a hostage to Germany, and freed in 1945 when American troops overran Dachau.

PAPANDREOU, George. b. 1888. During the internal unrest in Greece in 1944, Papandreou was brought by the Allies to form a Government-in-exile in Cairo. After a meeting of all the factions in Lebanon during May, Papandreou set up a representative government and this helped unite the military groups. He returned to Athens in October 1944 as Prime Minister after the Germans had withdrawn.

PARK, Air Marshal Keith. b. 1892. The highly able New Zealander on whose shoulders, as commander of No. 11 Fighter Group, fell the burden of the defence of Britain during the Luftwaffe raids of 1940. In 1941 he was appointed Air Officer Commanding to the Allied H.Q. in Egypt, and then, in July 1942, A.O.C. Malta. That was a transitional stage for Malta, and with fighters becoming more readily available, Park began to go over to the offensive against Axis convoys. He provided part of the air cover for the Allied landings in North Africa, and established a large air base for the Sicily and Italy operations. In January 1944 Park commanded all air forces in the Middle East, and a year later became Air C-in-C, S.E.A.C.

PATCH, General Alexander. b. 1889. The successful general who commanded U.S. forces in their first land victory over the Japanese in the battle of Guadalcanal. In 1944 he took command of the U.S. 7th Army for the August invasion of southern France. Patch deployed rearguard forces to besiege German concentrations, such as Marseilles, while the 7th Army advanced rapidly up the Rhône valley. He made contact with the right flank of Patton's 3rd Army, took northern Alsace, and began the battle of the Saar against the German Army Group G. In a move to counter the much-feared Nazi redoubt, Patch headed south-east from Munich towards Salzburg and the Brenner Pass. Army Group G surrendered on 5th May, and there was no concentration of forces between Munich and Brenner.

PATTON, General George. 1885–1945. One of America's best-known (and most flamboyant) commanders, who was also one of the war's greatest experts in mobile warfare. He took part in Operation Torch, and in the Sicily offensive he led the 7th Army in a rapid advance which soon captured Palermo and pushed the Americans ahead to capture Messina. In the Allied invasion of Normandy, Patton commanded the 3rd Army in the second wave, and rapidly smashed a path through France. In the Battle of the Bulge he outfought the Germans in fierce tank battles to break the siege of Bastogne, and then forged ahead across the Rhine to Czechoslovakia. His tactics were usually unorthodox and controversial, and they on occasion disrupted general offensives or overall plans. His strength of character and successful record, however, made him admired by most people, at all levels. Patton died after an accident in Germany in December 1945.

PAULUS, Field Marshal Friedrich von. b. 1890. Usually remembered as General Paulus, since he was an operative Field Marshal for only one day. As Chief of Staff of the German 6th Army, Paulus had taken part in almost every major campaign, and also assisted in planning Barbarossa. In the summer of 1942, as C-in-C of the 6th Army, Paulus was given the objective of capturing Stalingrad, an aim which might have been reached had Hitler not diverted Paulus's powerful Panzer flank across his path to the Caucasus. By November 1942 Paulus had taken nine tenths of Stalingrad, but was practically encircled. He was an intensely loyal officer, and though he repeated requests to break out again and again, he always refused to disobey Hitler's orders to remain in Stalingrad. His army was gradually killed off or starved to death until it was a third of its original size, and on 31st January, having been made Field Marshal that morning, Paulus surrendered to the Russians – and so became the first German Field Marshal to allow himself to be captured alive.

PEIERLS, Rudolf. b. 1907. A German-born scientist who was Professor of Applied Maths at Birmingham University in England in 1937. In February 1940 he wrote a paper with Otto Frisch indicating that Uranium 235 would be needed in far smaller quantities than natural uranium in nuclear weapons. They received a grant to continue their research in Britain, but in 1943 were sent to America to work on the Allied Manhattan Project.

PERCIVAL, Lieutenant General Arthur. b. 1887. Made G.O.C. Malaya in April 1941, and responsible for the defence of Singapore – then considered the Gibraltar of the East. Singapore's sea-facing defences were formidable, but it was totally vulnerable to land attacks. (Little could be spared for Singapore from the North African campaign.) The Japanese landings and movements down the Peninsula caused confusion among the retreating Allied forces, who had no air cover, and had never expected tanks to be used against them – let alone bi-

General George Patton, the frequently brilliant U.S. commander whose ability to wage fast armoured war crushed his opponents in Sicily and France, relieved beleaguered Bastogne in the Ardennes, and took the U.S. 3rd Army across the Rhine in energetic sweeps. In this picture his famous ivory handled revolver can just be seen; he sometimes also wore a highly-shined helmet, and was one of the most theatrical Allied leaders.

cycles. Percival's moves, when he made them, were too late and ineffectual, and there was no opportunity to evacuate women and children (though some had long argued that this should be done). Percival was eventually faced with surrender or the destruction of the city – already its water supplies were cut off – and on 15th February 1942 he surrendered Singapore and 85,000 foreigners to the slightly incredulous General Yamashita. Percival spent part of his captivity in Manchuria, but witnessed the surrender of Japan in Tokyo Bay in September 1945.

PÉTAIN, Marshal Henri Philippe. b. 1856. A legendary hero of World War I, Pétain seemed like a saviour in France's darkest hour. But Pétain agreed with Laval's assessment of Britain's poor chances, refused to consider further resistance, and signed the Armistice with Germany. Pétain was head of State of Vichy France, but his authority declined after Germany occupied that part in 1943. He began to collaborate with Britain, was arrested by the Germans in August 1944, and after Germany's defeat voluntarily returned to France to stand trial for treason. His death sentence was commuted by de Gaulle to life imprisonment.

PIUS XII, Pope. b. 1876. Having collected information for his predecessor's condemnation of the Nazis, Pope Pius was well aware of the type of people ruling half of Europe, and tried diplomatic intervention before the outbreak of war. His role in the war has consistently caused controversy. Some say that he should have done a great deal more than the many superficial charitable acts carried out, while others argue that strong condemnation and fierce opposition would have resulted in reprisals and the inability to carry out even limited acts of mercy.

PLACE, Lieutenant Godfrey. b. 1921. (See Cameron, Lt. Donald.)

PORTAL, Air Marshal Sir Charles. b. 1893. After a brief period as Chief of R.A.F. Bomber Command, Portal was Chief of Air Staff for the duration of the war. As such he directed the policy and operation of the R.A.F. and attended Allied war strategy conferences as the Air Member of the Chiefs of Staff Committee. Portal contributed much to the Casablanca Conference of January 1943, and he was greatly respected and totally relied on by the Americans. He also played major roles in the Washington and Quebec Conferences of 1943.

POUND, Admiral Sir Dudley. 1877–1943. Britain's First Sea Lord, and Admiral of the Fleet at the outbreak of war, Pound was highly experienced yet flexible in his thinking. Although the Admiralty at times caused confusion by interfering too greatly in actual operations, Pound was largely responsible for many of the R.N.'s significant successes in the first years of the war. He took on an enormous amount of work – Churchill was distressed to see him become so ill – but lived to see the U-boat peril conquered, the *Bismarck* sunk and other German capital ships confined in home berths, and the regaining of naval supremacy in the Mediterranean. Pound died – shortly after resigning as First Sea Lord – on, appropriately, Trafalgar Day, 1943.

PRIEN, Captain Günther. 1908–1941. Only six weeks after war was declared, Prien shook British morale with a highly skilled and daring U-boat attack in which he took his U-boat through the defences of Scapa Flow, torpedoed and sank the battleship *Royal Oak*, and escaped. He also had a number of successes in the Atlantic and off Narvik, but on 8th March 1941 *U47* was sunk by the R.N., all hands going down with the submarine.

QUISLING, Vidkun. 1887–1945. The Norwegian Fascist who has given his name to many languages as a synonym for "traitor". A political agitator before the war, Quisling tried to ingratiate himself with the Nazis, and he and a group of followers collaborated in the invasion of their country by Germany. Quisling declared himself the pro-German ruler of Norway, but his period of "power" lasted under a week, when many officials refused to serve under him. For the duration of the war he was a frustrated figurehead with no power, despised by the Norwegians and tolerated by the Germans. However he held onto his ideals and hopes until May 1945, and then surrendered to the Norwegian police. He was executed on 24th November that year.

RAEDER, Admiral Erich. b. 1876. Raeder was as perturbed by Hitler's invasion of Poland in 1939 as were the Army generals, for like them he was really preparing for war in 1944. Consequently his surface fleet was still relatively small, and he had far too few U-boats. But it was much through his urging that Hitler invaded Norway – for Raeder needed its ports – and the conquest of West Europe at last gave him unrestricted access to the Atlantic. However his navy was constantly deprived of the oil he wanted, and his surface fleet did little after 1941. The sinking of the *Bismarck* was a tremendous blow, and when *Hipper* and *Lützow* were driven off by the R.N. close-support escorts of an Arctic convoy in December 1942, Hitler threatened to break up the entire German surface navy. Raeder consequently retired at the end of January 1943. He was sentenced to life imprisonment at Nuremberg, but was released in 1955.

RAMSEY, Admiral Sir Bertram. 1883–1945. The Flag Officer at Dover who commanded the extraordinary evacuation of the B.E.F. from Dunkirk. Ramsey specialised in studies of amphibious landings, devised the North African landings and the Sicily invasion. He was appointed the naval C-in-C for the invasion of Europe, having to command not only the gigantic D-Day fleet, but the shipment of 1 million men plus millions of tons of equipment across the Channel in one month. On 2nd January 1945, on his way to see Montgomery in Brussels, Ramsey's plane crashed on take-off and he was killed.

REYNAUD, Paul. b. 1878. Reynaud had long argued, in vain, for an efficient, professional and mobile French Army, realising that the Great War methods were outdated. But although he replaced Daladier as Premier in March 1940, and also took over the Foreign and War Ministries, it was too late to begin any fundamental changes, and there were too many old-fashioned generals in command to implement them. Reynaud thought much more as Churchill did, sought an aggressive policy against Germany, and agreed with Churchill that there could never be a separate armistice. However after the invasion by Germany, Reynaud brought Pétain into high office and made Weygand C-in-C. His wish to fight on, if necessary from Algeria or from England, was turned down by his colleagues, and his Anglo–French Union suggestion was quickly snubbed. Reynaud resigned and was arrested by his former fellow-statesmen. He was tried at Riom for leading France into war, and deported to Germany in 1943; in 1945 he was released by the Allies.

RIBBENTROP, Joachim von. 1893–1946. A former wine salesman, none too intelligent, tactless and small-minded, the pompous Ribbentrop sprouted Nazi ideology from the earliest years, and was one of Hitler's trusted advisers and admirers. He negotiated, for what little it was worth, the Anglo–German Naval agreement of 1936 while he was Ambassador to Great Britain. In that period he developed a strong loathing of England, and, giving advice as Hitler's Foreign Minister from 1938 onwards, categorically maintained that Britain would never go to war over Poland. Hitler's trust in this contention fundamentally helped him to decide to invade Poland, and Ribbentrop's standing began to decline after this enormously wrong assessment. The other top Nazis had little time for him, and only his long association and friendship with Hitler kept him at the centre. He vanished after the defeat of Germany, but was discovered by the British in Hamburg in June 1945. At the Nuremberg trials Ribbentrop was sentenced to death, and was the first to be hanged on 16th October 1946.

ROKOSSOVSKY, Marshal Konstantin. b. 1896. One of Russia's top strategists, he became well known for his conduct of the defence of Moscow, under Marshal Zhukov, in November and December 1941. In 1942 he was sent to organise opposition to the German 6th Army at Stalingrad, and in December, having surrounded the Germans by smashing their Rumanian and Italian flanks, he launched a series of massive attacks which resulted in the surrender of the Germans in January 1943. One of the most successful commanders during the Russian offensives, Rokossovsky captured Lublin and Brest-Litovsk. He gained a certain notoriety in July 1944 when he halted his forces within sight of Warsaw and did nothing to help the Poles in their revolt against the Germans – a revolt urged by Moscow radio, and in which some 300,000 Poles were killed and their ancient city all but gutted. Rokossovsky only renewed his offensive after the Germans had quelled the uprising, and his troops took Danzig. In May he made contact with the British near Lübeck.

ROMMEL, Field Marshal Erwin. 1891–1944. Germany's best-known, most respected commander (by Allies and Axis), who achieved fame for his brilliant conduct of the war in North Africa when his Afrika Korps outfought forces far larger than his own. Despite his eventual defeat – by Allied forces which greatly outnumbered him – Rommel retained his prestige and in 1944 was entrusted with the defence, under Rundstedt, of the section of the French coast that was the probable destination of the inevitable Allied invasion. Rommel saw the importance of not allowing the Allies to establish a beachhead, and built formidable sea defences. But the area to be defended was too large, and there were so many arguments about where reserves should be placed, etc., that Rommel was still not satisfied with the defences when the invasion came. He was at home at the time (at Alamein he was also away when the blow struck) and it was two weeks before Rundstedt and Hitler allowed him to move Panzer divisions to the Normandy front. Early in July his car was machine-gunned by an R.A.F. fighter and Rommel was severely injured. He had become involved in the plot against Hitler, lending it his cautious support, and its failure led to his exposure as the Gestapo tortured known accomplices. Because of Rommel's tremendous popularity, Hitler was reluctant to try him or execute him. But by promising him the safety of his family, and an honourable burial, the Nazis persuaded Rommel in October 1944 to poison himself.

ROOSEVELT, Franklin Delano. 1882–1945. President of the United States of America for practically the whole war, and by his understanding of the global situation, one of the saviours of Great Britain. Roosevelt was at heart far more of an internationalist than most Americans would have tolerated in 1939, and he was frequently accused of "war-mongering". However, he gradually convinced America that her interests depended on Britain's survival, and began to establish the country as the "great arsenal of democracy". The Lend-Lease Act was America's most significant step away from her isolationist period, and she gradually became more and more affected by the conflict in Europe. Roosevelt began to build up the U.S. forces, and when Japan attacked Pearl Harbor, isolationism disappeared and Roosevelt was able to move America rapidly into full war production. His close relationship with Churchill and his affection for the British proved vitally important in achieving the most rapid defeat possible of Germany and Japan. Roosevelt's frequent meetings with Churchill and other Allied leaders – and eventually with Stalin – ensured that the Allies were committed to an agreed course of action, and his far-sightedness proved a great asset . . . though he did not see as clearly as Churchill the emergence of Russia as a massive and difficult power. Roosevelt died in April 1945, before the war against Germany was over, but when its outcome was in no doubt.

ROSENBERG, Alfred. 1893–1946. Russian-born ideologist and "philosopher" of the Nazi Party who impressed Hitler in 1919 with his diploma in architecture, albeit from the University of Moscow. Although Hitler liked to display him as the Party "thinker" and intellectual, Rosenberg had a mediocre intelligence at best. He dreamt even more than did Hitler of the dominant rule of a pure Nordic race, and introduced Quisling to Hitler. Rosenberg nursed an exceptional hatred for the Jews and Russians, and was rewarded with the Ministry for the occupied Eastern Territories, though Himmler and Goering held more senior positions. He helped bleed the Eastern areas of their riches and many of their peoples, and after trial at Nuremberg, was hanged on 16th October 1946.

RUNDSTEDT, Field Marshal Gerd von. b. 1875. Commanded Army Group South in the rape of Poland and then led Army Group A in the defeat of West Europe – the Group whose Panzers smashed through France from the Ardennes. Rundstedt commanded Army Group South in the invasion of Russia in June 1941, but in November he asked to be relieved of his duties, having been refused permission by Hitler to make a strategic withdrawal. In 1942 he was made C-in-C of the Western Front, and by D-Day he commanded the complete coast of Western Europe. His failure to stop the Allies led to his replacement in July, but in September he was re-instated. Although he himself thought the whole idea was absurd, he agreed to Hitler's request that he should launch an offensive against the Allies along the Ardennes. This too failed, but Rundstedt was only relieved of his command on the 10th March. He was captured by American forces in 1945.

SALAZAR, Antonio. b. 1889. Dictatorial Prime Minister of Portugal who remained neutral throughout the war, and though basically fascist in outlook sought American backing in August 1941 when Germany threatened occupation of her important sea bases. In 1943 Salazar eased his strict neutrality and granted Britain and America the use of the Azores as a naval and air base. Apart from this, Portugal and her colonies kept out of the conflict.

SANSOM, Odette. b. 1912. The famous S.O.E. agent who landed in southern France in November 1942 and worked with Peter Churchill's group. She was captured with Churchill, horribly tortured, and sent to Ravensbrück concentration camp. In the last days of the war, the camp commandant took her to the Allied lines, hoping for clemency. "Odette" was awarded the G.C.

SCHACHT, Hjalmar. b. 1877. The brilliant German economist and President of the Reichsbank until Hitler dismissed him in 1939 for his opposition to extremist views. Hitler owed a great deal to him, for it was his policy of massive Government investment which gave Germany full employment in the 30s and won Hitler such support. His early Nazi background made him only partially acceptable to the anti-Hitler plotters, though he was sympathetic to their aims. After the 20th July Plot, Schacht was arrested and interned in Ravensbrück and in Flossenburg (from which few left alive). But he was never executed, and U.S. forces freed him in April 1945. He was acquitted at the Nuremberg trials.

SCOBIE, General Ronald. b. 1893. The G.O.C. of the 6th Division which replaced the besieged Tobruk garrison in October 1941, and took part in Cunningham's November offensives by making sorties out of town. He became G.O.C. Malta in the crucial months of 1942, and was Chief of Staff, Middle East in 1943. In 1944 he was given the difficult task, as G.O.C. Greece, of quelling the communist-controlled resistance movements which refused to accept the new Greek Government. Tough military action intensive diplomacy brought peace by January 1945.

SEROV, General Ivan. b. 1908. As much dreaded, and as ruthless as many a Nazi, Serov was made responsible for the "Sovietisation" of Estonia, Lithuania and Latvia, and deported to labour camps (and likely death) all political "undesirables". Later made Commissar for Internal Affairs in the Ukraine under the ambitious Kruschev, and in charge of the N.K.V.D. (secret police), he wove a blanket of terror over the newly-annexed areas and is said to have sent some 3,500,000 Ukrainians to Eastern Russia. Serov's N.K.V.D. also shot hundreds of Russian soldiers suspected of deserting their units and imposed a Gestapo-like tyranny at every level. In 1941, under the monstrous Beria, Serov became Deputy Commissar for State Security, and arranged more mass deportations to Siberia of whole areas and peoples whose loyalty was simply suspect. In 1945, as Deputy Supreme Commander of Soviet Forces in Germany, Serov was also head of *Smersh* in Germany, which gave him further opportunity to exercise his talents.

SEYSS-INQUART, Arthur von. 1892–1946. The vicious Austrian Nazi Party leader (until the *Anschluss*) who was Commissioner of the Third Reich in the Netherlands from 1941 until the end of the war. Seyss-Inquart made the Dutch economy work entirely for Germany's benefit, and gradually bled the country of its wealth, strength, justice, art treasures and property of every kind. Some 5,000,000 Dutch workers were sent to work in Germany, and 117,000 of Holland's 140,000 Jews were deported – most of them, like Anne Frank, to certain death. Most of Holland's consumer goods were sent to Germany, and in the winter of '44/45 over 15,000 civilians died of starvation. He carried out brutal reprisals for acts of resistance and some of his troops still resisted after Germany's official surrender. He was captured by Canadian forces, tried at Nuremberg, and hanged on 16th October 1946.

SCHIRACH, Baldur von. b. 1907. Hitler Youth leader from 1931 to 1940, when he became *Gauleiter* and Defence Commissioner of Vienna. Although he denied full knowledge at the Nuremberg trials, he was implicated in the removal of thousands of children and youths from occupied territories to Germany, and in the deportation for eventual murder of some 60,000 Jews from Vienna. He fled Vienna before the Russians arrived, worked for the Americans under an assumed name, but eventually surrendered himself. Partly penitent at the war crimes trials, he was sentenced to 20 years imprisonment.

SIKORSKI, General Wladyslaw. 1881–1943. Refused a command by Warsaw when Poland was invaded, he went to Paris and got together a force of Polish miners. After Poland's defeat he became Premier of the provisional Polish Government-in-exile, and C-in-C of Polish forces – first in France and then in London. In 1941 he signed the Polish–Russian declaration of collaboration which repudiated the partition of 1939 and ended the war. He hoped this would enable the formation of a large Polish army from the p.o.w.s and deportees held by Russia. Sikorski's attention was drawn by the scarcity of officers to the fate of 14,500 Poles – among them 8,000 officers – who had been held in camps near Smolensk since 1939, and of whom nothing was known beyond Spring 1940. In April 1943 Sikorski presented information to Churchill which indicated that the Russians had murdered many, if not all of the Poles, and buried them in the Katyn forests. Three months later Sikorski died when his aircraft crashed taking-off from Gibraltar.

SIX, Professor Franz. The SS Colonel appointed by Heydrich to direct security matters in Britain following the intended invasion. He was officially appointed in September 1940, was to have his H.Q. in London, and an order of 9th September directed him to arrest and deport to Europe all males aged 17 to 45. Heydrich authorised Six to organise *Einsatzgruppen* (the action groups which murdered and plundered their way through Russia) which would be responsible for taking hostages, capturing "undesirable" people, appropriating treasures for the SS coffers, etc. When "Sealion" was cancelled, Six – an intellectual strangely drawn to the terrors of the SS and SD – had the opportunity to carry out these operations among the *Einsatzgruppen* in Russia. (In 1948, Six was sentenced at Nuremberg to 20 years imprisonment, but was freed after four years.)

Field Marshal Sir William Slim went to Burma after successful campaigns in the Middle East, where his division was the first to meet up with Russian allies. His excellent qualities of leadership made him popular with the very mixed troops in Burma, where he completely restored the morale of the 14th Army and led it in the greatest land victories achieved over the Japanese.

SLIM, General Sir William. b. 1891. After distinguished service in North East Africa and the Middle East, he led the retreat of the Allied armies in Burma (under Alexander) from Rangoon and Mandalay to Assam. Under S.E.A.C., Slim formed the 14th Army, and with his ability and personality matching that of his superior commanders, built up a formidable force. After successfully breaking the siege of Imphal, the 14th Army went on to defeat the Japanese at Arakan, and recaptured Mandalay in March 1945. Slim led the forced march to Rangoon which the Japanese evacuated before the Allies arrived. He was made C-in-C of Allied Land Forces in S.E. Asia.

SMIGLY-RYDZ, General Edward. 1886–1943. The virtual ruler of Poland when Germany invaded, he directed the futile resistance. He had planned on a fall-back to the south-east corner, but the Russian invasion threw his plans awry. With the Government, Smigly-Rydz fled to Rumania where he was interned, and was dismissed as C-in-C by Sikorski. In 1941 he escaped and went back to Poland where he was active in the Polish Underground. He is thought to have been killed by the Germans in 1943 – at that time probably regarded by the Germans as an anonymous corpse.

SMUTS, Field Marshal Jan Christiaan. b. 1870. The South African statesman of international repute who was made a British Field Marshal, but known universally as General Smuts. Against considerable opposition, Smuts argued for South African support of Britain, and became Prime Minister and Commander of the Union's forces, which fought mainly in North Africa, Abyssinia, and Italy. He was a trusted confidant of Churchill's and sat on the British War Cabinet. Smuts, Brooke and Churchill met in Cairo to elect the new commanders for the final offensive against Rommel, and he went to Britain four times during the war, as well as visiting numerous fronts. In 1945 he went to the United Nations Conference in San Francisco, and drafted the preamble to the U.N. Charter. In 1946 he attended the Versailles peace conference – the only person there who had also attended the 1919 Treaty of Versailles.

SOMERVILLE, Admiral Sir James. b. 1882. The Commander of the very effective R.N. Force H of the Mediterranean Fleet operating out of Gibraltar. He was forced to fire on the French Fleet in July 1940 when it refused to come over to the Allies, or sail beyond the reach of the Axis. Force H played a decisive role in the sinking of the *Bismarck*, and had the onerous task of escorting the Malta convoys. In 1942 Somerville was appointed C-in-C of the Eastern Fleet, originally intended to be based in Ceylon, but which withdrew to East Africa under the threat of considerable Japanese superiority. His force took part in the capture of Madagascar from the Vichy-French in 1943, and in August 1944 he became head of the British Naval Delegation in Washington.

SORGE, Richard. 1895–1944. The German journalist in Japan who became one of Russia's best spies. As senior reporter on the *Frankfurter Zeitung* in Tokyo he had access to diplomatic circles, and was a confidant of the German ambassador. He witnessed Japan's war preparations, but in 1938 the Japanese intercepted a radio message and began to hunt for "a spy". Sorge warned his superiors about Barbarossa, and told them of the planned attack on Pearl Harbor. He was arrested in October 1941, and hanged in 1944.

SPAATZ, General Carl. b. 1891. Commanding General of the U.S. (Army) 8th Air Force, based in East Anglia. He established close co-operation with the R.A.F. and laid the groundwork for the U.S.A.A.F.'s major role in the Allied air offensive over Europe. In February 1943 he commanded the N.W. African Air Force in the Tunisian, Sicilian and Italian campaigns. In January 1944 Spaatz was appointed C-in-C of the U.S. Strategic Air Forces, and supervised the massive daylight raids on German industrial targets, and on communications, prior to D-Day. In March 1945, he joined the H.Q. of the Army Air Forces, and in July commanded U.S. Strategic Air Forces in the Pacific – which included the A-bomb attacks on Hiroshima and Nagasaki.

SPEER, Albert. b. 1905. German architect who was taken into Hitler's favour and sympathetically carried out Hitler's monumental concepts mirroring the Third Reich – among them the Chancellery and the huge Nuremberg Stadium. In 1942 Speer's considerable administrative and organisational talents were put to use when he was made Minister for Armaments and Munitions, and in 1943 he was given overall direction of the war economy. It was largely due to Speer's abilities that the Allied air offensive was not more effective. He spread production throughout Germany, adopted prefabrication methods and found alternative materials, and for some items level of production was higher in 1944 than 1940. Speer repeatedly tried to persuade Hitler to stop the war, from as early as 1944, but for some reason Hitler never condemned him for this. At the Nuremberg trials Speer was practically the only high ranking prisoner who admitted and regretted his crimes (he had had the advantage of almost unlimited slave labour in his production efforts) and his involvement in the whole tragedy; he accepted his 20 year sentence without rancour.

SPEIDEL, General Hans. b. 1898. A successful German Staff Officer who saw most of his service in France, Speidel was in contact with the anti-Hitler conspirators, but took no part in the plots. He did, however, try to seek an armistice, and constantly tried to generate support. When the Allies advanced through France, Hitler ordered Speidel to destroy Paris. He and Choltitz refused, but re-

Above: Two German paratroopers being escorted into the British lines at Cassino by an unarmed Tommy (Photo: Imperial War Museum). Below: A Churchill tank of the 51st Royal Tank Regiment in "harbour" north of Rome, summer 1944 (Photo: Imperial War Museum).

ported that its destruction was proceeding. Speidel was arrested by the Gestapo and interrogated, but escaped after seven months imprisonment and went into hiding until freed by the Allies.

SPRUANCE, Admiral Raymond. b. 1886. Took over command in the Battle of Midway and was made Chief of Staff by Nimitz. In November 1943 he led the assault on Tarawa and in February 1944 directed the attacks on the Marshall Islands and on Truk. In the Battle of the Philippine Sea in June, Spruance almost totally destroyed the Japanese carrier force, and his carriers made air strikes on Tokyo in February 1945. The naval section of the Iwo Jima invasion came under his command, and the rapid ascendancy of U.S. naval supremacy in the Pacific owed much to Spruance's tactical abilities.

STALIN, Marshal Joseph. b. 1879. The cold, powerful, calculating dictator of Russia transformed his country from a strife-riddled lesser power to the position of the second most powerful nation within the duration of the Second World War. Stalin's terrible purges of the '30s, in which untold millions died, also left him with a disorganised army, and that, plus his foolish faith in Hitler's integrity despite every warning, led to Russia's rapid defeats in 1941. But Stalin had enormous manpower reserves, and, while he took overall military command himself, there were still enough highly competent generals to unify the army and prepare powerful defences. Stalin engendered a spirit of nationalism in almost a Churchillian manner, and the image of a "threatened motherland" brought wide support from Britain and America. Russian ruthlessness and hardiness demanded tremendous sacrifice, but made them formidable defenders and horrifying attackers. Stalin seemed to portray most of these aspects, together with a cunning and an appreciation of the West's dependency on his opposition to Germany that made him a negotiator who called for the utmost tact and skill. Churchill recognised Stalin's enormous and ruthless ambition, but could only hope to contain it as far as possible. Stalin's disregard for pacts and charters rivalled only Hitler's, and consequently he emerged from the war leading a vastly bigger country than he had begun with, the subjugator of millions of people who had fought to escape the clutches of one dictator, only to fall into the iron grip of another.

STAUFFENBERG, Lieutenant Colonel Count Klaus von. 1907–1944. After losing an eye and his right hand in the Afrika Korps, Stauffenberg became Chief of Staff to General Olbricht, while his anti-Hitler sentiments grew in intensity. He worked tirelessly to build up an organisation to remove and take over from Hitler. Later, as Chief of Staff to General Fromm of the "Home Army", Stauffenberg attended Hitler's Staff conferences, and he volunteered to be the assassin. Two attempts miscarried, but on the 20th July 1944 the bomb he planted exploded successfully – but only injured Hitler. As the coup fizzled out with the broadcast of Hitler's survival, Stauffenberg was one of those shot that night in the courtyard of the War Ministry.

STILWELL, General Joseph. b. 1883. An expert on China and possessing a powerful and intractable personality, "Vinegar Joe" commanded the U.S. Army forces in China and S.E. India in 1941, and was later made Chief of Staff to Chiang Kai-shek. Difficulties in the division of command led to Chiang requesting his transfer, and Stilwell was recalled in November 1944. In June 1945 he commanded the U.S. 10th Army in the Pacific.

STIMSON, Henry. b. 1867. At the age of 70, Stimson became U.S. Secretary of War, and was strongly against the American mood of isolationism. He argued for the early repeal of the Neutrality Act, and after Pearl Harbor was in strong support of defeating Germany before Japan. Churchill adamantly refused Stimson's urgings for an invasion of Europe in 1943, and the American eventually saw the need for greater preparation. Stimson was forward-thinking and actively supported scientific research, being particularly concerned about the possibilities of nuclear fission. He took overall responsibility for the atom bomb project, and resigned as soon as Japan was defeated.

STIRLING, Lieutenant Colonel David. b. 1915. The energetic, unconventional Scots Guards officer who became the founder of the SAS commandos in North Africa. The SAS eventually became recognised as a new regiment, and it caused widespread disruption to Rommel's forces in North Africa with daring raids deep into enemy territory. Stirling was captured in January 1943, but by then his men had destroyed some 250 aircraft, as well as numerous petrol dumps, trains, and military vehicles. Stirling escaped from the Italians four times, but his height usually led to his early recapture. He was eventually imprisoned in Colditz Castle.

STREICHER, Julius. 1885–1946. One of the most unpleasant of the Nazis – a sadist, pornographer, blackmailer and virulent anti-Semite who edited *Der Stürmer,* a publication which even his fellow Nazis found difficult to stomach, so obscene were its anti-Jewish writings. He initiated the hysterical rallies at Nuremberg and became the "uncrowned king" of Franconia. But soon after the war began he lost standing in the Nazi party, though he carried on his barbarous existence throughout the conflict. After trial at Nuremberg, his former seat of power, Streicher was hanged on 16th October 1946.

STÜLPNAGEL, General Karl Heinrich von. 1886–1944. Open opponent of Hitler from as early as 1938, he became Quartermaster General in 1939, and Deputy

Chief of Staff. He helped plan a coup for November 1940, but this collapsed – as did other attempts. (The numerous Army plots against Hitler were able to go undiscovered for a considerable period since, even if they did not support the plotters, officers still felt greater loyalty to other officers than to the Gestapo.) In 1941 Stülpnagel commanded the encirclement of the Russians at Kiev, and in 1942 became Military Governor of France, where in May 1944 he made plans, with Speidel and Rommel, to seek an Armistice. He was, with Stauffenberg, a leading member of the 20th July Plot, and on receiving the incorrect news of Hitler's death, immediately arrested prominent Nazis in Paris. But Kluge countered Stülpnagel's orders and suspended him. He was called to Berlin by Keitel, and stopping at Verdun, attempted suicide. His shot, however, had only blown out one eye, and damaged the other so badly that it was removed in hospital. Nursed carefully to health, Stülpnagel was brought before the People's Court on Hitler's orders, and on 30th August strangled in Ploetzensee prison, as many others had been, by being hanged on a loop of piano wire.

SUZUKI, Admiral Kantaro. Already aged in 1936, Suzuki miraculously survived an assassination attempt by extreme militarists when he was one of the powerful influences trying to curb Japan's expansion-by-war. He returned to political life in a more or less honorary and traditional capacity, but was elected Prime Minister of Japan in April 1945 as the only compromise figure who would not be fiercely opposed by any faction. Suzuki was determined to seek peace, but conducted a delicate and skilled "juggling act" in placating the different factions to prevent himself being ousted or assassinated. He therefore frequently made warlike speeches while privately yearning for peace, and eventually manoeuvred the Cabinet into the situation where the Emperor was able to command a surrender.

SZABO, Violette. 1918–45. A half-French London girl who joined S.O.E. and parachuted into France in April 1944 with a companion on a reconnaissance trip after the circle she was due to join was broken up. After returning to England, Violette was again dropped in France with a group of four others to join a French Resistance team. She and the leader of the local agents were ambushed by a German unit, and in the attempt to escape Violette hurt her ankle. She asked to be left while her companion escaped, and for two hours she held off a considerable German force with deadly-accurate shooting, until her ammunition ran out. She was taken to the Gestapo in Paris, and having refused to talk, was sent to Ravensbrück with two other S.O.E. agents in August. She maintained an infectious cheerfulness even in that grim camp of death, but she and her companions were shot on 26th January 1945.

TEDDER, Air Marshal Sir Arthur. b. 1890. The A.O.C. in the Middle East who became Allied Air Commander in the Mediterranean from mid-1942, Tedder was appointed as Eisenhower's Deputy for Overlord. He kept the position of Deputy Supreme Commander of the Allied Expeditionary Force for the rest of the war, and his strategic skills played an important part in the liberation of north-west Europe. As Eisenhower's representative, Tedder signed the formal surrender of Germany in Berlin on 8th May 1945.

TERAUCHI, Field Marshal Juichi. b. 1879. In 1942 the commander of Japanese troops in Indo-China, Siam and Malaya, and responsible for the construction of the

"Vinegar Joe" Stilwell: the corruption and inefficiency of Chiang Kai-shek's staff made his task very frustrating and no doubt explained the abrasive manner for which he was famous, particularly among British officers who had imagined that he and they were on the same side.

Siam–Burma road of 250 miles, built by Allied p.o.w.s. Some 50,000 men were made to work on the road under the most punishing natural conditions, and under brutal treatment from their captors. Almost one third of those prisoners died. In Singapore on 12th September Mountbatten accepted a ceremonial sword of surrender from Gen. Itagaki, in place of Terauchi, who had suffered a stroke.

TIMOSHENKO, Marshal Semyon. b. 1895. Successful in the Finnish campaign, Timoshenko commanded the central sector of the front with Germany, and prevented the attainment or encirclement of Moscow. He was sent to command the southern sector in September 1942 but failed to stop the Germans taking the Crimea and from advancing towards Stalingrad. For these failures he was removed to a quieter sphere, and finally held a staff position in Stalin's H.Q.

TITO, Marshal Josip. b. 1892. Chief of the Yugoslav Communist Party and heroic wartime leader of the partisans who waged a long and bitter struggle against the Germans (and initially against opposition Yugoslav groups as well). Tito's Partisans won support from the British after Maclean's visit, and with the aid of British arms and ammunition, his army forced the Germans out of Yugoslavia at the same time as the Russians swept in to assist. By then Tito had been accepted as leader of Yugoslavia by the Allies, and immediately took control of his country.

TODT, Major General Dr. Fritz. 1891–1942. The German civil engineer responsible for many of Germany's massive projects, from the autobahns to the Siegfried Line defences and the submarine pens. Given the facilities of innumerable workers, this gigantic "construction gang" became known as the Todt Organisation. He was killed in an air crash in 1942, and Speer took over most of his work.

TOGO, Shigenori. Japanese Foreign Minister at the time of Pearl Harbor, he was opposed to the excessive militarist aims of Japan, and later resigned in protest against Tojo's "dictatorial and high-handed policies". In April 1945, however, the new Prime Minister Suzuki, chose him to be Foreign Minister again, and to handle the delicate topic of seeking peace. Togo was therefore another of the "doves" in the Big Six upper Cabinet in the last months of the war, but resigned when surrender was agreed.

TOJO, General Hideki. 1884–1945. As Japan's War Minister in 1940 he made the pact with Germany and Italy, but disappointed the western dictators by favouring expansion to the south, rather than take on Russia. After Konoye resigned, Tojo was a favoured choice, and although his militarist attitude upset him, Kido recommended Tojo to the Emperor. Tojo immediately began planning for war, but the constant setbacks made his popularity and influence decline, and after the fall of Saipan, Tojo and his Cabinet resigned in July 1944. At the end of the war, Tojo attempted suicide by shooting himself, but his life was saved; he stood trial and was hanged on 22nd December 1945.

"TOKYO ROSE", Iva D'Aquino. b. 1916. An American whose parents were Japanese, she became Japan's major propaganda broadcaster. After the war she was sentenced to 10 years imprisonment for treason.

TOVEY, Admiral Sir John. b. 1885. C-in-C of the British Home Fleet in Scapa Flow, and the officer who played a principal part in the pursuit and sinking of *Bismarck*. His responsibility later included the protection of the Arctic convoys.

TOYODA, Admiral Soemu. Japan's Navy Chief of Staff, and one of the three extremist members of the Big Six who urged rejection of all peace offers, and, if necessary, the death of the whole Japanese nation in one great last stand. He replaced Admiral Koga, whose plane disappeared during a storm not long after he had succeeded to Yamamoto's position.

TRUMAN, Harry. b. 1884. Elected Vice President of the U.S.A. in November 1944, he suddenly found himself head of the world's most powerful nation on 12th April 1945, when Roosevelt died. He had a notable Senate record, but there had been little to indicate the strong, clear-minded person who so ably took command. He continued most of Roosevelt's policies, including preparations for the United Nations, and attended the Potsdam Conference in July 1945. There he told Churchill of the successful test of the A-bomb, and intimated its existence to Stalin. Although Churchill agreed it should be used, the final decision on whether to drop the A-bomb rested with Truman, and on 6th August 1945 he authorised its immediate use.

UMBERTO, Prince of Italy. b. 1904. In 1940 he commanded the Italian armies that attacked France, and he was widely regarded as a loyal successor to Mussolini, and favoured by the Nazis. After Mussolini was deposed the Italian Royal Family moved to southern Italy, and in June, after the Allied occupation of Rome, became Regent of Italy. In August 1944 he met Churchill while he was commanding the Italian forces on the Allied front.

UMEZU, General Yoshijiro. Made Japan's Army Chief of Staff in the great reshuffle of April 1945, and one of the "hawks" in the Big Six, who had to be coerced by Hirohito into thinking in terms of peace. Under duress – and only after the Emperor's command – Umezu attended the surrender ceremony on board U.S.S. *Missouri* on 2nd September 1945.

USHIJIMA, Lieutenant General Mitsuru. The commander of the Japanese forces on Okinawa, in the last battle of the war. On 22nd June 1945, with the Americans approaching his cave H.Q., and most of his 110,000 troops already dead, Ushijima cut through the flesh of his stomach, and was immediately beheaded by an aide. But it was not until 2nd July that the battle was declared over – at a cost of the lives of 110,000 Japanese soldiers, 75,000 Japanese civilians, and 12,520 Americans.

VIAN, Admiral Sir Philip. b. 1894. As Captain of the destroyer H.M.S. *Cossack*, Vian made a dash into Jösingfjord in Norway and boarded the German raider supply ship *Altmark*, freeing 300 Allied seamen from her holds – all victims of *Graf Spee*'s activities. He commanded the 4th Destroyer Flotilla in operations against *Bismarck* and was made Admiral in July 1941. His ships made the commando raid on Spitzbergen and in July 1943 he took part in the invasion of Sicily. In Overlord he commanded a night patrol fleet and in 1945 joined the British Pacific fleet which took part in the assault on Okinawa.

VICTOR EMMANUEL III. King of Italy. b. 1869. Placed in the awkward position of being used as a figure head by the Fascists, he was opposed to the war, and withdrew from politics when he was unable to influence Mussolini. When the Fascist Grand Council voted to depose Mussolini, Victor Emmanuel authorised the dictator's arrest, and appointed Badoglio as Prime Minister. In June 1944 he declared his son Umberto Regent.

VLASOV, General Andrei. 1900–45. The pre-war military adviser to Chiang Kai-shek, Vlasov gained distinc-

---

General Hideki Tojo (in uniform, with his cabinet) was the virtual dictator of Japan from 1941 – when he planned war against America – until island defeats brought U.S. planes within bombing range of Japan, whereupon he resigned. He was one of the comparatively few Japanese tried and hanged for war crimes.

The far-sighted Admiral Yamamoto – pictured here in civilian clothes at a pre-war function – was one of Japan's most able leaders, who realised that his country lacked the resources for a long war.

tion in the defence of Moscow, but was captured by the Germans. He became an anti-Stalinist, and broadcast propaganda against Russia. He even recruited an army from Soviet p.o.w.s and fought against Russia. In May 1945 he surrendered to U.S. forces, who handed him over to the Russians – by whom he was executed.

WAINWRIGHT, General Jonathan. b. 1883. After MacArthur's departure in March 1942, took over the hopeless defence of the Bataan Peninsula, and finally withdrew with as many troops as possible onto the island fortress of Corregidor. Eventually forced to choose between obliteration and surrender, Wainwright gave up the Americans and Philippinos under his command in May, and spent the remaining 3 years as a prisoner of the Japanese. He was awarded the Congressional Medal of Honour, and attended the surrender ceremony on *Missouri*.

WALLIS, Barnes. b. 1887. British aeronautical engineer who designed among other things, the Wellington bomber, the "bouncing bombs" used to break the Ruhr dams, and the massive bombs which smashed *Tirpitz*, U-boat pen covers (over 12 feet of concrete), and essential viaducts and dock installations.

WAVELL, Field Marshal Sir Archibald. b. 1883. C-in-C Middle East with the formidable responsibility of overseeing the war in North Africa, Iran, Greece, and Abyssinia, Wavell nevertheless inflicted a number of crushing defeats on the Axis. In July 1941 he was given a well-needed break and made C-in-C India, followed in December by the appointment as Supreme Commander, S.W. Pacific. In June 1943 he was made Viceroy of India.

WEIZMANN, Chaim. b. 1874. Zionist leader who was a noted scientist, and became scientific adviser to the British Ministry of Supply. He devoted most of his energies to the Zionist cause, formed a unit of Jewish commandos, and in November 1944 was summoned by Churchill to discuss the partition of Palestine.

WEYGAND, General Maxime. b. 1867. Made Supreme Allied Commander in France after the German invasion of France, but saw resistance would achieve little, and persuaded Pétain to sign an armistice. He was sent to command the forces in France's African colonies, but was dismissed by the Vichy Government under German pressure. In November 1942 he was arrested by the Gestapo as a hostage for General Giraud. On May 1945 Weygand was freed by the Allies, but arrested by de Gaulle's Government for collaboration. He was acquitted in 1948.

WILHELMINA, Queen of the Netherlands. b. 1880. Left Holland with her Government on British ships the day before Holland's capitulation, and ruled in exile from London. Returned as Queen on 2nd May 1945.

WILSON, Field Marshal Sir Henry Maitland. b. 1881. In 1939 G.O.C. in Egypt under Wavell and planned early operations against the Italians. In March 1941 he commanded the British forces sent to assist the Greeks and later quelled the revolt in Iraq. In June 1941 he captured Syria from the Vichy-French, and held commands in the Middle East until early 1944 when he succeeded Eisenhower as Supreme Allied Commander in the Mediterranean. In November 1944 he was head of the British Chiefs of Staff in Washington, and he attended the Yalta and Potsdam Conferences.

WINANT, John. b. 1889. U.S. Ambassador in London for most of the war, succeeding Kennedy and being responsible for much of the enormous assistance given to Britain before America entered the war.

WINGATE, General Orde. 1903–44. Eccentric commander of a guerilla group in the Abyssinian campaigns. After being sent to Burma he set up the Chindits – the formidable guerilla fighters who penetrated deep into the

Burma jungle to harass the Japanese. The Chindits suffered terrible hardships and high casualties, but caused the Japanese considerable irritation. Wingate was killed in an air crash in March 1944.

YAMAMOTO, Admiral Isoroku. 1884–1943. Conceived the attack on Pearl Harbor, though opposed to war with America, and certain of Japan's defeat once the attack had taken place. He tried to lure the remainder of the U.S. Pacific Fleet – especially the carriers – into conflict, but failed. In April the Americans discovered he was to visit Japanese bases and they ambushed and shot down his plane. A hero of Japan, his death shook morale.

YAMASHITA, Lieutenant General Tomoyuki. 1885–1945. Captured Singapore with scarcely any losses to his own troops in February 1942, and then went to command the 1st Army in Manchuria. In 1944 he was appointed Supreme Japanese Commander of the Philippines and put up a tremendous defence on Leyte. Although Hirohito announced Japan's surrender on 14th August, Yamashita continued the battle until the 25th. He was tried for war crimes, and executed on 23rd February 1946.

ZHUKOV, Marshal Georgi. b. 1896. Russia's most prominent and powerful commander, and Stalin's trusted military "trouble shooter". He came to notice after the rapid destruction of the Japanese 6th Army in a Mongolian skirmish in 1939, and in 1941 was made Director of the Soviet Army High Command. Apart from playing a part in the overall strategy of the war, Zhukov personally organised the defence of Leningrad, and then of Moscow, where he used his fresh Mongolian troops to drive back the Germans. He was sent to organise the final defence and recapture of Stalingrad, prepared for the futile German offensive at Kursk, directed the Russian sweep across the Ukraine, and finally planned and directed the devastating Battle of Berlin. He signed the formal declaration of Germany's surrender in Berlin on 8th May 1945.

4. THE ARMED FORCES

The greatest changes in war tactics are generally due to technological development, but no war has ever been as strongly affected by technology as the Second World War. It began with cavalry charges against tanks and ended with nuclear bombs dropped from altitudes of 32,000 feet. Commanders unable to make use of new technology rapidly revealed their incompetence, while successful militarists sought ways of adapting developments to wage a different kind of war.

Technology vastly increased the arsenal of every commander and this led to another significant development of the war, which was the degree to which land, air, and sea forces worked in unison. The same technology which united the forces also brought into being the third, and most tragic innovation of this war – the concept and the degree of total war, in which everyone in the belligerent countries is a potential victim.

The effects of technological innovation

On land, technology led warfare away from the old "set pieces" – which had caused such misery and slaughter in the Great War – into the *blitzkrieg* era which was dominant with few exceptions – Alamein, for example, or Monte Cassino, or the yard by yard battles on the Pacific Islands. This form of attack only became possible when commanders realised the full potential of tanks and had sufficient vehicles to rapidly bring in mobilised divisions. Tanks also brought about another form of battle – between tanks themselves such as in North Africa, and later at Kursk and in the Ardennes. The progress of technology made hand guns lighter and more accurate; machine guns faster-firing and less bulky; artillery more deadly.

Opposite, Waffen SS corporal. This branch of the SS came formally into being in 1940, and initially fell under the control of the Army High Command. Later in the war Army defeats, and Party pressure, made it a virtually independent force.

In the air, planes developed from the Swordfish "String-bag" which had trouble reaching 100 mph when carrying a torpedo, to the superb Mustang fighter which easily passed 400 mph, and in the last stages to jet aircraft which flew at 500 mph and could reach a height of 44,000 ft. Bombers at the beginning of the war, with their operational ceiling of 15,000 ft, were vulnerable to AA guns and carried a modest bomb-load of 2,000 lbs. By the end of the war they were flying at 35,000 ft and able to deliver bombs weighing 22,000 lbs. The development of radar enabled fighters to locate enemy bombers in the blackest of nights, and night bombers to find their targets, whether blacked-out cities or the speck of a submarine at sea – while ground defences knew bombers were coming long before they could be seen or heard.

At sea indications from 1918 that the age of the dreadnoughts had ended rapidly became blatant declarations when battleship after "unsinkable" battleship sank to the ocean floor, or grew hesitant about leaving port. For surface ships, technology brought more danger from above or below than it brought from another surface ship, and again it was electronic wizardry that changed the nature of war at sea. The ships that survived were those which could find other ships in the dark, or could call up air defence against an approaching air attack, or could reach into cubic miles of water and find a lurking submarine.

Nothing however, made the Second World War differ more from any other war as much as the aeroplane did – even to the extent that a "naval" engagement between the U.S. and Japanese fleets took place in the Coral Sea without any ship firing on another, or even seeing another, the whole battle being fought by carrier-borne aircraft.

Interrelation of land, air and sea forces

Certain generals might claim glory without paying tribute to the seamen who brought them men and tanks and guns, or without acknowledging the pilots who kept enemy bombers from their lines . . . and there were certainly air-minded leaders who once thought that winning wars could safely be left to the air force. But it was not long before the full extent of interdependence became obvious on every front. The Germans, practically surrounded by land and never envisaging having to cross anything larger than a river, stared impotently at the narrow English Channel – which could not be crossed without also gaining air superiority. Even Russia's land-locked front with Germany had vital supports that stretched across the Arctic and Atlantic Oceans to factories in Britain and America.

Nowhere was this interrelation more relied on than in the island-hopping Pacific war, where nothing at all could have been achieved by any of the forces without the fullest support of the others. In the European theatre the Allied invasion of Europe was the biggest operation ever mounted which called for massive simultaneous power on land, sea, and air.

Technology gave World War II an unprecedented mobility which the territorial ambitions of the Axis exploited to the utmost. This gave the war a coverage that made the conflict truly global, which, even without the inhumanity of many of the Nazi edicts, involved civilians on a tragic and massive scale.

Since technology played such an important part in World War II, it was obviously one of the major factors determining the outcome of any conflict between opposing forces, and it is worthwhile looking at significant elements in the arsenals of the major belligerents – Germany, Great Britain, Russia, Japan and the United States. There are two other factors which played equally important roles in comparing opposing forces, namely: the nature, quality and organisation of the force; and the supply and provisioning of the force. The rest of this chapter is devoted to brief coverages of these three factors (organisation and qualities, "hardware", supply) among the armies, air forces, and navies of the five major belligerents – though only very few of the most notable weapons, planes, etc. can be mentioned here. (Quantities – whether of men or machines – obviously have a strong bearing on the outcome of individual conflicts, but too much attention to them is misleading. Ten elite paratroopers, for instance, might easily cope with 50 untried recruits; 45 men in a submarine, or 10 in aircraft could seal the fate of 2,000 aboard a battleship; five men in a tank need not be concerned by 100 men with basic rifles – and at some stages of the Russian conflict, army strengths changed by 650,000 overnight.)

THE ARMIES

While individual countries differed in various respects, the basic formation of "an army" was: five or six men in sections forming platoons, a number of which formed a company – one of several companies in a battalion. There would be a number of battalions in a regiment, while three regiments, plus various ancillary service units would form a division. Theoretically a division was made up to provide a balanced team able to conduct independent combat, and they generally numbered between 11,000 and 18,000 men. Commanders therefore tended to assess circumstances in relation to the number of divisions being used – this being a rough guide to an army's strength. There might be anything from 8 to 20 divisions in an army, and, except in Russia, armies with a large number of divisions would have them divided into two or more corps. There would also be a large number of staff and ancillary services connected with an army, and it would be important for the army to have a proper balance – thus it might have artillery divisions, armoured divisions, motorised divisions, and perhaps an airborne division as well (normally much smaller than an infantry division). As the war progressed and fronts grew larger it became the habit to form two, three or four armies into an army group, with a group commander and his staff. An army group might easily number 1 million men – Bradley's, in early 1945, numbered over 2 million. The Army Group commanders would be responsible to a supreme commander for the front or area, or to the army Commander-in-Chief.

GERMANY

The German Army suffered before long from weaknesses at the top of the ladder, and from the constant and inexpert interference of Hitler. It was called on to perform far too many functions, usually prematurely, and accompanied by too many alterations to strategy. It was far from ready for international conflict in 1939, and the outstanding successes it achieved against superior numbers is testimony to the highly trained, courageous troops and the expertise of their field commanders. (Of course other armies in Europe were even less prepared for war, and by the time they had reached trained combat status, and were well-equipped and led, the discrepancy was considerably narrowed.)

The German High Command of the Armed Forces (OKW) theoretically headed the three services, but Keitel, its chief, was ineffectual. Besides, Hitler had long ago set himself up as supreme commander of the German armed forces. In December 1941 Hitler confused the command situation even further by appointing himself C-in-C of the Army (Chief of OKH) – a position that was in theory subordinate to Keitel in OKW. OKW was frequently little more than a rubber-stamping operation, and by 1943 it played no further part in the running of the war against Russia. A further complication was the presence of Waffen SS – the military branch of the SS policing body and Himmler's state-within-a-state. Initially under Army control, it grew larger (and acquired reserves of poorer quality) and more autonomous.

The German Army eventually drew on more and more

Panzer company commander: gunner and loader: and briefing by a Russian roadside, 1941. Germany initially assembled tank crews from selected personnel and trained them into an elite. Panzer units spearheaded the new mobile operations which Germany had perfected long before her enemies. (Signal)

"foreign" troops, such as Hungarians and Rumanians, as it tried to maintain the huge numbers necessary to enforce occupation of Europe and fight on two fronts (Germany launched the Russian invasion with 3 million troops). The steady loss of the Army's better troops became combined with Hitler's indiscriminate sacking of experienced generals, at the same time that the Allies began to get into their stride; and the final outcome was never in doubt once Hitler failed to take Moscow in December 1941.

The German army was trained and equipped for land warfare, mainly in western European conditions, but it adapted extremely well to desert warfare – while it never properly came to grips with the winter conditions of Russia. Effective use was made of airborne divisions in the invasion of Holland and Belgium, but after the high casualties suffered on Crete, paratroopers were rarely used again in their proper role.

Weapons

Infantry Basic rifle was 7·9 mm KAR-98K with 5 round magazine. The submachine-gun – usually called a machine-pistol and eventually known as an assault rifle – was the MP40 with 32 rounds of 7·9 mm. It developed into the very efficient and widely used MP44.

The MG42 7·9 mm medium, general-purpose machine gun was an excellent weapon, its one disadvantage often being its extremely high rate of fire – 1,000 rpm. It was air cooled, and could also be used as an AA gun.

(Assorted items for causing death and destruction, such as mines, hand grenades, mortars, anti-tank grenade-launchers and rocket-launchers, etc., differed little in their variety and effectiveness between armies, altered constantly, and are not covered here.)

The Pzkw V "Panther" was Germany's first tank actually designed after the outbreak of war in the light of combat experience. It was a sound piece of equipment, but was rushed into service too quickly as a result of the crisis on the Russian Front. The entire first batch of some 300 tanks were lost during the Kursk battles of summer 1943, most of them due to mechanical failures. Although it was mass produced for the rest of the war, most Panzer units could still field only one battalion of Panthers and one of the ageing Pzkw IV even in the final campaigns.

Armoured The German tank superiority was in some measure due to the armoured division commanders' greater understanding of the capabilities of tank warfare, but the first German tanks were also technically superior to the first French and British tanks.

The backbone of the early divisions was the Pzkw (*Panzerkampfwagen*) MkIII with a 37 mm gun and two 7·9 mm machine guns. It had a maximum range of 100 miles, and could reach about 25 mph. For the Afrika Korps the MkIII received additional front armour plates. The next model was the MkIV, also with a crew of 5, two 7·9 mm machine guns (firing rate about 850 rpm), but now fitted with a much more powerful 75 mm gun. It weighed 24 tons and had a similar range and speed to the MkIII.

After these Panzers had met the Russian T-34s, great improvements were essential. However so much time and money was spent on disconnected research and experimentation, that at one stage in 1942 Germany only produced 100 new MkIVs in a month, while Russia built 900 T-34s. A successful medium tank was eventually produced – mainly as a result of close study of the T-34. This was the MkV – Panther D. Its range and armament was the same as the MkIV, but it was faster by 5 mph though it weighed 43 tons. Its well-shaped armour was up to 120 mm thick – against the 57 mm of the first MkIIIs. The Germans also built the massive MkVI Tiger – a 55 ton tank with an 88 mm gun.

Artillery The superiority of the T-34s put excessive emphasis on other armaments – self-propelled guns and tank-destroyers. These were simpler and quicker to produce, but since they had no turrets they were

Germany filled manpower needs by recruiting soldiers in occupied countries for the battle against the "Bolshevik hordes". Scores of thousands responded. This officer wears the uniform of the Norwegian Waffen-SS regiment; there were also Dutch, Belgian, French, Danish, and many Eastern European units. (Taylor)

The enormous casualties in Russia led to the call-up of younger and younger men. One unit which fought with great determination in Normandy, 1944, was the Waffen-SS "Hitler Youth" Division, formed from fanatical 17-year-olds with veteran officers and NCOs. They suffered 60% casualties by July 9th. (PK)

far less effective against tanks than a tank itself would be. Numerous models were built, ranging from the Guderian-specified *Jagdpanzer* 38 "Hetzer" of 16 tons, a 75 mm gun, one machine gun and a crew of 4, to the brute *Jagdpanzer* Tiger "Elephant" on the Tiger hull, weighing 68 tons, with an 88 mm gun and a top speed of 24 mph. What made matters worse for the tank commanders (while the guns took manufacturing preference) was that they were officially classed as artillery, and generally not under a panzer commander's authority.

The best and most famous artillery gun produced for the German army was the 88 mm which was effective as a mobile gun, an accurate anti-tank gun, a field-gun with a range of some 12,000 yards, or an AA gun firing eight rpm to a maximum altitude of well over 35,000 ft.

Apart from numerous other guns and howitzers, the Germans also manufactured some monstrous absurdities which could be moved on specially prepared tracks, on railways or were self-propelled (3 mph) – such as the "Karl" siege gun which fired a 4,850 lb shell; or the gigantic 800 mm "Dora" L 40·6, firing 10,500 lb shells 29 miles – a feat it could accomplish twice in an hour with the aid of 250 men.

Supply and Provisioning

The lack of consistent overall command or responsibility and of foresight soon caused many problems in the German army – most notorious of which was the foundering of ill-prepared armies in the snows of a Russian winter. The long fronts thousands of miles from home caused supply problems aggravated by such things as the different gauge of the Russian railways and partisan activity. The Allied bomber offensive caused further supply difficulties, already complicated by the great number of different weapons and types of machinery. In the last months the shortage of oil added to the disruption. The massive use of slave labour and considerable ingenuity limited the effects of many Allied efforts to totally disrupt the supplying and provisioning of the German army.

GREAT BRITAIN

As Prime Minister and Defence Minister, Churchill was in a position of considerable power, but most decisions and moves needed the approval of the War Cabinet. The "war planners" were the members of the Chiefs of Staff Committee who directed the commanders of relevant areas (eg. C-in-C Middle East). Interference in operations was avoided if possible, and the system worked well. Airborne troops were relied on extensively, and the British developed commando attacks to a high level. The war against Japan called for completely different skills, and after initial setbacks the British and Empire armies became highly efficient.

Weapons

Infantry Two basic infantry weapons became known for their rugged reliability, and the calibre standardisation helped. The basic rifle was the Lee Enfield ·303 in. No. 4, with a range of 2,000 yds and a 10 round magazine. The reliable light machine gun was the Bren ·303 which could also fire single shots or short bursts, and was therefore economical. It fired at 500 rpm and the magazine held 32 rounds.

The British sub-machine-gun was the Sten 9 mm with a magazine holding 32 rounds, firing at over 500 rpm (when it did not jam).

Britain's early heavy machine gun was the extremely reliable water-cooled Vickers ·303 in. It weighed 50 lbs (with water) and could fire the 250 rounds on each belt at up to 550 rpm.

Armoured The British tanks suffered from being slow and too thinly armoured, and their 2 pounders were far too weak. The early Infantry MkII "Matilda" was succeeded by the "Valentine" (MkIII) which was still not fast enough, nor did it have enough fire power.

The desert war took a dramatic turn for the British when they began to use the U.S. M3 General Grant tank, which had a 75 mm gun (with limited traverse, being hull mounted), a 37 mm turret gun and four ·30 in. machine guns. It weighed 28 tons and had a potential speed of 28 mph.

The IVth Infantry tank was the Churchill MkI, first tried at Dieppe. It was well armoured, weighed 38 tons, but still had the ineffective 2 pounder gun.

British commandos in 1944, heavily laden with arms, ammunition, and miscellaneous equipment. Early commando raids kept up British spirits in the years before major landings in Europe were possible, and some notable intelligence-gathering exploits were recorded. From 1944 onwards commando units acted as élite spearhead formations in co-operation with more conventional forces.

The Churchill later provided the basic structure for a large variety of specialist machines, such as flail-tanks for mine clearing, flame throwers, bridge carriers, etc. The U.S. later again came to the rescue with the excellent Sherman, and the massive Pershing (see below, U.S.A.).

Artillery The famous artillery piece of the 8th Army was the versatile 25 pounder. It had the same calibre as the German 88 mm, was sturdy and reliable, and could be used as a howitzer ("drop-shots") long-distance gun, or anti-tank gun. A shorter, lighter version was produced for jungle warfare.

Anti-tank guns were important weapons in any artillery division: the 6 pounder replaced the 2 pounder in 1940, and was itself replaced by the powerful 17 pounder, which had a range of 3,000 yds and could stop a Pzkw Tiger at $\frac{3}{4}$ mile.

A good heavy gun of late 1941 was the 5·5 in. field gun which fired an 82 lb high-explosive shell 18,200 yards.

The 3·7 in. AA gun was similar to the German 88 mm, and there were far more of these at Alamein than there were 88s. But for some strange reason, they were only used as AA guns – even when the Allies ruled the skies.

Other AA guns were the famous 40 mm Bofors, which fired 2 lb shells at 120 rpm to a maximum altitude of 12,000 ft, and the Oerlikon 20 mm which had drum magazines of 60 rounds and fired at 650 rpm. It was widely used on naval and merchant ships and was adopted by U.S. forces.

Supply and Provisioning

For Britain, the early years of war involved sea and air war, and the desert war. The Mediterranean was a hazardous sea for the Allies, and most supplies initially had to follow the long Cape route. Once Mediterranean superiority was established there were few supply problems. Nothing made a greater difference than the assist-

The British 14th Army was manned by troops from many parts of the British Empire, welded into a very efficient force by Gen. Slim. This defensive group is using the three most widely used infantry weapons of the British army – a Sten 9 mm submachine-gun, a Lee-Enfield ·303 rifle, and a Bren ·303 light machine-gun.

ance of America, from where came an endless supply of weapons and supplies, and the ships to carry them in. Except for tanks, however, the two countries tended to keep to their own weaponry.

RUSSIA

The enormous manpower resources of Russia resulted in the war's biggest fully-equipped army – at its height it numbered some 12 million. The line facing Germany was divided into 12 Fronts which came directly under the General H.Q. headed by Stalin and usually consisting of about 10 senior commanders, the most prominent of whom was Zhukov. In the field each Front (equivalent to an Army Group) generally consisted of four armies with up to 2 million men in 100 Divisions. There were no corps between the divisions and the army commanders and this gave each army the stamp of its commander's personality. In a major campaign, a senior general and his staff would be despatched from General H.Q. to co-ordinate the activities of several fronts. The Russian soldiers were trained with a ruthlessness unknown in the West, and, since many of them came from the harsh lands of central and eastern Russia, they formed an incredibly tough fighting force. Their large numbers, the nature and history of the country frequently resulted in a disregard for casualties only comparable with the Japanese and Chinese "human wave" tactics.

Many Poles managed to escape from their country immediately before and after its defeat, and served with distinction in many theatres of war. Particularly large numbers joined the R.A.F., and many were decorated for valour.

Weapons

Infantry The Russians benefitted from a decision to make simple weapons with a high degree of standardisation. The basic rifle after 1942 was the M-1930 7·62 mm with 5 round magazine, and this calibre was kept for the 71 round drum-magazine of the PPSH sub-machine gun and the Tokarev TT automatic pistol.

The standard heavy machine-gun was an air cooled 12·7 mm weapon with a firing speed of 600 rpm.

Armoured Again motivated by the need for simplicity owing to the low levels of education and skills of large numbers in the army, the Russians built strong, unsophisticated tanks that were nevertheless more than a match for German tanks. Most formidable, and probably the best tank of the war, was the T-34. It was fast, had wide tracks which suited snow and mud, and weighed 26·3 tons. The maximum range was 250 miles, and the low silhouette and excellent

contours of the 45–75 mm hull and turret made it very difficult to destroy. The T-34 had a 76·2 mm gun, and two 7·62 mm machine-guns.

The Russians also produced the gigantic Joseph Stalin range (JS1, 2 and 3) which used 122 mm guns and had armour up to 160 mm thick.

Tank divisions were also supported by tank destroyers or self-propelled guns which were very effective. Most destructive was the SU-122 built on the T-34 hull. It weighed 31 tons, carried a 122 mm gun, and could reach 34 mph. Its maximum travelling range was a very useful 375 miles.

Artillery The Russians were the undisputed masters of artillery, and produced barrages of fearsome intensity at Stalingrad and Berlin. Again simplicity and standardisation ruled, and the most prolific guns were those which matched the tank guns.

The 122 mm Type 31/37 howitzer had a range of 22,000 yards, while the Type 38 76·2 calibre reached 14,800 yards.

A light anti-tank gun was the Type 32 45 mm with a range of almost 10,000 yards, or half that with a high-explosive shell.

The Russian artillery also made extremely effective use of their *Katyusha* rockets – this form of weapon only becoming widely used elsewhere later in the war, when batteries of them were mounted on tank hulls, lorries, ships, etc.

Supply and Provisioning

The simplicity and standardisation of weapons, the vast labour resources of Russia, and unstinting effort produced a massive output. Added to this was the assistance provided by Britain and America (5,000 tanks from Britain alone), and the failure of the Germans to completely isolate the rich oilfields of the Caucasus. War (and her own scorched-earth policy) ravaged much of Russia's industrial heart, but the country had little difficulty after 1942 in establishing a vast superiority which flung back the Germans.

JAPAN

The types of operations required by Japan to fulfil her territorial ambitions required considerable co-operation between the services, though the China and Burma wars were "army wars". Overall direction came from the Supreme Council for the Conduct of the War – the Big Six – comprising the Prime Minister, the Foreign Minister, the War Minister, and the military chiefs. Japan's rampant militarism and the traditions encouraged by the militarists placed surrender as the greatest dishonour and elevated suicide and death for the Emperor and Japan to the highest plane. This, plus carefully sown propaganda that prisoners of war were automatically shot, produced a deadly fanaticism. The Japanese soldiers therefore continued to inflict high casualties and to delay conquest far beyond the stage when any other army would have surrendered. Complete disregard for death enabled commanders to deploy suicide rear-guards covering retreats, or to launch massed attacks to win objectives by sheer weight of numbers. Technology, however, seems to have given little to the army, and there were few airborne or tank units.

Weapons

Infantry Basic rifle was the Model 38 6·5 mm, which was produced in three different lengths for different operations. The submachine-gun was the Model 11 6·5 mm holding 30 rounds and firing at 500 rpm.

The standard heavy machine-gun was the effective Type 99-1 air cooled 7·7 mm, firing at 550 rpm.

Jungle and island warfare called for extensive use of mortars – the Model 97 81 mm fired a 7 lb explosive-head 3,100 yards.

Armoured Virtually the only tank used by the Japanese, and encountered mainly in China and Burma was the light CHI HA Type 97. With a maximum armour of 25 mm, it weighed only 15 tons and could reach 25 mph. Its armament was a 57 mm gun and two 7·7 mm machine-guns.

Artillery Relying on ships' guns and dive-bombers for barrages, the Japanese artillery was devoted to howitzers whose "lobbing" action was more suitable for jungles and hilly island warfare. They ranged from the Model 92 70 mm with a range of 3,075 yards (firing a very heavy shell) to the Model 91 105 mm and the Model 4 150 mm which had a range of over 10,000 yards.

Supply and Provisioning

As the Japanese gradually lost their control of the Pacific, and then even their ability to use it without alarming shipping losses, garrisons on the many islands which were invaded soon ran short of ammunition. On islands which were "leap-frogged" by the Americans, the main shortage was eventually food. The supply lines for the columns fighting in Burma were long, and while much was dropped from transport planes, the Japanese had to learn to be sparing with all supplies.

U.S.A.

America entered the war when Britain had already been at war for two years, and in Europe U.S. forces always took part in combined operations. In the Pacific, it was agreed that the island war would be America's concern, while the S.E. Asian war would be run by S.E.A.C. largely under British direction. The U.S. armed forces' C-in-C was the President, and strategy was determined by the U.S. Joint Chiefs of Staff. For European combined

Above:

U.S. infantry moving forward across a wide front. Apart from individual weapons, they carry a mortar, a water-cooled machine-gun, and an anti-tank recoilless projector. During the war a doctrine of increased firepower for infantry squads was generally accepted.

Below:

U.S. Airborne troops being briefed during the invasion of Normandy. In the latter half of the war both the Americans and the British made far greater use of paratroopers and gliders than did the Germans, who seemed never to forget the slaughter on Crete.

operations the U.S. Joint Chiefs and the British Chiefs of Staff had representatives which formed the Combined Chiefs of Staff Committee, which reported to, and advised Roosevelt and Churchill. Backed by the country's enormous resources, the U.S. armies became extremely powerful, and by the end of the war numbered over 4 million. The famous Marine Corps fought most notably in the Pacific and numbered nearly 500,000 at the height of its power.

Weapons

Infantry and Marines The first basic rifle was the P-17 ·30 in. calibre which was replaced by the M-1 Garand ·30 in with an 8 round magazine – a rifle that became as well-known and trusted as the British ·303.

The ·45 in. Thompson submachine-gun was replaced by the M-3 which fired ·45 in. bullets from a 30 round magazine at 400 rpm. It had an extra barrel which could use German ammunition.

Another well-known weapon was the M-1 Carbine semi-automatic ·30 in. with a 15 round magazine.

The American heavy machine-gun was the Browning air cooled ·50 in. M-2, a formidable gun firing 100 round belts at 450 rpm and suitable as an infantry or AA weapon.

Armoured After the M3 (see above – Gt. Britain) the main, and very successful U.S. tank was the Sherman. Hardy and reliable, it had a 75 mm gun, 80 mm armour, a ·30 in. machine-gun in the hull and a ·50 in. on the turret.

The Sherman Firefly improved the range up to 120 miles and had similar armour, but was fitted with the more powerful British 17 pounder gun.

A major development was the low silhouette, very rugged 35 ton Pershing T-25 El. It had well contoured armour of up to 89 mm, and a 90 mm gun.

The M-10 gun motor carriage was an effective "tank-killer" whose 3 in. gun on a Sherman hull fired armour-piercing shells which could penetrate 100 mm armour at 100 yards.

Artillery The 37 mm anti-tank gun was also used for

U.S. Marines help a wounded comrade on the beach of Iwo Jima. The "island-hopping" war in the Pacific forced America to develop the equipment and techniques of amphibious warfare to a high level of sophistication.

firing anti-personnel canisters, and had a range of 12,800 yards.

Principal howitzers were the tough 105 mm and the very accurate 155 mm which had a range of 16,000 yards and could fire 2 rounds per minute.

The most-used long range artillery piece was the highly manoeuvrable 155 mm gun, with a range of 25,715 yards.

Supply and Provisioning

"Bigger and better" applied throughout the U.S. armed forces. Provisioned regularly and backed by the wealth and sophisticated industry of the U.S., even the daunting task of supply across the Pacific was more than adequately met (though the first six months of the war was a difficult period). In addition, through Lend-Lease America supplied a large proportion of the arms and supplies of many Allied countries.

THE AIR FORCES

GERMANY

From 1935 until five days before Hitler's death Goering was C-in-C of the German Air Force. Except for the 1940 effort to destroy the R.A.F., the Luftwaffe was envisaged in an army-support role, and it therefore had no heavy bombers. Light bombers and dive-bombers, heavily escorted by fighters, were essential components of *blitzkrieg* tactics, while they were also effectively used against Arctic and Mediterranean convoys. By 1943 fighters were taking on an increasingly defensive role, and production of bombers decreased – some light bombers finding a new role as night fighters. The greatest disadvantage shared by most Luftwaffe planes was a short range, and since the planners envisaged a short war, co-ordinated development fell behind that of the Allies –

A U.S. Army tank platoon in Europe, winter 1944–45. The Sherman tank, in its various developed versions the standard equipment of virtually the entire American armoured force, was the most widely used tank in the world, and was supplied to all Allied nations in great numbers.

Although crippled by the losses among trained aircrew by mid-1944, the Luftwaffe fighter arm began the war as the most effective in the world. Easy victories in Spain and Poland gave many pilots the perfect opportunity to perfect their tactical skills under fire. (Obert)

what innovation there was being squandered among a bewildering variety of experimental planes, from push-pull propellor craft to no less than 12 jet or rocket design concepts. The Luftwaffe also suffered from the Army's imbalance in the quality of its top leaders compared to its operative commanders.

Major aircraft

Fighters *Messerschmitt Bf 109E*. At 357 mph as fast as the Spitfire but less manoeuvrable and limited by a short range. Eventually replaced by the 109G models – the "Gustav".

Focke-Wulf Fw 190A. Germany's most successful fighter – top speed 408 mph, a range of over 500 miles and armament of four 20 mm cannons and two 13 mm machine-guns.

Messerschmitt Bf 110G. Twin-engined light bomber/fighter eventually finding a role as a night fighter. 342 mph, range of 1,305 miles and well armed with four cannons and two machine-guns. A crew of three.

Bombers *Ju 87 "Stuka"*. Only effective if not opposed by fighters, the Stuka dive-bomber is remembered mainly for its banshee scream. Slow and easily outflown. It normally carried 1,500 lbs of bombs.

Junkers Ju 88. One of the war's most versatile planes – twin-engined light or medium bomber, dive-bomber, night fighter, etc. Speed up to 311 mph, range up to 2,130 miles.

Heinkel He 111. Twin-engined, up to 258 mph and 5,500 lbs of bombs, but not successful as a bomber, being very vulnerable to fighters. Some usefulness at night bombing, torpedo-carrying, mine-laying, and as a paratroop transport.

Focke-Wulf Fw 200 Condor. A four-engined transporter which played a major role in guiding submarines to convoys or lone ships, and as a long distance light bomber (3,000 lbs). Range almost 4,000 miles.

Supply and Provisioning

The Allied air offensive disrupted aircraft production, but not as much as did changes of policy, and the lack of long-term planning and firm direction. Vacillating leadership prevented any sensible rationalisation of effort, and towards the end of the war a critical shortage of fuel kept most operative aircraft grounded.

GREAT BRITAIN

Britain was fortunate in having an air force prepared for a defensive role and in Air Marshal Dowding having insisted on withdrawing a substantial fighter force from Europe for the defence of Britain. Technology played an important part in the balance; superior radar and excellent fighters helped win the early battles, and then the concentration on developing heavy bombers as the only way of making an attack on Germany, built up the power of Bomber Command. The resources of the U.S. played an important role, and the R.A.F. benefitted by the development of the greatest aircraft engine of all time – the Rolls Royce Merlin.

Major aircraft

Fighters *Hawker Hurricane*. Sturdy and reliable. 328 mph, with great versatility of roles and armament. Tank-buster, fighter, dive-bomber, catapult-launched sea escort, etc. Range up to almost 1,000 miles. Altogether 14,533 Hurricanes were built in the war.

Supermarine Spitfire. Highly manoeuvrable, and the most famous fighter of the war. Built in numerous models, and highly adaptable and versatile. By the end of the war, with the RR Griffon engine, its speed had increased from 360 to 448 mph, in which form it shot down V1s and the first Me 262 jet.

Hawker Typhoon 1B. The best ground-attack plane of the war. 417 mph with four 20 mm cannon or two 500 lb bombs, and a range of almost 1,000 miles.

Multi-purpose In a category all of its own, the wooden-framed, twin-engined de Havilland Mosquito appeared in a bewildering variety of models to fulfil every role from a fast transporter to a night fighter, a solitary bomber or a low level attacker. Up to 408 mph, maximum range 1,830 miles. Up to 4,000 lbs of bombs; four cannons; rockets; etc.

Bombers *Wellington.* Very sturdy twin-engined bomber which could take tremendous damage. 255 mph; range 1,325 miles; bombs – 6,000 lbs.

Short Stirling and *Halifax* were the first and second four-engined heavy bombers. 260 and 282 mph; range up to 2,000 miles; bombs – over 13,000 lbs.

Lancaster. Bomber Command's most famous and useful four-engined heavy bomber. 275 mph; range up to 2,530 miles; bombs – 18,000 lbs. (specially developed to take 22,000 lb bomb).

Supply and Provisioning

The R.A.F. enjoyed the facilities of the U.S., with R.R. Merlin engines being manufactured by Packard. Numerous American planes, such as the Douglas Boston and the Consolidated B-24 Liberator were also used, as was the superlative P-51 Mustang with the Merlin engine.

RUSSIA

The Russian Air Force played an essentially army-support role, and therefore the majority of its planes were

A Focke-Wulf Fw 190A fighter ready for take-off from an airfield in the west in 1943. This was regarded by both sides as among the finest fighters of the war. Its maximum speed was over 400 mph, and later versions carried very heavy armament.

fighters, or fighter/ground attack planes. Like the army, the air forces were caught out by Barbarossa, and a large number of planes were destroyed on the ground. The principles of rationalisation strictly applied to ground weapons were apparently forgotten for aircraft, and a variety of planes were built.

Major aircraft

Fighters *Yak-1*. Succeeded the MiG-3, which lacked manoeuvrability. 364 mph; range 435 miles. The later Yak-9D increased the range, but was slower.

Lavochkin La-7. The most widely used fighter. 413 mph; range 394 miles; three cannon, and six rockets or two bombs.

Sturmovik Il-2. A famous ground-attack and close-support plane. 257 mph. Eight rockets or cannons and machine guns.

Bombers *Illyushin Il-4*. Twin-engined, 265 mph; range up to 2,500 miles; bombs – up to 4,400 lb.

Petlyakov Pe-2. Also used as a night fighter. 335 mph; range 1,200 miles; bombs – 2,200 lbs.

Supply and Provisioning

After their initial losses, the huge output of the Russian factories quickly redressed the balance against the Luftwaffe, which by then suffered from supply difficulties at the front line. The Russians were also helped enormously by America and Britain, who sent them some 22,000 aircraft during the war.

JAPAN

The Japanese air strength fell under the command of the Navy, and aircraft were envisaged as an extension of sea power – in which Japan was formidable – though it was not an ancillary service, and played a major role in the Pacific war. Range, for that type of warfare, was very important. The Japanese also tried a bewildering variety of aircraft, and in final desperation committed some 3,000 of them to *kamikaze* attacks.

Luftwaffe fighter-bomber crews during 1943, when the force was at its greatest. Towards the end of the war thousands of Luftwaffe men were transferred to the infantry. Aircraft production was maintained, but shortages of fuel and experienced aircrew were crippling.

Major aircraft

Fighters *Mitsubishi A6M Zero Sen.* "Zeke". Most famous Japanese fighter, fighter-bomber, and superior to any other plane in the Pacific in the first years of the war. 351 mph; range up to 1,200 miles. Over 10,600 were built.

Aichi D3A "Val". The Pearl Harbor dive bomber (816 lbs).

Nakajima B5N "Kate". Torpedo-bomber. Range 1,400 miles.

Nakajima Ki-84 "Frank". Superior to the Zero, and almost outflew the Hellcat and the Mustang. 388 mph; range 1,815 miles.

The Russian Air Force of 1941 – an aircrew briefing is pictured here – was no match in skill or equipment for the experienced Luftwaffe. After huge initial losses, with many aircraft destroyed on the ground before they could even take off, the force was gradually built up into an effective tactical arm of great strength. Later designs by Yakovlev and Lavotchkin proved outstanding, particularly at low altitude.

Bombers *Mitsubishi G4M "Betty"*. 276 mph; range 2,620 miles; bombs – 1,765 lbs.

Nakajima B6N "Jill". Replaced "Kate". 299 mph; range 1,600 miles. Two machine-guns plus one torpedo or six 220 lb bombs.

Supply and Provisioning

The steady destruction of the Japanese carrier fleet reduced both the number of planes, and the number of "airfields". Fuel shortage became an added problem for the Japanese, and many cut-off island bases which had planes and airfields ran out of fuel. A drastic shortage of strategic materials and the U.S. bombing raids on Japan from March 1945 rapidly curtailed the replacement of the Japanese air strength, and pilots were eventually also in short supply.

U.S.A.

The air force officially came under the control of the army, and its back-up services were dependent on army units. But the U.S. (Army) Air Force was in no way merely an army-support force, and resembled the R.A.F. more than it did the air forces. In the Pacific war, the U.S. Navy

U.S. 8th A.A.F. officers pose with their charmingly decorated B-17G Flying Fortress. The American daylight bomber offensive from England forced Germany to call home units of her overstretched fighter arm, thus contributing to further problems on the Eastern Front.

planes took on a major share of the fighting until air bases could be established on land, as they were on Guadalcanal, Iwo Jima, Leyte, Okinawa, etc. The bombing offensive against Japan itself was carried out by the Air Force.

Major aircraft

Fighters *Curtis P-40.* The first mass-produced U.S. fighter. The "Tomahawk" and then the "Kittyhawk" were mediocre fighters, but very good ground-attack planes. Maximum speed 357 mph; range 1,400 miles.

P-38 Lightning. One of the best long distance escort fighters in Europe in the early stages. 414 mph; numerous versions and armaments.

P-47 Thunderbolt. Big and heavy, but unexpectedly nimble. 426 mph. Capable of carrying bombs, or drop-tanks for long range escort flying.

P-51 Mustang. The war's best long range escort fighter, which made feasible the daylight bombing of Germany. 441 mph; range 1,300 miles or up to 2,700 miles with drop tanks. Four machine guns – or 2,500 lbs bombs on short range flights. It was not a successful plane until fitted with the Merlin engine.

Gruman F4F Wildcat. The standard carrier-borne fighter at the beginning of the war. 331 mph; range 860 miles.

Bombers *Douglas SB Dauntless.* Very hardy carrier-borne light bomber. 275 mph; range 875 miles; one 500 lb bomb.

B-24 Liberator. Very versatile – maritime reconnaissance, bomber, transporter, etc. 300 mph; range 2,100 miles; bombs – up to 12,800 lbs on short range.

B-17 Flying Fortress. The main U.S.A.A.F. bomber in the European war. Up to 287 mph; range 2,100 miles; bombs – 8,000 lbs.

B-29 Superfortress. Only flown against Japan. 357 mph; range 3,250 miles; ceiling 33,600 ft; bombs up to 12,000 lbs.

Supply and Provisioning

The American aircraft industry was already large before the war, and it turned into a gigantic industry which no other country could remotely match. Like the other countries, however, America also produced constantly revised and refined models which added to logistics problems.

THE NAVIES

GERMANY

The Treaty of Versailles forbade Germany to construct naval ships of over 10,000 tons, and the *Kriegsmarine* produced the ingenious solution of pocket-battleships which had a battleship's calibre guns and armour but in tonnage conformed to the Treaty. Hitler however soon flaunted the Treaty, and began to produce heavy cruisers and eventually battleships. The Navy suffered in that it was planning for war in 1944, not 1939, and it was ill-prepared. It also had the disadvantage of having to take commands, via Raeder, from a man who was wary of navy people and took little real interest in the service. U-boats were an exception, as they were a basic weapon in the war against the economy of Britain. The surface navy was given no proper objective, found no sensible role, and was largely a huge waste of money and man-power.

The Ships

Two great battleships were produced – *Bismarck* and *Tirpitz*. Both displaced approximately 50,000 tons, could reach 29 knots and were armed with eight 15 in. guns, twelve 5·9 in. and thirty-two AA guns. They carried 2 aircraft and some 2,200 men. *Tirpitz* fired her big guns in anger once at a remote Arctic island, and *Bismarck* was sunk on her maiden voyage. Four other capital ships were built in defiance of the Versailles Treaty, and all were fast, very heavily armoured, and had formidable armament. All of them, however, and the three pocket battleships, were expected to work as surface raiders, and avoid contact with any Allied fleet. Construction of one aircraft carrier was begun, but not completed. The German fleet never sailed as a fleet, with its capital ships, destroyer escorts, etc., and so there was never a major confrontation between almost equal forces. From 1941, in fact, the capital ships only made the briefest of sorties, and none at all sailed after *Scharnhorst* was sunk in December 1943 – a year after the last venture-out by two ships had ended in retreat and the resignation of Raeder.

However, the mere presence of the great ships in French or Norwegian ports constituted a threat which tied-up the British Home Fleet – which could have been out hunting U-boats, the major force in the German Navy. These too, were affected by Hitler's early start to the war but saw some development, though the Allied perfection of radar could never be countered, and U-boats never successfully went to sea in great quantities after June 1943.

U-boat types included the early Type II-B, a short-range boat 140 ft long, with a displacement of 279 tons; a range of 1,800 miles and a speed of 13 knots (43 miles and 7 knots submerged); and an armament of 3 tubes for which 6 torpedoes were carried. The main class was the Type VII, which more than tripled the range and more than doubled the armament. Later came the Type IXD2. 287 ft long; 1,616 tons; 19 knots (7 submerged); range 23,700 miles (57 submerged); one 4·1 in. gun, two AA guns; 6 torpedo tubes, 24 torpedos; crew 57.

E-boats (motor torpedo boats), mine layers and mine-sweepers were numerous in the Channel and formed the most active branch of the surface fleet.

Supply and Provisioning

The surface fleet was severely restricted by Hitler in its use of fuel, and the early successes of the armed merchant raiders was not followed up for this reason. Most of the German navy therefore became little more than floating AA platforms, as even their big guns were seldom put into operation. Development work on new submarines continued under tremendous difficulties, but once Overlord had removed Germany's direct access to the Atlantic, any hope for success at sea vanished.

GREAT BRITAIN

The immediate impact made by U-boats suggested that the R.N. had remembered little of the dangers of submarines from World War I, and hurried attempts were made to build escort vessels to enable convoys to be formed – the only possible defence against massive U-boat losses. The first special escorts were corvettes and while they were incredibly seaworthy they were no faster than a surfaced U-boat, and were horribly uncomfortable. From the corvette, the frigates were developed, and in them a reliable and effective escort was found, supplementing the traditional destroyers which combined speed and submarine-killing ability with considerable fire-power for surface conflict.

The British Navy was directed by the First Sea Lord and the commanders at the Admiralty who gave varying degrees of autonomy to the C-in-C's of the various Fleets, co-ordinated joint operations, and managed the escorting of convoys. By mid-1943, supremacy of the Atlantic and the Mediterranean had been attained – at the cost of four carriers, three capital ships, and numerous destroyers, submarines, and small escorts, MTBs, etc. In the war against Japan, lack of appreciation of the vulnerability of capital ships to aircraft was made immediately apparent by the loss of *Repulse* and *Prince of Wales*. One more aircraft carrier was lost, also sunk by Japanese aircraft.

The Ships

The length of time taken to design and build a ship meant that most of the British heavy fleet was a number of years old when war began, and there were only five capital ships (*Prince of Wales* and four sister ships) which were completed after 1938 and which saw service. The smaller the ship, the less this applied, of course, and the vulnerability of battleships focused attention far more on aircraft carriers, escort carriers, and smaller, attacking craft. War-derived experience was naturally slow in being put into practice, though all classes of ships constantly underwent modification – particularly the addition of AA guns and heavier deck armour.

A U-boat undergoing maintenance on a slipway in a French port. Control of the west coast of Europe gave the German submarines greatly increased range, with easy access to the Atlantic. This is a Type VII-B, the main sea-going class of submarine. Its surface speed was $17\frac{1}{4}$ knots (8 knots submerged) and its maximum operational radius was over 6,000 miles.

No improvement to a ship's design, however, could have made such a difference to the capabilities of R.N. ships as did the development of micro-wave radar, and the modifications which reduced the sets' bulk to proportions suitable for medium and smaller escorts. This greatly benefitted convoy escorting as well as submarine hunting. The invention of devices to project depth charges in front of the hunter, while holding a submarine in asdic contact (instead of dropping depth charges over a blind patch) greatly increased the "kill" rate, as did the asdic development which enabled depth calculations to be made.

Supply and Provisioning

The British shipyards produced a great number of new vessels during the war, but nothing strengthened the R.N. at its most critical time as much as the Lend-Lease Act which brought into action hundreds of escort vessels. However the natural overlap between "ordering-wants" and "delivery-needs" meant that the R.N. began the war weaker than was safe, and ended it twenty times stronger than was necessary.

RUSSIA

The vastness of Russia – her isolationism made permissible by abundant reserves of raw materials – and a scarcity of good, all-weather access to major shipping routes resulted in a navy of minor importance compared with Russia's other two services, and particularly her army. A large portion of the fleet was in the Black Sea, which was also the site of the major ship-building yards. Annexation of the Baltic States and the defeat of Finland had improved Russia's access to the Baltic, however, but the launching of Germany's attack in June 1941 was too soon, and too violent for the Russian navy to play a significant part. Overpowered by German ships and planes in the Baltic, the Russians suffered heavy defeat in their withdrawal from the Baltic States, and few ships reached Kronstadt undamaged – if they made it at all. A small number of more heavily-armed ships were able to lend their guns to the defence of Leningrad, but the Gulf of Finland was extensively mined and totally blockaded by the Germans. In the Black Sea the retreating Russians destroyed their shipyards and all incomplete ships, but though a number of warships were able to shell the advancing German ground troops, and assist in the siege and evacuation of Sebastopol, Luftwaffe superiority caused heavy damage. In the Arctic, the protection of the Russian-bound convoys was left almost entirely to the RN, with some assistance from the USN. Russian destroyers rarely met the convoys west of North Cape.

By early 1942, Russia had lost a substantial part of her navy, the Germans having destroyed two battleships, four cruisers, some 20 destroyers, about 30 submarines, and almost 75 MTBs and other small craft.

JAPAN

The Japanese navy was extremely powerful, and far exceeded the limits ostensibly laid down by the Washington Naval Treaty. It commanded the same (or greater) prestige and influence as the army, and in addition controlled the air force. In many respects Japan was similar to Britain – an island reliant on imports and exports, and her territorial ambitions gave her added reason to emulate the power of the R.N. She eventually surpassed it, with a massive fleet relying heavily on aircraft carriers and led by highly capable but unassertive Admirals. The Japanese navy's downfall came from an American fleet vastly superior in numbers and directed by a command structure not equalled in the argumentative Japanese high command.

The Ships

The Japanese navy had 16 aircraft carriers, as well as five escort carriers. The bigger carriers were about 26,700 tons, could reach 34 knots, carry 84 aircraft, and were manned by a crew of over 1,600.

Capital ships also played an important role, though they were to prove even more vulnerable than the U.S.N. battleships at Pearl Harbor. Twenty battleships and heavy cruisers were lost – the biggest was the world's biggest battleship, *Yamato*, which was 863 ft long, had nine 18 in. guns, twelve 6·1 in. guns and thirty-six AA guns. Its deck armour was 16 ins. thick (turret armour up to 25 ins.), and the 64,170 ton ship could reach 27 knots. Yet it too, was sunk by aircraft without ever causing a wave of destruction.

With planes such as these U.S. Navy Douglas Dauntless dive-bombers, and a massive shipbuilding programme, America rapidly overcame the disaster of Pearl Harbor and established air and sea superiority over Japan.

Japanese submarine ambitions were also expansive – one was designed to carry three aircraft and have ten AA guns, but the standby was the type KD7, whose specifications resembled the German Type IXD2.

Supply and Provisioning

Japanese ship production was severely curtailed by the very effective blockade of Japan carried out by U.S. ships, planes and submarines, and it never came anywhere near matching the depletion of the navy, even as regards smaller craft. The navy was simply destroyed ship by ship until its last suicidal voyage to Okinawa after which, like the air force, it ceased to exist.

U.S.A.

The main power of the U.S.N. lay in the Pacific, and after the frightening shake-up of Pearl Harbor an extremely effective fleet was put into operation. The commanders under King – Nimitz, Halsey, Spruance, etc. – were very skilled and the backing of the huge manufacturing resources, which took only months to produce results, made the U.S. Pacific Fleet the most powerful navy the world had ever seen.

The Ships

Apart from the fact that seven U.S.N. aircraft carriers escaped the Pearl Harbor destruction, the production of a further 32 during the war gave the U.S.N. an overwhelming superiority. (Less emphasis went on battleships, but even so 10 joined the 11 remaining in the whole fleet after Pearl Harbor.)

Two of the big carriers were *Saratoga* and *Lexington*: 888 ft; 33,000 tons; speed 34 knots; 90 aircraft; crew 3,300.

The carrier-of-all-work, however, was the sturdy *Essex* class of 27,100 tons, carrying 100 aircraft and only slightly slower and shorter than the bigger carriers.

The battleships, cruisers and destroyers were extensively used in pre-invasion shelling, as well as for their AA fire and surface-fleet protection.

Smaller vessels, in particular MTBs, played important roles in the war of the islands.

Supply and Provisioning

Apart from supplying many ships for other Allied navies, and keeping up a high production of merchant ships, U.S. shipyards produced 162 carriers, capital ships, escort carriers (basically converted merchantmen), and cruisers during the war, as well as hundreds of destroyers, MTBs, frigates, and other smaller craft.

CASUALTIES IN THE FORCES

In the war between Germany and Italy and the Allies who formed the United Nations, over 19,000,000 servicemen died: at least 13,500,000 Russian soldiers were killed; 3,250,000 Germans; 330,000 Italians and as many from Britain. In the Pacific War between Japan and the United Nations, nearly 6,000,000 members of the armed forces died: over 3,500,000 Chinese; at least 1,700,000 Japanese. Britain lost another 40,000 as did Australia and New Zealand. Heavily involved in both conflicts, America lost over 400,000 servicemen. (In World War I over 8,500,000 servicemen died.)

5. THE CIVILIAN EXPERIENCE

Over 30,000,000* civilians died in the Second World War. This is some five million more than in all the armed forces – a horrible illustration of the meaning of total war. The aeroplane, rocket and heavy gun made total war possible, and total war decrees that the person who makes a bullet, or grows the food to sustain the soldier who fires the bullet, is as much a threat as the soldier himself. The sadness of this decree is that the bombs which destroy factories, or the homes of the people engaged in war work also kill completely innocent people, such as young children. However, a nation at war enlists the aid of whoever it can, and so total war also makes a justifiable victim of the groups of young children who hunt for scrap metal and give in their metal toys to help the manufacture of, perhaps, a bomb casing (which may drop in some back yard two thousand miles away and kill a mother and her children as they cower beneath a rudimentary shelter).

Unable to do anything else, the world wearily accepts that war can now bring death to anyone, and remembers the Second World War for having demonstrated this.

Unfortunately, that horrifying figure of 30 million bears witness to a further, more sickening tragedy, for at least one third of those civilians were cold bloodedly, even enthusiastically murdered to satisfy the ideals and ambitions of the Nazi tyrants and the whims of scores of men drunk with the power of their uniforms, with propaganda and the assurance of licence, who smothered any hesitancy beneath servile obedience to orders.

The Nazi Terror

THE JEWS The Nazi persecution of the Jews began long before the party came to power, and by 1936 Hitler had managed to isolate – into concentration camps and ghettoes – most of the Jews who had not already left what was to them their homeland. It was a fundamental belief of the Nazis that the Jews were responsible for practically all social and economic ills, and were therefore to be removed from society. The execution of this task in Germany and in each occupied country was entrusted to the special para-military force, the SS, which was controlled by Himmler and could not be curbed or influenced either by the civil courts, the police, or the Army.

The "removal from society" usually followed a pattern. Jews were identified (by sight, questioning, house searches, local authority records, informants, etc.) and Jewish-owned businesses closed down or taken over by the SS. Personal wealth and property was also siezed. (In this way the SS grew to become one of Europe's most wealthy organisations, owning shops and factories – whose labour costs were minimal – and vast amounts of gold and jewellry, for Jewish custom and the inflation of the previous years meant a large proportion of wealth in this form, rather than in paper money. The majority of SS wealth was turned into tangible form or into other currencies, and many gold bars and loose precious stones were sent for safe-keeping outside Germany – by no means all of it ever to be recovered by the Allies or by Jewish dependants.) Jews were made to sew a yellow Star of David on their clothing, and were not entitled to normal rations, transport, choice of labour, or ownership of any property.

The next stage usually involved confinement to a ghetto in a central town, where the first split-up of families could occur, as many ghettoes segregated the sexes. Movement in and out of a ghetto was forbidden except for labour parties. The Jews had to erect the enclosing walls and adapt or build whatever accommodation they could. Rations were brought in by the Germans, and were minimal. Overcrowding soon became a serious problem, and though deaths were frequent due to starvation and exhaustion, they could not keep pace with the daily arrival of Jews from outlying areas. The SS therefore began to enlarge existing concentration camps in Germany and Austria (which also contained political prisoners, such as German communists), and to build new ones in Poland. As each train-load of Jews arrived at a

* This will always be an approximate total. The greatest unknowns are for China and Russia, and the figure of 30 million-plus allows for 10 million Chinese civilians, and 6 million non-Jewish Russian civilians dead as a result of the war. Some sources suggest 15 million Chinese civilians may have died.

ghetto (perhaps after five or six days travelling in closed cattle-trucks, packed together without food or water), a number equal to the survivors on the incoming train would be selected for transfer to a concentration or death camp. Variations of the system existed. Instead of going from a ghetto to a camp, it soon became cheaper to kill the older, weaker Jews at the ghettoes to make room for new arrivals. Most west European Jews went direct to concentration camps where they worked in labour gangs until the miserable rations made them useless to the Germans. They were then shot or hanged. In some ghettoes and camps, sections were marked off and those people left to die by starvation. Trains bound for camps were given the lowest priority of movement which ensured that great numbers were already dead at the end of the journey. Others were "transported" in large trucks which had their exhaust pipes leading into the enclosed rear bodywork; the victims were dead when the truck arrived at the disposal point.

Death on a small scale was constant too – beatings or clubbings followed such crimes as smiling (rare) or talking during assembly and inspection periods, or simply for daring to look in an SS officer's eyes. In eastern Europe the SS recruited many locals, half-educated brutes who fell to their task with a will, overjoyed to be "superior" to other humans at last. The cold, exhaustion, starvation and disease took their daily toll in the ghettoes of Warsaw, or Riga, in the camps of Belsen, Dachau, Treblinka, Mauthausen, Ravensbrück, Buchenwald, and Auschwitz.

Although by autumn 1941 Jews were already dying at the rate of thousands each week, and were efficiently being moved towards the east (where the occupation of Russian and Baltic lands opened another chapter of Nazi brutality), it was apparent to Hitler, Goering, Himmler and others that there were still millions of Jews in German territory. Instructions went out to begin the "Final Solution" to the Jewish "problem". The SS commandants of the camps systematically began to murder the inmates – whose numbers never seemed to diminish as train after train arrived from Poland, from Holland,

The murder of hostages, killings "as examples", and summary trials and executions were frequent atrocities committed by German troops, and the Poles probably suffered more than any race from these particular barbarities. This Polish citizen has been hanged in the doorway of his own home, with a notice of his "crime" pinned to his clothing.

Hungary, Rumania, Czechoslovakia, Lithuania, Belgium, the Ukraine. It was not easy to kill them all – hanging was slow and machine-gunning used even more ammunition than individual shots, which were, again, too slow. Starvation cost nothing, but it took days and space was at a premium. Gassing proved to be an inexpensive method which was also highly productive, and at Auschwitz Rudolf Hoess was soon able (with the aid of the inventiveness of engineers in German factories) to gas up to 6,000 people in a day. (An added refinement was that the inmates were led to believe they were going to communal showers – their co-operation did away with the time-consuming task of removing clothes, shoes, spectacles, etc. from corpses. This left only gold-filled teeth to be extracted and hair to be shorn, all these items being other sources of income for the SS organisation. Often gold teeth were extracted before gassing – another time saver.) As big a problem as the killing of the Jews, was the destruction of their bodies. In spite of competitive efforts by various German companies, no special crematoria were made which could deal adequately with Auschwitz's horrible daily tally, and many corpses were thrown into deep pits, hasty attempts made at burning them, or covering them with quicklime, and then the earth was bulldozed over the site.

Towards the end of 1942, the shortage of slave labour led to a decrease in the amount of deliberate killings, for Himmler realised that a live Jew was worth something as a labourer, as long as little was spent on food. Factories were set up near the camps (Krupps, for example, built one near Auschwitz), and generally inmates were only killed when they were no longer capable of a full day's work. Other Germans began to realise the value of Jews (as well as Russians, gypsies, and other "subhumans") and bizarre, horrifying "medical" experiments were carried out on thousands of victims at Belsen, Ravensbrück, Dachau and Natzweiler by intelligent, fully qualified doctors.

Efforts to kill concentration camp inmates were stepped up in 1945 when the end of the war became inevitable, but many tens of thousands died on forced marches towards the west as the Russians advanced. Food grew scarcer and scarcer, and eventually (after the murder of many special political prisoners) the SS officers and guards handed the starving prisoners over to the *Volkssturm* ("home guard") and then tried to cover their tracks – which many of them succeeded in doing.

Although the killings were recorded with Teutonic thoroughness, many camp records were burnt in the last days of the war, and tens of thousands of inmates still died of disease and starvation in the first days after liberation. It is generally accepted that between 5,500,000 and 6,000,000 Jews died under the Nazi tyranny. About 2,700,000 came from Poland; 1,400,000 from Russia and the Baltic States; 490,000 from Rumania; 180,000 from Germany; 103,000 from Holland; 800,000 from Bulgaria, Hungary and Czechoslovakia; 40,000 from Belgium; 118,000 from Yugoslavia and Greece.

The enormity of this barbarism, almost in the middle of the 20th Century, perpetrated by a country rich in cultural and intellectual achievement, was not simply a case of isolated racial fanaticism, for similar treatment was also inflicted on millions of people who were not Jews, but East Europeans, Russians, and central-Asiatics – even Germans and Austrians were not immune.

THE RUSSIANS AND EAST EUROPEANS In the minds of the Nazis there were few people apart from true Aryans who had the right to any life other than one of subservience, and among the lowest on their scale were the peoples of Russia, especially if they were politically active Communists. It was, the Nazis believed, as essential to "eliminate" these people as it was to kill the Jews. So the German campaign against Russia spread another bloody stain on the record of man; a stain spread regrettably yet further when the revenging Russian army, 12 million strong, crashed its way into the heart of Europe.

The occupation of eastern Europe and of Russia was the way Hitler intended winning his *lebensraum* and simultaneously finding large numbers of workers who could be harnessed to German industry. It was first essential, however, to get rid of Jews, Communist commissars and any likely troublemakers, and once again Hitler, Himmler and Goering found in the SS the means to carry out the executions and the exploitation. Under Heydrich's direct supervision (and with the German Army's consent) special SS *Einsatzgruppen* (action groups) followed on the heels of the Army as it overran Russia, and rounded up Jews and Communist functionaries. At first the SS groups shot these people close to their villages – usually getting them to climb into great pits (which they had dug themselves) after undressing and sorting-out their clothes. They were then machine gunned in batches, each batch first having to clamber over the bodies of their family, friends and colleagues, to await their own death. Men, women and children were killed together.

Later on – especially when Russia proved no easy conquest – the "undesirables" were sent to death camps nearer Germany, or in Poland. Hundreds of thousands were also rounded up to be used as slave labour, and indiscriminate killings of the elderly and of very young children were frequent, since they complicated the smooth organisation so ardently sought. The German army had been encouraged to treat the Russians with complete ruthlessness, and was assured no punishment would follow any criminal act against a Russian. Treatment of Russian civilians – not simply by the SS *Einsatzgruppen*, but by Army units as well – was therefore often barbaric. Few women escaped multiple rape, and thousands of ordinary people were needlessly slaughtered.

Over the period of the occupation, starvation grew widespread and the country was constantly scoured for people for the work camps (women as well as men). On top of that, there were the ordinary civilians caught up in war – bombed and shelled, squashed in the path of two great armies. Altogether (but excluding the Jews already mentioned), 6,000,000 Russian civilians died as a result of the war, and 2,500,000 Poles. From the Baltic States 430,000 died. Large proportions of these were deliberate murders or deaths from maltreatment.

FORCED LABOUR FOR GERMANY One of the reasons why Germany was able to field a large army and also maintain high war production was through its use of slave labour. By the autumn of 1944, there were well over 7,250,000 foreign civilians being forced to work for the German war effort. In addition about 2 million p.o.w.'s frequently had to work in armament factories, or even carry ammunition to front line troops – both contrary to the Geneva and Hague conventions. The Germans' treatment of their labour gangs was as inhuman as their methods of gathering labour in the occupied countries. Children aged 10–14 were often taken to be trained as apprentices, and together with men and women were simply rounded up at will and sent by "cattle-trains" to Germany, where they were kept in squalid conditions, close to the factories they worked in, or, on farms, in barns and bare sheds. Russians in particular, were brutally treated and Russian p.o.w.'s were only treated as yet another source of labour – though often they were forced to spend weeks without food or shelter, even in midwinter, before being sent into Germany. Whenever food became scarce, it was ensured that German people had sufficient before anything was given to the workers. Only when even the enormous number of slave labourers began dying in numbers which threatened production did Himmler order that more food be given to essential workers.

RESISTANCE, SABOTAGE AND HOSTAGES Part of Hitler's rapid undoing lay in his inability to realise that brutal occupation would cause him ceaseless trouble and tie down thousands of troops. In West

There was no occupied country in which the Axis did not have to contend with resistance fighters. Among the most numerous and effective were the partisans in Russia, where groups such as this constantly ambushed and disrupted the long supply lines through hostile territory.

Europe, any form of occupation was abhorrent to the general masses of the public, and even Vichy France bred discontent. In the east, however, Hitler really did have a chance to add new territory to Germany and considerably strengthen the German nation, for many sections of the rich Ukraine were discontented with their years under Stalin, and the Baltic States resented the Russian invasion. But when Hitler's mobs of murderers, looters and rapists arrived, even Stalin's iron claw became a touch they longed to feel again. Apart from the front line battles, therefore, the Germans had to constantly fight against subversion, highly effective bands of Resistance fighters and Partisans, secret agents, and sabotage by forced-labourers.

Partisans in Yugoslavia became so powerful under Tito that, armed by the British, they drove the Germans out of their country – though not before more than 1,500,000 civilians and soldiers had died. In Russia, partisans harassed the long supply lines, ambushed transports, blew up depots, and killed thousands of soldiers. In France, Holland and Norway, very strong Resistance movements were formed, run from London both by émigré governments and by the British S.O.E.

It was not only organised resistance that proved an embarrassment to the Germans. As their treatment of civilians grew worse, as they tried to sow more and more terror (by, for instance, "lifting" hundreds of men in a week, sending them to labour camps, and giving anxious relatives no information at all), they came up against higher and higher walls of petty sabotage, of obstruction, non co-operation – hundreds of small, individual acts that worried away at the gross figure of Nazidom like maggots, and gradually contributed to its disintegration.

The inevitable Nazi reaction to sabotage, and especially to the killing of any German, was the taking of hostages – and few hostages were ever given back alive. The Nazis' estimate of the worth of Aryans is reflected in a decree that hostages were to be taken in the ratio of 100 to 1 – this was frequently applied in the east, while in southern and western Europe a 50 to 1 ratio was common,

---

Largely as a result of the extensive use of private shelters, deaths in the air raids on London were proportionately lower than they were in the cities that were bombed before London – particularly Warsaw and Rotterdam. As severe as the Blitz of London was, it was mild compared to the utter devastation of most of Germany's large cities, of Leningrad and Stalingrad, and of the Japanese conurbations.

though in Denmark it was only 5 to 1, and then done secretly rather than with the bold proclamations in France, Italy (after the surrender of the Italians), Poland and other countries. A great deal depended, of course, on the crime. The midnight stabbing of a solitary German soldier on a country road might have led to the shooting of five men in the village square, but the assassination of Heydrich in Czechoslovakia resulted directly in the deaths of some 2,500 Czechs and Jews. In France, nearly 30,000 hostages were murdered during the war, and a further 40,000 "died" in Gestapo cells and German prisons – usually as a result of Resistance work. In Holland about 2,000 were killed, and Poland lost 8,000 hostages.

A particularly abhorrent form of "revenge" and rule by terror practised by the Nazis was the destruction of complete towns and their occupants. Lidice, part of the Heydrich retribution in June 1942, was one instance; only a few women and children survived, the village itself was reduced to rubble and the site ploughed over. Lezhaky suffered a similar fate in that country, as did several villages in Greece, Poland, Russia and Yugoslavia. In France, exactly two years after the Lidice tragedy, the village of Oradour-sur-Glane, near Limoges, was invaded by a unit of the *Das Reich* division of the Waffen SS. The women and children were herded into the church, the men into barns. Then the soldiers set fire to the whole village, and shot anyone trying to escape from windows. Of the 652 people in the village that morning, 10 survived.

Civilian Death in Total War

Dawn on 1st September 1939 brought death for hundreds of Polish civilians as the Nazi monster began its journey of destruction, and within hours of the Second World War's commencement on 3rd September 112 civilians and merchant seamen from the liner *Athenia* died in the cold Atlantic. Patterns had been set that were to be repeated around the world for almost six years. Excluding Jewish totals (as do all national figures in this section) another 2,500,000 Poles were to die before the end of the war – many through murder, starvation and deprivation, but many in the remorseless march of war as first the Germans, and then the Russians ravaged their way across the land. When *blitzkrieg* was unleashed on Western Europe, war caused the death of 50,000 Belgians, 100,000 Hollanders (15,000 from starvation in the winter of 1944/45), 270,000 French.

At sea, British merchant seamen, Norwegians, Poles, Americans, Swedes, Indians and many others risked their lives on every voyage. By the time the war was over, nearly 32,000 British seamen had died through hostile action. Warsaw and Rotterdam had already shaken and crumbled beneath German bombs; in the autumn of 1940 it was the turn of London, Southampton, Coventry, Plymouth, Birmingham, Liverpool. In Britain, 60,000 civilians died. Then the Swastika was stamped on Yugoslavia and Greece, and 1,400,000 Yugoslavs and 80,000 Greeks were to be killed before their nations were free. Thousands of miles away, Japanese bombs, shells and bullets were leaving a trail of death in China, and millions of people ran into the interior. At least 10 million Chinese were killed by the war.

On 22nd June 1941, in eastern Europe 3 million German soldiers faced east and at dawn the first of at least 6,000,000 Russian civilians died in the clamour and misery of war. More than 1 million died in the 900 day siege of Leningrad, a tragic, heroic battle in which over 600,000 people died from cold, exhaustion and starvation – many on the pavements, or at work, many while trying to drag away the bodies of friends and relatives – while the remainder were killed by the endless shells and bombs. Hundreds of thousands died in the savage battles for Kharkov, Kiev, Smolensk, Stalingrad, Sevastopol.

Then retribution came to Germany, and one by one her cities were blown to rubble. Ill-prepared civilians, ruled by madmen who seemed to care little about their fate, died in Hamburg, Essen and the Ruhr, Hanover, Berlin, Dresden, Frankfurt, Mannheim, Cologne . . . the bombs fell and people died, then shells began to explode amid the rubble, and in the end some 3,500,000 German civilians were dead – together with their Fuehrer and practically the same number of Germans in the services.

In the Pacific, islanders died in their hundreds, and then – against the assurances of their Premier (as Hitler and Goering had assured the people of Berlin) – thousands of U.S. bombs fell on Tokyo, Osaka, Kobe, Yokohama. In Tokyo, a firestorm killed tens of thousands; and then the atomic bombs fell on Hiroshima and Nagasaki, the war was over, and some 400,000 Japanese civilians had died.

Civilian Life in Total War

At the first signs of war, civilians naturally try to escape it, and in Britain, where apprehension over gathering war clouds was keenly felt, the Government worked out plans for the evacuation of children and expectant or nursing mothers from cities to safer country homes. In the first days of the war considerable numbers were evacuated and billeted with private families in the country – a traumatic experience for many, though obviously less damaging than bombs could have been. The summer and autumn of 1939 saw a massive upheaval and resettling of people throughout Britain. Some 2 million moved privately to less likely target areas, and great numbers of civil departments were placed out of harm's way. After the Blitz on London began in September 1940, the population of London dropped by almost one third. The British, however, escaped invasion and the terrified flight of families away from the crashing guns and soldiers in strange uniforms. Getting refugees on the move was part of the *blitzkrieg* tactics. Terror bombing – especially with the screaming Stuka – and artillery barrages sent the civilians out onto the roads in their tens of thousands, carrying their few bundles, pushing prams, pulling carts, going, constantly going. Thousands of refugees blocking the roads delayed the arrival of reinforcements and disrupted counter-attacks, and that was a great help to the invaders.

In 1945, however, half the population of Europe (now including Germans) seemed to be in flight – this time from the rapidly moving Russian Army which, for a large part, murdered, raped, and pillaged its way with revengeful and ambitious brutality across Poland, Czechoslovakia and the eastern provinces of Germany. Among the Germans, almost 2 million fled westwards from East Prussia; 700,000 from Poland; 3·2 million from Silesia; 1·4 million from Eastern Pomerania; 3 million from the Sudetenland. The American and British zones of Germany teemed with people with no homes, few possessions, lost and bemused after years of killing, destruction and forced labour. 1·2 million Frenchmen, and even more Russians; 600,000 Poles; 350,000 Italians; 200,000 Belgians and as many Hollanders; 60,000 Czechs, and tens of thousands of others. There can be few more pitiful figures in war than the lost and bewildered refugee, stripped of dignity and, all too often, hope. The leaders of the Third Reich made almost everyone in Europe, including the German people, into such figures.

In time of war, only supremely confident or stupid governments do not introduce strict rationing, centralised buying and distribution, and rigid price controls. Britain was fortunate in being well prepared for war, and in rapidly implementing necessary restriction. The Ministry of Food controlled the movement of over 90% of the food in the country – utilising gigantic warehouses for non-perishables – and brought in a rationing system that was carefully designed to provide everyone with the essential calories to carry on functioning at high efficiency. Even the choice of material and design of clothing was by the Government, and the result was that while

"Action is transitory . . .
. . . and in the after vacancy
We wonder at ourselves like men betrayed:
Suffering is permanent, obscure and dark,
And shares the nature of infinity."
William Wordsworth: The Borderers

British civilians may often have been hungry, they were healthy and well clothed.

Occupied countries, of course, had no opportunity to carry out sensible rationing schemes, for that was done by their "masters". It basically worked on the principle of "first feed the German troops" then feed the civilians. Consequently, although few things were obtainable in Europe without ration cards, the possession of ration cards did not mean that the goods were necessarily available. Towards the end of the war, as products grew scarcer and rail movement became practically impossible, sheer survival grew desperately difficult. Berlin in its last days was even without water, and very little food was available. There was widespread starvation in Holland, and in places such as Malta and Leningrad, on many of the Pacific islands and eventually in most of Japan, rations fell to bare subsistence level. With few exceptions, however, populations were resolute in the face of common crisis, although inevitable forgers and blackmarketeers did turn common hardship to private advantage.

The emancipation of women took a great step forward during the war, especially in Britain and the Empire and in America. Women played an increasing role, not only by taking on jobs that were traditionally the jobs of men (such as factory work, shipbuilding, farm labouring, clerical and organisational work), but by forming branches of the services, undertaking great varieties of jobs in the services – clerical and cypher work, maintenance engineering, driving, ferrying aircraft, etc. – and so freeing thousands of men for active service. In Britain, conscription for women was introduced, and it was only in Germany that women (that is, German women) were not made an essential part of the war effort until the late stages. (Germany had the 7 million slave labourers to help her, although many of these were women.)

Rulers-in-Waiting

London became a refuge for the governments-in-exile and royalty of countries occupied by the Germans. In most cases, principal members of the governments managed to flee in time, and the presence of their leaders comparatively close by provided hope and reassurance to millions of people living under Nazi tyranny. The B.B.C. gave opportunities to émigré governments and royalty to broadcast to their people, and apart from the assurance given to their own peoples, these governments were able to offer valuable assistance to Britain. It was not always simple for the British Government however, since some governments-in-exile were not recognised by all their people. Norway, Belgium and the Netherlands worked closely with Britain (though no foreign governments took part in the actual planning of the war, being only involved in assisting Resistance work and providing information). The Balkan States, however, and Poland, presented Britain with numerous headaches. Yugoslavia switched allegiance from King Peter in London to the highly competent communist Partisan leader, Tito, and eventually Britain had to face the fact that Tito was more likely to oust the Germans than the supporters of the émigré government. France provided another problem, with Britain hoping that the Vichy Government would change allegiance, while a comparatively-young "upstart", Gen. de Gaulle, proclaimed himself leader of a new France. Whatever the final determination of each country, however, the émigré governments were a constant reminder to the Nazis of how far they were from bringing the Third Reich to the position they intended it to hold.

* * *

Approximately 55,000,000 people died in the Second World War, and millions more were injured, scarred, blinded or crippled for life. The minds of millions live constantly with memories of terror and misery that nothing can drive away. The gigantic catastrophe utilised the technological brilliance of 20th Century scientists and brought the industrial world to a new age. It provided countless examples (from Axis and Allied alike) of everything that is admirable, courageous, and generous in mankind – and of the terrible, vicious barbarism that everyone thought "civilised" man had banished hundreds of years ago.

And yet within three years great nations were again confronting each other; and country after country, group after group, constantly embark on ventures to gain for themselves by force what they cannot obtain by reason.

Index

(The names of persons mentioned only in the alphabetical biographies are not included in this Index.)